EARTHQUAKE PREDICTION

FURTHER TITLES IN THIS SERIES

1. *F.A. VENING MEINESZ*
THE EARTH'S CRUST AND MANTLE

2. *T. RIKITAKE*
ELECTROMAGNETISM AND THE EARTH'S INTERIOR

3. *D.W. COLLINSON, K.M. CREER and S.K. RUNCORN*
METHODS IN PALAEOMAGNETISM

4. *M. BÅTH*
MATHEMATICAL ASPECTS OF SEISMOLOGY

5. *F.D. STACEY and S.K. BANERJEE*
THE PHYSICAL PRINCIPLES OF ROCK MAGNETISM

6. *L. CIVETTA, P. GASPARINI, G. LUONGO and A. RAPOLLA*
PHYSICAL VOLCANOLOGY

7. *M. BÅTH*
SPECTRAL ANALYSIS IN GEOPHYSICS

8. *O. KULHANEK*
INTRODUCTION TO DIGITAL FILTERING IN GEOPHYSICS

Developments in Solid Earth Geophysics
9

EARTHQUAKE PREDICTION

TSUNEJI RIKITAKE

Professor of Earth Sciences
Department of Applied Physics
Faculty of Science
Tokyo Institute of Technology, Tokyo, Japan

ELSEVIER SCIENTIFIC PUBLISHING COMPANY
Amsterdam - Oxford - New York   1976

ELSEVIER SCIENTIFIC PUBLISHING COMPANY
335 JAN VAN GALENSTRAAT
P.O.BOX 211, AMSTERDAM, THE NETHERLANDS

AMERICAN ELSEVIER PUBLISHING COMPANY, INC.
52 VANDERBILT AVENUE
NEW YORK, NEW YORK 10017

ISBN 0-444-41373-1

WITH 138 ILLUSTRATIONS AND 24 TABLES

PRINTED IN THE NETHERLANDS

A Nishiki-e (colored wood-block print) showing the people running away from the fire caused by the earthquake of magnitude 6.9 that struck Edo (now Tokyo), Japan, in 1855 (anonymous painter).

PREFACE

Academic as well as social attention has recently been drawn to earthquake prediction especially in countries like Japan, the U.S.A., the U.S.S.R., the People's Republic of China and so on which have been suffering from destructive earthquakes from time to time. Intensive work on earthquake prediction study in these countries has brought out some clues that enable us to believe that prediction of some earthquakes, if not all, will be put into practice in the foreseeable future.

The present author, who has been working in the Earthquake Research Institute (ERI), University of Tokyo for over 30 years has become involved in the national program on earthquake prediction in Japan although he was originally a geomagnetician. As one of the senior members of the ERI, which is one of the most powerful agencies of earthquake research in Japan, it was natural to take part in such a nationwide program.

As international interest in earthquake prediction grew in the 1960s, the author was also asked to organize a number of international symposia on earthquake prediction and has been working as the secretary of the International Commission on Earthquake Prediction attached to the International Association of Seismology and the Physics of the Earth's Interior.

All through his activity mentioned in the above, he began to feel that a textbook on earthquake prediction is needed not only by students who want to study prediction-oriented seismology but also by non-professional people who are concerned with the present status of scientific earthquake prediction. It would also be a matter of utmost importance to let administrative and legislative people know about the feasibility of earthquake prediction.

This is the reason why the author has undertaken the writing of a book on earthquake prediction. A number of friends of his said that it would not be the right time to write a book on the subject because earthquake prediction study is rapidly developing and relevant data are accumulating with an immense speed at the moment. The author agrees with them. But he still thinks that it might be worthwhile writing a book on the subject because it would doubtless stimulate further study. In order to have a variety of readers, the author tried not to use much mathematics. Although some mathematics will be found in a few chapters of this book, the author hopes that what he writes can be understood even if those mathematical expressions are skipped.

Many earthquake prediction studies have appeared in classical documents as well as current journals and books written in Japanese which are too difficult for people outside Japan to read. As there is no doubt that Japan has played the leading part in promoting earthquake prediction study, what the author writes about Japanese work in this book may be of some help to overseas readers.

A number of Chinese achievements are also included in this book although the author reads Chinese writings very poorly. As for literature written in Russian, only translations either in Japanese or English can be referred to because the author does not read Russian. The author fears, therefore, that important literature written in Russian might be missing. He sincerely hopes that a similar book on earthquake prediction would be published in a popular language such as English by someone who can extensively refer to literature written in Russian.

At this point the author would like to pay a tribute to Professor T. Hagiwara, the Chairman of the Coordinating Committee of Earthquake Prediction in Japan and the Ex-chairman of the International Commission on Earthquake Prediction for his vigor in promoting earthquake prediction study. The author was stimulated very much by discussions almost every day with Professor Hagiwara while he was working at the ERI. The author has also been inspired in many respects of geophysics by Professor Takesi Nagata, now the Director of the National Institute of Polar Research in Japan. The author is very thankful to these senior colleagues. The author has also been influenced by many colleagues in the ERI. Among them, he should like to extend his thanks especially to Professors I. Tsubokawa, K. Mogi and Y. Hagiwara whose geodetic and laboratory work has been most important in developing a theory of earthquake prediction.

Drs. Y. Harada, T. Dambara, M. Tazima, N. Fujita and other members of the Geographical Survey Institute also inspired the author through personal talks. The author would like to thank them. Many data were supplied to the author by observers and researchers who are working at the frontier of earthquake prediction study in Japan. The author is particularly indebted to Drs. T. Matsuda and K. Nakamura at the ERI for geological information, Drs. T. Mikumo and K. Oike at the Kyoto University for microseismic data, and Drs. Y. Tanaka and T. Tanaka at the Kyoto University for crustal movement data.

Dr. Y. Yamazaki at the ERI performed a unique observation of resistivity change at the author's suggestion. He also assisted the author in many ways in promoting earthquake prediction study. The author sincerely thanks Dr. Yamazaki for his help.

Turning to the support given by overseas colleagues to the author's work, he should first of all like to thank the members of the Cooperative Institute for Research in Environmental Sciences (CIRES) operated by the University of Colorado and the National Oceanic and Atmospheric Administration (NOAA). The author is especially grateful for many inspiring discussions with Professor C. Kisslinger, the Director of the CIRES. Chinese literature, which he brought back from China as one of the members of the U.S. seismology delegation sent to China in 1974, was of great help to the author.

Dr. E.R. Engdahl critically read the manuscript and Mrs. J. Trebing kindly checked the English. Dr. T. Chan helped the author in reading Chinese literature. The author would like to extend his sincere thanks to them. Substantial portions of this book were completed while the author was holding a Senior Visiting Fellowship at the CIRES in 1974 and 1975.

Some of crustal movement data were supplied to the author by Dr. G.J. Lensen of the New Zealand Geological Survey and Dr. S.R. Holdahl of the National Ocean Survey, NOAA. The author is very grateful to them.

In conclusion the author should like to thank Drs. F.W.B. van Eysinga of Elsevier Scientific Publishing Company who urged the author to write this book and constantly encouraged him in the course of writing.

T. RIKITAKE

CONTENTS

PREFACE VII

CHAPTER 1. INTRODUCTORY REMARKS   1

CHAPTER 2. FORETELLING EARTHQUAKES — VARIOUS LEGENDS . . .   9
  2.1. Unusual behavior of fish and animals   9
    2.1.1. Catfish and other fish   9
    2.1.2. Animals   17
    2.1.3. Frogs and snakes   18
    2.1.4. Birds   19
    2.1.5. Insects and worms   19
  2.2. Unusual weather   19
    2.2.1. Mist and fog   19
    2.2.2. Rainbow and mysterious light   21
  2.3. Underground water   23
  2.4. Magnet   23
  2.5. Position of celestial bodies   24
  2.6. Supernatural instinct   25
  2.7. Other indicators   26

CHAPTER 3. BIRTH OF PREDICTION-ORIENTED EARTHQUAKE SCIENCE   27
  3.1. Beginning of earthquake research in Japan   27
  3.2. The 1891 Nobi earthquake and the Imperial Earthquake Investigation
    Committee   27
  3.3. The 1923 Kanto earthquake   28
  3.4. Earthquake Research Institute   29

CHAPTER 4. EARTHQUAKE PREDICTION PROGRAMS   33
  4.1. The "blueprint"   33
  4.2. Japanese program   34
    4.2.1. Initiation and development   34
    4.2.2. Geodetic work   39
    4.2.3. Tide-gauge observation   41
    4.2.4. Continuous observation of crustal movement   42
    4.2.5. Seismicity   43
    4.2.6. Seismic wave velocities   44
    4.2.7. Active faults and foldings   44
    4.2.8. Geomagnetic and geoelectric work   44
    4.2.9. Laboratory work and rock-breaking tests   46
    4.2.10. Data processing   46
  4.3. U.S.—Japan cooperation   46
  4.4. American program   49
  4.5. Soviet program   54
  4.6. Programs in other countries   55
  4.7. International Commission on Earthquake Prediction   57

CHAPTER 5. LAND DEFORMATION AS DETECTED BY GEODETIC SUR-
VEYS   59
    5.1. Classical reports on land deformation   59
    5.2. Triangulation survey techniques   59
    5.3. Land deformations as detected by triangulations   61
        5.3.1. Kanto earthquake   64
        5.3.2. Tango earthquake   65
        5.3.3. North Izu earthquake   67
        5.3.4. Tottori earthquake   68
        5.3.5. Mikawa earthquake   69
        5.3.6. Nankai earthquake   71
        5.3.7. Fukui earthquake   72
        5.3.8. San Francisco earthquake   74
        5.3.9. Imperial Valley earthquake   77
        5.3.10. Kern County earthquake   78
        5.3.11. Fairview Peak earthquake   79
        5.3.12. Alaska earthquake   81
        5.3.13. Rhombus base lines at Mitaka, Tokyo   82
    5.4. Geodimeter survey techniques   83
        5.4.1. Horizontal strain over the South Kanto area   84
        5.4.2. Horizontal strain over the North Izu area   87
        5.4.3. Traverse surveys of high precision across the Japan Islands . .   89
        5.4.4. Surveys over the San Andreas fault   92
    5.5. Levelling survey techniques   94
    5.6. Land deformation as detected by levellings   96
        5.6.1. Nobi earthquake   96
        5.6.2. Ugosen earthquake   97
        5.6.3. Omachi earthquake   97
        5.6.4. Kanto earthquake   98
        5.6.5. Tango earthquake   99
        5.6.6. Ito earthquake swarm   100
        5.6.7. North Izu earthquake   101
        5.6.8. Nagano earthquake   102
        5.6.9. Tottori earthquake   102
        5.6.10. Mikawa earthquake   103
        5.6.11. Nankai earthquake   103
        5.6.12. Fukui earthquake   104
        5.6.13. North Miyagi earthquake   104
        5.6.14. Matsushiro earthquakes   104
        5.6.15. Kern County earthquake   107
        5.6.16. Alaska earthquake   107
        5.6.17. South Bulgarian earthquakes   109
        5.6.18. Ashkhabad earthquake   109
        5.6.19. Inangahua earthquake   110
        5.6.20. Meckering earthquake   111
    5.7. Anomalous land uplift forerunning an earthquake   112
        5.7.1. Sekihara and Nagaoka earthquakes   112
        5.7.2. Tonankai earthquake   113
        5.7.3. Niigata earthquake   114
        5.7.4. Tashkent earthquake   116
        5.7.5. Dunaharaszti earthquake   116
        5.7.6. San Fernando earthquake   117

5.8. Relationship between earthquake magnitude and area of land deforma-
tion 118
5.9. Non-seismic crustal deformation 119

CHAPTER 6. LAND DEFORMATION RELATIVE TO SEA LEVEL 121
6.1. Anomalous sea retreat before an earthquake 121
6.1.1. Ajikazawa earthquake 121
6.1.2. Sado earthquake 121
6.1.3. Hamada earthquake 121
6.1.4. Tango earthquake 122
6.2. Tide-gauge observation 122
6.2.1. Noise to observation of uplift and subsidence of land 122
6.2.2. Precursory and coseismic changes 123
6.2.3. Comparison between levelling and tide-gauge observation 124

CHAPTER 7. CONTINUOUS OBSERVATION OF CRUSTAL MOVEMENT . . 125
7.1. Tiltmeter 125
7.1.1. Horizontal pendulum tiltmeter 125
7.1.2. Water-tube tiltmeter 126
7.1.3. Borehole tiltmeter 126
7.2. Strainmeter 127
7.2.1. Quartz-tube strainmeter 127
7.2.2. Super-invar-wire strainmeter 127
7.2.3. Laser-beam strainmeter 128
7.2.4. Sacks-Evertson strainmeter 128
7.3. Crustal movement observatory 129
7.4. Secular changes in tilt and strain and their relation to regional crustal
movement 130
7.5. Coseismic strain step 133
7.6. Site effect 136
7.7. Tilt and strain changes forerunning an earthquake 137
7.7.1. Japanese examples 137
7.7.2. Soviet examples 143
7.7.3. American examples 145
7.7.4. Other examples 147
7.8. Earth tides 147

CHAPTER 8. SEISMIC ACTIVITY 151
8.1. Implication of plate tectonics 151
8.1.1. Extrusion 152
8.1.2. Mantle convection 152
8.1.3. Creation of sea bottom 153
8.1.4. Magnetic lineation observed at sea 153
8.1.5. Reversals of the geomagnetic field 153
8.1.6. Ocean-floor spreading 154
8.1.7. Plate tectonics 154
8.1.8. Subduction 155
8.1.9. Compression and rebound 156
8.1.10. Transcursion 157
8.2. Regional seismicity and microearthquakes 158
8.2.1. Gutenberg-Richter formula 158
8.2.2. Microearthquake studies in Japan 158

8.2.3. Microearthquake studies in the U.S.A. 164
8.2.4. Microearthquake studies in other countries 165
8.3. Foreshock 166
8.3.1. Small shocks or rumblings forerunning a main shock 166
8.3.2. Nature of foreshocks 166
8.3.3. Foreshocks in a broad sense 168
8.3.4. Characteristics of foreshocks pertinent to earthquake prediction . . 171
8.4. Seismicity gap 177
8.4.1. San Francisco and Fort Tejon areas, California, U.S.A. 177
8.4.2. South Kanto area, Japan 177
8.4.3. Eastern Hokkaido area, Japan 179
8.4.4. Tokai area, Japan 181
8.4.5. Kurile—Kamchatka—Aleutian—Alaska zone 183
8.4.6. Central and South Americas 183
8.4.7. A paradox 184
8.5. Deep-well observation of microearthquakes 185
8.6. Submarine seismology 186

CHAPTER 9. CHANGE IN SEISMIC WAVE VELOCITIES 189
9.1. Changes in the V_p/V_s ratio 190
9.1.1. Findings in the U.S.S.R. 190
9.1.2. U.S. work 192
9.1.3. Japanese work 193
9.1.4. Chinese work 193
9.2. Changes in seismic wave velocities and residual times 194
9.3. V_s anisotropy 196

CHAPTER 10. GEOMAGNETIC AND GEOELECTRIC EFFECTS 197
10.1. Classical observations of changes in the geomagnetic field associated
      with an earthquake 197
10.2. Modern magnetometers and present-day magnetic survey 200
10.3. Problems of noise elimination 200
10.4. Seismomagnetic effect 204
10.4.1. Matsushiro earthquakes 204
10.4.2. Southeast Akita earthquake 205
10.4.3. Work related to the faults in California 205
10.5. Geomagnetic changes associated with water impounded in a man-made
      lake and explosion 206
10.6. Precursory geomagnetic change 207
10.6.1. Japanese examples 207
10.6.2. U.S. examples 208
10.6.3. Chinese examples 209
10.6.4. Soviet examples 209
10.7. Theory of tectonomagnetism 209
10.7.1. Piezo-remanent magnetism 209
10.7.2. Interpretation of seismomagnetic effect 210
10.8. Anomalous changes in earth currents 211
10.9. Changes in earth resistivity 212
10.9.1. Soviet observation 213
10.9.2. U.S. observation 214
10.9.3. Chinese observation 214
10.9.4. Japanese observation 215
10.10. Changes in geomagnetic variation anomaly 218

CHAPTER 11. ACTIVE FAULTS AND FOLDING 221
  11.1. Creep of fault 221
    11.1.1. San Andreas fault 221
    11.1.2. Anatolian fault 222
  11.2. Faults that often moved in the past 223
    11.2.1. Movement of the Tanna fault 223
    11.2.2. Active faults in Japan 223
  11.3. Active folding 226
  11.4. Coastal terraces 226

CHAPTER 12. OTHER ELEMENTS FOR EARTHQUAKE PREDICTION . . . 227
  12.1. Gravity 227
  12.2. Underground water 229
  12.3. Oil flow 232
  12.4. Radon content 232

CHAPTER 13. LABORATORY EXPERIMENTS 235
  13.1. Rock-breaking experiments 235
    13.1.1. Microfracture and main rupture 235
    13.1.2. Experiments under a confining pressure 236
    13.1.3. Further developments in rock-breaking experiments 237
  13.2. Physical properties of highly stressed rocks 238
    13.2.1. Dilatancy 238
    13.2.2. Change in elastic wave velocities 238
    13.2.3. Change in electric resistivity 239

CHAPTER 14. DILATANCY MODELS 241
  14.1. Wet model 241
  14.2. Dry model 243

CHAPTER 15. THEORY OF EARTHQUAKE PREDICTION 245
  15.1. Statistical prediction of earthquakes 245
    15.1.1. 69-year period recurrence of large earthquakes in the Tokyo area . 246
    15.1.2. Earthquake statistics and their limitation 248
    15.1.3. Statistics based on the theory of extreme values 253
    15.1.4. Correlation between earthquake occurrence and other phenomena . 254
  15.2. Empirical approach to earthquake prediction based on actually ob-
      served premonitory effects 255
    15.2.1. Prediction of magnitude 255
    15.2.2. Prediction of occurrence time 258
    15.2.3. Rating of earthquake risk based on probabilities 260
  15.3. Ultimate strain and probability of earthquake occurrence 263
    15.3.1. Statistics of ultimate strain 263
    15.3.2. Probability of earthquake occurrence as estimated from crustal
      strain 264
  15.4. Prediction based on a dilatancy model 270
  15.5. Statistics of earthquake precursors 270
    15.5.1. Classification of precursors 271
    15.5.2. Histograms of the precursor time 290
    15.5.3. Histograms for different magnitude ranges 293
    15.5.4. Characteristics of A-type precursors 295
  15.6. Four stages of earthquake prediction 297
    15.6.1. Statistical prediction — preliminary stage 297

15.6.2. Long-term prediction — strain accumulation stage   297
15.6.3. Medium- and short-term prediction — dilatancy generation stage .   297
15.6.4. Prediction of extremely short range — stage immediately prior to
         main rupture   298
15.7. Operations research related to earthquake prediction   299
    15.7.1. Most effective way of carrying out levelling surveys for earthquake
             prediction in Japan   299
    15.7.2. Where should we set up a new crustal deformation observatory in
             Japan?   301

CHAPTER 16. EARTHQUAKE MODIFICATION AND CONTROL   303
16.1. Denver earthquakes   303
16.2. Water-injection experiment at Matsushiro   304
16.3. Man-made lakes and earthquakes   304
16.4. Experiments at Rangely Oil Field   306
16.5. Program on earthquake modification and control   307

CHAPTER 17. WHAT TO DO WITH AN EARTHQUAKE WARNING?   309
17.1. Experience at Matsushiro   309
17.2. How should an earthquake warning be issued to the public?   310
17.3. Socioeconomic and political study of response to earthquake prediction   311

REFERENCES   315

AUTHOR INDEX   339

SUBJECT INDEX   345

Chapter 1

INTRODUCTORY REMARKS

Predicting an earthquake is certainly a matter of deep concern for seismologists as well as the general public. In a highly seismic country like Japan, where people have long suffered from earthquake disasters, the desire to foretell an earthquake was so strong that people were tempted to rely on superstitious fortune-telling in earlier years. It is only recently that earthquake prediction on a scientific basis became known as one of the branches of earth science. A nationwide program on earthquake prediction started only in the early 1960s in Japan. Intensive studies on the subject seem to have started in the U.S.S.R., the People's Republic of China, the U.S.A. and other countries some time later.

Although many papers on earthquake prediction came out in recent years, not very many reviews, by which we can see the overall development of the subject, have so far been published. It is perhaps better to draw up a list of them in the following so that those who want to trace the progress of earthquake prediction study may refer to them:

1962:   Hagiwara, T., Earthquake prediction (in Japanese).
        Tsuboi, C. et al., *Prediction of Earthquakes — Progress to Date and Plans for further Development* (Report of the Earthquake Prediction Research Group in Japan).

1964:   Oliver, J., Earthquake prediction.

1965:   Press, F., Earthquake prediction: a challenge to geophysicists.
        Press, F. et al., *Earthquake Prediction: a Proposal for a Ten Year Program of Research.*

1966:   Båth, M., Earthquake prediction.
        Lomnitz, C., Statistical prediction of earthquakes.
        Press, F. and Brace, W.F., Earthquake prediction.
        Rikitake, T., A five-year plan for earthquake prediction research in Japan.

1967:   Hagiwara, T. and Rikitake, T., Japanese program on earthquake prediction.

1968:   Press, F., A strategy for an earthquake prediction research program.
        Rikitake, T., Earthquake prediction.
        Savarensky, E.F., On the prediction of earthquakes.

1969:   Hagiwara, T., Prediction of earthquakes.
        Hagiwara, T. and Rikitake, T., La previsione dei terremoti.
        Hagiwara, T. and Rikitake, T., Neue Entwicklungen in der Erdbebenprognose.
        Pakiser, L.C. et al., Earthquake prediction and control.

1970:   Kanamori, H., Recent developments in earthquake prediction research in Japan.
        Nersesov, I.L., Earthquake prognostication in the Soviet Union.
        Oliver, J., Recent earthquake prediction research in the U.S.A.
        Rikitake, T., Prévision des tremblements de terre.

1971:   Coe, R.S., Earthquake prediction program in the People's Republic of China.
          Pakiser, L.C. and Healy, J.H., Prédiction et contrôle des tremblements de terre.

1972:   Healy, J.H. et al., Prospects for earthquake prediction and control.
          Rikitake, T., Earthquake prediction studies in Japan.
          Rikitake, T., Problems of predicting earthquakes.
          Rikitake, T., An earthquake prediction operation in an area south of Tokyo.
          Sadovsky, M.A. et al., The processes preceding strong earthquakes in some
          regions of Middle Asia.
          Savarensky, E.F. et al., Geophysical principles for studying forerunners of earth-
          quakes.

1973:   Hagiwara, T., The development of earthquake prediction research (in Japanese).

1974:   Bolt, B.A., Earthquake studies in the People's Republic of China.
          Johnston, M.J.S. et al., Earthquakes — can they be predicted or controlled?
          Kisslinger, C., Earthquake prediction.
          Rikitake, T., Japanese national program on earthquake prediction.
          Sadovsky, M.A. and Nersesov, I.L., Forecasts of earthquakes on the basis of
          complex geophysical features.
          Savarensky, E.F., Introductory remarks and Soviet national program on earth-
          quake prediction.

1975:   Press, F., Earthquake prediction.

Complete references of the above reviews will be found in the bibliography toward the end of this book. Perhaps there are other review papers which were overlooked by the author. Schmidt (1971, 1973) published comprehensive lists of earthquake prediction-oriented papers including those written in Russian. As the author does not read Russian, it is likely that he missed review papers written in Russian. It is also regrettable that many papers published in China are at the moment inaccessible to the author, so that it is possible that there are important reviews in Chinese that have not come to the author's attention.

On the basis of those reviews and numerous individual papers, the author tried to summarize the most up-to-date knowledge about earthquake prediction study in this book. Emphasis will especially be put on Japanese work, much of which has not been known outside Japan because of linguistic difficulties. The author is convinced that data taken in Japan play an important role in promoting earthquake prediction study because seismicity is high there and a well-organized program on earthquake prediction is underway.

First of all, many of the legends about non-scientific prediction of earthquakes will be presented in Chapter 2 mostly on the basis of Japanese sources. Being picked up from historical documents, most of these legends are hard to believe. However, what is written in this chapter might be of some interest especially for non-Japanese readers because Japanese classical writings are quite inaccessible to most overseas people. At any rate, what is written in this chapter demonstrates how strong the longing of mankind to have the ability to forecast a disastrous earthquake was even in medieval time.

The science of earthquakes in early years was developed mostly in Japan after its new civilization about 100 years ago. Chapter 3 is devoted to describing how prediction-oriented earthquake science developed in Japan. It is rather surprising that no strong appeal for earthquake prediction study was proposed until about 15 years ago in spite of many disastrous earthquakes occurring in Japan. As a matter of fact, it used to be a taboo for a seismologist to talk about earthquake prediction some 30 years ago when the author was a student. A seismologist was supposed to work on less ambitious subjects and write papers.

However, data relevant to earthquake prediction have been accumulating over a period of scores of years. As will be mentioned in Chapter 4, a research group for earthquake prediction was formed in Japan around 1960. Japanese seismologists have now started to discuss ambitiously a possible approach to earthquake prediction at many meetings. The outcome of the group's discussion was published as a now-famous report named *Prediction of Earthquakes — Progress to Date and Plans for further Development* (Tsuboi et al., 1962). Being called the "blueprint" of earthquake prediction research, the report became a milestone of earthquake prediction study in later years.

It appears to the author that no remarkable effort toward earthquake prediction was made in the U.S.A. until a U.S.—Japan conference on earthquake prediction was held in Tokyo and Kyoto in 1964. Soon after the conference, a highly destructive earthquake of magnitude 8.4 hit Alaska giving rise to much damage there. In the following years, earthquake prediction has become one of the important subjects of earth science in the U.S.A. Although no nationwide program was set up until 1974, much money funded by the National Science Foundation (NSF) and the U.S. Geological Survey (USGS) was spent in promoting earthquake prediction study in the U.S.A.; some of the American work such as microearthquake monitoring became more advanced than that in Japan despite the fact that the project started only recently.

On the other hand, it becomes apparent that intensive earthquake prediction studies are progressing in Central Asia and Kamchatka, the U.S.S.R. (Rikitake, 1968b, 1970b; Savarensky, 1974; Savarensky and Rikitake, 1972). Coe (1971) and Bolt (1974) reported on intensive work on earthquake prediction that is in progress in the People's Republic of China.

Programs on earthquake prediction in these countries will be given in a summarized form in Chapter 4 although only limited knowledge about the programs in the U.S.S.R. and China was available to the author.

From Chapter 5 on, the author reports on various geophysical elements that are thought to have something to do with earthquake prediction. One of the most outstanding discoveries by Japanese workers, who vigorously took up intensive studies of earthquake phenomena after the great Kanto earthquake of 1923, was certainly the crustal deformation that occurs in association with a large earthquake. Although it has been known in Japan since A.D. 679 that a crustal deformation is accompanied by a strong earthquake, the precise characteristics of earthquake-associated crustal movement have become clear only by repetition of geodetic surveys.

In Chapter 5 are summarized almost all reported examples of land deformation associated with an earthquake as revealed by repetition of triangulation, levelling and geodimeter surveys in an encyclopedic manner. These studies have an important bearing on estimating the ultimate strain of the earth's crust. Even a number of precursory land deformations forerunning an earthquake have been found by the geodetic method.

A few classic reports on anomalous sea retreats are reproduced in Chapter 6. Curiously enough, only a very few examples of precursory land uplift or subsidence relative to sea level have been found through modern tide-gauge observations.

In order to supplement geodetic work, that is essentially intermittent, continuous observations of crustal movement have long been made by making use of tiltmeters and strainmeters of various models as readers will see in Chapter 7. General agreement between crustal deformations as revealed by geodetic surveys and those observed by water-tube tiltmeters have been reported in Japan. Although quite a few precursory effects have been reported by tiltmeter and strainmeter observations, it seems likely that signals observed by horizontal pendulum tiltmeters as well as highly sensitive strainmeters are often contaminated with noise as the statistics in Chapter 15 indicate. However, water-tube and borehole tiltmeters seem fairly reliable.

Chapter 8 is reserved for seismicity research, which plays one of the most fundamental roles in earthquake prediction. Current theory on plate tectonics had a strong impact on the basic idea of earthquake prediction. Extremely large earthquakes occurring in front of an island arc are interpreted as the result of crustal rebound following a tremendous compression or shearing by plate motion. Although no detailed mechanism of medium or small earthquakes beneath an island arc has been worked out, there is no doubt about the importance of monitoring strain accumulation in the earth's crust for earthquake prediction. The implication of plate tectonics on earthquake prediction will be reviewed in the first section of Chapter 8.

Present status and recent achievements of intensive microearthquake observation in Japan and the U.S.A. is also dealt with in Chapter 8. Several characteristics of foreshock activities, i.e. decreases in b-value and seismicity, reorientation of the axis of compression for small shocks prior to a main shock and the like will be described along with the concept of seismicity gaps which plays an important role in determining probable locations of large earthquake in the near future. Brief mention will be made about deep-well observations of microearthquakes, which seem to be the only way to obtain highly sensitive observations in a noisy city such as Tokyo, and sub-marine seismology, too.

It is still hard to say that much about foreshock activities is well under-stood. In some cases many microearthquakes forerun a moderately large earthquake as observed a number of times during the 1965—1967 Matsushiro earthquake swarm in Japan. On the contrary, it is believed, according to the concept of a seismicity gap, that areas of very low seismicity at present, such as the San Francisco and the South Kanto (a district to the south of Tokyo) areas, would become the seat of a large earthquake some day. Such apparently conflicting views must be understood by taking different condi-tions in the earth's crust of respective zones into account.

Quite an exciting discovery pertinent to earthquake prediction was report-ed from studies of seismic wave velocities in the Garm area, Middle Asia, U.S.S.R. It was found that the ratio of P-wave velocity V_p to S-wave velocity V_s of small earthquakes in an area considerably decreases before a moderate-ly large earthquake that occurs in the same area. As will be seen in Chap-ter 9, it was really hard for the present author to believe that V_p changes by 15% or so when he was first informed by Professor E.F. Savarensky (1968) who talked about Soviet discoveries at a symposium in Zurich in 1967. It was ascertained, however, by the later work in the U.S.S.R. and the U.S.A. that the V_p/V_s ratio drops and recovers prior to an earthquake in many cases. The length of anomalous period of the V_p/V_s ratio seems to be closely correlated with the magnitude of the coming earthquake. As similar findings were later reported from Japan and China, changes in the V_p/V_s ratio or V_p itself have become one of the most powerful elements of earthquake predic-tion. Intensive study of the physical mechanism for such a change led us to a dilatancy model as will be seen in later chapters.

Changes in the geomagnetic field and earth currents, which are reviewed in Chapter 10, have long been supposed to have something to do with earth-quake occurrence. Modern studies made it clear, however, that most of the data in earlier years are spurious because of inadequate measuring and noise-elimination techniques. It seems now established that a seismomagnetic effect hardly exceeds the order of 10 gammas (about 1/500 of the intensity of the earth's magnetic field). A precursory geomagnetic change may well be a little smaller. According to a recent development in the measuring tech-nique of the geomagnetic field, however, it is not quite hopeless to monitor a magnetic forerunner in a low-noise circumstance. In spite of many reports of anomalous changes in earth currents associated with an earthquake, no clear-cut overall character of precursory signals in earth-currents has been brought to light. Remarkable changes in electric resistivity forerunning an earthquake have been reported first in the Garm region followed by a similar observation on the San Andreas fault, California, U.S.A. On the other hand, precursory and coseismic changes in earth resistivity associated with large earthquakes at a teleseismic distance have been observed by an unusually high-sensitivity resistivity variometer in Japan. It now turns out that resistivity monitoring provides a means by which long- and short-term precursors can be detected.

Recent observations made it clear that faults such as the San Andreas and Anatolian faults are continually creeping. There are also many faults which often moved in historical and geological times. Studies of these active geological structures as are reviewed in Chapter 11 indicate the potential danger for the occurrence of large earthquakes at active faults which should be watched as targets of earthquake prediction research.

Chapter 12 presents current views on gravity, underground water, oil flow and radon emission as tools of earthquake prediction. Not much attention has so far been paid to these elements partly because of difficulties in measuring techniques, but recent work seems to suggest that an important contribution to earthquake prediction study might emerge from studies of these elements.

Earthquake prediction research has been mostly developed on empirical bases. This could not be helped in the early stage of study because the knowledge about earthquake mechanism was extremely poor. However, the study of "laboratory earthquakes" that began in the early 1960s brought out many important points relevant to earthquake prediction. Study of highly stressed rock specimens provided explanations of dilatancy generation, premonitory changes in seismic wave velocities, electric resistivity and so on. Rock-breaking experiments also brought out some clues to understanding the role of pore pressure, the relation between foreshocks, main shock and aftershocks and the like. It may be said that laboratory experiments on rock specimens provide a theoretical background of earthquake prediction study. All these points relevant to laboratory experiments are discussed in Chapter 13.

In view of the importance of the dilatancy model in the current theory of earthquake prediction, Chapter 14 is saved for a review of the dilatancy theory.

It is attempted in Chapter 15 to put forth a theory of earthquake prediction on the basis of what is learned in the preceding chapters. One might think that it would be premature to work out such a theory because necessary data have not yet been aquired. It is the author's belief, however, that an attempt to form an earthquake prediction theory, no matter how premature it is, would stimulate further investigation.

No attempt to review the statistical prediction of earthquakes in detail is made in this chapter because the author is of the opinion that a realistic prediction must be made on the basis of physical changes. But some comments on periodicities of earthquake occurrence are undertaken because the author is afraid that there are widespread misunderstandings about the so-called 69-year periodicity of large earthquakes in the Tokyo area.

A purely empirical approach for estimating probabilities of the magnitude and occurrence time of a coming earthquake is first described in this chapter

along with the limitation of such an approach. Secondly, some more realistic
way of estimating occurrence time in terms of probability is introduced on
the basis of monitoring of strain accumulation combined with the statistics
of ultimate strain of the earth's crust. Thirdly, extensive statistics of earthquake precursors are presented. From such a study, it seems likely that we
may distinguish long-term and short-term precursors.

The above studies will lead us to four stages of earthquake prediction; i.e.
statistical, long-term, medium- and short-term, and extremely short-term predictions. These may be assigned preliminary, strain accumulation, dilatancy
generation and immediate precursory stages, respectively.

There will still be many difficulties in applying the above theory to
actual prediction because necessary data will never be satisfactory. As data
accumulation will further be strengthened, it is highly likely that the above
theory of earthquake prediction will be improved through actual tests.

Chapter 16 is devoted to a brief account of earthquake modification and
control, one of the most ambitious projects of earth science. Although it will
take some time to materialize the project, promotion of the project would
doubtless stimulate studies relevant to earthquake prediction.

Even if a practicable method of earthquake prediction is established, it is a
matter of great difficulty to let the public know the prediction. In Chapter
17 is presented a very incomplete debate about "how to issue an earthquake
warning to the public". Such a subject involving sociology, economics, poli-
tics, psychology and the like is obviously beyond the scope of this book. The
author believes, however, it is high time to start studies on such a complicated subject because some sort of earthquake prediction will become possible
in the foreseeable future.

There are a few points to which the author would like to ask the readers
to pay attention. First of all, there are instances in this book where the same
notation is used for different quantities. For example, σ means either stress
or standard deviation depending upon circumstances. The author believes,
however, such usage of notations would not cause confusion because they
are defined every time. If the author tried to make use of unified notations
throughout the book, some strange notations, which differ from the customary usage, must necessarily be adopted.

Magnitude of an earthquake could be different from report to report
because it can be estimated on the basis of data taken at different observatories. In order to avoid confusion, therefore, magnitudes of large earthquakes which are given in the *Rikanenpyo* (Science Calendar, Tokyo Astronomical Observatory) edited by Usami (1975) are used. In spite of the fact
that the magnitude of the 1960 Chilean earthquake is reported as 8.5, or
over, in many references, a value of 8.3 is always cited in this book because
it is so indicated in the *Rikanenpyo*. Some of the readers may think it
strange that the magnitude of earthquakes in historical time, when we had
no seismometrical observation, is indicated. This is somehow estimated from

historical documents, so that the accuracy of the estimated value is not high.

A number of abbreviations are used in this book. They are summarized in the following:

AEC	Atomic Energy Commission
AGU	American Geophysical Union
CCEP	Coordinating Committee for Earthquake Prediction
CERECIS	Centro Regional de Sismologia
CIRES	Cooperative Institute for Research in Environmental Sciences
EHRP	Earthquake Hazards Reduction Program
ERI	Earthquake Research Institute
ESC	European Seismological Commission
ESSA	Environmental Science Services Administration
GSI	Geographical Survey Institute
HUD	Housing and Urban Development
IAG	International Association of Geodesy
IAGA	International Association of Geomagnetism and Aeronomy
IASPEI	International Association of Seismology and Physics of the Earth's Interior
IAVCEI	International Association of Volcanology and Chemistry of the Earth's Interior
ICEP	International Commission on Earthquake Prediction
ICG	Inter-Union Commission on Geodynamics
ICSU	International Council of Scientific Unions
IUGG	International Union of Geodesy and Geophysics
IUGS	International Union of Geological Sciences
JMA	Japan Meteorological Agency
JSPS	Japan Society for Promotion of Science
NCER	National Center for Earthquake Research
NOAA	National Oceanic and Atmospheric Administration
NSF	National Science Foundation
PPBS	Planning-Programming-Budgeting System
UMC	Upper Mantle Committee
UMP	Upper Mantle Project
USGS	United States Geological Survey

Chapter 2

FORETELLING EARTHQUAKES — VARIOUS LEGENDS

Often it has been reported, prior to an earthquake, that fish and animals behave unusually, that a mysterious rainbow is sometimes observed, that a magnet loses its attracting power, and so on. These legends have been probably told over a period of several hundred years, and we still read non-scientific foretellings of great earthquakes in today's journals and magazines for amusement. Probably the desire of mankind for forecasting a disastrous earthquake is so strong that some people are tempted to rely on such things.

Although the author intends to describe in this book the present status of earthquake prediction study based on scientific grounds, it is of some value to deal with some of the classical legends, many of which are derived from Japanese literature. As Japanese literature is not easily accessible to people outside Japan, and it is especially so in the case of classical Japanese writings which are hard even for present-day Japanese people to read, what follows may be of some interest for non-Japanese readers. Not that we believe in all these legends, but it is important for scientists to look into things, which might contain some truth, without being biased.

2.1. UNUSUAL BEHAVIOR OF FISH AND ANIMALS

2.1.1. Catfish and other fish

In medieval time Japanese people believed that an earthquake was caused by sudden movements of a big catfish living in the earth. We can find documents written in the 17th century in which a catfish is correlated to an earthquake occurrence: In many Nishiki-e's (colored wood-block prints) published soon after the great Edo (now Tokyo) earthquake of 1855, we see various descriptions of catfish which are thought to have given rise to that earthquake. It is not at all clear, however, why catfish are correlated to earthquakes. Probably a catfish, which is usually submerged in mud at the bottom of rivers and ponds, gives people some impression of apprehension because of its grotesque appearance, so that superstitious Japanese people might be induced to presume that an earthquake, which is terribly dreadful and hazardous, could be caused by a gigantic catfish.

It has also been said that the catfish becomes active and bubbles are formed around its barbels prior to an earthquake, although no exact sources of such sayings are known. In *Nihon Jishin Shiryo* (Musha, 1951, p. 623), we find a report which describes unusual behavior of catfish before the 1855 Edo earthquake. In downtown Edo, there was a man who was so fond of fishing that he went to a river every night. He tried to catch eels as usual on the evening of November 11, 1855, but, strangely enough, he saw many catfish making a fuss, so that most of the eels seemed to run away. As he had heard that a catfish becomes active before an earthquake, he hurried back home. He then brought all his household effects out in the courtyard. His wife laughed at him because she did not believe what he said. After a while, however, a strong shock took place as he expected. His properties were thus kept safe though his house was damaged. One of his neighbors, who also went fishing, watched the catfish making a fuss, too. He ignored this and continued fishing. Having been surprised by the quake, he ran back home only to see his house and godown lying in ruins.

According to Musha (1957), it is said that a high official of the Ministry of Education saw many fish jumping in a pond at a restaurant in downtown Tokyo on August 31, 1923, i.e. one day before the great Kanto earthquake (see section 3.3). A waitress at the restaurant told him that the catfish had recently become unusually active. He later told the story to a famous painter who happened to keep a few big catfish in a tub in order to sketch them. The painter recalled that they jumped around before the earthquake.

Another official of the same Ministry was enjoying himself fishing by casting a net at a pond near the coast south of Tokyo on the day before the earthquake. To his astonishment, he got three buckets full of catfish, each fish being about 30 cm in length.

The catfish activity forerunning an earthquake as reported in the above may well be mere coincidence. In order to establish a firm correlation between catfish activity and earthquake occurrence, it should be proved that a catfish is inactive when there is no earthquake. Hatai and his group (Hatai and Abe, 1932; Hatai et al., 1932) were the first who investigated the response of catfish to earthquakes. They kept a few catfish in a water tank in which they placed mud and water plants. Usually, the catfish were so inactive that they hid themselves under mud or the roots of plants. The catfish neither swam around nor jumped up from the water surface before or after earthquakes.

It was observed, however, that the catfish sometimes became sensitive to shocks which were given by a few light taps at the table on which the tank was placed. After some experiments, it was concluded that the catfish responded nervously to finger knocks within several hours of an earthquake. Hatai and his associates classified the reaction of the fish into the following grades:

(1) *Very sensitive.* Jump once and then remain quiet.

(2) *Somewhat sensitive.* Move their bodies slightly but soon remain quiet.

(3) *Less sensitive.* No response to sound. Stronger knock may induce slight motion.

(4) *Insensitive.* No response whatsoever even with a very strong knock.

When the response of the catfish to finger knocks was that described by grades 1 and 2, the Hatai group observed an earthquake within several hours with a probability amounting to 80%. On the contrary, no earthquake was observed when the fish behaved in the manner as described by grades 3 and 4. When the water temperature was very low, an earthquake occurrence was reported even in the case of grade 3.

Hatai and his associates made predictions every day by putting up a notice on a blackboard at the Asamushi Biological Station, Aomori Prefecture in the northeastern part of Japan during a period from October 15, 1931 to May 15, 1932. Earthquake occurrence was checked by a seismograph having a magnification of 50.

It was suspected by the Hatai group that some sort of electric stimulus might forerun an earthquake occurrence because they knew that a catfish is extremely sensitive to electric currents of the order of microamperes. They actually found that the above response of catfish did not occur when the tank in which the fish were kept was insulated from the ground. It was also found out that a V-shaped change on the earth-current record was correlated to the catfish activity and earthquake occurrence. It was also believed that the catfish felt something prior to the main earth-current changes because they became active before the signals. The catfish reacted strongly to an earthquake which occurred at a place close to the station, no matter how small it was. When the distance between the station and the epicenter was larger, the reaction of the catfish was weak even if the earthquake was fairly large.

The above study suggests strongly that the catfish is sensitive to a signal, probably of electric origin, that seems to occur prior to an earthquake although it is difficult to dispatch an actual prediction of an earthquake only on the basis of the behavior of catfish. Logically speaking, it seems better to conduct a high-sensitivity observation of earth-currents rather than to rely on catfish.

There are many reports on unusual behavior of fish other than catfish. Even today, a majority of people believe that some fish can foretell coming earthquakes. In Japan, it was reported in the summer of 1973, the year of the 50th anniversary of the 1923 Kanto earthquake, that many mackerel pikes, which are usually found in an open ocean, came to Yokohama where people could fish for them from the quay. Newspapers and weekly magazines wrote that this might be a premonitory phenomenon of a large earthquake although nothing happened in the Tokyo–Yokohama area in that year.

As the readers will see in later paragraphs, some of the reports cannot be ruled out because they are based upon reliable observations by scientists. It is of some value, therefore, to look into legends about fish and earthquakes. Most of the following are due to Musha (1957) although the present author did see a number of original reports. Musha, who was specially interested in fish movements in relation to earthquakes, classified what people regard as unusual into the following four cases:

(1) People see fish, which are not usually seen in the area, before an earthquake.

(2) Fish come up to the water surface or jump up from the surface before an earthquake.

(3) Swarms of fish come to the seashore before an earthquake.

(4) Some fish disappear before an earthquake.

Case 1

Countless loaches appeared in paddy fields near the epicenter of the 1891 Nobi earthquake having a magnitude (M) in the Richter scale of 7.9 immediately before the earthquake according to a document of local history in Aichi Prefecture.

Before the 1896 earthquake ($M = 7.1$) that was accompanied by a great tsunami which killed 27,122 local inhabitants along the Pacific coast of northeastern Japan, an enormous number of eels were found along that coast. It was said that someone caught more than 200 eels at one time there.

We had a severe earthquake ($M = 7.7$) off the Pacific coast of northeastern Japan and a great tsunami struck the coast of Hokkaido and northeastern Japan in 1857. It was reported in *Nihon Jishin Shiryo* (Musha, 1951, p. 676) that many eels were caught at the seashore before the earthquake.

On the west coast of Izu Peninsula, which is located about 100 km southwest of Tokyo, many fish were found dead along the seashore after the 1854 earthquake ($M = 8.4$) off the Pacific coast of Central Japan and the accompanying tsunami. Most of the fish were unknown to the local people. They must usually have lived deep in the sea (Musha, 1951, p. 231).

A Belgian ambassador to Japan, who was at a summer resort looking over Sagami Bay, scores of kilometers southwest of Tokyo, saw a reddish deep-sea fish floating on the surface of the sea before the 1923 Kanto earthquake ($M = 7.9$) which is believed to be caused by a faulting beneath the bay. Some sort of deep-sea fish, probably a kind of cod, was also found close to the water surface by fishermen at the western coast of the bay along Izu Peninsula before the quake.

Many lobsters and cuttlefish, which usually live at the bottom of the sea, were taken by fishing nets at the water surface off the Japan Sea coast of Kyoto Prefecture before the 1927 Tango earthquake ($M = 7.5$).

On the occasion of the 1933 Sanriku earthquake ($M = 8.3$) that was accompanied by a tsunami which struck the same area as that in the case of the 1896 tsunami, we had a number of reports on unusual fish movements. It was reported that a large number of eels came out at various places along the Pacific coast of northeastern Japan, so that even children could catch them with their hands. Ear shells were reported to have moved to shallower sea bottoms before the tsunami. Sardines, *Sardina melanosticta*, found close to the seashore in the seawater, which was only about 20 cm in depth because of the ebb-tide, were reported from a bay in Miyagi Prefecture several days prior to the earthquake. It was extremely rare to see sardines around there. Along the seashore of Hachinohe, a town facing the Pacific Ocean in Aomori Prefecture, local people could fish for mackerel on the beach before an earthquake. They said that they had never fished for mackerel on the beach. About 15—16 days preceding the quake, fishermen were surprised to catch a kind of crab off the coast of Iwate Prefecture where they had previously never caught that kind of crab.

We have had many, perhaps too many, reports on abnormal movements of fish like the above. It should be borne in mind, however, that most reports of this kind are told after the earthquake event. People try to recall things to which they did not pay special attention at the time. Hence, the description is usually vague and sometimes erroneous. On top of this, it is highly proba- ble that most of what people feel is unusual is mere coincidence with earth- quake occurrences. In order to establish a firm correlation between them, it must be proved that what people called anomalous did not occur when we had no earthquakes. In this sense we must be careful in believing reports on unusual behavior of fish, animals and the like.

Suyehiro (1934), a famous ichthyologist, reported on the following inter- esting facts which probably have something to do with the 1933 Sanriku earthquake. Unlike what was written in the preceding paragraphs, what fol- lows is an observation by a professional specialist. The earthquake occurred at about 2.30 (local time) on March 3. At about seven o'clock in the morn- ing a rare deep-sea fish called *Nemichthys avocetta* was caught alive on the coast of Odawara, Kanagawa Prefecture, several hundred kilometers distant from the epicenter. According to Suyehiro, the sample was an adult fish 78.8 cm in length and 7.5 g in weight. This species is an eel-like fish with an elongated body, and usually lives on the deep-sea bottom at a depth of more than 300 fathoms. Therefore, if we suppose that the fish swam to the beach from such a depth, we must come to the conclusion that the fish had left its haunts previous to the earthquake. Suyehiro suspected that there most probably occurred a certain change at the deep-sea bottom, so that the fish was driven away from there. It is also interesting to note that some other deep-sea fish were caught at the same place on the same day and afterwards.

Suyehiro (1934) also paid attention to the fact that adult sardines, *Sar- dina melanosticta*, which were caught by a purse seine in the upper layer of the sea near Misaki, Kanagawa Prefecture, on the evening previous to the day of the Sanriku earthquake, had eaten many bottom-adherent diatoms. It had been known that sardines of this species usually eat plankton in the upper layer of the sea. It was also observed that the sardines had eaten five times as much food as their average amount. It was thus concluded that the bottom- adherent diatoms, prior to the earthquake, must have appeared in a large quantity in the upper layer of the adjacent sea of Misaki. Suyehiro analyzed the food contents in stomachs of sardines caught at the same area on

March 6, three days after the quake, but nothing unusual was found in this case.

Tago, a professor at the Imperial Fisheries Experimental Station, who was collecting plankton at the mouth of Tokyo Bay on the very morning of the September 1, 1923 Kanto earthquake, observed an unusual abundance of plankton in the surface layer together with a scantiness of them in the middle layer. At the same time, an unusual swarm of bonitos was observed in the vicinity of an island near the mouth of Tokyo Bay where such things occur quite rarely (Terada, 1932; Suyehiro, 1934; Musha, 1957).

On the occasion of the 1939 earthquake (M = 7.0) at Oga Peninsula, Akita Prefecture, facing the Japan Sea, it was observed that tuna weighing about 15 kg, which had never come to the shore, were caught on the beach before the quake. It was also reported that many octopuses, which seemed as if they were drunk, came ashore at a number of places near the epicenter. Octopuses were not usually caught near there.

Case 2

It has already been written in the preceding paragraphs that catfish became so active that they swam around and jumped up from the water surface before the 1855 Edo and the 1923 Kanto earthquakes. When we had an earthquake (M = 6.5) near Fukuoka City in northern Kyushu in 1898, fishermen observed many fish jumping about over sea waves off the north coast of Kyushu. While they were wondering what these were, they saw ripples coming from an eastsouth direction. Subsequently, all the fish suddenly disappeared. The fishermen gave up fishing and went home when a large earthquake occurred.

On the day before the 1923 Kanto earthquake, a man, who was working for a movie company located at the southern part of Tokyo, saw many fish which were jumping about over a tiny pond on his way back home. As he liked fishing, he and his friends looked for a fishing net at the movie studio. They consequently got many fish which half-filled a big barrel of some 70 liters. He went home with the fish and drank too much while enjoying the dishes that his wife prepared with the fish. It was said that he slept so well that night that he was awakened by the shock of the earthquake at about noon next day.

Many carp and crucian carp came up to the water surface of a pond in downtown Tokyo at seven or eight o'clock in the very morning of the Kanto earthquake. It seemed as if these fish suffered from shortage of oxygen. It is said that the fish recovered when they were put in fresh water.

Local fishermen observed mackerel jumping about over the surface of the sea near the epicenter the morning of the day on which we had the 1927 Tango earthquake. Mackerel seldom jump over the sea surface in this season.

Many carp that were kept in a pond at Shichinohe, Aomori Prefecture, got quite active on the day before the 1933 Sanriku earthquake although they did not jump over the water surface. It was also reported that before the earthquake crucian carp jumped out from the river on the ground at Kuji, a fishing town in Iwate Prefecture.

When an earthquake (M = 6.5) occurred in Northern Yunan Province, China on July 31, 1917, it was reported that the level of river water became high and countless fish jumped up on the bank a few days before the earthquake (Musha, 1957, p. 30).

Case 3

That many eels appeared along the beach before the 1857, 1896 and 1933 earthquakes and tsunamis has already been reported in the foregoing paragraphs. Before these tsunamis, it was reported that many sardines were found off the Pacific coast of northeastern Japan.

Fishermen caught many sardines of a certain kind off Boso Peninsula, south of Tokyo, before the 1923 Kanto earthquake, but they did not get any after the quake. As has already been written in one of the preceding paragraphs, sardines came very close to the seashore before the 1896 and 1933 Sanriku earthquakes and tsunamis, so that fishermen along the Pacific coast of northeastern Japan benefited from the large catch of sardines. After the tsunamis, however, they usually caught many cuttlefish. In the district there is a saying "Sardines bring calamity, but cuttlefish save people".

It is said that before the shock many sardines came along the seashore of Kanagawa Prefecture in the vicinity of the epicenter of the 1923 Kanto earthquake. Some of them went up rivers there. On the same occasion an unusual swarm of bonitos was observed near the mouth of Tokyo Bay as has already been written. Unusual movements of fish were also reported in Lake Yamanakako, a lake located north of Mt. Fuji. The lake water became muddy since May of the year of the earthquake, and many crucian carp were caught immediately before the quake.

It is tedious to write all the reports of this kind, but it seems important that we still have some reports of this nature even in the case of quite recent earthquakes. Off Kii Peninsula facing the Pacific Ocean in Central Japan, local fishermen caught many bonitos prior to the 1944 Tonankai earthquake (M = 8.0) which occurred off that peninsula. The same thing happened in 1946, so that they foretold the 1946 Nankai earthquake (M = 8.1) whose epicenter was a few hundred miles more to the west than that of the previous earthquake. Before the Nankai earthquake, many halfbeaks and cuttlefish were caught on the south coast, and lobsters on the east coast of Kii Peninsula.

A few hours before the 1948 Fukui earthquake (M = 7.3), a fisherman got as many as 80 sweetfish on the River Kuzuryu near the epicenter. The normal amount of fish in a catch there was reported to be around 30.

The author does not have much information about reports of this kind in countries outside Japan. Musha (1957) wrote that many fish came to the shore when Naples was struck by a great earthquake in 1058. It is said that many fish gathered at the shore of Sicily before the Calabrian earthquake of 1783 (Milne, 1886, p. 301).

Case 4

We have many reports that fish disappeared before a large earthquake. For example, it was noticed in northeastern Japan that no cods and sharks were caught before the 1896 Sanriku earthquake. That is also the case for trepang, dace and other fish before the 1933 Sanriku earthquake. People said that their catch of fish in Sagami Bay became poor several days before the 1923 Kanto earthquake.

Cause of unusual behavior of fish

Terada (1932), an outstanding physicist and geophysicist, presented an interesting study on the relation between earthquake occurrence and fish catch. He was interested in reports that the kinds of fish most abundantly caught on the east coast of Izu Peninsula before the remarkable earthquake swarms there in 1930 were quite different from those caught after the earthquakes and similarly for the 1923 Kanto earthquake. Terada undertook a

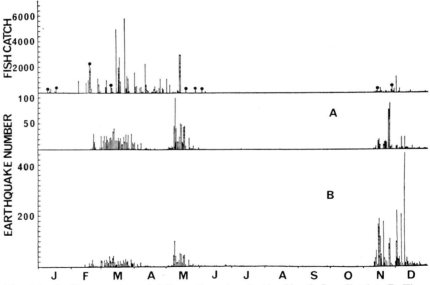

Fig. 2-1. A. The number of felt earthquakes in the North Izu district. B. The sum of the numbers of earthquakes, felt and unfelt earthquakes in Izu Peninsula and Suruga Bay, east of the peninsula, plus the number of conspicuous or moderately conspicuous earthquakes in Tokyo, Kanagawa, Shizuoka and Yamanashi Prefectures. The upper diagram gives the correlation with fish catch. A solid circle indicates that the catch, although abundant, was not exactly known (Terada, 1932).

statistical study on the relation between the daily fish catch in the fishing grounds on the west coast of Izu Peninsula as recorded by the Imperial Fisheries Institute and the daily frequency of earthquakes around there. A rather remarkable fact that can be seen in Fig. 2-1 is that the epochs with an abundant catch of horse mackerel, *Caranx*, coincided very well with the periods in which the seismic activity was very high. Terada extended the statistics over a six-year period from 1924—1929, and after statistical tests, came to the conclusion that earthquake occurrence has a positive correlation with the amounts of fish catches.

Unlike numerous reports of fragmental character in the preceding paragraphs, Terada's work, which is based on modern statistics, may suggest some relationship between earthquakes and fish catch. Terada speculated three possible causes of the relation:

(1) The seismic shocks or some kind of mechanical stimuli associated with them may be directly felt by fish and induce them to approach the fishing ground in a manner different to their usual.

(2) The shocks may somehow affect the depth of the layers with the greatest density of plankton that the fish eat.

(3) The earthquakes may affect the chemical nature of the coastal seawater due to the disturbance of the subterranean water and thus indirectly affect the plankton and fish.

In addition to these possibilities, something of electric origin, which may stimulate a catfish, cannot be ruled out. The present author is of the opinion, however, that it would be better to try to understand the physical changes by which fish are excited, rather than to rely on fish behavior resulting from such changes.

2.1.2. Animals

It has long been told that small animals run away before a large earthquake as if they foresee the occurrence of the quake. Among the legends relevant to the 1891 Nobi earthquake, it was said that there was a restaurant called the "Rat House" in Nagoya City. The restaurant was famous for many rats which were kept in the house. The rats always ran about in the house even in the presence of patrons. In the evening of the day prior to the earthquake, however, many of the rats disappeared somewhere.

It was reported that weasels and rats ran about a town in Akita Prefecture nearby the epicenter of the 1896 Rikuu earthquake ($M = 7.5$) on the day prior to the shock.

Someone noticed that rats disappeared suddenly before the 1923 Kanto earthquake. A few days prior to the quake, a storyteller who had been informed of the sudden disappearance of rats from an inn in downtown Tokyo foretold an earthquake occurrence because he knew that the same thing had happened immediately before the 1855 Edo earthquake.

We have numerous reports of this sort from a number of towns and villages in northeastern Japan on the occasion of the 1933 Sanriku earthquake and tsunami. Probably rats and mice have been most familiar to Japanese people among animals because traditional wooden houses are easily invaded by rats and mice, and provide a comfortable living place for them. Hence it is natural to hear about movements of the rat and mouse in relation to earthquake occurrence. It should be borne in mind, however, that most people remember the behavior of rats and mice only in association with an unusual happening such as an earthquake. The author suspects that rats and mice sometimes make a fuss even when earthquakes do not occur.

Unusual behavior of rats was reported before the 1966 Hsingtai earthquake ($M = 6.8$) that occurred in Hopei Province, 300 km distant from Peking (Coe, 1971).

It has also been said that cats sometimes make a fuss before an earthquake. Immediately before the 1891 Nobi earthquake, a cat ran about restlessly in a house in the epicentral area. The owner of the cat unlocked the door and let the cat go out. He and his family thus ran out safely from that door when the shock attacked a few moments later. The cat went somewhere and came back after several days. When cats mew in a strange way, it is believed by some people that an earthquake may well occur.

There are many reports on unusual barking of dogs, neighing of horses, braying of donkeys, etc., prior to earthquakes. It is said that monkeys made a fuss a few hours preceding the 1972 Managua earthquake ($M = 6.25$) in Nicaragua. Restless movements of horses, pigs, raccoon dogs and other animals are sometimes correlated to forthcoming earthquakes. Milne (1886, p. 303) wrote "Before the catastrophe of 1812 at Caracas, a Spanish stallion broke out from its stable and escaped to the highlands, which was regarded as the result of the prescience of a coming calamity." He also wrote that all the dogs escaped from the city of Talcahuano in Chile before an earthquake in 1835.

2.1.3. Frogs and snakes

There is a saying in Japan that an earthquake is expected when snakes, centipedes, frogs and the like come out from holes in the ground where they usually live. At the time of the 1855 Edo earthquake on November 11, many grass snakes came out of the ground near the focal area although they hardly moved about because it was too cold. A blue-green snake was caught in Ginza, the most prosperous street in Tokyo, in the summer of 1973. As this was the year of the 50th anniversary of the 1923 Kanto earthquake, Tokyoites became nervous about the possibility of an earthquake occurring although nothing happened that year.

2.1.4. Birds

About ten days preceding the 1855 Edo earthquake, hens and cocks near the focal area became so restless that they did not enter the henhouses. Cocks crowed and hens clucked in the epicentral area approximately one hour prior to the 1896 Rikuu earthquake. Many geese cackled at the time of the 1783 Calabrian earthquake. Immense flocks of sea birds flew inland before the 1822 and 1835 Chilean earthquakes (Milne, 1886, p. 303).

Many pigeons that used to nest at a bell-tower of a Buddhist temple near the epicenter of the 1891 Nobi earthquake went somewhere in the evening of the day prior to the earthquake. It is also said that swallows, macaws and the like seem to feel something prior to an earthquake. It is believed in Japan that pheasants foretell an earthquake by making noise. It appears to seismologists, however, that these birds are sensitive to very small tremors in the beginning of an earthquake motion, so that they make a fuss after the arrival of P waves.

2.1.5. Insects and worms

It has been said in Japan that we may well expect an earthquake when a swarm of red dragonflies is observed. Some Tokyoites became terrified in the summer of 1973 because they saw many dragonflies in the area, though no earthquake occurred that year.

Earthworms, millipedes, centipedes and the like are said to come out from holes in the ground before an earthquake.

2.2. UNUSUAL WEATHER

2.2.1. Mist and fog

There are many writings about unusual weather preceding an earthquake. It has often been said that it turns sultry immediately before an earthquake, sometimes with mysterious mist and fog in the sky.

On the occasion of the 1802 earthquake (M = 6.6) that struck Sado Island, Niigata Prefecture, in the Japan Sea, a businessman went up to a hill to see the weather for sailing. A boatman, who accompanied him that day, pointed out that the weather was extraordinary, unlike any that he had seen before. It was misty in a strange manner: mountain skirts were covered by mist, while their upper halves could be seen fairly clearly. The boatman, who used to forecast weather by watching the sky, could not say anything on this occasion. The businessman recalled what his father had told him many years ago. "Prior to an earthquake, a strange air called 'Chiki' (literally means 'air from the earth') comes up from the ground". They hurried back to an inn where they had been staying and, after picking up their belongings, they left. After they walked a distance of about 15 km, they felt a terrible shock of the ground.

The businessman, who later visited a gold mine on the island, was surprised to see that none of the miners was injured by the earthquake. In reply to his question, the miners told him that they had foretold the earthquake three days prior to its occurrence by watching the appearance of Chiki just as they had been doing over many years, so that no one entered the mine on the day of the earthquake. It was said that, when they observed the Chiki in the mine, they could hardly see their companions working nearby.

The present story of Chiki was found in *Dai Nihon Jishin Shiryo* (Imperial Earthquake Investigation Committee, 1904, 1973, Part 1, p. 509). The book was first published in 1904 and reprinted by a publisher in 1973. *Dai Nihon Jishin Shiryo* was later revised, notably by Musha who added many newly found documents to the book. They were published under the title *Zotei Dai Nihon Jishin Shiryo* in three mimeographed volumes during World War II, and they are difficult to obtain nowadays. Only one volume following them was published entitled *Nihon Jishin Shiryo* (Musha, 1951).

In *Dai Nihon Jishin Shiryo* is also found a description of Chiki in relation to the 1830 Kyoto earthquake (M = 6.4).

There is a story of an old gatekeeper who foretold the 1855 Edo earthquake (Musha, 1951, p. 625). He had been hired by a Samurai (warrior) of high rank many years ago. In the early evening of November 11, he had been looking around outside the gate, and told his fellow workers that there would be a strong earthquake that evening. He then boiled some rice for emergency use. Most of the servants in the Samurai residence did not believe what the old man said.

The old gatekeeper sat with some of his colleagues on a straw mat spread in the courtyard. At about ten o'clock in the evening, it became somewhat misty or foggy with clouds covering half of the sky. Yet, ridiculously enough, stars could be seen very close to the people. Suddenly the ground began to shake with terrific force. When the shock became a litte quiet, they saw that the houses had collapsed. The well-prepared gatekeeper and his friends immediately extinguished the fire which had started.

Having been impressed by what the gatekeeper did, the Samurai, the gatekeeper's master, praised him to the skies, and asked him how he could foretell the quake. The gatekeeper said that, when he experienced the 1828 Echigo earthquake (M = 6.9) and the 1847 Shinshu earthquake (M = 7.4) respectively in the districts which are nowadays called the Niigata and Nagano Prefectures, he observed, prior to the quakes, stars shining so brightly in the misty sky that he felt that they were unusually close to him. As he observed similar things for a day or two this time, he simply told the people that an earthquake was impending.

Most seismologists, including the present author, do not think that an earthquake can be foretold by watching the weather. The legends cited in the above may well be fiction. Unusual weather forerunning an earthquake can well be a mere coincidence. There are many misty days, but people only remember the days before a terrible earthquake.

2.2.2. Rainbow and mysterious light

It has been told in Japan that a rainbow of short length is a precursor of an earthquake, that a rainbow appears very low in the sky before an earthquake, and that a rainbow consisting of three colors, i.e. black, yellow and indigo, is a warning of a coming earthquake. H. Mukuhira, an amateur predictor who lives in the northern part of Kyoto Prefecture, insisted that he could foresee earthquake occurrence by watching a sort of rainbow which appears from time to time in a particular direction from a village where he lives. It is said that earthquakes that occur not only in Japan but also in some other parts of the world can be foretold by his rainbow method. Mukuhira often sent a postcard forecasting an earthquake to the Japan Meteorological Agency, a seismological institute of a certain university and so on. It is hard to believe, however, that an earthquake can be foreseen by observing a rainbow because no physical relationship between an earthquake and a rainbow has been established. The author suspects that Mukuhira's prediction sometimes was correct because we may well expect a coincidence between two things, i.e. the frequent sending of postcards and the frequent occurrence of earthquakes. It is also impossible to believe that an earthquake which occurs at a far corner of the world, thousands of miles away from where the predictor lives, can be foretold by an observation of a rainbow in Japan.

Numerous reports on mysterious light associated with an earthquake can be seen in classical and modern documents related to earthquakes (Terada, 1931; Derr, 1973). At the time of the 1965—1967 Matsushiro earthquakes, occurrence of such light was reported so often that even many colored photographs were taken by amateur photographers. The present author and his colleagues conducted electric and magnetic observations on the summit of Mt. Minakami situated at the center of the earthquake area. The author is afraid, however, that he and his co-workers have never observed anomalous luminosity and no anomalous trace whatsoever has been found on the records of earth-current observation at the times when mysterious luminosity was reported.

Probably luminous phenomena accompanying earthquakes were best observed in association with the 1930 North Izu earthquake ($M = 7.0$). On that occasion we had numerous reports on luminous phenomena which were observed by people, some of whom lived at places more than 100 km distant from the epicentral area. Even a number of scientists reported on light which they observed. It is therefore hard to deny the occurrence of anomalous luminosity in this case although no physical explanation of it can be put forward. Terada (1931) presented a very detailed review on luminous phenomena accompanying earthquakes. Those who are particularly interested in the phenomena may refer to his paper.

It has sometimes been reported that some unusual light is observed preceding an earthquake. In the case of the 1703 Genroku earthquake ($M = 8.2$), which caused tremendous damage in an area south of Edo (now Tokyo), luminous bodies and air were frequently seen in the nights preceding the day of the severest shock, and afterwards (Imperial Earthquake Investigation Committee, 1973, Part 1, p. 285). At the time of the 1830 Kyoto earthquake, it was stated that in the night preceding the earthquake, luminous phenomena were seen in the whole sky and some kinds of luminosity were so bright that they could be compared with daylight (Imperial Earthquake Investigation Committee, 1973, Part 1, p. 583), also emitted from the ground.

The statements in the last paragraph and the following ones are taken from Terada (1931). The present author checked the descriptions by examining *Dai Nihon Jishin Shiryo*, too. Although the author could not find the original, Terada quoted a document related to the 1847 Shinshu earthquake which reads as follows: "Under the dark sky, a fiery cloud appeared in the direction of Mt. Iduna. It was seen to make a whirling motion and then disappeared. Immediately afterward, a roaring sound was heard, followed by severe earthquakes." (Musha, 1957, p. 56).

A party of 19 persons went to sea on the eve of the 1855 Edo earthquake. Before the time of the shock a sudden luminosity was seen towards the northeast, which was so bright that the colored patterns of their clothes could be well discerned. Soon afterwards, a horrible roaring sound was heard from underneath the sea, which gave them the impression that a mass of gravel was impinging upon the bottom of the boat. At the same time a mass of flame, accompanied by sounds, went flying through the sky (Musha, 1957, p. 60).

In the preceding night of the 1891 Nobi earthquake, lightning was seen towards the west from a village near the focal region. A woman in downtown Tokyo saw a flashing light on the sea in the morning, i.e. several hours prior to the shock, of September 1 on the occasion of the 1923 Kanto earthquake.

On the occasion of the 1930 North Izu earthquake, it was reported that a watchman who was in charge on the top of the watch-tower of a fire-brigade station in downtown Tokyo, observed a flash of light towards the south about ten minutes before the shocks, and afterward four or five spark-like flashes during the earthquake. A number of fishermen who were about to set their boat afloat in the evening prior to the earthquake observed a spherical luminous body to the west of Mt. Amagi which moved towards the northwest with a considerable speed.

In Terada's paper (1931) numerous examples of luminous phenomena relevant to earthquake occurrences outside Japan are found. On the occasion of the Yunan earthquake of March 1925 ($M = 7.1$), for instance, immediately before each of the severe shocks, a sulphurous smell arose, and a fiery light which moved from north to south appeared in the sky.

As the present author has never observed a luminous phenomenon related to an earthquake occurrence, he cannot really believe in precursory luminosity. Indeed, Terada (1931) wrote "With regard to all these testimonies of witnesses, it must be always kept in mind that people are naturally alive to all kinds of phenomena observed at the time of a severe earthquake and apt to regard them as something connected with the catastrophal occurrence, while they forget to consider that the same phenomena are frequently observed on many other occasions not at all connected with earthquakes."

2.3. UNDERGROUND WATER

(1) When the water of a fountain decreases, an earthquake is approaching.

(2) When well water suddenly decreases, we may well expect an earthquake occurrence.

(3) Sudden lowering or rising of the head of subterranean water may well be a precursor of an earthquake.

(4) When well water suddenly becomes muddy, an earthquake is forthcoming.

These are picked up from Japanese legends related to underground water.

It was reported (Imperial Earthquake Investigation Committee, 1973, Part 1, p. 360) that a Samurai noticed that the fountain water at a farmer's, which used to be very clear, became muddy on the day of the 1751 Takata earthquake ($M = 6.6$) in a district which now belongs to Niigata Prefecture. He found that the water from several fountains around there were also muddy, and foretold that an earthquake would occur in the evening.

On the morning of the day of the 1855 Edo earthquake, a Samurai found that well water had become muddy and had a salty taste. He then suggested a coming earthquake, but nobody believed him (Musha, 1951, p. 623).

As we will see in a later chapter, changes in underground water may sometimes have something to do with a forthcoming earthquake in a way which can be accounted for on the basis of a scientific theory.

2.4. MAGNET

Reports that a magnet loses its attracting power before an earthquake can often be found in classical literature.

There was an optician in downtown Edo in 1855. The proprietor was proud of a horseshoe magnet which was as large as 3 shakus (1 shaku is equal to 30.3 cm). All nails and iron pieces attached to the magnet suddenly dropped to the ground on the day of the 1855 earthquake. The proprietor was surprised and terribly disappointed because the magnet used to be a good advertisement for his shop. He thought that the magnet had lost its magnetism because it was too old. About two hours later, however, a destructive earthquake struck Edo. After that, the proprietor found that the magnet recovered its attracting power (Musha, 1951, p. 625). On the basis of his experience, it was said that the proprietor had invented an apparatus that could foretell an earthquake. According to Milne (1886, p. 16), however, it does not appear that this instrument has ever performed with success.

Probably one of the most complete summary reports on magnetic and electric phenomena related to earthquakes in early days would be the one due to Milne (1890). It was reported that iron pieces had fallen from a number of horseshoe magnets on the occasion of an earthquake in Rome. Around 1870 Count Malvasia watched a magnet to which a small iron piece was attached for a long period. The iron piece sometimes fell down from the magnet in association with an earthquake, but there were instances when the piece did not fall.

In those early days, the above phenomena were thought to be caused by changes in the earth's magnetic field. But present-day knowledge about geomagnetism does not support the association of such a large change with an earthquake.

2.5. POSITION OF CELESTIAL BODIES

Much has been conducted about the statistical study of earthquake occurrences in relation to moon phase. It has thus been reported that numbers of earthquake occurrences are usually larger for the new and the full moon than those for a young moon. A. Perrey reported on such a tendency as early as 1875 (Milne, 1886). During a certain period of the 1965--1967 Matsushiro seismic activity, the author had an experience that proved the above tendency very well. Even more, the correlation between geomagnetic storm and earthquake occurrence was unbelievably high during that period although such a high correlation period did not last a long time.

Statistics of earthquake occurrence in relation to the position of the stars, the sun and the like have also been studied by seismologists, but the present author does not intend to review such statistical studies in this subsection. Those who are interested in such studies can find many references elsewhere (e.g. Sadeh and Meidav, 1973). Studies of this kind suggest that earthquakes can be triggered by mechanical forces arising from particular combinations of celestial body positions.

Apart from such statistical results, some say that a large earthquake can occur when a few planets take on a certain combination of their positions although the author does not understand the physical basis of such a prediction. This may be a kind of astrology.

Terada (1931) quoted a story of an astronomer who premonitored the 1703 Genroku earthquake. It is stated in a document recorded in *Dai Nihon Jishin Shiryo* that on the eve of the great earthquake, Sukezaemon Shibukawa, the astronomer of that age in service of Shogun, the governor of Japan, gave a positive warning to the officers in the residence of Shogun to the effect that a severe thunderstorm or earthquake could be expected in the course of the night. It is also stated that he was constantly in the habit of watching the night sky, as is natural for an astronomer. Terada suspected that the astronomer's premonition was based on some luminous phenomena although it is not at all clear to the present author, who also read the original document, whether the prediction was based on some sort of astrology or luminosity observation.

2.6. SUPERNATURAL INSTINCT

In Japan, there are stories of lunatics who foresaw an earthquake occurrence by means of their supernatural instinct. On the very day of the 1855 Edo earthquake, a man, who said that he was possessed by a fox spirit, told his neighbors that a great earthquake would come that evening and ran away somewhere. Superstitious Japanese people at that time seemed to believe that a man's soul could be replaced by that of a fox which has a supernatural power to take the form of a man or woman, to turn leaves into notes and coins, and so on.

There was an elderly woman in downtown Edo who could talk with gods. She was suffering from epilepsy. About three months before the 1855 Edo earthquake, she told everybody that the town would be burnt down because a god would become angry for some reason. The rumor of the woman widely spread all over Edo at once. She was arrested by the police and expelled from Edo because of her demagogy.

It is said that the 1896 Sanriku tsunami was foretold by an old woman who lived in a village in Iwate Prefecture. She believed in Buddhism so deeply that she prayed at a temple every day. A few months prior to the earthquake and tsunami, she began to say that the village would turn into a muddy field. She announced what she foresaw all over the village by playing a drum. People thought that she had become a lunatic because of her crazy business. However, they actually had a large earthquake and tsunami some time later.

It is said that a lady named Mrs. J. Budd, the wife of an ex-governor of San Francisco, foretold the occurrence of the 1906 San Francisco earthquake (Bronson, 1971, p. 274) although the author does not know the details of the story. A crazy lifeguardsman prophesized that an earthquake would take place in London on April 4, 1691 (Milne, 1886).

It might be possible for lunatics, who could be very sensitive to particular things, to feel some unusual sounds, smells, lights and the like which are so feeble that no ordinary people can feel them. Although some of what these people can feel cannot be ruled out, it is useless to put much stress on such supernatural things for the purpose of predicting an earthquake on scientific grounds.

2.7. OTHER INDICATORS

A confectioner in Tokyo insists that he can predict an earthquake by observing colors of steamed rice for Japanese sweets. Someone says that candles at Buddhism temples or Shintoism shrines bend or crush in a strange way forerunning an earthquake. All these premonitions of an earthquake are hard to believe from the standpoint of a physically plausible theory. It is rather surprising, however, that these things are still widely believed by people even in the 20th century. In the author's experience, letters and telephone calls concerning amateur prediction of earthquake have come to him from time to time from not only Japanese people but also from people living in foreign countries. It may be said that there are many people whose hobby is earthquake prediction, and this in turn reflects that the desire of mankind for earthquake prediction is very strong.

Chapter 3

BIRTH OF PREDICTION-ORIENTED EARTHQUAKE SCIENCE

As far as the forecasting of an earthquake occurrence relies on what the author described in the last chapter, it hardly can be said that such a warning is based on modern science. As a matter of fact, prediction of earthquakes had long been the business of astrologers, fortune-tellers, and sometimes lunatics until the science of earthquakes was set forth about a hundred years ago. Because the progress of earthquake research was not very rapid, we are still suffering from misleading forecasts of earthquakes by amateurs even today.

3.1. BEGINNING OF EARTHQUAKE RESEARCH IN JAPAN

At the beginning of the new civilization in Japan about one hundred years ago, the Japanese government invited many scientists from western countries in order to accelerate modernization of Japanese science. Some of the professors who came over to Japan on the invitation of the Japanese government were surprised by strong earthquakes which often occurred in the Tokyo—Yokohama area.

The 1880 Yokohama earthquake ($M = 5.4$), which gave rise to damage to chimneys, tombs and so on, provided an opportunity for the scientists invited from western countries to set up the Seismological Society of Japan. Among these scientists, special mention should be made of J. Ewing and J. Milne who invented seismographs for practical use based on the principle of a horizontal pendulum. It may be said that this is the very beginning of modern seismology. Although it is beyond the scope of this chapter to deal with the history of seismology in general, it should be mentioned that P (primary) and S (secondary) waves were first discovered on the seismographs constructed by them.

Milne, who married a Japanese woman, spent almost 20 years in Japan. He not only promoted earthquake research but also trained a number of Japanese seismologists such as K. Sekiya, F. Omori, A. Imamura and others, who later became leading members of the seismological community in Japan.

3.2. THE 1891 NOBI EARTHQUAKE AND THE IMPERIAL EARTHQUAKE INVESTIGATION COMMITTEE

A large earthquake with an estimated magnitude of 7.9 struck the Mino-Owari district (now Gifu and Aichi Prefectures) in Central Japan on October 28, 1891 (Richter, 1958, p. 563). Having been called the Nobi (an abbreviation of Mino-Owari) earthquake, it is famous for the Neodani fault, which appeared in association with the quake, running over a distance of 40 km in a WNW—ESE direction. The largest difference in the height between both the sides of the fault was as large as 6 m. It was reported that 7,273 people were killed, that 142,177 houses totally collapsed and that landslides took place at more than 10,000 places. Aftershocks were felt during a period of 10 years or so. It was remarkable that many of the western style brick buildings were heavily damaged in Nagoya, the largest city in Central Japan.

Because of the earthquake, the Japanese government set up the Imperial Earthquake Investigation Committee. The main job of the committee is to investigate into seismic and volcanic phenomena and to find a way to lessen earthquake hazards. The committee also made every effort to collect historical documents relevant to earthquake and volcanic eruption throughout the history of Japan. It was possible to trace earthquake records way back to A.D. 416. The accumulation of seismic history over such a long period, which has been achieved only in Japan, plays an important role in estimating the earthquake risk in a certain district. It is regrettable, however, that only the last portion of the historical documents thus collected has been published as already stated in Chapter 2.

Seismic history in China is also extensive (e.g. Lee, 1974). But, unlike Japan, the country is too vast for a complete coverage of the seismic records.

3.3. THE 1923 KANTO EARTHQUAKE

Like the Nobi earthquake, the Kanto earthquake of 1923 was a terrible shock to Japanese people. Kanto (sometimes written as Kwanto) means the district surrounding Tokyo. The author does not intend to repeat a detailed account of the Kanto earthquake because excellent reports are available elsewhere (e.g. Richter, 1958, p. 567). The following is a brief summary of the damage caused by the earthquake.

On September 1, 1923, an earthquake with an estimated magnitude of 7.9 struck the South Kanto area including Tokyo and Yokohama, the economical, political, as well as cultural centers of Japan. The damage caused by the

TABLE 3-I

Damage caused by the 1923 Kanto earthquake

	Number
Totally collapsed houses	128,266
Partly collapsed houses	126,233
Houses burned down	447,128
Deaths	142,807

earthquake was incredibly large as can be seen in Table 3-I. Many of the deaths were caused by the fire which started soon after the earthquake. Violent tsunami waves also hit the seashore along Sagami Bay as well as Izu, Miura and Boso Peninsulas (see Fig. 5-29), the height of the waves was reported to exceed 10 m at some places.

The extremities of Boso and Miura Peninsulas uplifted by 1—2 m at the time of the earthquake. It is believed that the earthquake was caused by a fault movement which took place along a submarine canyon called the Sagami Trough running through Sagami Bay somewhere between Oshima Island and Boso Peninsula in a NW—SE direction.

The social impact of the earthquake was so strong that in 1925 the Japanese government hurriedly founded the Earthquake Research Institute which was attached to the Tokyo Imperial University (now University of Tokyo). A number of seismological institutes were also set up in Imperial Universities in other cities such as Kyoto and Sendai. The seismic observation network of the Central Meteorological Observatory (now Japan Meteorological Agency) was also intensified.

3.4. EARTHQUAKE RESEARCH INSTITUTE

It cannot be said that the Earthquake Research Institute (ERI) was a large organization in the beginning. Most of the members, consisting of physicists, architects, civil engineers, geographers and geologists, were part-time. Year by year that followed, however, fresh graduates in physics, seismology and geology joined them in forming a unique research team whose energetic work opened a new phase in earthquake research.

In the early days of the ERI, there was much to learn about the earthquake phenomena. Although the work achieved by the Imperial Earthquake Investigation Committee was invaluable, the knowledge accumulated was descriptive rather than scientific. The founders of the ERI thus began to study earthquake phenomena on a physical basis. For example, measurement of ground motions as well as vibrations of a building during an earthquake was first accomplished by developing new techniques. M. Ishimoto designed and constructed a then revolutionary accelerometer by means of which the acceleration of earthquake motion was first measured. He also invented a quartz horizontal-pendulum tiltmeter for measuring extremely small tilts of the earth's surface. Theoretical work was also intensively conducted by a few researchers led by K. Sezawa who set out a general equation of elastic waves in spherical polar coordinates. His theory subsequently had many applications to problems concerned with the propagation of body and surface waves.

A few large-scale earthquakes such as the 1927 Tango and the 1930 North Izu took place soon after the establishment of the ERI, so that the staff had the opportunity to make observations over the earthquake area and learn much about earthquake phenomena. It is of particular importance that marked land deformations were discovered by analyzing levelling and triangulation surveys carried out before and after an earthquake.

It was really remarkable that many new facts about earthquake phenomena were discovered during the first 10-year period of the ERI. Much of earthquake study based on new ideas and techniques has been promoted very intensively in the following years, so that it may be said that seismology was established as one of physical sciences by that time. However, further development of studies at the ERI was curtailed by World War II.

The activity of the ERI soon after the war was inevitably not very high because funds for research were extremely limited as a result of the war. However, as the staff of the ERI, who survived the war, came back to the institute, the ERI recovered its activity gradually. Since the early 1950s, it has become possible to send younger members of the research staff to foreign countries. This was good for the ERI because much internationally-minded work in later years was thus founded.

Japan showed a marked recovery in its economic situation in the late 1960s. The ERI was also revived in a more modernized form. Although only 30 to 40 people, including technicians, clerks in the administrative section and porters, had been working in the ERI before the war, the numbers of employees increased so tremendously by the middle of the 1960s that some 200 people were working there. The ERI also runs eighteen observatories, scattered all over Japan, for seismic, crustal deformation, geomagnetic and tsunami observations.

Probably the ERI activity reached its maximum when an earthquake swarm activity occurred in Matsushiro, a small town in Central Japan (see Fig. 5-55), which experienced an incredibly large number of shocks during the 1965—1967 period. At the most violent stage some 600 shocks per day were felt, including moderately large shocks from time to time which gave rise to slight damage. The ERI carried out all sorts of observations, i.e. seismometric, geologic, geodetic, geomagnetic and the like, over the Matsushiro area. On the basis of these observations, warnings of coming earthquakes were sometimes released to local inhabitants.

As the national program for earthquake prediction in Japan made progress, as will be presented in the following chapter, the ERI expanded very much in scale after the Matsushiro event. Since the administration of the ERI, as one of the institutes attached to the University of Tokyo, has not been changed, a serious labor problem was to arise sooner or later. Since 1970, the ERI has been involved in serious trouble. In spite of its famed history, the ERI could not function properly during the first half of the 1970s.

Through the activities of foreign and domestic seismologists in the earlier period, those of the Imperial Earthquake Investigation Committee, the ERI, the Central Meteorological Observatory and the seismological institutes of provincial universities, data which suggest the possible existence of premonitory effects of large-scale earthquakes have been accumulated in Japan.

Earthquake study that aims at searching for phenomena forerunning an earthquake has also been conducted in countries outside Japan for the last scores of years. However, it is certain that the Japanese effort must be the most intensive in the world (Rikitake, 1972b). The seismology that has developed in western countries was mostly aimed at clarifying the internal structure of the earth by making use of seismic waves rather than by investigating into the physical cause of an earthquake.

Chapter 4

EARTHQUAKE PREDICTION PROGRAMS

4.1. THE "BLUEPRINT"

Accumulation of observations relevant to earthquake occurrence gradually led Japanese seismologists to the recognition of probable precursors of an earthquake. Some 20—30 years ago, however, it was still unusual for a professional seismologist to talk about the prediction of an earthquake. That kind of thing was wholly the business of fortune-tellers, astrologers and the like at that time. But the situation has been drastically changing in recent years.

Since around 1960, a movement to discuss a possible approach to earthquake prediction has arisen among Japanese seismologists. Scores of them met many times and eventually formed a research group for earthquake prediction. The outcome of the group's discussion was published in a summarized review called *Prediction of Earthquakes — Progress to Date and Plans for further Development* (Tsuboi et al., 1962). The now famous report has been colloquially called by the Japanese seismologists the "blueprint" of earthquake prediction research.

The blueprint describes what the Japanese seismologists believe is the best way of achieving prediction of earthquakes, and provided the guiding principle of an earthquake prediction program in the following years. The most important point emphasized in the blueprint was to make every effort to obtain basic data for possible prediction rather than to hasten the actual forecasting. In the blueprint were stated probable merits and drawbacks of work in various disciplines, i.e. geodetic work, continuous observation of crustal movement, seismic activity, seismic wave velocity, active fault, geomagnetic-geoelectric work and so on. The following is a few paragraphs quoted from the concluding chapter of the blueprint which not only summarizes the role of various disciplines but also mentions the anticipated outcome of the proposal.

"It is proposed, with regard to investigations by geodetic methods, that the time interval for nationwide repeated surveys be 5 years for levelling and 10 years for triangulation. Hence, it would be some 10 years or so before the program really got under way. For certain special areas, a considerable amount of information should be obtained within 5 years. But when we realize that during the initial years of the project much work in instrumentation and education of personnel will be demanded, 5 years should reasonably be allocated for the preparatory stage.

Tide-gauge stations would be completed in 2 years, but data covering several years would be necessary to be really useful.

Continuous observation of crustal deformation: six base stations would be established under a 3-year project, and personnel trained in these stations. Then, such trained personnel would construct the proposed 100 stations under an 8-year scheme. If things work out as planned, completion of stations would be accomplished in 11 years.

Observation of microearthquakes: twenty branch stations and their subsidiary stations would be established under a 10-year project.

Observation of ultra-microearthquakes: a small network of stations in six special areas would be carried out under a 6-year project.

Determination of seismic wave velocity by means of explosion seismology: regular operation would be combined with explosions at six places under a 6-year project.

Investigation of active faults would be completed in 2 years.

Investigation of geomagnetism and earth currents: several fixed stations in special areas would be completed in 3 years.

Provided that the project is promoted as planned above, an amount of useful information would be obtained in 5 years and after 10 years the amount of data should be fairly adequate for earthquake prediction.

In other words, it will take at least 10 years before the survey and observations under the present proposal really get under way. After that, the stage for processing data would start. At present, statistics show that earthquakes with magnitude $M > 6$ occur about five times every year in and near Japan. Among these, one is usually destructive. If we aim at predicting earthquakes with magnitude $M > 6$, it seems highly probable that we would be able to find some significant correlation between earthquake occurrence and observed phenomena merely by accumulating data for several years."

Nothing was mentioned in the blueprint about the expenses needed for the proposal. It was unofficially estimated that, if a sum of 10,000 million yen (ca. 30 million U.S. dollars) should be spent for promoting the program within 10 years' time, it would become possible to see whether or not prediction of an earthquake is feasible. Journalists tended to believe that this amount of money to be spent during this 10-year period would result in achieving the prediction of major earthquakes.

4.2. JAPANESE PROGRAM

4.2.1. Initiation and development

In spite of the public interest in earthquake prediction in Japan, it took some time to actually launch a national program on earthquake prediction because there was much red tape to be cut.

In 1963 a subcommittee for earthquake prediction research was set up by the Geodetic Council, Ministry of Education, which is responsible for administrative coordination of geodetic and geophysical work in Japan. On the other hand, the Science Council of Japan, which is in a position to discuss important scientific projects in Japan, resolved that the government should take proper action in promoting earthquake prediction research later in the same year.

Quite unexpectedly on June 16 of the next year, a destructive earthquake ($M = 7.5$) hit the Niigata City and its surroundings, the most industrialized area on the Japan Sea coast. In view of the strong public demand for earthquake prediction as a result of the Niigata earthquake, the Japanese government decided to launch a government-supported long-term program on earthquake prediction research.

It was fortunate that a guideline of the program had already been worked out in the blueprint. The above-mentioned subcommittee hurriedly worked on forming the program for the first year although a more comprehensive 5-year one was later put forward by a newly established Committee for Earthquake Prediction, associated with the National Committee for Geodesy and Geophysics, Science Council of Japan. It cannot be helped, of course, that the actual program differed somewhat from the blueprint because the amount of the governmental budget was limited.

The 5-year program (Rikitake, 1966a) originally consisted of the following disciplines:

(1) Detection of premonitory crustal movement by geodetic observation
(2) Detection of premonitory crustal movement by tide-gauge observation
(3) Continuous observation of crustal deformation by strainmeters and tiltmeters
(4) Seismic observation: overall seismic activity in Japan
(5) Observation of changes in seismic velocities
(6) Detailed survey of active faults and foldings
(7) Geomagnetic and geoelectric observation
(8) Laboratory work and rock-breaking tests
(9) Establishment of data processing centers

Just as the earthquake prediction program started, it was to be tested by the Matsushiro earthquakes in 1965—1967. As has been mentioned in section 3.4, the swarm activity centering on Matsushiro Town, Nagano Prefecture (see Fig. 5-55), was at one time so high that it became an urgent matter for the local people to know whether or not a bigger shock was to strike them. The mayor said to the press: "What we badly need is a science of earthquakes."

Because no extremely large earthquakes had taken place there in spite of the incredibly large number of small shocks, the ERI and other organizations could perform all sorts of observations without being interrupted by electric power failure, road closing and the like. It was demonstrated that changes in ground tilt, as observed by water-tube tiltmeters, were closely correlated to the growth and decay of seismic activity. Precursory changes in tilting prior to a moderately large earthquake were often observed. Mobile observations of microearthquakes proved that numerous small shocks had been occurring at places where moderately large shocks occurred a few months later.

On the basis of these observations, warnings relevant to occurrences of a moderately large earthquake were issued to the public by the Japan Meteorological Agency (JMA).

The Matsushiro experience suggested possible improvements of the prediction program. The importance of quick data processing as well as of field patrols which could be sent to the area of emergency at any time was recognized. These points were subsequently amended (Hagiwara and Rikitake, 1967; Rikitake, 1968a; Kanamori, 1970).

North Japan was violently shaken by the Tokachi-oki earthquake ($M = 7.9$) on May 16, 1968. As a consequence, the necessity of earthquake prediction was discussed at cabinet level, and a drastic intensification of earthquake prediction was proposed. The public now required actual prediction rather than prediction research, wherever possible. The 5-year program was thus modified into a semipermanent one (Rikitake, 1972a).

In response to such a public demand, it was decided to set up three centers in order to accelerate the processing of earthquake prediction data. They are the Crustal Activity Monitoring Center (geodetic, tide-gauge data, etc.) at the Geographical Survey Institute (GSI), the Seismicity Monitoring Center (for earthquakes of $M > 3$) at the JMA, and the Earthquake Prediction Observation Center (microearthquakes, crustal deformation, magnetic and other data from university sources) at the ERI, University of Tokyo.

After processing at these centers, data are sent to the newly established Coordinating Committee for Earthquake Prediction (CCEP) which was also attached to the GSI. The CCEP, which consists of about 30 specialists from universities and governmental organizations, is responsible for analyzing the data sent through the above three channels, so that it is actually functioning as the headquarters of earthquake prediction in Japan. The CCEP is in a position to issue information to the public about anomalous phenomena, if any, such as crustal deformation, seismic activity and so on which might be correlated to the danger of a large earthquake occurring in a particular area although no actual issue of a definite earthquake alarm has as yet been put forward.

In addition to the nationwide routine observations of various disciplines, intensified observations are to be carried out over the *area of special observation*, which: (1) have experienced destructive earthquakes in the past, (2) include active faults, (3) are characterized by the frequent occurrences of earthquakes, or (4) are sociologically or economically important, such as the Tokyo area. Every effort is to be made in these areas to detect anomalous premonitory effects by establishing observatories for crustal movement and microearthquakes, along with frequent repetitions of geodetic surveys. The CCEP nominated the nine areas shown in Fig. 4-1 as the ones of special observation in 1969.

Fig. 4-1. The areas of special observation as selected by the CCEP. The shaded areas, i.e. the South Kanto and Tokai areas, were selected as areas of intensified observation, respectively in 1969 and 1974.

Whenever the CCEP confirms that something anomalous is taking place in a certain area, it is designated an *area of intensified observation*. The area will then be monitored by teams of various disciplines. In case these intensified observations lead to a conclusion that the anomaly seems likely to be correlated to an earthquake occurrence, then the CCEP will designate the area as an *area of concentrated observation*. Every effort will then be made toward possible earthquake prediction by concentrating all kinds of observations there. The South Kanto district was nominated as an area of intensified observation because of an anomalous land uplift found in an area south of Tokyo in 1969. Geodetic, seismic and other data suggest the possibility of having a large-scale earthquake off the Pacific coast of Central Japan (the Tokai district), so that the area was designated as an area of the same rank in 1974.

The above strategy may sound splendid. However, there are difficulties in actual performance. The CCEP handles only "coordination"; it is not authorized to issue an "order", so that it is not always possible to conduct timely observations.

In 1973, the year of the 50th anniversary of the horrible Kanto earth-

TABLE 4-I

Yearly budget of the Japanese program on earthquake prediction

Year	Amount (yen)
1965	212,539,000
1966	290,035,000
1967	334,362,000
1968	328,559,000
1969	496,116,000
1970	596,120,000
1971	805,720,000
1972	898,900,000
1973	761,164,000
1974	1,552,674,000
1975	2,007,638,000
Total	8,283,827,000 (ca. 28 million U.S. dollars)

quake of 1923, the importance of earthquake hazard reduction was especially stressed in Japan. The public was warned of the earthquake risk in parts of Japan through campaigns of newspapers, weekly magazines, TV programs and so on. A special committee for promoting new techniques attached to the National Diet summoned specialists and asked them whether there was an immediate danger of occurrence of destructive earthquakes. On that occasion the present author pointed out that he would not be surprised if a large-scale earthquake occurred off eastern Hokkaido and off the Pacific coast of Central Japan on the basis of his investigation of the probability of earthquake occurrence.

As an earthquake having a magnitude of 7.4 actually occurred off eastern Hokkaido on June 17, 1973, it became a strong social demand to strengthen the existing program of earthquake prediction. Accordingly, the Geodetic Council proposed to the government to intensify the program by two or three times its present funding. New instrumentation, such as sea-bottom seismographs, telemetering of microearthquake data, establishment of precise geodetic networks and so forth were included in the new proposal.

It was also an urgent matter to have an agency which would act as earthquake prediction headquarters and which would be much more powerful than the existing CCEP. At the moment, however, nothing definite has been decided about a new agency which should eventually be established.

In Table 4-I is listed the yearly budget which has been allocated for the Japanese program on earthquake prediction since 1965. It cannot be said that the total amount is very large. As a matter of fact, it is much smaller than the budget of the Japanese space project. Because the money cited in the table was spent purely on earthquake prediction research, it had quite an impact in promoting solid earth science in Japan. It should be mentioned that expenses for salaries for personnel working on the program, for constructing observatory buildings and the like have been defrayed from other sources. The present-day level of earthquake prediction research in Japan would certainly not have been reached without the government-supported money mentioned in this subsection.

The development in each discipline of the program will be briefly described in the following subsections.

4.2.2. Geodetic work

A first-order triangulation survey was first carried out over the Japan

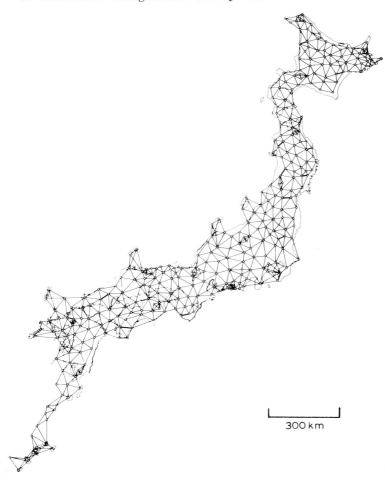

Fig. 4-2. First-order triangulation network over Japan.

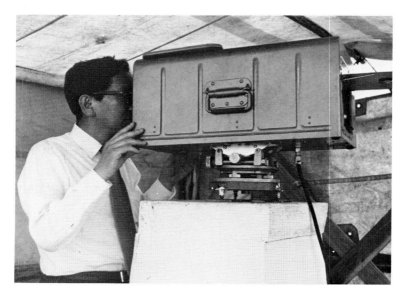

Fig. 4-3. Geodimeter Type 8. The photo was taken by the author in 1972.

Islands in the years towards the end of the last century. Fig. 4-2 shows the triangulation network for some 330 first-order stations covering Japan. Triangulation surveys are so laborious and expensive that the second survey in Japan was completed only quite recently. It seems difficult to repeat first-order triangulation surveys every 10 years as proposed in the blueprint.

It is fortunate, however, that the geodimeter technique, by which we can measure distance over a few tens of kilometers, made progress by introducing a laser light source (Fig. 4-3) in recent years. It is expected that most triangulation surveys will be replaced by geodimeter ones in the coming years. The GSI is proposing to establish a precise geodetic network to be observed by geodimeters every 5 years. The network consists of not only first-order triangulation stations but also second-order stations. The total number of stations amounts to some 6,000. The average distance between two stations is about 8 km. It is thus anticipated that the accumulation of crustal strain may well be made clear all over Japan provided that the plan goes well.

It is now possible to conduct first-order levelling surveys every 5 years along routes 20,000 km in total length (Fig. 4-4) as proposed in the blueprint. As will be described in later chapters, a number of premonitory land deformations have been detected by the surveys, along with those observed by triangulation and geodimeter surveys.

It is interesting to note that the strain accumulation revealed by the

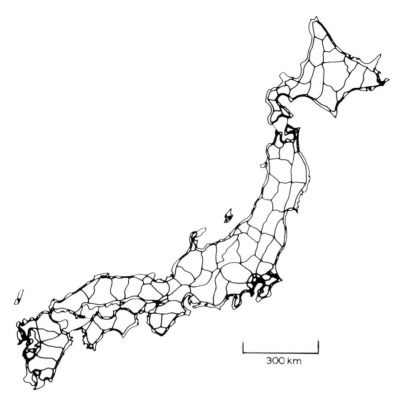

Fig. 4-4. First-order levelling routes in Japan.

repetition of geodetic surveys is a factor in estimating the probability of earthquake occurrence in a certain area.

4.2.3. Tide-gauge observation

Land uplift or subsidence relative to sea level can be detected by tide-gauge observation. It was originally planned to establish tide-gauge stations along the coastlines of the Japan Islands with intervals of approximately 100 km. Some twenty stations were newly constructed under the earthquake prediction program in addition to the existing ones, so that 80 tide-gauge stations are now operating. The observed data are sent from these stations to a center at the GSI for processing.

No remarkable precursor has been observed by these tide-gauges since the beginning of the program. It is apparent that fluctuations of sea level due to oceanographic origins such as changes in the temperature and density of seawater are so large that land uplift or subsidence less than several centimeters can hardly be detected.

4.2.4. Continuous observation of crustal movement

Twelve crustal movement observatories equipped with strainmeters and tiltmeters were completed in addition to the existing five observatories. The locations are shown in Fig. 4-5. The number of observatories constructed under the present program is substantially smaller than that originally proposed in the blueprint because it turns out that the construction of many observatories of underground-gallery type is not practicable, judging from the expense and labor needed. Borehole strainmeters and tiltmeters will play an important role in the future program.

In some cases it is found that results of a continuous observation agree very well with the patterns of crustal movement revealed by geodetic surveys conducted in the vicinity of the observatory concerned. A number of precursory changes in ground tilting have also been reported as can be seen in a later chapter.

Fig. 4-5. The distribution of crustal deformation observatories in Japan.

4.2.5. Seismicity

Seismographic observation by the JMA has been much modernized in the last years. The classic Wiechert seismographs at 55 weather stations are to be replaced by visual-recording electromagnetic seismographs. Replacement of half of them was completed by 1973. Installation of tape-recording seismographs has been completed at 67 stations, along with semi-automatic data processors at five regional centers.

Through the observations under the earthquake prediction program, it is clear that monitoring all earthquakes of $M > 3$, as originally proposed in the blueprint, is extremely difficult. It seems practicable to aim at monitoring earthquakes of $M \geqslant 3.8$.

Nineteen microearthquake observatories, of which the locations are shown in Fig. 4-6, are now in operation. As each observatory has several satellite stations, the coverage over Japan by a microearthquake observation network is now fairly complete. The overall microseismicity has thus been brought to light except for a few parts of Japan where the coverage is not as yet quite complete. As little effort has been made in establishing a telemetering system

Microearthquake
observatories

Fig. 4-6. The distribution of microearthquake observatories in Japan.

for handling microearthquake data, the labor necessary for processing the data becomes enormous. It is urgent that something is done to improve the observation system.

Seismographic observation in the Tokyo area is difficult to carry out because of the noise due to building construction, traffic, etc. The National Research Center for Disaster Prevention dug a borehole of 3,510 m in depth at a location some 28 km north of Tokyo, and placed a seismograph in it. It turns out that the diminution of noise with depth is so remarkable that the magnification of the borehole seismograph can be 1,000 times as large as that of a similar seismograph placed at the ground surface. Monitoring of microearthquakes occurring beneath the Tokyo area has now been intensified.

4.2.6. Seismic wave velocities

Seismic waves from an explosion source on Oshima Island, a volcanic island about 100 km south of Tokyo, have been observed at a number of stations distributed over the South Kanto district including Izu, Miura and Boso Peninsulas. The explosions were made approximately once a year. Although the purpose of the observation is to detect possible changes in seismic wave velocities associated with the stress accumulation in the earth's crust underneath Sagami Bay, from where the 1923 Kanto earthquake was originated, no significant changes have so far been reported.

In the light of changes in seismic wave velocities associated with a dilatancy model of the focal region (see Chapter 9) as developed in recent years, Japanese seismologists have been working on such changes in relation to natural earthquakes although nothing definite has as yet been found.

4.2.7. Active faults and foldings

A few groups of geologists and geographers have been working on identifying geological faults which indicate evidence that they had moved in recent geologic time. This is also the case of foldings which are believed to be going on today. A number of active faults, which might move suddenly in the future resulting in a large earthquake, have been listed.

4.2.8. Geomagnetic and geoelectric work

Much stress has been put on observing the geomagnetic secular variation with a high accuracy by a nationwide array of proton precession magnetometers. Although conspicuous changes in the geomagnetic field associated with an earthquake have sometimes been reported in the past, it is feared that those reports may not be reliable because of various difficulties in measuring the absolute values of the geomagnetic field. This is the reason why an

Proton precession
magnetometers

Fig. 4-7. The distribution of stations equipped with a proton precession magnetometer in Japan.

organized observation is undertaken with newly developed, highly stable magnetometers. Digital proton precession magnetometers have been operating at the stations shown in Fig. 4-7. Comparisons between the observations at these stations made it clear that the natural noise involved in the observed values of the total intensity of the geomagnetic field is unexpectedly large, so that it would be no easy matter to detect a seismomagnetic effect in Japan.

Magnetic surveys by the GSI have been intensified. Although no conclusive results have so far been obtained, changes in the magnetic field of the earth which seemed to be correlated to earthquake occurrence have sometimes been reported.

Changes in earth resistivity have been observed at a station about 60 km south of Tokyo. Precursory and coseismic changes in the resistivity have often been observed. Earth-current measurements are difficult in Japan because of stray electric currents from d.c.-operated electric railways and other artificial sources, so that no systematic observation of telluric currents has been undertaken.

Soundings of electrical conductivity in the earth's crust and mantle from observations of temporal geomagnetic changes have indicated a possible change in the electrical conductivity of a deep layer in association with the occurrence of a large earthquake.

4.2.9. Laboratory work and rock-breaking tests

Mogi (1962a) performed a series of rock-breaking experiments. When a rock specimen is moderately nonuniform, numerous shocks associated with microfracture production take place prior to the main shock, or rupture. When the specimen is extremely nonuniform, no main shock occurs. On the other hand, no microshocks precede the main shock for a highly uniform specimen. As this kind of study provides a physical basis for the relation between foreshocks and main shock, it has been planned to conduct similar experiments under the conditions prevailing within the earth's crust. The apparatus for the experiments has been provided by the ERI and a few geophysical institutes of other universities.

Experimental work for measuring the changes in the physical properties of rocks under mechanical stresses has been carried out. Interesting results for electric and magnetic properties were reported.

4.2.10. Data processing

An IBM 360-40 computer was installed at the Earthquake Prediction Observation Center at the ERI for processing the earthquake prediction data. The computer was supposed to process data from university sources. In view of the rapidly developing computer facilities at Japanese universities, however, data taken by provincial university people have been processed mostly by their own computers.

The need for regional centers with adequate manpower, at which preparatory work can be done before computer processing, has been stressed by workers of provincial universities. A few such centers were established by 1974.

Large organizations such as the JMA, GSI and so on, of course, have their own computers that can be used for processing the earthquake prediction data.

4.3. U.S.–JAPAN COOPERATION

In 1961 a special arrangement to start a scientific cooperation program between the U.S.A. and Japan was made through talks between the U.S. President and the Japanese Prime Minister. Among many fields of the scientific cooperation conducted in the framework of the U.S.–Japan Scientific Cooperation Program, seminars on earthquake prediction problems were a great success for seismologists of both countries.

Having been interested in the blueprint (see section 4.1) published in 1962, J.E. Oliver, then a professor of seismology at the Lamont-Doherty Geological Observatory, Columbia University, wrote to C. Tsuboi, a professor of geophysics at the University of Tokyo and one of the authors of the blueprint, about the possibility of having a conference on earthquake prediction research. It was mentioned in that letter that it would be of great benefit, not only to the U.S.A. and Japan, but also to the whole world, if the interested seismologists of the two countries could meet and exchange knowledge and information they have relating to the problem of earthquake prediction.

The reaction of Japanese seismologists to the proposal was favorable because they naturally wanted to know of the developments in the U.S.A. It was thus agreed that a conference on the research related to earthquake prediction problems be held in Tokyo and Kyoto on March 9—20, 1964, sponsored jointly by the U.S. National Science Foundation (NSF) and the Japan Society for Promotion of Science (JSPS).

It was impressive to listen to Oliver who said the following in his introductory speech: "Those of us from the United States come here, I assure you, with some humility. We know that research related to earthquake prediction is more widespread and in many ways more advanced in Japan than in the U.S.A. We are grateful that you are to share this knowledge with us at these meetings, and we hope that we can in part repay you by providing information from our own efforts in related branches of seismology. Within the U.S.A. there are at present very few seismologists who devote even a small fraction of their time to direct consideration of the problem of earthquake prediction..." (Hagiwara, 1964).

Throughout the conference and associated field trips, the American seismologists could see the Japanese effort toward earthquake prediction in detail. Soon after the conference, a destructive earthquake ($M = 8.4$) occurred in Alaska on March 28, 1964. The earthquake gave rise to public concern which later resulted in a proposal for earthquake prediction research as will be seen in the following section. The knowledge acquired by the American participants at the conference was doubtless of some help in forming the proposal.

The second U.S.—Japan conference on earthquake prediction research was held at the Lamont-Doherty Geological Observatory, Columbia University, on June 6—9, 1966. There was much to talk about: the 1964 Niigata earthquake and the Matsushiro earthquake swarms which were still occurring at that time concerned Japan, and the 1964 Alaska earthquake, the man-made earthquakes in Denver since 1962 and the proposed 10-year earthquake prediction research program concerned the U.S.A. (Page, 1966).

A post-conference trip was undertaken to the earthquake areas in Nevada and California. Many of the Japanese participants were impressed by the gigantic faults which had appeared in association with large earthquakes in the past. It is extremely interesting to note that the field party was able to observe fresh cracking of the ground in Parkfield, California, so that it was joked on the site that a large earthquake would soon occur there. The Parkfield earthquake ($M = 5.3$) in fact occurred there 2 weeks later. As Oliver wrote in the introduction of the proceedings of the conference, this is "the first observation of a phenomenon which may indeed bear upon earthquake prediction".

In view of the fast development of earthquake prediction research, the third conference was held at the National Center for Earthquake Research (NCER) of the U.S. Geological Survey in Menlo Park, California from October 28 to November 1, 1968 with a post-conference field trip to southern California. The conference was this time named "the Joint U.S.–Japan Conference on Premonitory Phenomena Associated with Several Recent Earthquakes and Related Problems" (Alsop and Oliver, 1969).

Much of the outcome of the intensive observation of the Matsushiro earthquakes, the Denver earthquakes and so forth was reported, together with many interesting topics in various disciplines.

Earthquake prediction-oriented study made remarkable progress in the early 1970s. Through a talk between J.P. Eaton, the Director of the NCER, and the present author, who was in the U.S.A. for other business, in 1972, the fourth U.S.–Japan conference on earthquake prediction problems was planned after a 5-year interruption. Because of the university trouble in the ERI and due to the intention of Japanese seismologists to see the recent development in the U.S.A., a "U.S.–Japan Seminar on Earthquake Prediction and Control" was held at the Cooperative Institute for Research in Environmental Sciences (CIRES), University of Colorado in Boulder, Colorado, with C. Kisslinger as the host on August 13–15, 1973 with a pre-conference tour via Salt Lake City, Wasatch fault system, Rangely Oil Field and Rocky Mountains (Kisslinger and Rikitake, 1974).

Earthquake prediction studies based on intensive geodetic work in Japan were reported, as well as those of other disciplines. The Japanese participants were very much impressed by the monitoring system for microearthquakes over the San Andreas fault zone in California. Controlled experiments of man-made earthquakes which have been performed at Rangely Oil Field were also interesting to the Japanese participants. In view of the current interest in the dilatancy model of earthquake mechanism (see chapter 14) and its application to earthquake prediction, much time was spared for that topic.

Throughout these conferences, seismologists from both countries inspired each other. It can be said that the U.S.–Japan conferences played a crucial role in the advancement of earthquake prediction research. In addition to these seminars, a number of actual observations of microearthquakes, crustal strains and the like have been conducted under the auspices of the U.S.–Japan Scientific Cooperation Program, so that an extensive exchange of geoscientists and scientific instruments was made between the two nations.

4.4. AMERICAN PROGRAM

Americans did not seem to pay much attention to earthquake hazards until recently. This is partly because of the low seismicity, partly because of the short history of the country and partly because of the sparse population. The situation has been changing, however, in recent years: the population in California is rapidly increasing. There is every reason to believe that in the future parts of California may be the target of a destructive earthquake such as the 1906 San Francisco earthquake ($M = 8.3$).

As U.S. seismologists were well aware of the situation, they paid attention to the Japanese "blueprint", and some of them came over to Tokyo for the 1964 U.S.–Japan conference on research related to earthquake prediction problems in order to learn Japanese ideas. The Alaska earthquake, that took place immediately after the conference, seemed to accelerate the effort towards prediction research in the U.S.A.

In 1965, a group of scientists presented a report of a 10-year research program (Press et al., 1965). The program consisted of the following five categories: it is not only aimed at earthquake prediction but also at preventing earthquake hazards.

  (1) Field studies:
      (a) detailed geologic mapping
      (b) rates of deformation
      (c) tectonic mechanisms
      (d) gravity surveys
      (e) aeromagnetic surveys
      (f) seismic profiles
      (g) miscellaneous geophysical studies
      (h) aftershock studies
      (i) geodetic surveys.
  (2) Instrumentation of seismic zones:
      (a) microearthquake arrays
      (b) other "cluster" instruments
      (c) special survey devices
      (d) deep-hole instruments
      (e) telemetry
      (f) systems operation and management
      (g) movable "clusters"
      (h) central analysis system.
  (3) Physical basis of earthquakes:
      (a) theoretical studies

    (b) experiments in fracture and flow

    (c) field measurements

    (d) seismic source studies

    (e) seismic propagation studies.

(4) Earthquake engineering:

    (a) seismic zoning

    (b) soil mechanics and foundation engineering

    (c) structural dynamics

    (d) design techniques

    (e) economic studies.

(5) Miscellaneous projects:

    (a) tsunami studies

    (b) heat flow

    (c) tide gauges

    (d) psychological and practical aspects

    (e) analysis and prediction

    (f) earthquakes and fluid injection.

The estimated expenses for completing the proposed plan in the California—Nevada region are given in Table 4-II. The 10-year totals for the whole project amount of 137 million U.S. dollars. It may be said that the proposed American program was about one order of magnitude larger than the Japanese one in funding.

Much stress is put on geophysical observation along the seismic belts in

TABLE 4-II

Estimated cost for the American plan in the California—Nevada region (Press et al., 1965)

Discipline	10-year total (U.S. dollars)
Microseismicity arrays	3,000,000
Development and installation of other cluster instruments (tiltmeters, magnetometers, strainmeters, gravimeters and meteorological instruments)	3,050,000
Development and installation of special survey devices (laser strain seismograph, optical surveying devices, etc.)	9,050,000
Development and installation of super-cluster instruments (including drilling)	7,800,000
Installation of telemetry	5,000,000
Operation and management of instrument system	2,500,000
Total	30,400,000

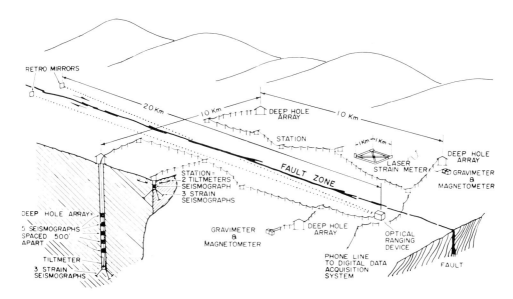

RETRO MIRRORS

20 Km

10 Km

DEEP HOLE
ARRAY

10 Km

STATION

~1Km~/1Km~

FAULT ZONE

LASER
STRAIN METER

DEEP HOLE
ARRAY

GRAVIMETER
&
MAGNETOMETER

STATION =
2 TILTMETERS
SEISMOGRAPH
3 STRAIN
SEISMOGRAPHS

DEEP HOLE ARRAY=

5 SEISMOGRAPHS
SPACED 500'
APART

TILTMETER

3 STRAIN
SEISMOGRAPHS

GRAVIMETER
&
MAGNETOMETER

DEEP HOLE
ARRAY

OPTICAL
RANGING
DEVICE

PHONE LINE
TO DIGITAL DATA
ACQUISITION
SYSTEM

FAULT

Fig. 4-8. Schematic view of the proposed super-cluster (Press et al., 1965).

California—Nevada and Alaska—Aleutian areas. An idea to set up observatories called clusters or super-clusters was put forward. Fig. 4-8 indicates the idea about how a super-cluster will be equipped with various instruments. Such clusters or super-clusters shall be set up from place to place along seismic belts, to hopefully catch premonitory signals with adequate sensitivity.

A symposium on earthquake prediction organized by the Environmental Science Services Administration (ESSA) was held at Rockville, Maryland, in February, 1966. Possible contributions from the ESSA to earthquake prediction were discussed there (Environmental Science Services Administration, 1966a).

In spite of increased public as well as academic interest in earthquake prediction in the U.S.A., implementation of the 10-year program has never taken place, probably because of financial difficulties. But the program has doubtless given rise to an increasing interest in earthquake prediction research in the U.S.A. Thus research in universities and governmental organizations has been intensified, although no unified project on earthquake prediction was established. Funds for this research have been provided by the NSF and other sources. As a result, striking developments in certain disciplines of earthquake prediction research have been achieved. For example, a microearthquake monitoring network covering parts of the San Andreas fault zone was completed by the early 1970s. In spite of its slow start, the U.S. earthquake prediction research has made outstanding progress in some aspects, so that now it may be said that some disciplines of research are more advanced than those of the Japanese program.

The spirit of the 10-year program proposed by Press et al. (1965) came to a revival when the earthquake research programs of the National Oceanic and Atmospheric Administration (NOAA) and the U.S. Geological Survey (USGS) were administratively merged in September, 1973. Called the Earthquake Hazards Reduction Program (EHRP), the combined program to be handled by the USGS includes major efforts of the Federal Government in earthquake-related studies such as the seismic-engineering research supported by the NSF (Wallace, 1974). It may be said that a unified national program on earthquake prediction has actually started in the U.S.A., along with other related projects such as earthquake engineering.

The EHRP of the USGS consists of the following seven disciplines:

(1) Earthquake hazard mapping and risk evaluation.

(2) Earthquake prediction research and implementation.

(3) Earthquake modification and control.

(4) Seismic engineering.

(5) Earthquake information services.

(6) Postearthquake studies.

(7) Application and demonstration projects.

What each discipline aims at is self-explanatory. This book is naturally concerned with disciplines 2 and 3. The program is implemented by utilizing not only the USGS capabilities, but also those of the universities, States and the private sector. Research projects outside the USGS are supported by extramural grants and contracts, proposals being reviewed by a grants review panel made up of outstanding non-USGS scientists.

The goals of discipline 2, i.e. earthquake prediction research and implementation, are described as follows (Wallace, 1974):

(a) Develop the physical understanding and instrumental means required for forecasting the time, place, and magnitude of earthquakes and to implement and evaluate experimental earthquake prediction systems in highly seismic regions.

(b) Develop the historical and geological background for estimating earthquake probability and recurrence characteristics.

In order to reach such goals, much stress should be put on the following lines of research:

(a) To establish telemetered microearthquake monitoring systems which are useful for providing data on the physical properties and elastic regime of the earth's crust and also for search for premonitory seismic velocity changes.

(b) To install telemetered tiltmeters at many places for monitoring slow deformations as well as rapid precursory changes.

(c) Geodetic work for monitoring crustal deformation across major fault zones.

(d) Creep measurements within fault zones.

(e) Intensification of studies of active faults by geologic mapping.

(f) Laboratory experiments on physical properties of rocks under the conditions found in the crust.

(g) Computer modeling of deformation and faulting in realistic earth models.

(h) Multiparameter correlation of microearthquakes, strain patterns, strain events and the like to search for propagation of strain or slip events.

(i) Use of portable seismograph networks for studying crustal structure, aftershock monitoring and so on.

(j) Use of geothermal logging to develop information on changes in temperature with depth.

(k) Analysis of geologic and tectonic characteristics of highly seismic area.

(l) Exploratory deep drilling for direct examination and instrumentation of fault zones at depth.

(m) Analysis of geologic record of active faults.

(n) Testing of earthquake prediction methods developed in Japan, the U.S.S.R., the People's Republic of China and other countries.

(o) Exploration of global plate systems that control earthquake generation.

The following are believed to be still in a testing stage. Nevertheless every effort must be made in developing them:

(a) In-situ stress measurement.

(b) Short-base shallow-burial strainmeter.

(c) Multibeam laser-ranging instrument for high-precision distance measurement.

(d) Seismograph for recording a broader spectrum of ground motion.

(e) Water-level recorder and volumetric strainmeter.

(f) Stable high-sensitivity magnetometer for search for magnetic precursors.

(g) Monitoring of water composition in relation to geochemical precursors.

The selected projects under the EHRP cover almost all items which appeared in the proposal by Press et al. (1965). They are in many ways similar to the Japanese equivalents although emphasis is naturally put on monitoring seismicity, crustal movement, geomagnetic and geoelectric changes along the San Andreas fault zone in California.

It is interesting to see that prediction techniques by pattern recognition methods are going to be developed. Investigation of radon and helium as possible fluid-phase precursors is also promoted. In addition to studies in California and Nevada, prediction work in the Aleutian Islands is being undertaken, so that prediction techniques for island-arc earthquakes are going to be sought. Earthquake prediction studies in Utah, Montana, Missouri and so on are also being undertaken, although the seismicity of these regions is not quite as high as that of California and Nevada.

It is the author's understanding that a sum of 19.4 million dollars is allocated for the EHRP for the 1974 fiscal year, i.e. 8.7 for the USGS, 8.0 for the NSF, 1.4 for the NOAA, 0.6 for the Atomic Energy Commission (AEC) and 0.7 for the Department of Housing and Urban Development (HUD), all in million dollars. Some 2.1 million dollars will be spent from the USGS budget for supporting universities and other researchers through grants and contracts.

The USGS budget of the present category for the years 1972 and 1973 was respectively 1.7 and 4.7 million dollars, while that for the NSF was 2.9 and 4.8 million dollars for those years, respectively. It may be said that the U.S. effort toward earthquake hazard reduction is drastically intensified.

Intensification of international cooperative programs in earthquake prediction has also been stressed in the U.S.A. Much of the U.S.–Japan cooperation was stated in the last section. As one of the subjects of an agreement for the protection of the environment between the U.S.S.R. and the U.S.A., which was set forth as a result of the U.S. President's visit to Moscow in May, 1972, a cooperative program on earthquake prediction has been promoted. The Schmidt Institue of Earth Physics and the USGS are responsible for implementing the program. Exchange of working groups was made in 1973. Some American seismologists are going to spend some time in Garm to see and learn earthquake prediction work there.

A delegation of ten seismologists visited the U.S.A. from the People's Republic of China in 1974, and a return visit of a U.S. delegation to China, planned by the National Academy of Sciences, was actualized later in that year.

4.5. SOVIET PROGRAM

So far no published report of a national program on earthquake prediction in the U.S.S.R. with the exception of Savarensky (1974) has been available to the present author who does not read Russian. The following is a summary of the U.S.S.R. effort toward earthquake prediction as gathered from rather fragmentary information obtained through his contacts with Soviet colleagues.

The progress in relation to earthquake prediction work in the U.S.S.R. was first disclosed in a summarized form to western researchers by Savarensky (1968) who read a paper at a symposium on earthquake prediction held in Zürich in 1967. He also reported on earthquake prediction-oriented work in the U.S.S.R. at a symposium in Madrid in 1969. A summary report on the Soviet work on earthquake prediction was also presented by Savarensky (1974) at the Lima symposium on earthquake prediction.

In the U.S.S.R., earthquake prediction work has concentrated on the

Middle Asia and the Kurile—Kamchatka zones. The seismicity in the former zone is connected with tectonic processes in Tien Shan and Pamirs. Important cities such as Alma-Ata, Frunze, Dushambe, Ashkhabad and Tashkent are under the threat of destructive earthquakes.

Investigations in the Middle Asia zone are carried out by the Institute of Physics of the Earth, Academy of Sciences of the U.S.S.R., and by the Academies of Science of the Kazakh, Kirghiz, Uzbek, Tajik and Turkmen Republics of the Soviet Union. Under the leadership of I.L. Nersesov, intensive work on changes in the ratio of longitudinal wave velocity (V_p) to shear wave velocity (V_s), changes in focal mechanism, changes in electric resistivity and the like has been carried out there in the hope of detecting possible forerunning effects. Geodetic work, strainmeter observation and observation of the radon content of underground water have also been carried out. As can be seen in later chapters, some of these observations have been successful in detecting remarkable precursors. Trials of actual prediction are being made on the basis of these observations.

When Savarensky (1968) discussed the premonitory changes in the V_p/V_s ratio at the 1967 Zürich symposium, the present author (and probably most of the audience) simply could not believe what he reported. If the changes are interpreted in terms of changes in elasticity of the earth's crust, it must be presumed that some 30% change takes place in order to account for the observed results. After the 1971 General Assembly of the International Union of Geodesy and Geophysics (IUGG), held in Moscow, a number of seismologists from the U.S.A. and Japan had a chance to visit the Garm area in the Tajik Republic. Some of the U.S. seismologists, who had been interested in the V_p/V_s work conducted there, reported a similar observation in the U.S.A. In fact they found large changes in the V_p/V_s ratio preceding local earthquakes. Precursory changes in focal mechanism, earth resistivity and the radon content in underground water were also reported for the first time by the Soviet workers in the Middle Asia. These data play an important role on development of the dilatancy theory as can be seen in a later chapter.

Work in the Kurile—Kamchatka zone has been led by S.A. Fedotov. Being an island arc, the zone has been a target of strong earthquakes in a similar fashion to the Alaska—Aleutian and Japan arcs. It appears that a statistical investigation of large earthquakes can be applied to actual prediction to some extent. Some work has also been conducted on telluric current observation, changes in the V_p/V_s ratio by observing seismic waves from explosion sources and the like.

4.6. PROGRAMS IN OTHER COUNTRIES

In spite of tremendous earthquake hazards, the effort towards earthquake prediction has not been quite strong in developing countries, probably because of financial difficulty together with the lack of intellectual manpower. Most of the Latin American countries are in a stage of establishing seismographic networks which monitor seismicity there. This is also the case for countries in the Middle East, Southeast Asia and so on. Under these circumstances no well-established programs on earthquake prediction have been reported from these countries. Much international funding will certainly be needed for promoting earthquake prediction research in developing countries.

The present author understands, however, that an intensive program on earthquake prediction is under way in the People's Republic of China, although he has never managed to see modern China. The following is a summary of what the author learned from Coe (1971), Wilson (1972), Bolt (1974) and Lee (1974), and through conversations with members of a Chinese seismological delegation, led by Ku Kung-hsu, that visited the U.S.A. in 1974. Professor C. Kisslinger, who visited China in 1974 as one of the members of the U.S. seismological delegation also provided much information to the author.

According to Coe (1971), a Chinese program on earthquake prediction was set up soon after the visit of Premier Chou En-lai to Hsingtai, Hopei Province, 300 km southwest of Peking, where a destructive earthquake ($M = 6.8$) had occurred on March 8, 1966. Three institutes of the Academia Sinica, i.e. the Institute of Geophysics, the Institute of Geology and the Institute of Engineering Mechanics at Harbin, and the Peking University are involved in the program.

China is characterized by its long history, so that a fairly complete record of historical earthquakes has been compiled in a chronological table as thick as 1653 pages (Lee, 1974), although the author as yet has had no chance to see it. China has suffered from many great earthquakes in its long history. Bolt (1974) listed 16 earthquake of $M \geqslant 8$ in China in the period 1303–1951. It was reported that more than 800,000 people, some of them had been living in loess caves, had been killed at the time of the 1556 Shensi earthquake near Hsian. The next worst earthquake was the one that occurred in Kansu Province in 1920 when 180,000 people died. A statistical analysis of the historical records has been performed by Chinese seismologists. The application of the extreme-value statistics sometimes led to a successful prediction of large earthquakes (see subsection 15.1.3).

It is interesting to note that seismically active zones in China such as the Taiyuan–Hsian zone extending to the southwest of Peking are characterized by a relatively quiet period of several hundred years followed by a highly active period of shorter duration.

Bolt (1974) reported that triangulations and levellings are in progress over certain fault zones such as the Pa Pao Shan fault near Peking. Coe (1971) noted that a tiltmeter has been operating at the Hongshan provincial station, 40 km from the epicenter of the 1966 Hsingtai earthquake. Metal and quartz pendulum-type tiltmeters are operating at the Peking Observatory (Bolt, 1974).

Seismographic observations are carried out at seventeen national observatories. The Institute of Geophysics has a telemetry network of eight seismographic stations around Peking. Geomagnetic and geoelectric observations aimed at detecting possible precursors have been conducted. At the Hongshan station, much stress is put on earthquake prediction by means of geomagnetic methods (see subsection 10.6.3). Investigations of water level at many wells around the Hongshan station also seem to provide a basis of earthquake prediction (see section 12.2). Changes in seismic wave velocities are also an item of prediction research (see subsection 9.1.4).

From time to time, actual prediction of the occurrence time of an earthquake and its magnitude has been preliminarily undertaken with some success at the Hongshan station (Coe, 1971).

4.7. INTERNATIONAL COMMISSION ON EARTHQUAKE PREDICTION

In view of the rapidly rising interest in many countries, an international symposium on earthquake prediction was held in Zürich during the 14th General Assembly of the IUGG in 1967. Following general discussions on earthquake prediction programs in a few countries, highlights of earthquake prediction research in various disciplines were reviewed (Rikitake, 1968b).

After the symposium, members of a Working Group on Earthquake Prediction were nominated. The working group, which is attached to the International Association of Seismology and Physics of the Earth's Interior (IASPEI), is to work on the international coordination of research relevant to earthquake prediction. The working group was initially started with thirteen members representing various countries (Japan 3, U.S.S.R. 3, U.S.A. 2, Chile 1, New Zealand 1, Turkey 1, U.K. 1, Yugoslavia 1) and various bodies belonging to IUGG such as the International Association of Geodesy (IAG), the International Association of Geomagnetism and Aeronomy (IAGA), the International Association of Volcanology and Chemistry of the Earth's Interior (IAVCEI) and the Upper Mantle Committee (UMC). T. Hagiwara was appointed chairman and T. Rikitake secretary.

In 1969 the working group convened a symposium on earthquake mechanics (Rikitake, 1970b) at the IAGA-IASPEI Scientific General Assembly in Madrid. A symposium on forerunners of strong earthquakes (Savarensky and Rikitake, 1972) was also organized by the working group during the IUGG General Assembly in Moscow in 1971.

At the Moscow Assembly, the working group became an International Commission on Earthquake Prediction (ICEP), and E.F. Savarensky was nominated as the new chairman.

The 1973 IASPEI Scientific General Assembly in Lima provided an opportunity to have a symposium on focal processes and earthquake prediction convened by the ICEP (Rikitake, 1974c). The following are the recommendations resolved by the ICEP in Lima.

The Commission on Earthquake Prediction recommends:

(1) That the Commission collect information on national programs of earthquake prediction and prepare a draft of international recommendations on the most effective methods of searching for forerunners of strong earthquakes; and that the draft of international recommendations be put into circulation prior to the discussion to be held during the Tashkent symposium.

(2) That the final version of such recommendations be ready for discussion and approval during the Grenoble meeting of the Commission in 1975.

(3) That the scheduled symposium of the Commission at Tashkent in 1974 be endorsed, along with the plan to invite the European Seismological Commission to join in the symposium; and, as a general rule, the Tashkent symposium be organized on the basis of invited scientific communications.

(4) That the Association be asked to organize a multidisciplinary symposium at Grenoble in 1975 devoted to the various geophysical events which precede or accompany strong earthquakes, as well as to the hazardous geological consequences of such earthquakes.

(5) That regional or national cooperative organizations (such as CERESIS in South America and ESC in Europe) be requested to help in the compilation of information on their cooperative, and their national, programs to search for earthquake forerunners.

(6) That the Commission be asked to establish close contacts, in programming, with bilateral or multilateral working groups, on earthquake prediction and with other special national or international committees (such as the Inter-Union Commission on Geodynamics) whose work significantly involves earthquakes or the processes that generate them.

(7) That special notice be taken of the need to broaden membership in the Commission to include representatives from the major seismic zones of the world at the Grenoble meeting of the Commission.

(8) That Prof. G.J. Lensen be thanked for his letter and report on results of earth deformation studies in New Zealand that are closely related to the search for earthquake forerunners.

At the 1971 Moscow meeting, an ICEP policy to have symposia at places where large earthquakes had occurred, was recommended, so that Tashkent was chosen following Lima.

As can be seen in the first of the above recommendations, the ICEP puts much stress on forming international recommendations on the most effective methods of searching for forerunners of strong earthquakes. The recommendations will be adopted at a Commission meeting in Grenoble during the 16th General Assembly of IUGG.

Chapter 5

LAND DEFORMATION AS DETECTED BY GEODETIC SURVEYS

5.1. CLASSICAL REPORTS ON LAND DEFORMATION

It has long been noticed that large earthquakes are often accompanied by some land deformation. There are many historical documents in Japan which describe land deformations associated with great earthquakes. The following are some of such reports taken from the earliest records.

A ground crack, 6 m in width and 10 km in length, appeared at the time of the A.D. 679 earthquake (M = 6.7) in North Kyushu. This seems to be the oldest report on an earthquake fault in Japan. In 684, a great earthquake accompanied by a tsunami struck Japan. As the magnitude was estimated as 8.4, this quake must have been one of the largest occurring off the Pacific coast of Southwest Japan. An area amounting to 12 km^2 subsided under the sea surface in South Shikoku. In the case of the 701 earthquake (M = 7.0) in the northern part of the Kyoto Prefecture, an island having a 2.4 km × 4 km dimension was submerged into the sea leaving only its top above the sea surface.

Countless reports of land deformation of this kind are available in association with major earthquakes in many countries. As those historical reports are hard to prove quantitatively, most cannot be used for purposes of scientific analysis. Only land deformations that are monitored by geodetic surveys are adequate for such an analysis.

5.2. TRIANGULATION SURVEY TECHNIQUES

Most countries are covered by triangulation networks which are necessary for producing topographical maps. A triangulation survey is an operation to determine the positions of the triangulation stations very accurately, primarily for mapping. The principle of triangulation is simple although actual operation is laborious.

First of all, the length of a base line set up on flat ground is measured very accurately. Such a measurement used to be made by an invar-wire scale of 25 m in length, and the length of such a base line was usually 3—4 km in Japan. The invar-wire scale must be calibrated from time to time by a 5-m standard scale which is standardized by comparing it to the national standard scale of 1 m. It became popular in recent years, however, to make use of an electro-optical method for such a calibration by a technique as will be described in section 5.4.

Let us suppose that we take a point P and look at that point from the two end points of a base line, A and B. If the angles between the base line and the lines connecting point P to A or B can be measured, the size of a triangle formed by these three points is determined, and accordingly the position of point P is fixed relative to base line AB. On repeating a similar operation taking line PA as the reference in place of AB, a new triangle QPA forms, and so the position of a point Q can be determined. A series of similar operations leads to a line having a length of 40–50 km, the positions of terminal points being well established.

We call such a line the base line for the first-order triangulation, and a terminal point the first-order triangulation station. All other triangulation stations are then surveyed in reference to such base lines. As it became possible in recent years to measure the length of a base line for the first-order triangulation directly by an electro-optical method, about 60 base lines have been set up in Japan.

The Japanese first-order triangulation network, formed by some 300 triangulation stations, has been shown in Fig. 4-2, Fig. 5-1 shows a Japanese first-order triangulation station. It is customary to use a granite block of about 20 cm $\times$ 20 cm $\times$ 100 cm in size. Another marking stone is also buried immediately beneath the block, so that the station cannot be destroyed even if the block is lost. During a survey operation, a temporary tower (e.g. Fig. 5-2) is set up immediately above the station marking.

Fig. 5-1. Granite block for the first-order triangulation station at the Kanozan Geodetic Observatory several tens of kilometers southeast of Tokyo, Japan.

Fig. 5-2. Temporary tower to aid in a triangulation survey.

A triangulation survey is so laborious and expensive that the Japanese first-order net was only completed in 1915, 32 years after the start of the work. The second survey, that was started in 1949, was finished in 1967. In practice, extremely complicated numerical work is required for adjusting errors necessarily involved in the measurements.

Although the present author does not know much about geodetic work outside Japan, it is his belief that there would be no principal difference between the survey operations of Japan and those of other countries. For the purpose of producing detailed maps, triangulations of second-, third-, ... order, which are less accurate than the first-order one, are carried out. These triangulation surveys are also useful for detecting land deformation associated with an earthquake.

5.3. LAND DEFORMATIONS AS DETECTED BY TRIANGULATIONS

Whenever a great earthquake occurs, it is necessary to conduct a triangulation survey over the seismic area in order to recover the positions of triangulation stations. In Japan, remarkable land deformations associated with large earthquakes were often found by the Military Land Survey (Hagiwara, 1974a) and its successor, the GSI, by comparing triangulation surveys over the seismic areas carried out before an earthquake to those after it. Probably the oldest example of land deformation detected in this way would be the one associated with the 1891 Nobi earthquake (Sato, 1973), which clearly disclosed fault movement, although the pre-earthquake survey north of the Neodani (Neo valley) fault (see section 3.2) was incomplete.

It is sometimes useful to calculate the two-dimensional strains in the horizontal plane from triangulation results. Let us take the x- and y-axes in the directions of east and north respectively and denote the displacement of a triangulation station in these directions by u and v. In that case the dilatation, rotation and shear can be defined by:

$$\Delta = \frac{\partial u}{\partial x} + \frac{\partial v}{\partial y} \qquad\qquad\qquad [5\text{-}1]$$

$$\omega = \frac{1}{2}\left(\frac{\partial u}{\partial y} - \frac{\partial v}{\partial x}\right) \qquad\qquad\qquad [5\text{-}2]$$

$$\sigma = \frac{\partial u}{\partial y} + \frac{\partial v}{\partial x} \qquad\qquad\qquad [5\text{-}3]$$

The maximum shear is then given by:

$$\Sigma = \left[\left(\frac{\partial u}{\partial x} - \frac{\partial v}{\partial y}\right)^2 + \left(\frac{\partial u}{\partial y} + \frac{\partial v}{\partial x}\right)^2\right]^{1/2} \qquad\qquad\qquad [5\text{-}4]$$

The following is a method devised by Terada and Miyabe (1929) to calculate these strains from actual data. A triangle ABC as can be seen in Fig. 5-3 is considered for the strain calculation. The coordinates of points A, B and C

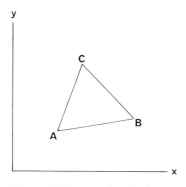

Fig. 5-3. Triangle for the horizontal strain calculation.

are given as (x_1, y_1), (x_2, y_2) and (x_3, y_3), while the displacement components are given as (u_1, v_1), (u_2, v_2) and (u_3, v_3), respectively. It is assumed that the displacements are correlated linearly to the coordinates, so that:

$$u = ax + by + c$$
$$v = a'x + b'y + c' \qquad\qquad [5\text{-}5]$$

It is therefore possible to have six linear equations for u_1, u_2, u_3, v_1, v_2 and v_3 which are similar to those of [5-5]. Solving them with respect to a, b, c, a', b' and c', we obtain:

$$a = \frac{(y_3 - y_1)(u_2 - u_1) - (y_2 - y_1)(u_3 - u_1)}{(x_2 - x_1)(y_3 - y_1) - (x_3 - x_1)(y_2 - y_1)}$$

$$b = \frac{(x_2 - x_1)(u_3 - u_1) - (x_3 - x_1)(u_2 - u_i)}{(x_2 - x_1)(y_3 - y_1) - (x_3 - x_1)(y_2 - y_1)}$$

$$a' = \frac{(y_3 - y_1)(v_2 - v_1) - (y_2 - y_1)(v_3 - v_1)}{(x_2 - x_1)(y_3 - y_1) - (x_3 - x_1)(y_2 - y_1)} \qquad [5\text{-}6]$$

$$b' = \frac{(x_2 - x_1)(v_3 - v_1) - (x_3 - x_1)(v_2 - v_1)}{(x_2 - x_1)(y_3 - y_1) - (x_3 - x_1)(y_2 - y_1)}$$

The combination of equations from [5-1] to [5-4] and [5-6] then leads to:

$$\Delta = a + b'$$
$$\omega = \tfrac{1}{2}(b - a')$$
$$\sigma = b + a' \qquad\qquad [5\text{-}7]$$
$$\Sigma = [(b + a')^2 + (a - b')^2]^{1/2}$$

These are regarded as the values of respective strains at the geometric center of the triangle.

Tsuboi (1933) devised a simpler method for calculating two-dimensional strains when the number of triangulation stations is large. The above calculation can easily be extended to those of the pricipal strains, ϵ_1 and ϵ_2, and their directions, θ_1 and θ_2, by making use of the following formulas:

$$\left.\begin{array}{c}\epsilon_1 \\ \epsilon_2\end{array}\right\} = \frac{\partial u}{\partial x} + \frac{\partial v}{\partial y} + \left[\left(\frac{\partial u}{\partial x} - \frac{\partial v}{\partial y}\right)^2 + \left(\frac{\partial v}{\partial x} + \frac{\partial u}{\partial y}\right)^2\right]^{1/2} \qquad [5\text{-}8]$$

$$\left.\begin{array}{c}\tan\theta_1 \\ \tan\theta_2\end{array}\right\} = \frac{\dfrac{\partial v}{\partial y} - \dfrac{\partial u}{\partial x} + \left[\left(\dfrac{\partial u}{\partial x} - \dfrac{\partial v}{\partial y}\right)^2 + \left(\dfrac{\partial v}{\partial x} + \dfrac{\partial u}{\partial y}\right)^2\right]^{1/2}}{\dfrac{\partial u}{\partial y} + \dfrac{\partial v}{\partial x}} \qquad [5\text{-}9]$$

Earlier results of crustal deformation brought to light by triangulations were compiled by Tsuboi (1933) who demonstrated that the crustal strains associated with an earthquake never exceed 10^{-4} except for strains over faulting zones. Similar studies have been conducted mostly in Japan and the U.S.A., so that a certain number of crustal deformations relevant to earthquake occurrence have been accumulated these scores of years. These data provide the basis for understanding the focal mechanism, the ultimate strain of the earth's crust, etc.

It should be borne in mind, however, that certain assumptions must be made in determining the displacements of triangulation stations. For instance it has been customary to assume that two or more stations far from the epicentral region do not move. Some other assumptions may also be made instead of this. Because of these assumptions, no absolute displacements can be deduced from a comparison between two triangulation surveys. However, we may well derive meaningful displacements on the basis of a physically acceptable assumption.

5.3.1. Kanto earthquake

A brief account of the 1923 Kanto earthquake has been given in section 3.3. Muto (1932), who compared the results of the two surveys respectively made in 1891 and 1925, found displacements of triangulation stations as shown in Fig. 5-4. There is every reason to surmise that the earthquake was caused by a fault movement along a submarine canyon, the Sagami Trough, running in a NW–SE direction through Sagami Bay somewhere between Oshima Island and Boso Peninsula (see Fig. 5-31). The fault plane having a length of 130 km and a width of 65 km dips in a NE direction with an angle

Fig. 5-4. Horizontal displacements of the first-order triangulation stations associated with the 1923 Kanto earthquake (Muto, 1932).

of 30°. The displacements parallel and perpendicular to the strike are estimated respectively as 6 and 3 m (Ando, 1971, 1974b). Seismometric analyses support this interpretation (Kanamori and Miyamura, 1970; Kanamori,
1971).

Sato and Ichihara (1971), who reexamined the geodetic data related to
the Kanto earthquake, presented a graph in which the mean diminution of
horizontal displacement parallel to the submarine fault with distance from
the fault was shown. A diminution rate amounting to 7.5×10^{-5} was
obtained in the immediate neighborhood of the fault.

Tsuboi (1933) analyzed the third-order triangulation results and calculated
the two-dimensional strains for the 1923 Kanto earthquake.

5.3.2. Tango earthquake

An earthquake having a magnitude of 7.5 occurred in the northern part of
Kyoto Prefecture, Japan, on March 7, 1927. Two remarkable seismic faults,
the Gomura and the Yamada faults, appeared as can be seen in Fig. 5-5 in
which the displacements of triangulation stations as obtained by the 1884—
1888 and 1927 surveys (Tsuboi, 1932, 1933) are also shown.

Fig. 5-5 provides one of the best demonstrations of crustal movement
associated with an earthquake, and so the deformations have been analyzed
in many ways. Kasahara (1957) interpreted the triangulation data in terms of
a vertical left-lateral fault having a dimension of 30 km (length) $\times$ 15 km
(width in depth direction) and a surface dislocation of 3 m. Such a model
was obtained by a best fit to the diminution of horizontal displacement with
distance from the fault as can be seen in Fig. 5-6. Chinnery (1961) presented
an improved model of the fault on the basis of dislocation theory.

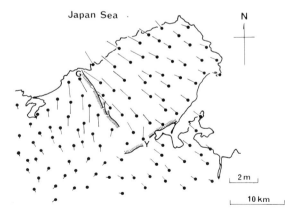

Fig. 5-5. Horizontal displacements of the third-order triangulation stations associated
with the 1927 Tango earthquake (Tsuboi, 1933). Two faults, i.e. Gomura (G) and Yamada (Y), are also shown.

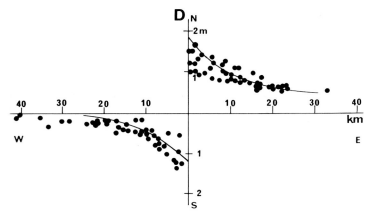

Fig. 5-6. Diminution of horizontal displacement parallel to the Gomura fault with distance from the fault (Kanamori, 1972a). Reproduced, with permission, from "Mode of strain release associated with major earthquakes in Japan". *Annual Review of Earth and Planetary Sciences*, Volume 1. Copyright © 1972 by Annual Reviews Inc. All rights reserved.

Kanamori (1972a), who analyzed a seismogram of the Tango earthquake recorded at Tokyo, found that a seismic fault having the dimension cited above can well be the origin that produced the observed seismic waves, the seismic moment and the stress drop, estimated as 4.6×10^{26} dyne cm and 100 bars, respectively.

Tsuboi (1932, 1933) calculated the two-dimensional strains from the triangulation data which has been shown in Fig. 5-5. In Fig. 5-7 the distribution of maximum shearing strain is reproduced. The conclusion that the

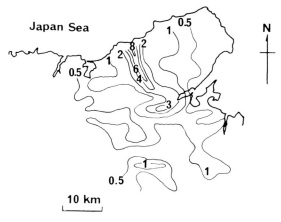

Fig. 5-7. Maximum shearing strains in units of 10^{-4} associated with the 1927 Tango earthquake (Tsuboi, 1932, 1933).

earth's crust ruptures when the crustal strain exceeds 10^{-4} or thereabout
has thus been deduced.

5.3.3. North Izu earthquake

Intensive geodetic work was undertaken after the North Izu earthquake
($M = 7.0$) that occurred on November 26, 1930. The epicenter was located
about 100 km southwest of Tokyo. Tsuboi (1933), Yamaguti (1937) and
Sato (1973) analyzed the geodetic data. In Fig. 5-8 are shown the displace-

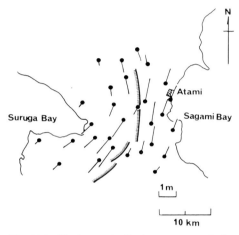

Fig. 5-8. Horizontal displacements of the second- and third-order triangulation stations
associated with the 1930 North Izu earthquake (Sato, 1973). Thick lines indicate the
traces of the Tanna fault that appeared at the time of the earthquake.

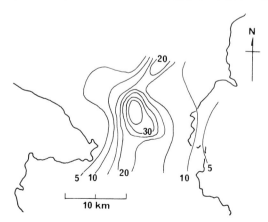

Fig. 5-9. Maximum shearing strains in units of 10^{-5} associated with the 1930 North Izu
earthquake (Tsuboi, 1933).

ments of triangulation stations over the seismic area as obtained by comparing the survey results of 1933 to those of 1925. In the figure, the Tanna
fault that appeared at the time of the earthquake is also shown with thick
solid lines, the fault movement being almost left-lateral strike-slip with a
displacement amounting to 2—3 m.

The diminution of horizontal displacement parallel to the strike was estimated by Kasahara (1957) and Chinnery (1961). The mean rate of diminution was estimated as 4.0×10^{-5} in the immediate neighborhood of the
fault.

Two-dimensional strains were calculated by Tsuboi (1933) from the geodetic data. In Fig. 5-9 the distribution of maximum shearing strain is reproduced. The figure suggests that the maximum strain which the earth's crust
can bear without rupturing would be around 10^{-4}.

5.3.4. Tottori earthquake

At the time of the Tottori earthquake ($M = 7.4$) that occurred in Tottori
Prefecture, Japan, about 150 km west of Kyoto on September 10, 1943, two
seismic faults, the Shikano and the Yoshioka faults, appeared, both having a
right-lateral horizontal displacement of 2—3 m. The retriangulation carried
out in 1957 brought to light horizontal crustal movements during the period
1891—1957, most of which must be associated with the earthquake, as can
be seen in Fig. 5-10. The rate of diminution of horizontal displacement from
the fault can be obtained from a graph as shown in Fig. 5-11 in which only
the absolute values of displacement on both sides of the faults are plotted.

According to Kanamori (1972a), the triangulation data can be interpreted
in terms of a near-vertical right-lateral fault with a surface offset of 2.5 m.
The length and the strike of the fault are estimated as 33 km and N80°E

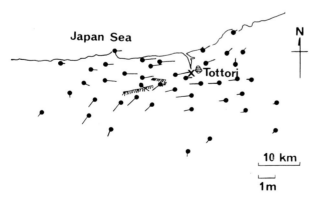

Fig. 5-10. Horizontal displacements of first-, second- and third-order triangulation stations, associated with the 1943 Tottori earthquake. The cross indicates the epicenter
(Kaminuma et al., 1973). Two fault traces are also shown.

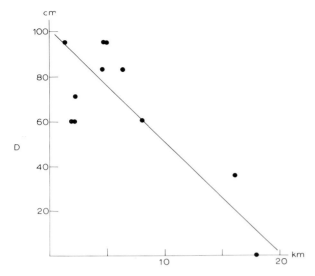

Fig. 5-11. Decrease of horizontal displacement parallel to the fault with distance from the fault for the Tottori earthquake (Rikitake, 1975c).

respectively. An analysis of the seismogram recorded at a station at an epicentral distance of 140 km suggests a model in which the fault depth is estimated as 13 km, the average dislocation 2.5 m, the seismic moment 3.6×10^{26} dyne cm, and the stress drop 83 bars.

There is evidence (Matsuda, 1968) that the rate of the right-lateral displacement along the Shikano and Yoshioka faults is of the order of 3 m/10,000 years or so. There is no evidence, however, of a significant slip during the several thousands of years preceding the earthquake. It may be that the Tottori earthquake is a sudden rupture of the earth's crust in which the tectonic stress has been built up to some 100 bars over a period of 10^4 years or so.

5.3.5. Mikawa earthquake

An earthquake of magnitude 7.1 occurred in the Mikawa Bay, Aichi Prefecture in Central Japan, facing the Pacific Ocean on January 12, 1945. It was reported that 1,961 lives were lost and that 5,539 houses were totally destroyed. A curved earthquake fault of 9 km in length appeared on land.

The triangulation network over the area was resurveyed by the GSI 10 years after the earthquake. Like the Tottori earthquake, no resurvey immediately after the shock was possible because the earthquake took place during the war. The displacements of second- and third-order triangulation stations during the period 1887—1955 are illustrated in Fig. 5-12 which is

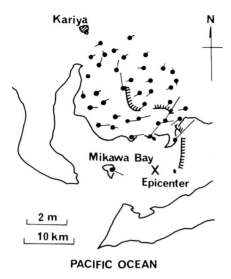

Fig. 5-12. Horizontal displacements of the second- and third-order triangulation stations associated with the 1944 Mikawa earthquake (Ando, 1974a). Fault traces and epicenter are also shown.

redrawn from Ando (1974a). The fault traces are also shown in the figure. As the bay is so shallow that the maximum depth amounts to only 20 m, the fault could be traced even on the sea bottom.

Ando (1974a) presented a graph in which the diminution of horizontal

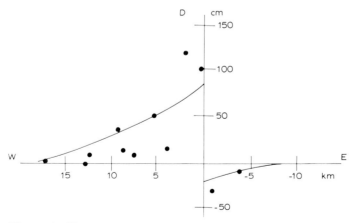

Fig. 5-13. Horizontal displacements parallel to the fault strike versus distance for the Mikawa earthquake. Solid lines represent the displacements calculated for a model having a right-lateral strike-slip component amounting to 1 m (Ando, 1974a).

displacements parallel to the fault strike with distance from the fault is shown as reproduced in Fig. 5-13. If a fault plane striking N—S of 12 km in length and 11 km in width dips westwards with $30°$ dip angle, 2 m reverse dip-slip and 1 m right-lateral strike-slip, the observed crustal deformation can be accounted for. Such a focal model seems to fit the seismographic and tsunamigenic data.

5.3.6. Nankai earthquake

An earthquake ($M = 8.1$) that occurred off Shikoku, Japan on December 21, 1946, was certainly one of the great ones which have repeatedly hit Southwest Japan in the past. 1,330 deaths were reported along with 102 missing people. 11,591 houses totally collapsed. The tsunami that accompanied the earthquake was also so violent that waves as high as 6 m were observed at some places. The earthquake has been called the Nankai or Nankaido, which means South Sea in Japanese, earthquake.

Fig. 5-14 shows the horizontal displacements of the first-order triangulation stations for the period 1899--1949 (Geographical Survey Institute, 1952, 1954). The straight line shown in Honshu represents the base line which is assumed not to have been affected by the earthquake. No geodetic surveys were carried out over the area after the 1944 Tonankai earthquake ($M = 8.0$), of which the epicenter had been located some 100 km northeast of the present one. Fig. 5-14 may reflect a combined effect of these two earthquakes.

Sato (1973) presented a similar study in which not only the displacements

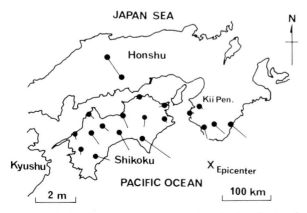

Fig. 5-14. Horizontal displacements of the first-order triangulation stations associated with the 1946 Nankai earthquake. The straight line connecting two stations in Honshu represents the base line which is assumed not to have been affected by the earthquake. The epicenter is indicated by a cross (Geographical Survey Institute, 1952, 1954).

of the first-order stations but also those of the second-order stations were obtained.

The extremities of the peninsulas on Shikoku uplifted about 1 m, while subsidence amounting to a few tens of centimeters was observed over a large inland area as will be seen in subsection 5.6.11. It is remarkable that the area affected by the earthquake is extremely wide. Fitch and Scholz (1971) interpreted the geodetic data by assuming an elastic rebound mechanism consistent with an underthrusting. A fault, whose surface trace coincides with a submarine canyon, the Nankai Trough running in a WSW—ENE direction, is assumed to be about 100 km off the coast. The fault plane was estimated as 2.5×10^4 km^2, while the dislocation varying from 5 to 18 m is required to account for the coseismic deformations. Kanamori (1972b) pointed out on the basis of analyses of seismograms that the Nankai earthquake can be explained in terms of a low-angle thrust whose size and dislocation are about 10^4 km^2 and 3 m respectively.

It is apparent that the slip deduced from the seismometric study is significantly smaller than that from the geodetic analysis. Kanamori (1972a,b) suggested that the discrepancy between the seismographic and geodetic analyses can be accounted for by taking the anelasticity of the rebound mechanism into account.

5.3.7. Fukui earthquake

Fukui City in Central Japan bordering the Japan Sea was hit by a severe earthquake of magnitude 7.3 on June 28, 1948. 3,895 people were killed, and 35,420 houses were totally destroyed. Although no surface offset was observed, resurvey of triangulation stations made it clear that there should be a subsurface left-lateral fault striking N10°W to N20°W (Muto et al., 1950; Nasu, 1950). Several ground fissures arranged en echelon were observed in the direction of the fault which was probably smeared out by a thick alluvial. The length of the fault is estimated as about 25 km with the maximum offset amounting to about 2 m as can be seen in Fig. 5-15.

Kanamori (1972a) presented a focal model of the Fukui earthquake. A fault plane of 30 km (length) $\times$ 13 km (width in depth direction) having 2 m offset is thus supposed. The seismic moment, the stress drop and the effective stress determined from seismic data are 3.3×10^{26} dyne cm, 83 bars and 36—120 bars, respectively.

The focal model seismically determined seems to agree very well with the geodetic data. The horizontal displacement as a function of distance from the fault as shown in Fig. 5-16 can well be accounted for by the model. Only the displacements of triangulation stations in an area close to the central portion of the fault are shown in the figure.

Inland earthquakes in Japan, such as the Fukui, Tango and Tottori, may well have been caused by almost purely elastic rebound judging from the

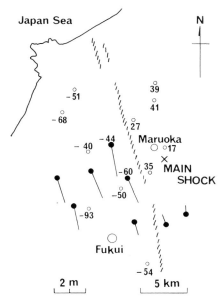

Fig. 5-15. Horizontal displacements of triangulation stations associated with the 1948 Fukui earthquake. Numerals denote vertical displacements in units of centimeters. Shaded belts indicate the subsurface fault; the epicenter is marked by a cross (Kaminuma et al., 1973).

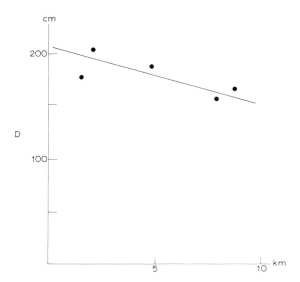

Fig. 5-16. Diminution of horizontal displacement parallel to the fault with distance from the fault for the Fukui earthquake (Rikitake, 1975c).

good agreement between seismic and geodetic analyses. In contrast to these earthquakes, extremely large earthquakes occurring off and along the Pacific coast of Japan, such as the Kanto and Nankai earthquakes, seem to have something to do with an anelastic process in the crust because the fault plane geodetically deduced is much larger than that due to seismic analysis.

5.3.8. San Francisco earthquake

One can trace the earthquake history for California, U.S.A., way back to July 28, 1769, when a strong earthquake was felt somewhere around Los Angeles. After that, many earthquakes were recorded in California and Nevada. Those who are interested in the American history of earthquakes should refer to Richter (1958) and the National Oceanic and Atmospheric Administration (1973).

The 1857 and the 1906 earthquakes which occurred respectively around Fort Tejon, about 100 km north of Los Angeles, and San Francisco, were probably the severest among many earthquakes in California and Nevada. No reports by trained observers were available for the 1857 earthquake. But there is evidence that a fault of 40 miles (64 km) in length appeared in association with the earthquake. There is every reason to believe that the Fort Tejon earthquake was a great one, having a magnitude of 8 or thereabouts.

Fig. 5-17. Major geologic fault systems in California and Nevada, U.S.A.

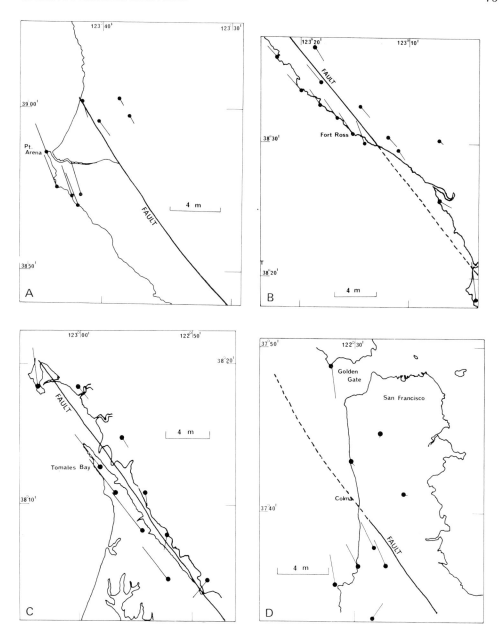

Fig. 5-18. Horizontal displacements of triangulation stations associated with the 1906 San Francisco earthquake (Hayford and Baldwin, 1907). A. Pt. Arena area. B. Fort Ross area. C. Tomales Bay area. D. San Francisco—Colma area.

Earthquakes in California and Nevada are characterized by the fact that they are well correlated to geologic faults, and that new faulting is almost always observed whenever an earthquake of moderately large magnitude occurs. Fig. 5-17 shows the major faults in California and Nevada.

Tectonically speaking, the most predominant feature is represented by the San Andreas fault, which, according to the idea of current plate tectonics, is identified as one of transform faults (Wilson, 1965). There is evidence that the earth's crust along the San Andreas fault has been subjected to a right-lateral movement amounting to about 500 km over a period of 10^8 years since the Cretaceous (Allen, 1965).

The San Francisco earthquake (M = 8.3) that occurred on April 18, 1906, killed several hundred people in San Francisco and its vicinity although no exact number of deaths was known. The fire was terrible as was described in a documentary book (Bronson, 1971).

A fault movement over about 200 miles (ca. 320 km) from Pt. Arena southwards, which was predominantly strike-slip, was associated with the earthquake. According to Richter (1958), the largest displacements were in Martin County, north of the Golden Gate. The offset had a general maximum of about 15.5 ft (4.7 m); however, on the soft alluvial ground it attained 21 ft (6.4 m).

A new triangulation survey in California was undertaken during the interval July, 1906, to July, 1907. The results are compared to those of old triangulations carried out in the period 1851—1899. Remarkable displacements of triangulation stations associated with the earthquake (Hayford and Baldwin, 1907) were found. It is interesting to note that a remarkable land

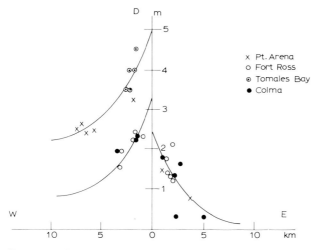

Fig. 5-19. Decrease of horizontal displacements with distance for the San Francisco earthquake (Chinnery, 1961).

movement probably associated with the 1868 Hayward Fault earthquake, that caused extensive damage at San Francisco, was also observed.

Fig. 5-18A—D shows the displacements associated with the 1906 earthquake as redrawn from Hayford and Baldwin (1907). It is apparent that the displacements of the triangulation stations are markedly parallel to the fault strike, and that large displacements are confined to a narrow zone along the fault.

Curves for the horizontal displacements parallel to the fault versus the distance from the fault are shown in Fig. 5-19 (Chinnery, 1961) for the four areas shown in Fig. 5-18. As the total discontinuity differs from place to place along the fault, the tendency of diminution of the horizontal displacements can only be shown with a few curves. The mean rate of diminution is estimated as 1.7×10^{-4} which is surprisingly larger than those for other cases.

5.3.9. Imperial Valley earthquake

An earthquake of magnitude 7.1 (9 deaths), that occurred in the Imperial Valley near El Centro, South California, on May 18, 1940, was accompanied by a faulting of 40 miles (64 km) or more in length extending to the south across the international border between the U.S.A. and Mexico. The fault, which is parallel to the San Andreas fault, was named the Imperial fault (Fig. 5-17). A fairly detailed report of the earthquake can be found in Richter (1958, pp. 487—495).

Triangulation surveys had been executed over the earthquake area in 1935 and supplemented in 1939. A new survey in 1941 disclosed an interesting

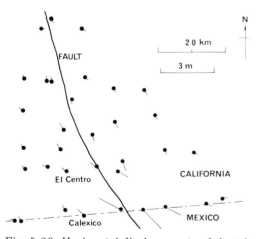

Fig. 5-20. Horizontal displacements of the triangulation stations associated with the 1940 Imperial Valley earthquake (Meade, 1948; reproduced with permission from *Transactions, American Geophysical Union*, Vol. 29, pp. 27—31. Copyright 1948 by American Geophysical Union).

feature of earth movement as can be seen in Fig. 5-20 (Meade, 1948; Whitten, 1955) in which the righthanded strike-slip is well demonstrated.

Analysis of the diminution of horizontal displacements parallel to the fault leads to a horizontal strain amounting to 8.5×10^{-5} in the immediate neighborhood of the fault.

5.3.10. Kern County earthquake

An earthquake of magnitude 7.7, which was the largest in California since 1906 and killed 12 people, took place on July 21, 1952, causing much damage to Bakersfield, Arvin and other towns. The epicenter was located quite close to the White Wolf fault which had been known to exist but had not been thought to be a possible seat of a major earthquake. New faulting could be traced over 20 miles (32 km), and a dip-slip movement could be observed unlike faulting associated with the San Andreas fault where the movement is essentially strike-slip. Details of the earthquake can be seen in Richter (1958, pp. 519—531).

Fig. 5-21 represents the horizontal and vertical displacements of the earth's crust associated with the Kern County earthquake as redrawn from Whitten (1955). It was fortunate that a triangulation survey had been completed several months before the earthquake, so that the horizontal displacements as shown in Fig. 5-21 are deduced from the two surveys respectively

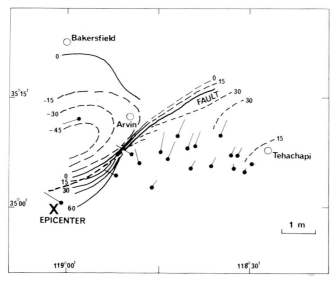

Fig. 5-21. Horizontal displacements of the triangulation stations associated with the 1952 Kern County earthquake. Numerals indicate the vertical displacements in units of centimeters. The epicenter is indicated by a cross (Whitten, 1955).

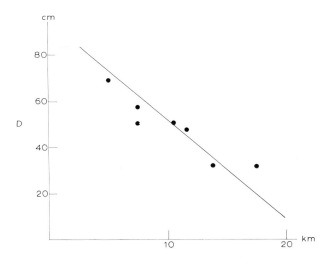

Fig. 5-22. Diminution of horizontal displacement parallel to the fault with distance from the fault for the Kern County earthquake (Rikitake, 1975c).

carried out in 1951—1952 and 1952—1953. The mean rate of diminution of the horizontal displacement parallel to the fault is calculated as 4.3×10^{-5} from the displacement versus distance from the fault plots as shown in Fig. 5-22.

5.3.11. Fairview Peak earthquake

The Dixie Valley area in Nevada was struck by a series of earthquakes in 1954. Only a few people were injured because of sparse population. A shock of magnitude 6.6 occurred at Rainbow Mountain, about 10 miles (16 km) east of Fallon on July 6 followed by a remarkably long series of aftershocks. On August 23, another strong shock of magnitude 6.8 occured a little north of the first one. The seismic activity reached its maximum when an earthquake of magnitude 7.1 followed after 4 minutes by another shock of magnitude 6.8 took place some 30 miles (48 km) east of the July earthquakes on December 16. These and the following descriptions are from Richter (1958, pp. 510—515).

Faulting, 65 miles (104 km) in total length, appeared in relation to the activity. At the time of the first shock on December 16, a spectacular fault scarp (Fig. 5-23) appeared at Fairview Peak. Unlike the San Andreas fault, fault movements to the east of the Sierra Nevada mountain range are characterized by a predominant dip-slip motion.

Triangulation work associated with these earthquake events provided one of the best opportunities to look into crustal deformation related to large earthquakes. A triangulation party was working over an area east of Fallon in

Fig. 5-23. The fault that appeared in association with the 1954 Fairview Peak earthquake. The photo was taken by the author in 1966.

the summer of 1954. The survey was completed just before the December earthquakes. In response to the requirements raised by seismologists, geologists and others, the same party went back to the area, and the entire network was reobserved in the summer of 1955.

The results obtained by comparing the two surveys are striking as can be

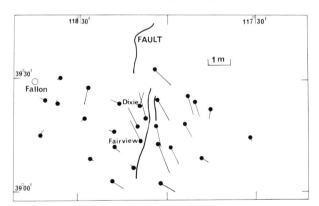

Fig. 5-24. Horizontal displacements of the triangulation stations associated with the 1954 Fairview Peak earthquake (Whitten, 1956; reproduced with permission from *Transactions, American Geophysical Union*, Vol. 37, pp. 393—398. Copyright 1956 by American Geophysical Union).

seen in Fig. 5-24 (Whitten, 1956, 1957). A right-lateral shearing movement can be clearly observed in the figure. The mean rate of diminution of the horizontal displacement parallel to the fault is estimated as 6.2×10^{-5}.

5.3.12. Alaska earthquake

The great Alaska earthquake ($M = 8.4$), that occurred in the region of Prince William Sound on March 28, 1964, caused much damage to Anchorage and the neighboring area. The number of dead or missing people amounted to 112, and 12 people were killed by the tsunami that accompanied the earthquake. The area subjected to crustal movement was so wide that land upheaval and subsidence could be observed over a distance of several hundred kilometers. The total area affected is estimated as 200,000 km^2 (Plafker, 1965; Environmental Science Services Administration, 1966b, 1969a,b).

According to Parkin (1969), the horizontal displacements of triangulation stations caused by the earthquake are something like those shown in Fig. 5-25 in which displacements exceeding 20 m are observed. Plafker (1972) interpreted such crustal movements by supposing a low-angle thrust fault beneath the Alaska--Aleutian arc with a movement of 20 m or so.

In order to estimate the mean horizontal strain over the focal region, changes in horizontal displacement from an arbitrary straight line AA' as indicated in Fig. 5-25 are obtained. Line AA' is striking in a direction approximately perpendicular to the general trend of horizontal displacement. Fig. 5-26 shows the relation between the horizontal displacement projected

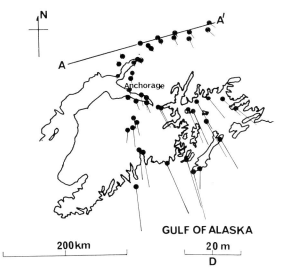

Fig. 5-25. Horizontal displacements of the triangulation stations associated with the 1964 Alaska earthquake (Parkin, 1969).

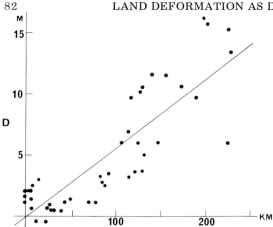

Fig. 5-26. Increase in horizontal displacement perpendicular to the straight line AA' as indicated in Fig. 5-25 with a distance from AA' in the case of the Alaska earthquake (Rikitake, 1975c).

on a direction perpendicular to AA' and the distance from AA', the straight line in the figure being determined by the least-squares method. The mean rate of diminution of horizontal displacement is thus obtained as 8.4×10^{-5}.

5.3.13. Rhombus base lines at Mitaka, Tokyo

In the compound of the Tokyo Astronomical Observatory at Mitaka in the suburbs of Tokyo, a set of geodetic base lines of a rhombic shape was set up in 1916. As can be seen in Fig. 5-27, the rhombus consists of four base lines of lengths very near 100 m (Tsuboi, 1933).

The lengths of the base lines were measured from time to time by invar-wire scales, mostly with one- to two-year intervals. It appeared that the

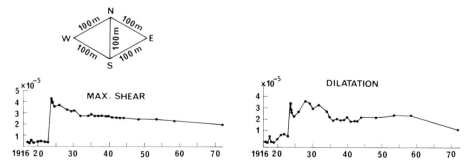

Fig. 5-27. Changes in the maximum shearing strain and dilatation as calculated from secular distance changes of the Mitaka rhombus base lines (Geographical Survey Institute, 1972c).

lengths fluctuate to a certain extent. The fluctuations in the dilatation and the maximum shearing strain as calculated from the changes in the base-line lengths are shown in Fig. 5-27 (Geographical Survey Institute, 1972c). It is interesting to note that an increase in the area of the rhombus amounting to 3×10^{-5} in its rate occurred in association with the 1923 Kanto earthquake whose epicenter was several tens of kilometers distant from the base lines.

Careful examination of Fig. 5-27 further tells us that an anomalous increase in the rhombus area started about 4 years prior to the earthquake. This might be a precursor of the earthquake.

It has nowadays become popular to set up a rhombus or quadrilateral having base lines of several kilometers in length over areas where significant crustal movements are expected (e.g. Harada, 1969; Meade, 1971).

5.4. GEODIMETER SURVEY TECHNIQUES

If one measures time T needed for a light beam, which is sent from point A to another point B, to go and to come back to A after being reflected at B, the distance D between A and B is obtained as:

$$D = cT/2 \tag{5-10}$$

in which c denotes the light velocity.

A geodimeter is an apparatus that works on the above principle. In practice, however, a light beam modulated by a high frequency ω of 10—30 MHz is sent to a reflector. As the modulated light is subjected to a phase change amounting to $2D\omega/c$, it is possible to obtain D by measuring the phase change. Geodimeters have been used for measuring a distance amounting to a few tens of kilometers since around 1950, although an earlier model was bulky and measurement of a long distance could be made only during nighttime.

A dramatic improvement has been achieved by the introduction of the He-Ne laser as the light source in recent years. The new model geodimeter is easier to handle (Fig. 4-3) as well as being more accurate. With the aid of a narrow-band filter, it becomes possible to measure a distance of 30—40 km with an accuracy of 10^{-6} even in daytime. Fig. 5-28 shows a reflector in a field operation. In an actual measurement certain corrections for temperature and other atmospheric effects must be made.

On introducing the geodimeter techniques, it has become possible to make a first-order triangulation survey by measuring the distances between stations forming a triangle instead of measuring the angles. The overall accuracy of survey becomes several times higher than that of the classic triangulation survey.

A geodimeter based on the simultaneous measurement with two colors of light has been under development. Because of adequate correction for the

Fig. 5-28. Field setting of the reflector of a geodimeter.

refractive index, such an instrument with red (He-Ne) and blue (He-Cd) laser sources seem to have a precision about one order of magnitude higher than that of a single-color instrument (Bouricius and Earnshaw, 1974).

5.4.1. Horizontal strain over the South Kanto area

It has been feared by Japanese people that a large earthquake might recur in the area southwest of Tokyo where the 1923 Kanto earthquake occurred which was certainly the worst one in the history of Japan. On the basis of his statistical study, Kawasumi (1970) proposed that there is a 69-year period between the strong earthquakes that strike the Tokyo area although there are objections to his statistics (e.g. Shimazaki, 1971a, 1972c). However, Kawasumi's point was taken seriously by the press. As 50 years had already past since the Kanto earthquake, newspapers, weekly magazines and the like wrote much about the possibility of having a large earthquake in the Tokyo area.

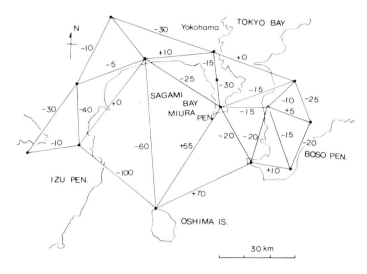

Fig. 5-29. Changes in distance in units of centimeters between triangulation stations in the South Kanto area during 1925—1971 (Geographical Survey Institute, 1972b).

Under these circumstances, the GSI undertook a revision of the triangulation survey for stations in the South Kanto area in order to investigate the crustal strain accumulating there (Geographical Survey Institute, 1972b). Fig. 5-29 shows the changes in horizontal distance between the first-order triangulation stations from 1925 to 1971. The changes were obtained by comparing the geodimeter survey results to those of a triangulation survey carried out a few years after the Kanto earthquake. It is striking that the distance between Oshima Island and a triangulation station on Izu Peninsula shortened by 100 cm and that the distance between the island and the extremities of Miura and Boso Peninsulas elongated by several tens of centimeters during the 46-year period. It is also apparent that a considerable contraction took place in a roughly N—S direction in Boso Peninsula.

It is extremely interesting to compare the land deformation thus detected to the one that occurred in association with the 1923 earthquake. In Fig. 5-30 (Geographical Survey Institute, 1972b) are shown the principal axes of horizontal strain over the South Kanto area as calculated from the results of triangulations for the periods 1887—1925 and 1925—1971. It can be clearly seen that the post-earthquake deformation is almost exactly opposite in direction to the co-earthquake deformation, and that approximately one-third of the co-earthquake deformation has been recovered in these 46 years. It may therefore be said that, if one assumes a simple extrapolation, the remaining two-thirds of the co-earthquake deformation might be accumulated within 92 years' time from 1971 onwards, so that we would not be

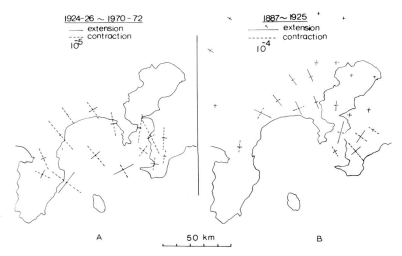

Fig. 5-30. Horizontal principal strains in the South Kanto area as obtained by comparing the results of triangulation or geodimeter surveys. A. 1925 (1924—1926) to 1971 (1970—1972), B. 1887—1925 (Geographical Survey Institute, 1972b).

surprised even if we had another large-scale earthquake originating from Sagami Bay at about that time.

The pattern of horizontal strain indicates that the motion of the Philippine Sea plate, which is shown in Fig. 5-31, in a NW direction seems to be the principal cause of the land deformation. The submarine fault, the surface trace of which is believed to coincide with the Sagami Trough seems to have

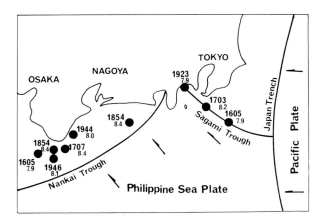

Fig. 5-31. Plates, troughs and a trench off the Pacific coast of Honshu, Japan. The arrows show the directions of plate motion. Epicenters of extremely large earthquakes since 1600 are indicated in the figure along with their year of occurrence and magnitude.

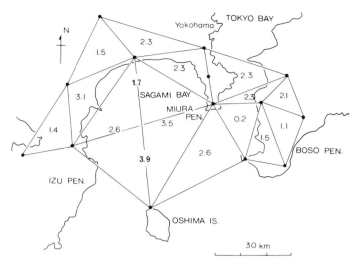

Fig. 5-32. Maximum shearing strains in units of 10^{-5} for each triangle in the South Kanto area as accumulated during 1925–1971 (Geographical Survey Institute, 1972b).

been locked after its movement at the time of the 1923 earthquake, so that a considerable amount of shearing strain has been accumulated around it as can be calculated and is shown for each triangle in Fig. 5-32. The mean rate of accumulation of the maximum shearing strain is estimated as 0.0568×10^{-5}/year.

The geodetic work repeated over the South Kanto area provides a unique observation of crustal strain over a focal region where a great earthquake has occurred and is expected to recur sooner or later. Measurements of the distances between the triangulation stations on Oshima Island, Izu, Miura and Boso Peninsulas have been repeated every year since 1971. At the moment, however, no significant changes have as yet been reported.

5.4.2. Horizontal strain over the North Izu area

The Geographical Survey Institute (1974b) has recently completed a geodimeter survey for second- and third-order triangulation stations in the North Izu district, Japan, where a destructive earthquake occurred in 1930 (see subsection 5.3.3). The horizontal displacements of each station during 1933–1973, obtained by comparing the results of the present survey to those of a triangulation survey conducted soon after the North Izu earthquake, are shown in Fig. 5-33.

It is interesting to note that the displacements are small around the Tanna fault, which moved at the time of the 1930 earthquake, and that the stations on both sides of the fault moved in directions which are the same as those

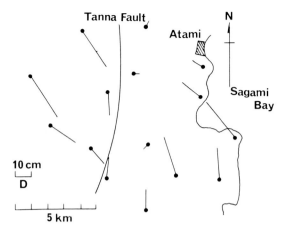

Fig. 5-33. Horizontal displacement (D) of triangulation stations in the North Izu district during 1933—1973 (Geographical Survey Institute, 1974b).

associated with the earthquake as shown in Fig. 5-8. It is clear that a shearing movement, the rebound of which may lead to the recurrence of an earthquake as suggested first by Reid (1910, pp. 16—32), has been taking place, the fault seeming to have been locked.

Dambara (1975) argued that displacements of triangulation stations such as shown in Fig. 5-33 are obtained with a certain assumption, so that no

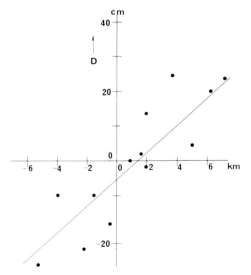

Fig. 5-34. Changes in the horizontal displacement parallel to the Tanna fault plotted against the distance from the fault (Rikitake, 1975c).

absolutely correct displacements can be obtained. It is tentatively assumed here, however, that the displacements in Fig. 5-33 are approximately correct.

Fig. 5-34 shows the displacements parallel to the fault as plotted against the distance from the fault. The slight curvature of the fault line has been ignored. In spite of the scatter, it is apparent that the area is subjected to a shearing stress. A straight-line fit by the least-squares method as shown in Fig. 5-34 leads to an averaged strain value amounting to 3.8×10^{-5}. Assuming that the strain has been accumulating with a constant rate since the 1930 earthquakes, the strain rate becomes 0.096×10^{-5}/year.

5.4.3. Traverse surveys of high precision across the Japan Islands

An internationally cooperative program on solid earth science called the "Geodynamics Project" was launched in 1972 following the very successful international effort called the "Upper Mantle Project" (UMP) in the 1960s. During the UMP, which aimed at clarifying physical and chemical states in the upper part of the earth's mantle, the ideas of sea-floor spreading and plate tectonics were developed. In view of such exciting findings, it was proposed to continue internationally cooperative work on the dynamics within the earth, and so an Inter-Union Commission on Geodynamics (ICG) sponsored by the IUGG and the International Union of Geological Sciences (IUGS) was formed under the auspices of the International Council of Scientific Unions (ICSU). Scores of nations are participating in the project.

One of the most important undertakings in the framework of the Geodynamics Project in Japan is to prove or disprove that the Japan Islands have been actually compressed by the motions of the Pacific and Philippine Sea

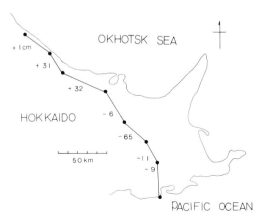

Fig. 5-35. Changes in distance in units of centimeters between adjoining triangulation stations along a traverse line in eastern Hokkaido during 1907—1972 (Geographical Survey Institute, 1973).

plates as plate tectonics suggests. The GSI undertook to conduct a number of traverse surveys of high precision along several nearly straight lines connecting triangulation stations across the Japan arc, and to see whether or not any significant land contraction has been taking place.

Fig. 5-35 shows a traverse line in Hokkaido (Geographical Survey Institute, 1973) which is approximately perpendicular to the axis of the Japan—Kurile Trench where the Pacific plate is believed to submerge. Changes in the length of the distances connecting neighboring triangulation stations are obtained by comparing the present survey in 1972 to the first-order triangulation survey conducted in 1907. It is interesting to note that the southern half of the traverse line indicates a contraction which might reflect the compression by the motion of the Pacific plate.

The result of a traverse survey along a line running west of Tokyo in an approximately N—S direction towards the Japan Sea is also of extreme interest as can be seen in Fig. 5-36 (Geographical Survey Institute, 1973). During the period 1900—1972 the distances between the stations on the southern half of the line were subjected to a fair amount of contraction. At

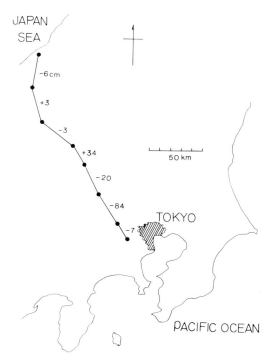

Fig. 5-36. Changes in distance in units of centimeters between adjoining triangulation stations along a traverse line across Honshu running from the western suburbs of Tokyo to the north during 1900—1972 (Geographical Survey Institute, 1973).

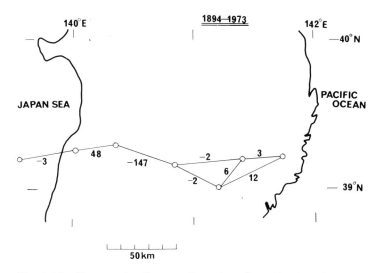

Fig. 5-37. Changes in distance in units of centimeters between adjoining triangulation stations along a traverse line running in an approximately E—W direction across Honshu near the 39° parallel during 1894—1973 (Geographical Survey Institute, 1974a).

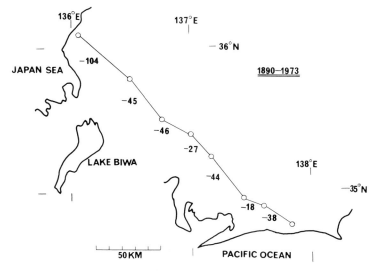

Fig. 5-38. Changes in distance in units of centimeters between adjoining triangulation stations across Honshu in Central Japan during 1890—1973 (Geographical Survey Institute, 1974c).

the time of the 1923 Kanto earthquake, however, these stations rebounded, namely the distances increased (see subsections 5.3.1 and 5.4.1). After that they were subjected to contraction again. In contrast to this, the northern half of the traverse line seems to be fairly stable, no significant deformation having been observed in these 72 years.

Traverse surveys of this kind have been extended to Northeast and Central Japan (Geographical Survey Institute, 1974a,c) in a subsequent year. No outstanding contraction was found along a line close to the 39° parallel during 1894—1973, although we see an anomalously large shortening of distance between two triangulation stations in the middle (Fig. 5-37). As the area is very far from the Japan Trench, the effect of compression by the Pacific plate might not be quite large.

A traverse survey across Central Japan indicates an extremely interesting result as can be seen in Fig. 5-38 which represents the changes during 1890—1973. An enormous compression in a NW direction is clearly demonstrated in the figure. A 3.22-m shortening is observed for the total length amounting to 230 km, so that the averaged strain rate is estimated as 1.6×10^{-7}/year.

There is every reason to believe that the probability is high for a large-scale earthquake to occur in the near future off the Pacific coast of Central Japan called the Tokai district (which means East Sea district in Japanese), as will be discussed later (see subsection 15.3.2). The crustal shortening as shown in Fig. 5-38 provides one of the reasons why such a high earthquake risk is assigned to the Tokai district.

A similar survey along the eastern coast of Kyushu (Geographical Survey Institute, 1974d) shows that almost all distances connecting neighboring triangulation stations elongated by a few tens of centimeters during 1899—1973. No physical interpretation of the results has as yet been put forward.

5.4.4. Surveys over the San Andreas fault

Intensive work on observing time variations of horizontal distances by making use of a geodimeter has been under way over the San Andreas fault zone since 1959. The work was begun by the California Department of Water Resources and later was transferred to the California Division of Mines and Geology and the USGS.

Most of the water in California is collected in the northern areas of the state and is delivered to the highly populated southern areas through aqueduct systems which cross the San Andreas fault from place to place. It is therefore of vital importance for Californians to know how the aqueducts are affected by the fault movements.

Many of the precise geodimeter distances, that cross the fault system, are set out in a fashion as shown in Fig. 5-39 in which the San Francisco—Hollister—Cholame portion of the San Andreas fault is illustrated (Meade, 1969).

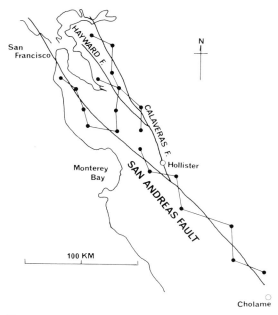

Fig. 5-39. Precise geodimeter distances covering the San Andreas fault system between San Francisco and Cholame (Meade, 1969).

As a result of frequent measurements of these distances, it turns out that the average annual fault movement on the San Andreas fault is greatest south of Hollister, amounting to 4.4 cm/year (Hofmann, 1968). Earthquakes are often preceded by changes in the rate of movement along nearby faults.

When an earthquake of magnitude 5.2 occurred at Corralitos, some 20 km

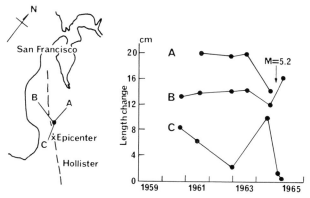

Fig. 5-40. Precursory length change in relation to the 1964 Corralitos earthquake in northern California (Hofmann, 1968, *Bulletin of the Department of Water Resources, State of California*, No. 116-6, p. 74, fig. 33).

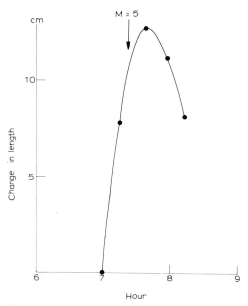

Fig. 5-41. Short-range anomaly in the length of a geodimeter distance immediately prior to and after the 1960 Hollister earthquake (Hofmann, 1968, *Bulletin of the Department of Water Resources, State of California*, No. 116-6, p. 83, fig. 40).

north of Hollister, in 1964, reversals of changes in distance were observed as can be seen in Fig. 5-40. When an earthquake of magnitude 5 occurred near Hollister on January 19, 1960, a measurement was in progress along a 25-km distance across the San Andreas fault just north of Hollister. The distance elongated as much as 8 cm during 15 minutes just before the shock, and an extension of several centimeters was observed by an observation 10 minutes after the shock. Within a following hour, it contracted by a few centimeters. Fig. 5-41 shows the short-range change in distance during the earthquake.

More recent data taken by geodimeter surveys have been analyzed by Scholz and Fitch (1969, 1970), Savage and Burford (1970, 1971, 1973), Savage et al. (1973) and Greensfelder and Bennett (1973). Scholz and Fitch pointed out a considerable accumulation of strain over portions of the San Andreas fault, although Savage and Burford mentioned that most of the changes in length may be caused by fault slippage resulting in little accumulation of strain. The author is not in a position to judge which is true.

5.5. LEVELLING SURVEY TECHNIQUES

Levelling bench marks are buried along the main roads in Japan at intervals of about 2 km. These bench marks provide height references for mapping. A levelling survey is carried out by reading a vertical scale with a telescope attached to a precise level placed at a certain distance, and then, after turning the level by almost $180°$ in a horizontal plane, reading another vertical scale which is placed at some distance. By subtracting the first reading from the second one, it is possible to obtain the difference in height between the two points where the scales are put. Repeating similar operations, heights of bench marks can be determined one by one in reference to a base bench mark. The Japanese base bench mark is located in the center of Tokyo, and its height is presumed to be 24.4140 m relative to the mean sea level of Tokyo Bay.

As has been shown in Fig. 4-4, the Japan Islands are covered by the first-order levelling routes of about 20,000 km in total length. When a levelling survey along a certain route is compared to a previous one along the same route, it is possible to see the changes in height of bench marks along the route during the period between the two surveys. It is necessary, however, to assume that the height of one of the bench marks has not been changed.

The author is not well acquainted with levelling work in countries outside Japan, but he believes that there should not be much difference between levelling work in various countries.

As levelling surveys are less laborious as well as less expensive than triangulation surveys, levelling surveys are repeated as often as possible along the routes shown in Fig. 4-4, according to the earthquake prediction program in Japan. As was written in subsection 4.2.2, it now becomes possible to conduct a first-order levelling survey along nationwide routes (Fig. 4-4) every 5 years. Levelling surveys with a shorter interval of 1—2 years have been and will be carried out over areas of particular importance such as the South Kanto and Tokai areas.

As Japanese industrialization became enormous in recent years, many bench marks tended to be destroyed by reconstruction of roads. Workers engaging in a levelling survey sometimes met with traffic accidents because of increasing motorization in Japan, so that it is getting difficult to carry out extensive levelling surveys in Japan. Probably the situation may still not be as bad as that in other countries.

It is also possible to determine the height of a triangulation station in the course of a triangulation survey by means of trigonometric levelling. Although the accuracy of such a height determination is considerably lower than that achieved by a levelling survey, it is sometimes useful to make use of trigonometric levellings in order to see changes in the height of triangulation stations over a wide area in association with a large earthquake.

5.6. LAND DEFORMATION AS DETECTED BY LEVELLINGS

It has been customary in Japan to conduct a levelling survey over an earthquake area soon after an occurrence of a large earthquake in order to recover the exact heights of bench marks in that area. A good deal of land deformation data connected with earthquake occurrences have thus been accumulated in Japan. The data before 1933 were compiled by Tsuboi (1933).

Changes in height as disclosed by levelling surveys before and after an earthquake have also been accumulated in the U.S.A., the U.S.S.R., Bulgaria, Hungary, New Zealand, Australia and other countries.

5.6.1. Nobi earthquake

A brief account of the 1891 Nobi earthquake ($M = 7.9$) was given in section 3.2. There were two levelling routes over the focal area north of Nagoya, the largest city in Central Japan. The routes cross the Neodani fault, that appeared at the time of the earthquake, at two points d and e as are shown in Fig. 5-42 (Tsuboi, 1933) in which the levelling routes around Nagoya are also shown. The present concern is the changes in height as disclosed by levelling surveys along routes a-d-b and a-e-c.

In Fig. 5-42 are also shown the changes in height as obtained by comparing the survey of 1895 to that of 1889. In addition to the discontinuities at the fault, land deformations in the vicinity of the fault are well demonstrated in the figure.

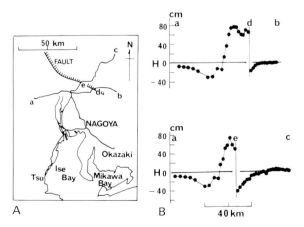

Fig. 5-42. A. Levelling route map around Nagoya, Central Japan, in which the Neodani fault that appeared at the time of the 1891 Nobi earthquake is also shown. B. Changes in height of bench marks along routes a-d-b and a-e-c (Tsuboi, 1933).

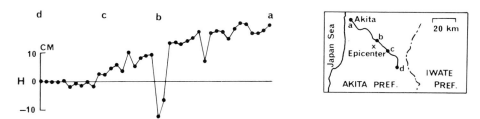

Fig. 5-43. Level changes associated with the 1914 Ugosen earthquake (Kaminuma et al., 1973).

5.6.2. Ugosen earthquake

An earthquake of magnitude 6.4 occurred in Akita Prefecture in northeastern Japan in 1914. It was reported that 94 people died and that 640 houses were totally destroyed. Although no levelling survey was carried out immediately after the earthquake, a survey in 1934 disclosed a ground depression in the epicentral area as can be seen in Fig. 5-43 (Kaminuma et al., 1973). The changes in height are obtained by comparing the 1934 survey to the 1900 survey.

5.6.3. Omachi earthquake

Omachi, a town in Nagano Prefecture, Central Japan (see Fig. 5-55), was hit by two earthquakes, each having a magnitude amounting to 6.1, on

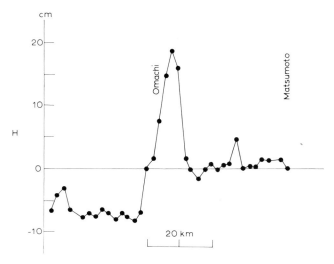

Fig. 5-44. Level changes associated with the 1918 Omachi earthquakes (Tsuboi, 1933).

November 11, 1918. Twenty-two houses totally collapsed. Although no crustal movement was witnessed after the earthquake a levelling survey in 1920 disclosed an uplift of about 20 cm in the immediate neighborhood of the epicenters (Fig. 5-44; Tsuboi, 1933). The post-earthquake survey was compared to the one carried out during 1891—1893. The levelling route runs along the foot of a mountain range called the Japan Alps in an approximately N—S direction starting from Matsumoto City at the southernmost end (see Fig. 5-55).

5.6.4. Kanto earthquake

Much of the damage and social impact of the Kanto earthquake has been stated in section 3.3. The crustal movement associated with the earthquake was extremely extensive as has been presented for horizontal displacement in subsection 5.3.1.

Relevellings along many routes over the South Kanto area made it clear that the Sagami Bay coast and Miura and Boso Peninsulas (see Fig. 5-29) suffered a considerable uplift of more than 1 m (Tsuboi, 1933). For the purpose of looking at the general features of uplift and subsidence over such a wide area, it is more convenient to make use of changes in the height of second- and third-order triangulation stations which, unlike levelling routes, are widely scattered over the South Kanto area. Miyabe (1931) obtained the vertical movements of the ground revealed by trigonometrical levelling for those triangulation stations during 1889—1925 as reproduced in Fig. 5-45 in which only the changes of major scale are illustrated after a kind of averaging procedure. The distribution of the vertical displacement as shown in the

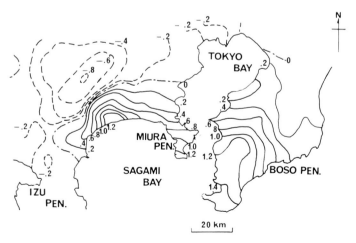

Fig. 5-45. Changes in height in units of meters in the South Kanto area associated with the 1923 Kanto earthquake (Miyabe, 1931).

figure is compatible with the fault model (Àndo, 1971, 1974b) as already
described in subsection 5.3.1.

5.6.5. *Tango earthquake*

The 1927 Tango earthquake is famous for very detailed geodetic studies
conducted in association with the earthquake. The horizontal deformations
and their analyses were presented in subsection 5.3.2.

The earthquake area was covered by levelling routes as shown in Fig.
5-46A. A comparison between the levelling of April, 1927, i.e. soon after the

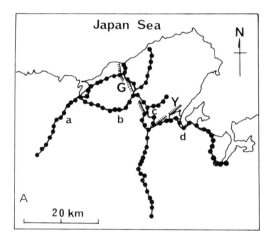

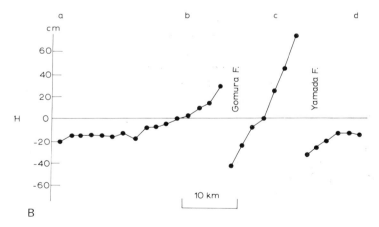

Fig. 5-46. A. Levelling routes covering the 1927 Tango earthquake area. G = Gomura
fault, Y = Yamada fault (Tsuboi, 1933). B. Level changes along the route *a-b-c-d* associated with the 1927 Tango earthquake (Tsuboi, 1933).

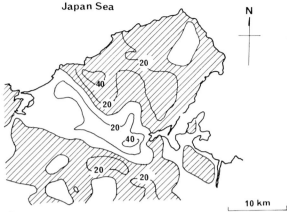

Fig. 5-47. Coseismic changes in height in units of centimeters in the 1927 Tango earthquake area as obtained from a trigonometrical levelling of third-order triangulation stations (Tsuboi, 1932). The land subsided and uplifted respectively in shaded and non-
shaded areas.

shock, and that of 1888 showed changes in the height of the bench marks as
can be seen in Fig. 5-46B (Tsuboi, 1933).

The changes in the height of the third-order triangulation stations are
summarized by Tsuboi (1932), so that an overall distribution of the vertical
displacement over the focal region is clearly brought to light as can be seen
in Fig. 5-47.

5.6.6. Ito earthquake swarm

A swarm activity of earthquakes occurred around Ito, a town famous for
its hot springs located on the east coast of the Izu Peninsula, Japan, in
February 1930. The activity increased progressively in both intensity and
frequency, reaching an apparent maximum toward the end of March, after
which the activity gradually declined. Further activity took place in May
although the activity disappeared by August. The activity had not quite gone
when it returned in November with increasing violence. On November 25, as
many as 690 shocks were recorded at Ito. On the next day the North Izu
earthquake occurred (M = 7.0) which has already been described in subsection 5.3.3. The number of earthquake occurrences during the activity has
been illustrated in Fig. 2-1 in relation to the statistics of fish catch.

At the request of the ERI, the Military Land Survey repeated levellings
along a route running along the east coast of the peninsula as shown in Fig.
5-48 (Tsuboi, 1933) in which changes in the height of bench marks during
the periods between respective pairs of levellings are also shown. Levelling 1
was carried out in 1923—1924, levelling 2 in March—April, 1930, levelling
3 in November, 1930, and levelling 4 in December, 1930, to January, 1931.

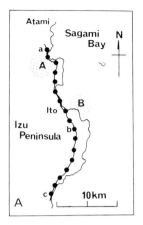
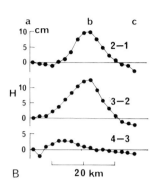

Fig. 5-48. A. Levelling routes running along the east coast of Izu Peninsula and epicentral areas of seismic activity in the autumn (A) and the spring (B). B. Changes in the height of bench marks during the respective periods. Levelling 1: 1923—1924; 2: March—April, 1930; 3: November, 1030; and 4: December, 1930, to January, 1931 (Tsuboi, 1933).

According to seismographic observations, earthquakes clustered in areas A and B respectively during the fall and spring activity. It is interesting to note that the maximum uplifts of the ground surface for both periods of activity are located close to the epicentral areas.

5.6.7. North Izu earthquake

A levelling survey across the Tanna fault that appeared in association with the North Izu earthquake (see Fig. 5-8) showed a depression amounting to 20 cm or so during 1924—1930 as can be seen in Fig. 5-49 (Tsuboi, 1933).

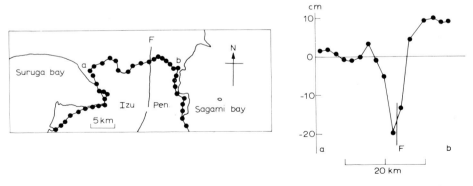

Fig. 5-49. Levelling route and changes in level associated with the 1930 North Izu earthquake (Tsuboi, 1933).

Yamaguti (1937) produced a map of the vertical deformation on the basis of changes in the height of the third-order triangulation stations.

5.6.8. Nagano earthquake

An earthquake of magnitude 6.2 occurred several kilometers northeast of Nagano City in Central Japan (see Fig. 5-55) on July 15, 1941. It was reported that 5 people were killed and that 29 houses were totally destroyed. In Fig. 5-50 (Kaminuma et al., 1973) changes in height of bench marks are shown along a route running in a NE direction starting from Nagano City for the periods 1894—1928 and 1928—1941. The changes for the latter period must reflect the effect of the earthquake.

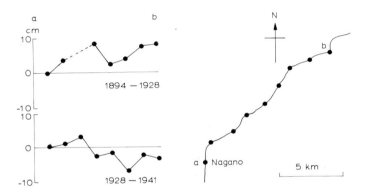

Fig. 5-50. Levelling route and changes in level for the periods 1894—1928 and 1928—1941. The changes associated with the 1941 Nagano earthquake may be shown by the latter (Kaminuma et al., 1973).

5.6.9. Tottori earthquake

The Tottori earthquake ($M = 7.4$) of September 10, 1943, gave rise to a loss of 1,083 lives along with complete destruction of 7,485 houses. The

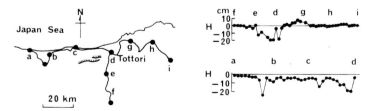

Fig. 5-51. Levelling routes and changes in level associated with the 1943 Tottori earthquake (Kaminuma et al., 1973).

horizontal displacements of triangulation stations have already been presented in subsection 5.3.4.

Relevellings in 1943 along the routes as shown in Fig. 5-51 (Kaminuma et al., 1973) resulted in changes in height of bench marks which are also shown in the figure. The surveys along routes *f-d*, *d-i* and *a-d* are compared to the surveys of 1935, 1927 and 1935, respectively.

5.6.10. Mikawa earthquake

Ando (1974a), who analyzed the crustal movement associated with the 1945 Mikawa earthquake, combined changes in the height of triangulation stations as obtained by trigonometric levellings with the depth changes in Mikawa Bay. An overall distribution of vertical displacement was thus obtained as reproduced in Fig. 5-52. The mean diminution rate of vertical displacement with the increase in distance from the fault is estimated as 1.3 $\times$ 10^{-4} or so.

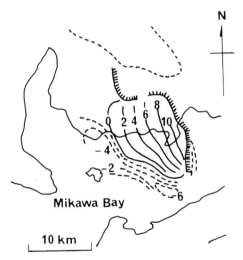

Fig. 5-52. Level changes in units of 10 cm associated with the 1945 Mikawa earthquake (Ando, 1974a).

5.6.11. Nankai earthquake

In subsection 5.3.6 a brief account of the 1946 Nankai earthquake of magnitude 8.1 was given. Horizontal displacements of the crust associated with this earthquake were also described in the subsection.

In Fig. 5-53 are shown the seismic uplift and subsidence associated with the earthquake as deduced from the first-order levelling surveys conducted

Fig. 5-53. Changes in height in units of centimeters associated with the 1946 Nankai earthquake (Geographical Survey Institute, 1967).

before and after the earthquake (Geographical Survey Institute, 1967). The pre-earthquake surveys were conducted during 1928—1939, while the post-earthquake survey was carried out in 1947.

It is apparent from the figures that the extremities of Muroto (Shikoku) and Kii (Honshu) Promontories jumped up by scores of centimeters. Meanwhile land subsidence amounting to several tens of centimeters at maximum took place over Kochi, Kagawa, Ehime, Tokushima, Wakayama and Mie Prefectures adjacent to the upheaved area.

5.6.12. Fukui earthquake

Fig. 5-15 shows the vertical displacements of triangulation stations along with the horizontal displacements. We clearly see the upheaval and subsidence bounded by the subsurface fault.

5.6.13. North Miyagi earthquake

An earthquake of magnitude 6.5 occurred about 50 km north of Sendai City in northeast Japan on April 30, 1962. Three deaths and 369 collapsed houses were reported. A relevelling along a route running in an approximately N—S direction brought to light changes in the height of bench marks as shown in Fig. 5-54 (Kaminuma et al., 1973) for the period 1954—1962. The epicenter is located at a distance of 5 km from the levelling route. The largest change in height occurred at a bench mark close to the epicenter.

5.6.14. Matsushiro earthquakes

Microearthquakes were first observed by the Matsushiro Seismological Ob-

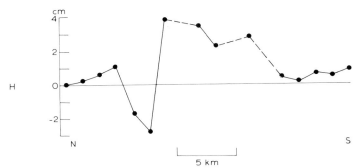

Fig. 5-54. Changes in level along a route running in an approximately N–S direction associated with the 1962 North Miyagi earthquake (Kaminuma et al., 1973).

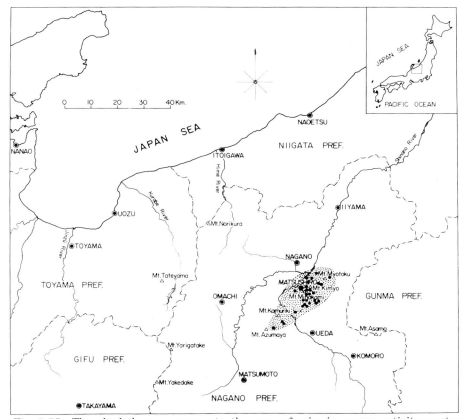

Fig. 5-55. The shaded area represents the area of seismic swarm activity centered on Matsushiro during 1965–1967. Moderately large shocks having a magnitude equal to 4.7 or larger are indicated by solid circles (Hagiwara and Rikitake, 1967, *Science*, Vol. 157, pp. 761–768, fig. 4. Copyright 1967 by the American Association for the Advancement of Science).

servatory attached to the JMA in August, 1965. The observatory, which is located on the outskirts of a town called Matsushiro, 10 km south of Nagano City, Central Japan, is primarily aimed at observing seismic waves from distant earthquakes. The swarm activity increased day by day, and the number of microearthquakes observed by a seismograph having a magnification of 10^4 reached several hundreds a day by October. The number of felt earthquakes increased, too.

A network of seismographs temporarily set up around Matsushiro town made it clear that these earthquakes were occurring in an area centered on Mt. Minakami, a Quaternary volcanic dome of dacite. The focal depths of these shocks ranged from 2 to 5 km. After November, moderately large earthquakes of magnitudes 4—5 tended to occur from time to time.

Starting in March, 1966, the swarm activity became so violent that more than 6,000 microearthquakes were observed in a day by the afore-mentioned seismograph while the daily number of felt earthquakes exceeded 600 in the middle of April. Cracks began to be noticed on the ground north of Mt. Minakami. It was later identified that those cracks were associated with a subsurface fault.

The earthquake area tended to expand to neighboring areas in an elliptic shape elongated in a NE—SW direction as can be seen in Fig. 5-55, which is also useful for finding the locations of various cities, towns, rivers, mountains and the like in the northern part of Central Japan. Moderately large earthquakes of magnitudes larger than 4.7 are also shown in the shaded area of the swarm activity.

The activity, which became somewhat calm in the June—July period,

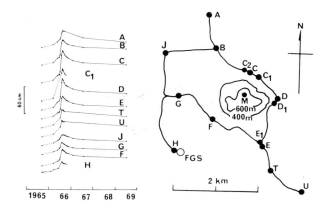

Fig. 5-56. Levelling routes and changes in the level of bench marks around Mt. Minakami (M) which is shown by the topographical contours. Bench mark J is located in the center of Matsushiro Town. FGS denotes the first-order gravity station at the Matsushiro Seismological Observatory. Some of the bench marks are for gravity observation only (Y. Hagiwara, personal communication, 1974).

recovered again toward August and September. Although the number of microearthquakes was not quite as large as that for the April activity, crustal uplift around Mt. Minakami was accelerated, and, at the same time, the ground produced much water giving rise to landslides. The amount of water was estimated in the order of 10^7 m^3 (Iijima, 1969).

The ERI conducted levelling surveys along a newly set up route around Mt. Minakami quite frequently in close cooperation with the GSI which carried out levelling surveys over a more extended area. As a result, an enormous uplift exceeding 70 cm was observed around the Mt. Minakami area. The results of these surveys were reported in a number of papers in Japanese, a summary of which was reported by Okada and Tsubokawa (1969).

Fig. 5-56 shows how the heights of bench marks in the central area of the swarm activity changed with time. The figure has been corrected for mistakes in the curves previously published (Y. Hagiwara, personal communication, 1974).

5.6.15. Kern County earthquake

It was fortunate that levelling routes over the Bakersfield—Arvin area had been surveyed a few months before the occurrence of the 1952 Kern County earthquake in California. As can be seen in Fig. 5-21, the depression of the land mass north of the fault is apparent indicating thrust faulting accompanied by left-lateral strike-slip.

Vertical crustal movements associated with large earthquakes in the California—Nevada region have also been reported for the 1933 Long Beach earthquake (Parkin, 1948), the 1954 Fairview Peak earthquake (Whitten, 1957) and other earthquakes although no account of them is presented here.

5.6.16. Alaska earthquake

As has already been stated in subsection 5.3.12, crustal deformation took place over an extremely wide area (Plafker, 1965), probably 700—800 km long and 150—250 km wide in association with the 1964 Alaska earthquake.

During the period from April to October, 1964, first-order levelling, totaling 956 miles (1,538 km) was undertaken by the U.S. Coast and Geodetic Survey in Alaska (Small, 1969). Some more levelling surveys were added in 1965. The levellings were compared to those carried out in 1922—23 and 1944 depending upon the portions of levelling routes. It appeared that the Seward—Anchorage area subsided 1—2 m. The levelling surveys were available only for a limited area which seems too small to reveal the overall aspect of such a vast land deformation accompanied by the earthquake.

Plafker (1965) measured the vertical movements along the seashore mainly by making more than 800 measurements of the displacement of intertidal sessile marine organisms. These measurements were supplemented at 16 tidal bench marks by coupled pre- and post-earthquake tide-gauge readings made by the U.S. Coast and Geodetic Survey. The maximum uplift on land is 10 m at the southwest end of Montague Island. The distribution of the vertical changes in land level accompanied by the earthquake is shown in Fig. 5-57 (Plafker, 1965) in which it is seen that the major area of uplift is about 800 km long and trends NE from southern Kodiak Island to Prince William Sound.

Plafker (1965) presented three schematic sections of land deformation as reproduced in the lower half of Fig. 5-57 for sections A-A', B-B' and C-C' which are shown in the upper half. Faulting associated with the earthquake

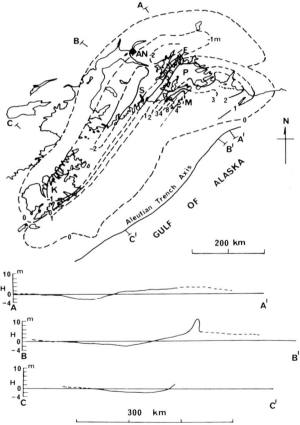

Fig. 5-57. Uplift and subsidence associated with the 1964 Alaska earthquake. Numerals are vertical displacements in meters. Profiles along A-A', B-B' and C-C' are shown in the lower figures. AN = Anchorage, E = Epicenter, P = Prince William Sound, S = Seward, M = Montague Island, and K = Kodiak Island (Plafker, 1965, *Science*, Vol. 148, pp. 1675–1687, figs 2, 6. Copyright 1965 by the American Association for the Advancement of Science).

was found at two localities on Montague Island. They are near vertical and reverse.

It seems likely that the earthquake was caused by a rebound of the land plate associated with a rupture at the interface of the land and sea plates, the latter tending to dip beneath the Aleutian arc.

Plafker (1972) pointed out a remarkable similarity in the crustal deformations associated with the 1964 Alaskan and 1960 Chilean ($M = 8.3$) earthquakes. It is concluded that these earthquakes resulted from release of near-horizontal compressional elastic strain oriented roughly normal to the trends of the eastern Aleutian and southern Peru—Chile arcs. A movement of the order of 20 m on the major thrust fault with an average angle of 9° occurs beneath the eastern Aleutian arc and 20° beneath the southern Peru—Chile arc.

5.6.17. South Bulgarian earthquakes

Richter (1958) described land deformations associated with earthquakes in southern Bulgaria on April 14 and 18, 1928, both having a magnitude amounting to 6.8. Faults were produced with a maximum throw of 3—4 m. The changes of level associated with the earthquakes as revealed by repetition of precise levellings are reproduced in Richter (1958, p. 620). The rate of diminution of vertical displacement from the fault amounts to an extremely large value of 1.5×10^{-4}.

5.6.18. Ashkhabad earthquake

An earthquake of magnitude 7.6 occurred southeast of Ashkhabad, Turkmenian S.S.R., on October 5, 1948, giving rise to serious damage to Ashkha-

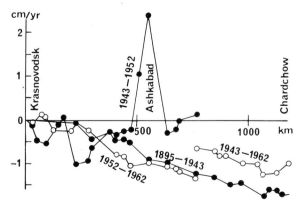

Fig. 5-58. Vertical crustal movements along the route Krasnovodosk—Ashkhabad—Chardchow, Turkmenian S.S.R. (Mescherikov, 1968).

bad and its vicinity where no strong earthquakes had been reported for centuries.

A relevelling along a route connecting Krasnovdosk on the shore of the Caspian Sea to Chardchow at the eastern part of the Turkmenian S.S.R. via Ashkhabad resulted in an uplift of land near the epicenter as can be seen in Fig. 5-58 (Mescherikov, 1968). The uplifted portion of the route seemed to have subsided during 1895—1943. The changes in level during 1952—1962 are just normal.

5.6.19. Inangahua earthquake

An earthquake of magnitude 7 occurred at Inangahua, South Island of New Zealand, on May 24, 1968, causing much damage to property and communications (Boyes, 1971; Lensen and Otway, 1971). Two fault traces having lateral and vertical displacements of several tens of centimeters to more than 1 m appeared as shown in Fig. 5-59. Regional surveys disclosed that an area of 1,000 km^2 was uplifted by an average of 1 m.

Vertical movements as shown in Fig. 5-59 (Lensen and Otway, 1971) were obtained by summarizing comparisons between levelling and trigonometrical surveys for 1954—1967 and those for 1968—1969. Lensen and Otway (1971) have shown a profile of vertical deformation along the line A-B-C.

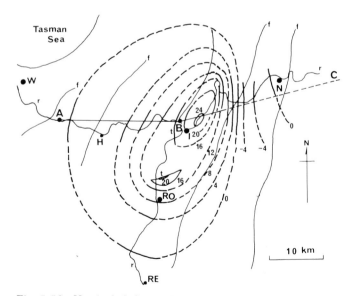

Fig. 5-59. Vertical deformation in units of 10 cm associated with the 1968 Inangahua earthquake. r, f, and t denote rivers, geological faults and newly appeared fault traces, respectively. W = Westport, H = Hawks Crag, I = Inangahua, N = Newton Flat, RO = Rotokohu, RE = Reefton (Lensen, 1971).

The mean rate of fall-off of vertical deformation is estimated as 2.0×10^{-4} and 4.0×10^{-4} respectively for the west and east portions of the profile centered on Inangahua.

Large horizontal displacements amounting to scores of centimeters were also found over the area shown in Fig. 5-59.

Many of the large earthquakes in New Zealand before 1942 have been described by Richter (1958). Levelling bench marks are associated only with railways in New Zealand, so that relevelling results are not quite appropriate for detailed geodetic analyses. However, a few reports on level changes can be found in Richter (1958).

5.6.20. Meckering earthquake

On October 14, 1968, an earthquake of magnitude 6.9 occurred in Western Australia. The shock had the greatest felt intensity and was accompanied by the first faulting to be reported from Australia (Gordon, 1971). A small town called Meckering, 132 km east-northeast of Perth, was destroyed, but no casualties were reported (see Fig. 5-60A).

A fault of an arcuate shape appeared to the west of Meckering, its length amounting to 37 km. The fault dips inward toward the center, at most places about 40°, and the inside was uplifted relative to the outside. A few shorter faults appeared around Meckering, too. A relevelling survey along a road running in an approximately E—W direction brought to light changes in level as shown in Fig. 5-60B (Gordon, 1971). The maximum throw reached 2 m

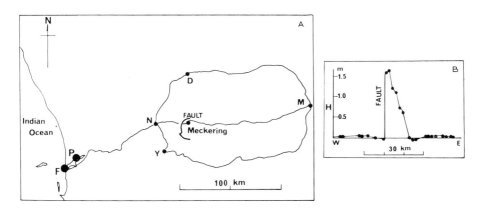

Fig. 5-60. A. The Meckering fault which appeared in association with the 1968 earthquake and the levelling routes. F = Fremantle, P = Perth, N = Northam, D = Dowerin, M = Merredin, Y = York. B. Changes in level along a route running in an approximately E—W direction connecting Northam to Merredin associated with the 1968 Meckering earthquake (Gordon, 1971).

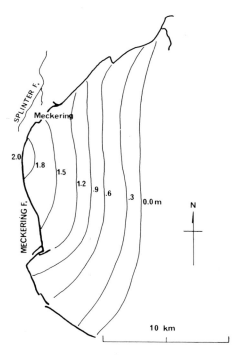

Fig. 5-61. Contour map for the level changes associated with the 1968 Meckering earth-quake (Gordon, 1971).

just south of Meckering. The distribution of vertical deformation is con-toured as seen in Fig. 5-61.

5.7. ANOMALOUS LAND UPLIFT FORERUNNING AN EARTHQUAKE

There are a number of instances in which some land deformations are detected by a repetition of levelling surveys prior to an earthquake.

5.7.1. Sekihara and Nagaoka earthquakes

On the occasion of an earthquake of magnitude 5.3 that occurred in October, 1927, at Sekihara, a small town near Nagaoka City in Niigata Prefecture, Japan, a levelling survey happened to have been completed along the route shown in Fig. 5-62 two months before the earthquake. Compari-son between this survey and a previous one made in 1894 made it clear that a land uplift as shown in Fig. 5-62 had taken place during the 33-year period. Another survey hurriedly made soon after the earthquake brought to light a

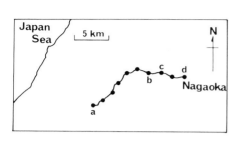

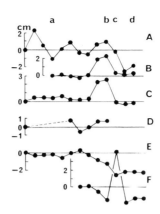

Fig. 5-62. Changes in level associated with the Sekihara (*b*) and the 1961 Nagaoka earthquakes. Periods *A*, *B*, *C*, *D*, *E* and *F* correspond respectively to 1894—July 1927, July 1927—November 1927, July 1927—1930, 1930—1955, 1955—1958 and 1958—1961 (Kaminuma et al., 1973).

further uplift within the 3-month period during which the earthquake occurred (Tsuboi, 1933; Kaminuma et al., 1973).

In the case of the 1961 Nagaoka earthquake (M = 5.2), that killed 5 people and destroyed 220 houses, the levelling surveys of 1955 and 1958 disclosed an anomalous level change around the epicentral area as is also shown in Fig. 5-62. An upheaval of 4 cm took place there in association with the earthquake. The precursor-like changes for the Sekihara and Nagaoka earthquakes could only be pointed out after the earthquake occurrences because the level changes had not been large enough. These examples encouraged Japanese seismologists who presumed that a much larger change would occur prior to an earthquake of greater magnitude.

5.7.2. Tonankai earthquake

The 1944 Tonankai earthquake (M = 8.0, 998 deaths and 26,130 totally destroyed houses) has not been well documented because Japan was in a state of disorder toward the end of the World War II. The following interesting fact was found only several years ago by the GSI while the survey records made during the war were reexamined.

A levelling survey was in progress around Kakegawa City, Shizuoka Prefecture, near the Pacific coast in Central Japan on December 7, 1944, the day of the earthquake, which occurred under the sea some 150 km southwest of Kakegawa at 13.36 local time (see Fig. 5-31). The survey, that was in progress along a route north of Kakegawa from 10 to 12 o'clock, indicated an apparent closing error amounting to 9 mm/2 km which is too large for an

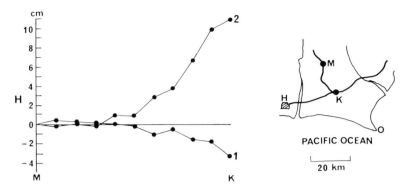

Fig. 5-63. Levelling route around Pt. Omaezaki and changes in level along route *M-K*. Level change 1 took place in the period from March, 1934, to November, 1944, while change 2 occurred from November, 1944 to December, 1944. The Tonankai earthquake occurred on December 7, 1944. H = Hamamatsu, M = Mikura, K = Kakegawa, O = Pt. Omaezaki (Geographical Survey Institute, 1969b).

observational error. It was surmised that a northward ground tilt must have been developing during the survey.

The levelling route of 20 km in length from Kakegawa to Mikura, located to the north of Kakegawa, was resurveyed immediately after the earthquake. To the great surprise of the surveyors, it was brought to light that Kakegawa uplifted relative to Mikura by 11 cm during the period from November to December, which includes the earthquake occurrence, as can be seen in Fig. 5-63 (Geographical Survey Institute, 1969b).

During the period from 1934 to November, 1944, a subsidence of a few centimeters of Kakegawa relative to Mikura is apparent as also shown in Fig. 5-63. Summarizing the results of surveys that cover a much wider area, there is every reason to believe that the speed of subsidence at the Kakegawa—Pt. Omaezaki area, which had been gradually subsiding over many years, tended to slow down about 10 years prior to the earthquake, and that the area suddenly began to uplift a few hours before the earthquake occurrence. Judging from the report, it is almost certain that a precursory land uplift took place preceding the Tonankai earthquake.

5.7.3. Niigata earthquake

Probably one of the most remarkable premonitory effects as observed by means of levelling survey is the ground uplift in relation to the 1964 Niigata earthquake ($M = 7.5$) which killed 26 people and totally destroyed 1,960 houses.

Since the first survey in 1898, a number of levelling surveys have been carried out along a levelling route running along the Japan Sea coast and

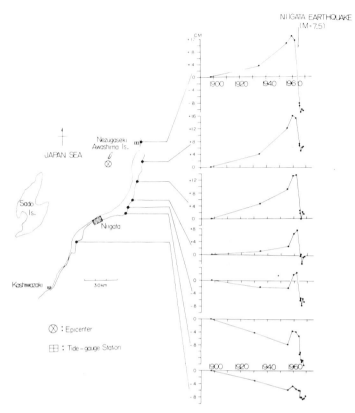

Fig. 5-64. Changes in height at levelling bench marks before and after the 1964 Niigata earthquake (Dambara, 1973).

passing through Niigata City. In order to check the ground subsidence which was said to be caused by the withdrawal of much water containing natural gases from the plain area, levelling surveys have been repeated with unusually short time intervals from 1954 onwards. As can be seen in Fig. 5-64 (Tsubokawa et al., 1964; Dambara, 1973), it is clear that the gradual change occurring since around 1900 changed its rate around 1954. The anomalous uplift seemed to reach its maximum around 1959. That state seemed to last a few years, and the earthquake followed. The bench marks were subjected to considerable subsidence at the time of the earthquake.

Should the sudden change in the rate of land deformation be a premonitory effect, an earthquake warning would have been provided 5—10 years before the earthquake. Some of Japanese seismologists were well aware of the anomalous crustal movement thus brought to light. However, nothing was officially said about the occurrence of an earthquake because at that time they were not quite certain whether it was a kind of precursory effect.

5.7.4. Tashkent earthquake

Tashkent in the Uzbek Republic of the U.S.S.R. was destroyed by an earthquake of magnitude 5.5 that occurred on April 25, 1966. Fig. 5-65 (Mescherikov, 1968) shows the changes in height at four stations in the Tashkent area. Stations A and B, located near the epicenter, have experienced an upheaval since 1900. The sign of movement changed around 1940 and a subsidence followed. During the period of seismic activity, an upheaval started again with a rate that was 10—20 times larger than the previous one. Changes in height at stations C and D, which are distant from the epicentral area, were not large, but a tendency of crustal uplift and subsidence similar to that at A and B can also be seen.

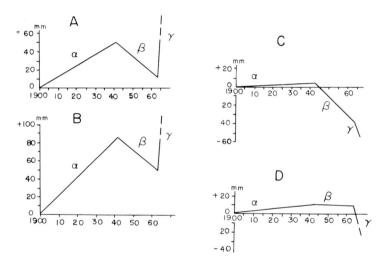

Fig. 5-65. Three phases of crustal deformation as revealed by the changes in height at four stations. Stations A and B are located in the epicentral area of the 1966 Tashkent earthquake; C and D are other non-epicentral stations (Mescherikov, 1968).

Summarizing the many examples of level change in a number of countries, Mescherikov (1968) concluded that three phases of crustal movements can be distinguished in seismic regions. They are: (1) slow movement revealed during the cycle between the bursts of seismic activity (α-phase); (2) preseismic crustal movement of a coming earthquake (β-phase); and (3) movement caused by the earthquake (γ-phase). These phases are also noted in Fig. 5-65.

5.7.5. Dunaharaszti earthquake

According to Lensen (1971), the best example of a vertical deformation

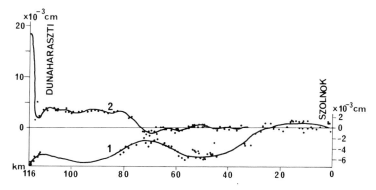

Fig. 5-66. Precursory (1) and co-earthquake (2) vertical deformations in units of 10^{-3} cm per day associated with the 1956 Dunaharaszti earthquake (Bendefy, 1966; Lensen, 1971).

sequence preceding and following an earthquake is that described by Bendefy (1966). The following is quoted from Lensen (1971).

"Early in 1955 surveyors in Hungary discovered large misclosures in their levelling circuits, the closing errors reaching 10 times the permissible ones. Parts of a 450-km route were subsequently relevelled four times in quick succession. In April of that year it became evident that elastic sinusoidal deformation was taking place, increasing in amplitude and decreasing in wavelength towards the end of that year. On 12 January 1956 an earthquake (M = 6) took place at Dunaharaszti where the large amount of elastic deformation of -55 mm had been observed a few days before the earthquake. Immediately after the earthquake a maximum uplift of +43 mm was measured, resulting in a maximum deformation of 98 mm.

Bendefy's main conclusions can be summarized as follows:

(1) Precursory crustal vertical deformation appeared as elastic sinusoidal waves, the wavelengths decreasing and amplitudes increasing both in time and place towards the epicentre.

(2) Elastic vertical precursory deformation took place as far as 70—80 km from the future epicentre."

Fig. 5-66 shows the rate of precursory (1) and co-earthquake (2) vertical deformation in association with the Dunaharaszti earthquake. The ordinate is scaled in units of 10^{-3} cm/day.

5.7.6. San Fernando earthquake

Castle et al. (1974) reported on level changes preceding the San Fernando earthquake (M = 6.4) on February 9, 1971. The epicenter of the earthquake is located in the San Gabriel mountain range running approximately in an E—W direction, and the focal depth was estimated as 8 km. Damage in the San Fernando area of Los Angeles County was severe because the epicentral

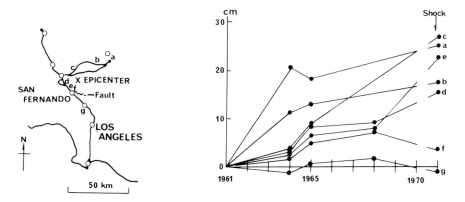

Fig. 5-67. Changes in height at a number of bench marks in association with the 1971 San Fernando earthquake (Castle et al., 1974).

distance of the center of San Fernando was only 14 km. Sixty-four deaths were reported. Two reverse fault traces, each having a length of 2 km, appeared to the east of San Fernando.

Examinations of levelling survey records in the past indicate that a 207 mm uplift occurred at south of Palmdale, about 28 km east-northeast of the epicenter, during 1961–1964. An uplift amounting to 96 mm was found at a point 13 km southwest of the epicenter for the period 1961—1968. A point 30 km northeast of the epicenter uplifted as much as 129 mm during 1964–1968.

Fig. 5-67 shows the changes in height at a number of bench marks plotted against time, together with a map of the levelling routes. The data have been taken from the graph published by Castle et al. (1974). It shows clearly that the area around San Fernando has been uplifting since 1964.

In addition to the examples above, Tsubokawa (1969) reported two more precursor-type examples found by levelling surveys. They are the 1961 North Mino ($M = 7.0$) and the 1967 Omi ($M = 5.0$) earthquakes that occurred in Central Japan.

5.8. RELATIONSHIP BETWEEN EARTHQUAKE MAGNITUDE AND AREA OF LAND DEFORMATION

It has been noticed that the larger the earthquake magnitude is, the wider is the area of land deformation associated with the earthquake. Dambara (1966) put forward an empirical relation between earthquake magnitude M and the mean radius of crustal deformation r measured in units of centimeters as:

$$\log_{10} r^3 = 8.18 + 1.53M \tag{5-10}$$

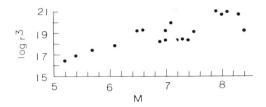

Fig. 5-68. $\log_{10} r^3$ vs. M, where r is the effective radius (in cm) of the area over which an anomalous crustal deformation associated with an earthquake is observed (Dambara, 1966).

which can be rewritten as:

$$M = 1.96 \log_{10} r + 4.45 \qquad\qquad\qquad [5\text{-}11]$$

when r is measured in units of kilometers.

Fig. 5-68 shows the empirical relation between the logarithm (to base 10) of the third power of the mean radius r of the land deformation area and magnitude M of the earthquake.

On the assumption that a land deformation takes place over an area under which the strain energy related to an earthquake is accumulating, equation [5-10] or [5-11] may be used for estimating the magnitude of a coming earthquake from the extent of a premonitory crustal deformation (Dambara, 1966; Rikitake, 1969a,b). Although the Dambara formula as given in [5-10] or [5-11] was obtained on the basis of a purely empirical study, Rikitake (1975b) suggested a physical process that can possibly lead to the formula on the basis of a dilatancy model (see section 14.1).

5.9. NON-SEISMIC CRUSTAL DEFORMATION

A crustal movement is not necessarily connected with the occurrence of an large-scale earthquake. For instance, post-glacier uplifts in Scandinavia do not result in a large earthquake. Even in a seismically active country like Japan, crustal movements which seem to have nothing to do with earthquake occurrence have been observed.

During the Matsushiro earthquakes, there occurred a few instances of crustal uplift over an area of several kilometers in its horizontal extent as detected by frequent levellings; however, no earthquake has occurred in the vicinity of such uplifted areas.

Probably some kinds of crustal movement are controlled largely by the plasticity of the earth's crust. In that case no sudden rupture of the crust would take place. Although the physical process of such plastic deformations has not been understood very well, crustal movements of a large extent may be caused by a non-seismic origin.

When one observes an anomalous crustal deformation, it is not at all clear whether or not the deformation is connected with an earthquake. It is generally believed, however, that an uplift having a speed exceeding 1 cm/year may well have something to do with an earthquake occurrence. It is therefore important for earthquake prediction to detect a land deformation such as described by the β-phase (see subsection 5.7.3; Mescherikov, 1968). Slow deformations having a small rate as classified by Mescherikov as the α-phase may not be directly related to an earthquake occurrence although strain must be accumulating even in that phase.

Chapter 6

LAND DEFORMATION RELATIVE TO SEA LEVEL

6.1. ANOMALOUS SEA RETREAT BEFORE AN EARTHQUAKE

There are a number of historical documents in Japan in which an anomalous sea retreat was reported before an earthquake. As the retreat seems to have taken place over a limited portion of the seashore, it seems highly likely that the land uplifted locally relative to the sea level. English texts of those retreats can be found in Imamura (1937).

6.1.1. Ajikazawa earthquake

One of the most marked examples of precursory sea retreat was reported in association with the Ajikazawa earthquake (M = 6.9) that took place in the northernmost part of Honshu, Japan, in 1793. The earthquake occurred at about 14.00 local time. The local inhabitants who noticed an extraordinary retreat of the sea in the morning were so afraid of tsunamis that they ran up into the mountains where they felt a strong shock in the afternoon. The terrified people ran back to the seashore where they were hit by tsunamis that arrived there some time later, and some children were carried away by the high waves. The story clearly indicates that an anomalous land upheaval occurred several hours prior to an earthquake.

6.1.2. Sado earthquake

On the occasion of the 1802 Sado earthquake (M = 6.6), which occurred somewhere around Sado Island (see Fig. 5-64) in the Japan Sea north of Niigata Prefecture, Japan, a remarkable sea retreat was noticed at about 10.00 local time at a harbor called Ogi where the water depth had usually been so deep that a fairly large ship could enter. As a fairly strong earthquake was also felt at about the time of sea retreat, the local people thought that tsunamis might come. In the meantime, the main shock struck the island destroying many houses.

6.1.3. Hamada earthquake

Small shocks or rumblings of the ground had been felt for several days before the 1872 Hamada earthquake (M = 7.1) that occurred in Hamada City, Shimane Prefecture, facing the Japan Sea in western Honshu, Japan. It was reported that the sea retreated there so considerably that it became possible to walk to an island about 140 m distant from the shoreline, and that people picked up ear shells on the dried-up beach. A severe earthquake occurred a few tens of minutes later, and a tsunami struck there.

The sea retreat seemed to have occurred along the shoreline of several tens of kilometers in length. Unlike the Ajikazawa and Sado earthquakes reported in the preceding subsections, this earthquake occurred after the new civilization of Japan, so that there was already a weather station at Hamada. The report on the earthquake must therefore be highly reliable. There is every reason to believe that the land around Hamada uplifted by about 2 m prior to the earthquake.

6.1.4. Tango earthquake

It was said that a lowering of sea level of 1 m or so had been observed a few hours before the 1927 Tango earthquake (M = 7.5) at a few places in the epicentral area. This was reported by fishermen in a few villages. They observed reefs, which used to be hidden under the sea surface, appearing above the surface.

Attention should be drawn to the fact that the above four examples of anomalous sea retreat were observed along the coast of the Japan Sea where the tide is generally small. Whether or not this is due to the small tide or due to the characteristics of earthquakes occurring there is not clear.

It is somewhat surprising that no such sea retreats have been observed since tide-gauge observations became popular. The author has not heard of a sea retreat preceding an earthquake in a country outside Japan.

6.2. TIDE-GAUGE OBSERVATION

6.2.1. Noise to observation of uplift and subsidence of land

Sea-level observations are nowadays carried out by a tide-gauge. The usual model of a tide-gauge works on the principle of recording the vertical motion of a buoy floating on the surface of the seawater which is led to a well where waves of short period are damped out. There is another tide-gauge model which measures the changes in water pressure at the sea bottom.

As has been stated in subsection 4.2.3, 80 tide-gauge stations are operating along the coast line of Japan Islands at intervals of approximately 100 km.

The height of sea level is influenced by various environmental elements such as atmospheric pressure, water temperature, wind, ocean currents and so on. An anomalously high tide, exceeding the normal level by about 20 cm, was observed along the Pacific coast of Japan in October, 1971. The event lasted about one week although it had nothing to do with earthquake occurrence. No reason for this phenomenon was given by oceanographers.

A conventional way of eliminating the noise in tide-gauge observations arising from such oceanographic and meteorological origins is to difference the observed height of sea level between neighboring tide-gauge stations on the assumption that both stations are affected by the noise to an approximately equal extent. It turns out, however, that there still remains some noise, probably of the order of several centimeters, even after making use of such a technique.

6.2.2. Precursory and coseismic changes

As can be seen in Fig. 5-64, there are two tide-gauge stations, Nezugaseki and Kashiwazaki, close to the epicentral area of the 1964 Niigata earthquake. Fig. 6-1 indicates the difference in the monthly means of tidal record between the two stations (Tsubokawa et al., 1964). A land uplift of a few centimeters of Nezugaseki relative to Kashiwazaki can be observed in the figure since around 1958; such an uplift is approximately compatible with the results of levelling surveys. In the middle of 1963, the land at Nezugaseki tended to subside, and the earthquake took place about one year later. The sea level indicated a sudden jump at the time of the main shock.

Nothing definite can be concluded from the changes as shown in Fig. 6-1 because of the noise due to sea level as discussed earlier, but the change of sign in the gradient that occurred about one year prior to the earthquake might be a premonitory effect. Although coseismic jumps of the sea level have been frequently observed in association with large earthquakes, not many examples of precursory change in the sea level have been reported.

Tsumura (1963, 1970), who made an extensive analysis of the tidal observation data accumulated in Japan over many years, concluded that extreme caution must be taken in talking about a precursory effect in terms of the tidal record.

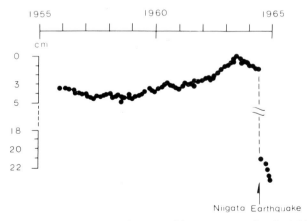

Fig. 6-1. Changes in the monthly mean sea level at Nezugaseki relative to Kashiwazaki (Tsubokawa et al., 1964).

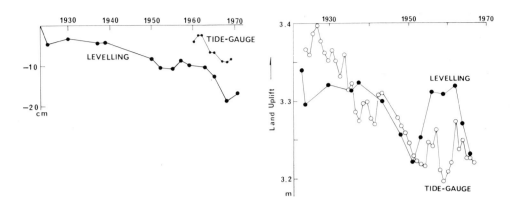

Fig. 6-2. The thick line represents the level changes of Aburatsubo relative to Yokohama as revealed by levelling surveys, while the thin line indicates the differences in yearly mean sea level between Aburatsubo and Yokohama (Fujita, 1971).

Fig. 6-3. Solid circles represent changes in the height of a bench mark at Aburatsubo relative to the Tokyo base bench mark as revealed by levelling surveys. Open circles indicate changes in the yearly mean sea level at the Aburatsubo tide-gauge station (Geographical Survey Institute, 1969a).

6.2.3. Comparison between levelling and tide-gauge observation

It is interesting to compare changes in sea level to those in height as revealed by levelling surveys. As a levelling survey along a long route can possibly be influenced by an accumulation of errors, it is important to check the result of a levelling survey by a tide-gauge observation. Fig. 6-2 shows the change in the height of a bench mark at the Aburatsubo tide-gauge station at the tip of Miura Peninsula, South Kanto (see Fig. 5-29) relative to a bench mark in Yokohama which is about 30 km north of Aburatsubo. In the figure is also shown the change in the yearly sea level at Aburatsubo relative to a tide-gauge station in Yokohama, although the record at the latter station has been available only since 1960. It may be seen that the land movement obtained by levelling surveys agrees fairly well with that obtained by tidal observations (Fujita, 1971).

The Geographical Survey Institute (1969a) presented a comparison between changes in the height of a bench mark at Aburatsubo relative to the base bench mark in Tokyo and those revealed by tide-gauge observations there. We see that the curves for both changes agree with one another in general as can be seen in Fig. 6-3. The distance between Aburatsubo and Tokyo amounts to about 60 km. However, it is apparent that the curve for tide-gauge observations suffers short-term fluctuations probably of meteorological and oceanographic origin.

Chapter 7

CONTINUOUS OBSERVATION OF CRUSTAL MOVEMENT

Repetition of geodetic surveys is certainly useful for detecting precursory and coseismic land deformations as has been presented in Chapter 5 in fair detail. As survey work is essentially intermittent, however, it is not possible to conduct a continuous observation of crustal movement by means of geodetic work only. As has been proposed in the "blueprint" of earthquake prediction research in Japan, it has been planned to watch crustal movement continuously by tiltmeters and strainmeters installed at crustal movement observatories. Use of arrays of borehole instruments will be popular in future observations.

7.1. TILTMETER

A tiltmeter is an instrument by which a very small tilting of ground surface can be measured. Three kinds of commonly used tiltmeters will be described in the following, reports on other models can be found elsewhere.

7.1.1. Horizontal pendulum tiltmeter

A pendulum, that can rotate about an axis, which deviates very slightly from the vertical, performs an oscillation having a long period because the restoring force due to the gravity is small. As the pendulum weight oscillates in an almost horizontal plane, such an oscillating system is called the horizontal pendulum.

When the axis of a horizontal pendulum undergoes a slight tilting, the weight tends to rotate with a fairly large angle. A horizontal pendulum has thus been used for measuring ground tilting as well as ground displacement caused by seismic waves. Actual construction of a horizontal pendulum tiltmeter of high sensitivity has been no easy matter because of the mechanical friction at the axis and other amplification mechanisms in earlier days.

It is not the intention of the present author to describe all the details of the horizontal pendulum tiltmeter. But the author should like to point out that a tiltmeter for practical use was designed and constructed by Ishimoto (1927) as has already been mentioned in section 3.4. As the tiltmeter is made of fused quartz and has a height of 20 cm or so, it is possible to have a period of free oscillation as long as several tens of seconds by means of a fine adjustment. The movement of the pendulum weight is amplified by an optical lever and recorded on a sheet of photographic paper.

It seems likely that a horizontal pendulum tiltmeter records a very local ground movement because the instrument is mounted on a small tripod. It has also been experienced that the tiltmeter undergoes a drift movement probably because of the instability of mounting. It thus turns out that a quartz tiltmeter may be used for monitoring a rapid tilting, but when it measures a long-term change over a period of months or years, it may be affected by a large drift.

7.1.2. Water-tube tiltmeter

When two water pots, interconnected with a pipe, are placed on the ground at a distance of several tens of meters, changes in the difference in height of water surface are proportional to the mean tilting of the ground on which the system is installed. This type of detecting device is called the water-tube tiltmeter, and various models have been constructed by many investigators. Among them, a model of water-tube tiltmeter developed by Hagiwara (1947) is simpler in its construction and more suitable for practical use than other models which are sometimes too sophisticated.

Extensive observations with water-tube tiltmeters have been undertaken by members of the ERI, notably by Yamada (1973). The height of the water surface is usually read by a micrometer with a sharp point for the Hagiwara-type tiltmeter. An effort has also been made to make a self-recording tiltmeter using the reflection of ultrasonic waves (Yamada, 1973).

Tiltmeters working on a principle similar to a water-tube one, but making use of mercury instead of water, have often been used. For instance, such models are operating at the Granite Mountain Observatory, University of Utah, which is located a few tens of kilometers south of Salt Lake City (Cook, 1973; Kisslinger and Rikitake, 1974). Changes in the height of mercury surfaces are detected in terms of the inductance change for these tiltmeters. This kind of tiltmeter is particularly popular in the U.S.A.

7.1.3. Borehole tiltmeter

In order to install a water-tube tiltmeter having a length of a few tens of meters, an underground vault having a length exceeding the span of the tiltmeter is necessary. It is at present becoming difficult to find a place which is suitable for constructing such a vault in a particular area of seismic interest, especially in a country like Japan where the population is very dense.

In view of this, use of a borehole-type tiltmeter whose installation does not necessarily require an extensive area of land has been considered. The principle of a borehole tiltmeter is simple. If a weight is hung with a fine string, a small deviation of the vertical relative to the ground can be detected easily with present-day techniques such as an inductance change. Many such borehole tiltmeters have a length ranging from 10 cm to 1 m. To set up an array of borehole tiltmeters with a telemetering system over an earthquake area would provide a powerful means for detecting possible precursors.

Another type of borehole tiltmeter called the buoy tiltmeter is under development at the ERI (Kasahara et al., 1973) and elsewhere. It is used to record the motion of a buoy floating on the surface of water filling a borehole of 50 m in depth relative to the ground, the buoy being connected at the bottom of the hole with a stainless steel wire of 0.5 mm in diameter. The motion of the buoy is recorded in two orthogonal directions, and it is hoped that the system records the tilting motion averaged over the length of the wire.

7.2. STRAINMETER

7.2.1. Quartz-tube strainmeter

Small extensions or contractions of the ground can be measured by a strainmeter, which is sometimes called an extensometer. A usual model of a strainmeter consists of a quartz tube of a few tens of meters in length mounted on a pair of piers. The tube is suspended by a number of suspenders which are free from friction. One end of the tube is fixed to one of the piers, and the motion of the other end relative to the ground is monitored by making use of a suitable detector such as a recording system with an optical lever, a variable inductance or capacitance transducer and so on.

Since the first workable strainmeter has been constructed by Benioff (1935), various models of strainmeters have been constructed by many workers. Quartz-tube strainmeters are widely used in Japan (e.g. Hagiwara et al., 1948), the U.S.S.R. (e.g. Latynina and Karmaleyeva, 1970) and the U.S.A. (e.g. Benioff, 1959; Wideman and Major, 1967; Cook, 1973).

It is customary to use a set of strainmeters installed in three directions in order to determine the strains completely in a horizontal plane. It is necessary to set up these instruments in an underground vault where the changes in temperature are very small.

7.2.2. Super-invar-wire strainmeter

Strainmeters making use of super-invar wire (e.g. Sassa et al., 1952) or rod (e.g. Ozawa, 1971) have been traditionally used by a research group of Kyoto University, Japan. For this instrument, a super-invar wire of 20 m in length under some tension interconnects two piers. When the distance between the piers changes, the middle point of the wire undergoes a vertical displacement which can be monitored with a high magnification by making use of a suitable device, for instance the optical bifilar method. The wire under tension, however, inevitably undergoes a drift, so that a strainmeter of this type is not suitable for observing long-term secular changes.

7.2.3. Laser-beam strainmeter

The stability of quartz-tube as well as super-invar rod or wire strainmeters is limited because of the effect of temperature fluctuations on the reference length. For this reason, it is difficult to attain a stable intensity of 10^{-10} even if they are installed in an underground fault. In addition to this, these conventional strainmeters are vulnerable to the high acceleration arising from the ground motion due to an earthquake.

Application of the electro-optical method, which has been used for measuring long distances (see section 5.4), to a continuous measurement of distance with a high accuracy is under development in recent years. Making use of a coherent light source, optical interferometry can be applied with a path of 1 km or more. It is beyond the author's capability, however, to go into the details of a laser-beam strainmeter. Those who are specifically interested in the topic are referred to a review by Berger (1973).

It is reported that stabilities of 10^{-12} strain per year may be expected by use of an iodine absorption-cell laser (Department of Geodesy and Geophysics, 1973). Comparing this to the stabilities estimated for conventional strainmeters installed in crustal movement observatories in Japan, it is found that the stability of the laser-beam strainmeter is higher by a factor of 10^5 to 10^6. Although overall stability of a laser-beam strainmeter may become somewhat low because of background noise, it seems worthwhile to make extensive use of such strainmeters.

7.2.4. Sacks-Evertson strainmeter

A strainmeter, that is sensitive to volume change, has been constructed by Sacks et al. (1971). A stainless-steel cylinder of 4 m in length and 11 cm in diameter is filled with degassed silicon oil, and buried in a borehole in such a way that it is bonded to the rock by cement whose volume expands after solidification. The apparent rigidity of the cylinder and its contents is made approximately equal to that of the surrounding rocks by choosing a suitable thickness of the cylinder wall. When the volume of the cylinder decreases, the fluid is pushed through a fine pipe at the upper end of the cylinder. Bellows connected to the pipe then extend, and the extension is detected by an appropriate means such as a differential transformer.

Three strainmeters of the type were installed in the Matsushiro area in 1971. As the local earthquake activity was still high after the violent 1965—1967 swarm, it was possible to compare the observed results to those observed by the 100-m quartz-tube strainmeters at the Matsushiro Seismological Observatory.

It turned out that, in many cases, no coseismic strain step (see section 7.5) was recorded by the Sacks-Evertson strainmeter while the quartz-tube ones recorded it. When a step is recorded by the Sacks-Evertson strainmeter, it is always one order of magnitude smaller than that recorded by the quartz-tube one. It is thus believed that some of steps recorded by a conventional strain-meter might be spurious. The way of constructing such an instrument is not appropriate for preventing the influence of mechanical shocks caused by a near earthquake that gives rise to a high acceleration.

7.3. CRUSTAL MOVEMENT OBSERVATORY

We have so far constructed seventeen crustal movement observatories in Japan as has been shown in Fig. 4-5. These observatories are usually equipped with two-component horizontal-pendulum tiltmeters, two-component water-tube tiltmeters, three-component quartz-tube strainmeters and other additional instruments such as thermometers and so on. A Japanese standard vault in which these instruments can be installed is schematically shown in Fig. 7-1. Much caution is taken in avoiding the influence of temperature changes by providing a number of shutters as can be seen in the figure.

Fig. 7-2 shows the interior of a crustal movement observatory. The picture was taken at the Nokogiriyama Observatory, about 70 km south of Tokyo. The observatory, that has been in operation since 1959, is slightly old-

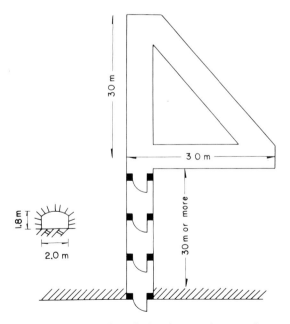

Fig. 7-1. Standard vault for the continuous observation of crustal movement in Japan.

Fig. 7-2. Interior of the Nokogiriyama Crustal Movement Observatory. An observer is measuring the height of the water surface of a 25-m water-tube tiltmeter. A 25-m quartz-tube strainmeter with a recording system can also be seen there.

fashioned. Observatories constructed in recent years are equipped with much more sophisticated instruments.

The author had the experience to see a few observarories in countries outside Japan. The way of constructing observatories in those countries is much the same as that in Japan.

7.4. SECULAR CHANGES IN TILT AND STRAIN AND THEIR RELATION TO REGIONAL CRUSTAL MOVEMENT

Whether or not changes as recorded by tiltmeters and strainmeters represent a general crustal movement over a fairly wide area around a crustal movement observatory where the instruments are set up was an open question when the earthquake prediction program started in Japan. If changes recorded by tiltmeters and strainmeters are too local, only indicating strains over the dimensions occupied by these instruments, we should not put much stress on what they record because we are interested in the strain state over a certain region of some spatial extent in which earthquake energy must be stored. It has been planned, therefore, to compare the changes recorded by tiltmeters and strainmeters to those deduced from geodetic surveys over the area in which the crustal movement observatory is located.

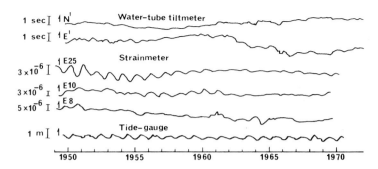

Fig. 7-3. Secular changes in ground tilt, horizontal strain and sea level recorded at the Aburatsubo Crustal Movement Observatory. Details of the length and azimuth of the instruments are given in the text. The arrows indicate tiltings in the N' and W' directions, extensions for respective strainmeters and land upheaval (Yamada, 1973).

First of all, let us look at the secular changes in earth strains as recorded at a typical observatory. Fig. 7-3 shows the smoothed monthly means of ground tilts, strains in the horizontal plane and sea level as observed at the Aburatsubo Crustal Movement Observatory, about 60 km south of Tokyo, during the period approximately from 1949 to 1970 (Yamada, 1973). The observation vault of the observatory is very close to the seashore. E_{25}, E_{10} and E_8 as shown in the figure denote respectively the records obtained by strainmeters having lengths of 25, 10 and 8 m, their directions being N22°E, N81°W and S64°W, respectively. The azimuths of the N' and E' tiltmeters are respectively N22°E and N81°W. Their lengths are 25 and 10 m, respectively.

It is apparent that annual variations, probably caused by temperature changes, are predominating. Such variations are readily eliminated by taking a 12-month running average or some other filtering operations. Although the significance of secular variations thus observed is not quite clear, the change in tilt recorded by the E' tiltmeter, for instance, seems to be significantly larger than possible errors. The W'-ward tilting of 1.0 second of arc or so during 1955—1961 and the following E'-ward tilting amounting to 2 seconds of arc or a little more during 1961—1967 may have reflected something related to the crustal activity in the area around Aburatsubo.

Fig. 7-4 shows the changes in elevation of a bench mark adjacent the crustal movement observatory relative to that in Yokohama, about 30 km north of Aburatsubo, which have already been shown in Fig. 6-2, and those in ground tilting in the N81°W direction as observed by the E' component of the water-tube tiltmeter. It is striking that the shape of both the changes roughly agrees with one another although the amount of tilting obtained by the tiltmeter is a few times larger than that of the levelling surveys.

It sounds strange, however, that agreement is seen between the tilting as obtained by the two methods for directions almost perpendicular to one

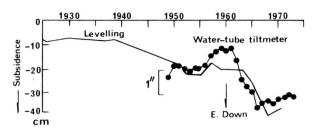

Fig. 7-4. Changes in ground tilt as measured by a water-tube tiltmeter in an almost E—W direction at the Aburatsubo Crustal Movement Observatory and changes in the subsidence of land there relative to a bench mark in Yokohama as revealed by levelling surveys (Yamada, 1973).

another. No such agreement can be found between the tilting deduced from the levellings and that from the N′ component (N22°E). It can be said that the ground tilting as observed by a tiltmeter may sometimes reflect a general crustal movement predominating over an area of a certain extent surrounding the observation point although a quantitative correlation between geodetic and continuous observations is hard to find. Changes in ground tilting as observed by a tiltmeter may merely be indicators of crustal movement. However, they might still be useful for earthquake prediction in some cases.

Similar agreement between changes in elevation of a bench mark near a crustal movement observatory in Niigata Prefecture and changes in northward tilting recorded at the observatory has been reported. The level change at a bench mark in a small town called Iwamuro has already been shown by the first curve at the bottom of Fig. 5-64 in association with the 1964 Niigata earthquake. About 7 km to the west of the town, an observatory called Maze (now Yahiko Crustal Movement Observatory; see Fig. 4-5) has been in operation since 1953. Comparison between level changes and ground

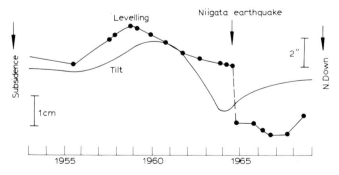

Fig. 7-5. Level changes at a bench mark at Iwamuro compared to changes in ground tilt at the Maze Observatory (Kasahara, 1973).

tilting is shown in Fig. 7-5 in which a general agreement between the two curves can be seen (Kasahara, 1973).

During the Matsushiro earthquakes, the development of tilting as observed by water-tube tiltmeters set up at the Matsushiro Seismological Observatory was compatible with that of land upheval as revealed by levelling surveys (subsection 5.6.14) as well as that of land extension observed by a geodimeter over the epicentral area (Kasahara, 1970). The tilting rate was in close agreement with the increase and decrease of seismic activity as has been stated in subsection 4.2.1.

Such agreement between ground tilting and land deformation as revealed by geodetic surveys is further seen for a number of cases in Japan. It is therefore concluded that ground tilting and strain observed at a crustal movement observatory may well represent the actual crustal deformation taking place around the observatory. Although no quantitative agreement may be possible, the changes observed by tiltmeters and strainmeters may be an indicator of actual movement. On the basis of the phase differences between tiltmeter and levelling results and a comparison of the tiltmeter records of nearby observatories, i.e. Aburatsubo and Nokogiriyama, the distance between them amounting to 20 km, Kasahara (1973) pointed out a possible migration of crustal movement with a speed of 10—20 km/year, although this is not necessarily the present author's view.

7.5. COSEISMIC STRAIN STEP

When an earthquake occurs, sometimes the trace of the record from tiltmeters and strainmeters deviates from that of the pre-earthquake level, after oscillations due to seismic waves are damped out. Such jumps or steps are called strain (or tilt) steps, and are sometimes observed even in association with earthquakes of teleseismic origin.

It has long been thought that such a step is caused by some defect of the observing system, especially in the case of a strainmeter making use of a long guartz rod because the devices connecting the rod to the amplifier system or supporting the rod are not invulnerable to a mechanical shock of high acceleration.

If one thinks of the fact that an earthquake is caused by a rupture in the earth's crust, however, it is natural that some sort of permanent deformation is accompanied by the earthquake. If so, a sudden deformation of the crust might take place at a distance from the seismic origin. It has thus been gradually believed that steps as observed by tiltmeters and strainmeters really exist although the possibility of spurious effects due to shocks cannot be ruled out in many cases (e.g. Press, 1965a; Wideman and Major, 1967; Takemoto, 1970).

Hagiwara et al. (1949a) made an observation of crustal movement by

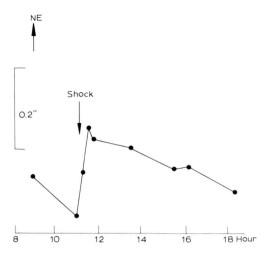

Fig. 7-6. A tilt step observed by a water-tube tiltmeter in association with one of the aftershocks of the 1948 Fukui earthquake (Hagiwara et al., 1949a).

setting up a temporary observation point at an unused mine called Bando-jima near the epicentral area soon after the 1948 Fukui earthquake (subsec-tions 5.3.7 and 5.6.12). When an aftershock probably having a magnitude between 4 and 5 occurred somewhere around Maruoka (see Fig. 5-15), the readings of a NE-oriented water-tube tiltmeter installed at a point about 17 km distant from the epicenter changed in a stepwise shape as shown in Fig. 7-6. Probably this must have been the first observation of a tilt step although no clear-cut interpretation was possible at that time. It is interesting to note that the step seems to have started prior to the shock.

Press (1965a) showed that the distant strain fields caused by a major earthquake are large enough to be detected by modern instruments. Wide-man and Major (1967), who summarized the strainmeter observations at the Cecil H. Green Geophysical Observatory, Colorado, U.S.A., presented curves for which a strain step of specified magnitude is to be observed totally on an empirical basis. The curves are approximately straight lines on an earthquake magnitude (M)—logarithmic epicentral distance (Δ) plane. The empirical rela-tionship:

$$M = 1.1 + 1.7 \log_{10} \Delta \qquad\qquad [7-1]$$

was derived from their analysis. The equation specifies the magnitude of the smallest earthquake for which strains of the order of 10^{-9} may be expected at a distance of Δ km.

Wideman and Major (1967) suggested that the amplitude of strain steps decreases as $\Delta^{-3/2}$ when the epicentral distance increases. Studies of the dislocation theory (Chinnery, 1961; Press, 1965a) indicate that the fall-off is proportional to Δ^{-2}. On the basis of the observations at three observatories operated by the Kyoto University, south of Kyoto in the Kinki district, Japan, Takemoto (1970) proposed $\Delta^{-2.4}$ for the fall-off.

In contrast to the fact that the above studies are based on observations of many earthquakes at a single or a few observatories, an analysis was made for strain steps simultaneously observed at fifteen crustal movement observatories mostly constructed under the Japanese national program on earthquake prediction (see Fig. 4-5; Japanese Network of Crustal Movement Observatories, 1970) in association with the Gifu earthquake ($M = 6.6$) that occurred in Central Japan on September 9, 1969. It seems that the signal-to-noise ratio is so low in Japanese observatories that steps smaller than 10^{-8} may not be reliable, and that scatterings of data are so large that no definite conclusions can be deduced. However, there seems to exist a fall-off tendency of the amplitude of steps which is roughly proportional to Δ^{-3}. In view of the scattering of data as observed at many stations, it is remarked that one must be careful in drawing a conclusion based on observations at a single observatory.

Judging from the different results by various workers of the fall-off vs. Δ

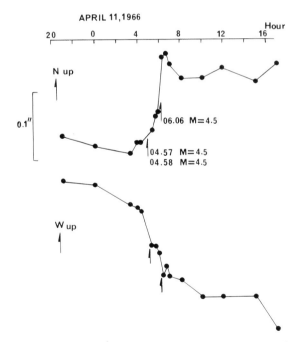

Fig. 7-7. A tilt step recorded by a water-tube tiltmeter at the Matsushiro Seismological Observatory on April 11, 1966 (Yamada, 1973).

relation, studies of strain steps are by no means well developed partly because of difficulties in the measuring system.

A laser strainmeter at La Jolla, some 200 km away from San Fernando,
California, where an earthquake of magnitude 6.4 occurred on February 9,
1971 (see subsection 5.7.5), recorded the oscillations accompanied by the
earthquake. When a low-pass filter was applied to the record, a clear offset of
1.6×10^{-9} was found at the time of the earthquake (Berger, 1971, 1973).
The quartz strainmeters and mercury tiltmeters at the Isabella facility of the
California Institute of Technology, 147 km north of the epicenter, also
recorded steps. They were of the order of 10^{-9} to 10^{-8}. Two strainmeters
near the Nevada Test Site 380 km to the northeast of the epicenter exhibited
offsets of the order of 3×10^{-10} (Jungels and Anderson, 1971).

When the Matsushiro seismic activity was extremely high, a few observers
worked day and night on reading the water-tube tiltmeters installed at the
Matsushiro Seismological Observatory. As a result scores of tilt steps were
observed, mostly in association with shocks of magnitudes 4—5. Yamada
(1973) presented an extensive catalogue of these steps. Fig. 7-7 shows one of
the most conspicuous examples of tilt steps. It is interesting to note that the
step seems to start a few hours prior to the shocks. At least five tilt steps
with clear forerunners were observed at Matsushiro. Probably this type of
steps might be different from purely coseismic steps which seem to terminate almost instantaneously. To the author's knowledge, no strain step of
premonitory character has been reported from strainmeter observations
except the one associated with an earthquake near Hollister, California, as
detected by a geodimeter observation (see subsection 5.4.4).

7.6. SITE EFFECT

Hagiwara et al. (1949b) discussed the effect of topography on ground
tilting and strain in association with observations at the Aburatsubo Crustal
Movement Observatory. Only a two-dimensional case in which a rectangular
elevation, that represents a mountain body through which the observation
vault was dug, overlies a semi-infinite earth was discussed. If the height of
the elevated part is much smaller than its length, it is concluded that the
topography effect is small when a uniform load is applied to the surface with
the exception of the elevated part. No detailed study of such an effect could
be carried out because of mathematical difficulty in those earlier days.

King and Bilham (1973) pointed out that the deformation of a vault,
where a tiltmeter is installed, under a uniform stress produces an anomalously large tilting depending upon the position where the apparatus is placed. It
has been simple-mindedly thought that a tiltmeter records a change in
ground tilting when it is placed on a flat horizontal surface and that it
measures the tilt of a horizontal element. If one takes the deformation of the

vault, or the cavity effect as it has been called by Harrison (1974), into account, it is seen that the apparent tilting can readily be amplified a few times depending upon the positions in the vault, and so tilts are different from place to place in a vault. In a strained medium, as pointed out by Harrison (1974), line elements of different orientation do not tilt by the same amount.

The cavity effect in the above may have an important bearing on the observation of tilt and strain. The fact that the tilting as measured by a tiltmeter is usually a few times larger than that deduced from geodetic measurements might be accounted for by this effect to some extent.

In addition to the cavity effect, the effect of topography sometimes play an important role on tilt and strain measurements (J.C. Harrison, personal communication, 1974). Recent development of the finite-element technique enables us to calculate the strain distribution in a medium having a complicated surface topography. When the surface of a medium consists of a hill and is under a uniform compression, it is demonstrated that an extension occurs in some part of the hill. In such a case, the general strain prevailing in the crust is hardly detected.

In the light of cavity and topography effects, it is evident that a quantitative discussion of tilt and strain may sometimes be meaningless. It is stressed, however, that an anomalous tilting or strain may well be amplified by several times by these effects in some cases, so that the measurement of tilt and strain may be used as an indicator of an anomalous condition such as dilatancy within the earth's crust.

7.7. TILT AND STRAIN CHANGES FORERUNNING AN EARTHQUAKE

There are many reports on anomalous tilts and strains that precede an earthquake. Although some of them may not be reliable, examples of tilt and strain precursors that came to the author's knowledge will be presented in this section.

7.7.1. Japanese examples

Kanto earthquake
Probably the oldest report of tilt precursor would be the one related to the 1923 Kanto earthquake ($M = 7.9$) (see section 3.3, subsections 5.3.1 and 5.6.4). Imamura (1928) pointed out that an Omori-type horizontal pendulum seismograph of long period at the Tokyo Imperial University had recorded a sudden westward tilt from about 04.00 local time on September 1, 1923. The Kanto earthquake occurred at 11.58 on that day. According to the author's experience, however, the seismograph suffers much friction and is unstable, so that the record as shown in Fig. 7-8 may not be quite reliable.

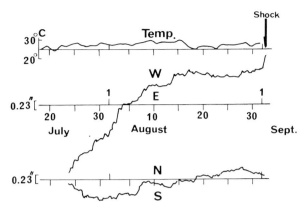

Fig. 7-8. Changes in ground tilt before the Kanto earthquake of September 1, 1923, as observed by Omori-type horizontal pendulum seismographs at the Tokyo Imperial University (Imamura, 1928).

Should the anomalous change in tilt be a precursor, however, seismologists may have some hope of expecting a short-range precursor of a large earthquake.

Tottori earthquake

Observation of tilt and strain has been traditionally carried out by the Geophysical Institute and the Disaster Prevention Research Institute, Kyoto University, so intensively that they operate a few tens of vaults equipped with tiltmeters and strainmeters at present. Although some of the stations are not as good as the present-day crustal movement observatories constructed under the earthquake prediction program, a number of precursory effects have been reported by the Kyoto group. A summary of the observations before 1951 was presented by Sassa and Nishimura (1951).

At the time of the 1943 Tottori earthquake (M = 7.4; see subsections 5.3.4 and 5.6.9), horizontal pendulum tiltmeters at the Ikuno copper mine, some 60 km southeast of the epicenter, recorded a remarkable change amounting to 0.1 second of arc or more some 6 hours prior to the earthquake as can be seen in Fig. 7-9A which shows the trace of the N43°W tilting component. Fig. 7-9B shows the tilt vectors there for the pre-earthquake period starting from a time 10 hours prior to the shock. The S-shaped trace is regarded by Sassa and Nishimura (1951) as one of the characteristics of precursors of this sort.

Tonankai earthquake

The Tonankai earthquake (M = 8.0) occurred off Kii Peninsula, Japan, on December 7, 1944. The location of the epicenter is shown in Fig. 5-31, and

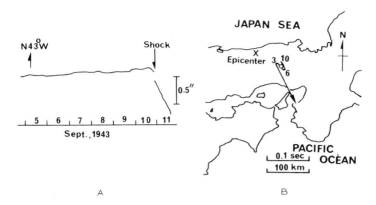

Fig. 7-9. Changes in ground tilt as observed by horizontal pendulum tiltmeters at a copper mine 60 km from the epicenter of the 1943 Tottori earthquake. A. The trace of the N43° W component. B. The arrowed curve indicates the direction and amount of the tilting motion. The numerals represent the time in hours counted back from the instant of earthquake occurrence (Sassa and Nishimura, 1951).

an episode about a premonitory effect as revealed by levelling surveys has been presented in subsection 5.7.2.

Horizontal pendulum tiltmeters at the Kamigamo Geophysical Observatory, Kyoto University, 160 km north-northwest from the epicenter, recorded a precursor-like tilting of the ground 5.7 hours prior to the earthquake. The amount of tilting was only 0.04 second of arc, but, according to Sassa and Nishimura (1951), an S-shaped trace of the tilt vector, as can be seen in the case of the Tottori earthquake, was observed.

Nanki earthquake

An earthquake ($M = 6.7$) occurred at the sourthern part of Kii Peninsula (33.9°N, 135.8°E) on April 26, 1950. The earthquake was called the Nanki (southern Kii) earthquake. Remarkable tilt precursors were observed at Tamamizu, Kamigamo and Kochi Observatories at epicentral distances of 80, 120 and 200 km, respectively. The precursor times were reported as 6.9, 6.8 and 5.4 hours, and the amounts of tilting were 0.15, 0.04 and 0.02 second of arc for the respective observatories (Sassa and Nishimura, 1951).

Daishoji-oki earthquake

When an earthquake called the Daishoji-oki earthquake ($M = 6.8$) occurred in the Japan Sea off Ishikawa Prefecture, Japan, on March 7, 1952, a tiltmeter observation was in progress at the Ogoya copper mine about 40 km southeast from the epicenter (Hosoyama, 1952; Nishimura and Hosoyama, 1953).

A tilting of 1 minute of arc or larger in a direction pointing to the epi-

center took place 3 months before the earthquake. The tilting was accelerated a little more 10 days prior to the earthquake occurrence. Should the
anomalous change in tilt be a kind of premonitory effect, we may say that
there are tilt precursors having a duration of a few months or thereabouts in
addition to those of which the time constant is several hours as mentioned
earlier in this subsection. However, there are views that such an extremely
large tilting might be caused by some local effect of unknown origin.

Yoshino earthquake

On the occasion of the Yoshino earthquake (M = 7.0) that occurred at a
depth of 70 km in the middle of Kii Peninsula, Japan, on July 18, 1952, an
anomalous extension of the ground was observed by a strainmeter installed
at the Osakayama Observatory, Kyoto University, 94 km north of the epicenter as can be seen in Fig. 7-10. The strain amounted to 2.5×10^{-6}. The
anomalous change started some 10 months before the quake, and recovered
after it within a year's time (Sassa and Nishimura, 1955).

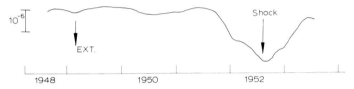

Fig. 7-10. Changes in horizontal strain in an S38° W—N38° E direction as observed at the
Osakayama Observatory in association with the Yoshino earthquake (Sassa and Nishimura, 1955).

Sassa and Nishimura (1955) and Takada (1959) also reported anomalous
changes in earth strain associated with the earthquake as observed at the Ide
Observatory, Kyoto University, 72 km distant from the epicenter. On the
same occasion precursor-like tilt changes were also observed at a few observatories (Tanaka, 1965).

Odaigahara earthquake

When an earthquake of magnitude 6.0 occurred on Kii Peninsula on
December 26, 1960, nine crustal movement observatories were in operation
within a distance of 100 km from the epicenter. Having a focal depth of 60
km, the general aspect of the shock was much the same as that of the
Yoshino earthquake. Tiltmeters at those observatories recorded characteristic changes during the 6 months before the shock. The marked turning
points of tilt vector trace were observed at about 30 and several days prior to
the shock. The amplitude of tilting exceeded 1 second of arc at most observatories, the maximum change reaching 6 seconds of arc at an observatory
on the western coast of the peninsula. Strainmeters also exhibited anomalous

changes. The above information is taken from Nishimura (1961) and Tanaka (1965).

Hyuganada earthquake

A precursory tilt change of 0.1 second of arc was observed 12 days prior to an earthquake, the Hyuganada earthquake, of magnitude 7.0 that occurred underneath the sea east of Kyushu, Japan, on February 27, 1961 (Nishimura, 1961; Tanaka, 1965). A change in sign of tilting seemed to have taken place about 4 days before the shock. The distance between the observation point and the epicenter was some 120 km. Looking at the tilt trace which was regarded as a precursor by Nishimura, however, the present author cannot help to think that its magnitude does not exceed very much that of the background noise.

In addition to the last seven examples, some more precursor-like changes in tilt and strain have been reported by the Kyoto University group, notably by Tanaka (1965). They were associated with the 1961 North Mino (M = 7.0), 1962 Shirahama-oki (M = 6.2), 1963 Echizenmisaki-oki (M = 6.9) earthquakes and the 1961 Western Hyogo earthquake swarm. These precursors will be summarized in the form of a table in a later chapter.

Niigata earthquake

In section 7.4, it was stated that general agreement in the pattern of time variation between the ground tilting as observed by a water-tube tiltmeter and the level change at a bench mark close to the Maze Observatory, where the tiltmeter was at work, can be seen as shown in Fig. 7-5. The observatory is situated near the Japan Sea coast, and is very close to a bench mark for which the changes in level are shown by the curve at the bottom of Fig. 5-64. The distance between the epicenter of the 1964 Niigata earthquake (M = 7.5) and the observatory is about 80 km. Looking at the tilt curve in Fig. 7-5, it might be said that a precursory change took place about 8 years prior to the earthquake. However, no premonitory change immediately prior to the earthquake was detected by either water-tube or quartz tiltmeters.

Central Gifu Prefecture and Atsumi Peninsula earthquakes

The Inuyama Crustal Movement Observatory, Nagoya University, that was constructed under the Japanese national program on earthquake prediction, has been in operation since 1967. The records of water-tube tiltmeters and strainmeters are affected by annual variations and other short-period variations. When these variations are eliminated by applying a low-pass filter to the original records, however, smoothed secular changes in tilt and strain can be obtained. Iida and Shichi (1972) further estimated the changes in rate of tilt and strain which are reproduced in Fig. 7-11. It is interesting to note that fairly rapid changes are observed before the Central Gifu Prefecture earthquake (M = 6.6) on September 9, 1969, which occurred at an epicentral

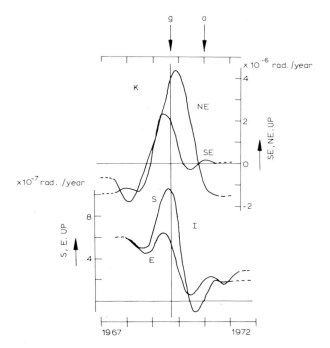

Fig. 7-11. The smoothed rates of tilt change at the Kamitakara (K) and Inuyama (I) Crustal Movement Observatories. The occurrences of the Central Gifu Prefecture and Atsumi Peninsula earthquakes are respectively denoted by g and a (Shichi, 1973).

distance of 48 km in a north-northeast direction from the observatory. It may be said that a change of similar sort, though a little smaller, took place before the Atsumi Peninsula earthquake ($M = 6.1$) on January 5, 1971 about 90 km south of the observatory. Should these changes be some sort of premonitory effects, precursor times are about 250 days for both earthquakes. The amount of anomalous changes is 0.5×10^{-6}/year in strain and 0.5×10^{-6} radian/year in tilt, respectively. Shichi (1973) reported that a precursor-like change of similar character was also observed at the Kamitakara Crustal Movement Observatory, Kyoto University, at an epicentral distance of 60 km in a northeast direction from the epicenter in association with the Central Gifu Prefecture earthquake. The curves for Kamitakara are also shown in Fig. 7-11.

As was mentioned in subsection 4.2.4, twelve crustal movement observatories were constructed under the earthquake prediction program in Japan, but no precursors have as yet been reported from these observatories except for the above examples. This is probably because the detectability of anomalous strain and tilt associated with an earthquake at an observatory is not quite as high as had been expected. As it is not practicable to increase drastically the number of crustal movement observatories, observation with arrays of borehole tiltmeters and the like should be intensified.

7.7.2. Soviet examples

Tiltmeter results

Observations of ground tilt and strain in the U.S.S.R. seem to be concentrated in Middle Asia where seismic activity is fairly high. The first work on ground tilting in relation to earthquake prediction was reported by V.F. Bonchkovskiy (see Ostrovskiy, 1972).

It was reported that an anomalous ground tilt of 0.1 second of arc was observed at the Ashkhabad station an hour before an earthquake of $M < 4$ occurred at an epicentral distance of 25 km on April 25, 1957.

At the Alma-Ata station, tiltmeters are installed in a mine tunnel at a depth of 15 m from the ground surface. The tilt records are free from noise due to changes in atmospheric pressure. An earthquake of magnitude 4.0 followed by another one of magnitude 4.7 after 30 minutes occurred at an epicentral distance of 250 km from the station on October 13, 1958. A tilt step amounting to 0.4 second of arc was observed starting 3 hours before the earthquakes as can be seen in Fig. 7-12. The direction of tilting was almost exactly opposite to the one of the epicenter.

When earthquakes of magnitudes 5.0 and 3.5 occurred in Afghanistan, respectively at epicentral distances of 245 and 300 km from the Kondara Observatory, Dushambe, on March 2 and 16, 1959, marked precursors with steps in tilt were observed at the observatory. Probably these are the most outstanding records of tilt precursors as can be seen in Fig. 7-13. The above three tilt precursors are described in Ostrovskiy (1972, 1974).

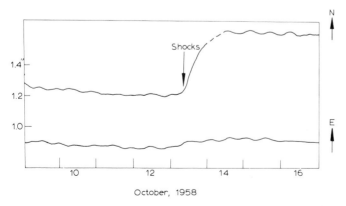

Fig. 7-12. Anomalous change in ground tilt at the Alma Ata station associated with earthquakes on October 13, 1958 (Ostrovskiy, 1972).

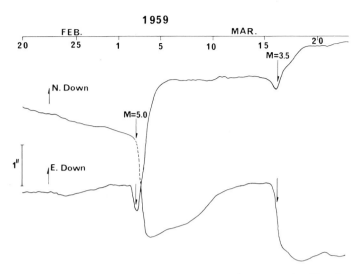

Fig. 7-13. Anomalous changes in ground tilt at the Kondara Observatory, Dushambe associated with two Afghanistan earthquakes on March 2 and 16, 1959 (Ostrovskiy, 1972, 1974).

Sadovsky et al. (1972) showed examples of tilt precursors observed at Naryn and Dushambe although no detailed discussion was presented.

Strainmeter results

The following is taken from Latynina and Karmaleyeva (1970, 1972) and Nersesov et al. (1974a). A quartz strainmeter having a length of 25 m was set up in the Talgar station in the spurs of the Zaliyskiy range of North Tien Shan in 1961. It was reported that the general trend of strain at Talgar changed from compression to dilatation a few months before the 1964 Alaska earthquake (M = 8.4) at an epicentral distance of 7,000 km from Talgar.

An earthquake of magnitude 6.0 occurred somewhere in southern Tien Shan (41.8°N, 79.4°E) at an epicentral distance of 250 km from the Talgar station on May 5, 1965. The strainmeter began to record a marked compression amounting to 9×10^{-8} about 15 days before the earthquake. The strain changed its sign 4 days prior to the earthquake, an extension of 4×10^{-8} having been recovered by that time. Such an anomalous strain change seems to have terminated within 15 days' time after the shock. However, no marked strain change was observed in association with an earthquake of magnitude 6.6 that occurred at almost the same locality on February 11, 1969.

There was another instance when an earthquake of magnitude 5.0 occurred at Djungarskoie Ala-Tau (45.4°N, 80.4°E) at an epicentral distance of

320 km from Talgar on August 20, 1967. The mode and amplitude of the strain change was more or less the same as the one mentioned above. A sudden change in strain was found 10 days before the shock.

Two strainmeters having lengths of 26 and 20 m have been operating at the Garm station since 1968. In association with an earthquake of magnitude 3.0 on January 9, 1969, an anomalous strain of 3×10^{-8} or thereabouts was observed 2 days prior to the shock. The epicentral distance was 5 km in this case.

It is sometimes pointed out that the secular variation in strain changes its rate prior to an earthquake. An earthquake of magnitude 7.5 occurred at an epicentral distance of 300 km from the Kondara station near Dushambe on March 14, 1965. A marked change in the rate of ground compression from 4.5×10^{-8} to 1.5×10^{-8} was observed 4 days prior to the earthquake. An anomalous tilt of the ground was also recorded by tiltmeters installed at a station, some 50 km distant from Kondara, before the earthquake.

On the occasion of an earthquake of magnitude 4.5 that occurred at an epicentral distance of 100 km from the Kondara station, a sudden change in the rate of deformation was observed 3 days before the earthquake.

Although some of the Soviet examples presented here are very clearly correlated to earthquake occurrence, there are a number of examples of which the correlation to an earthquake is not quite clear. Likewise in many of the Japanese examples, it is feared that in many cases the signal-to-noise ratio of the continuous observation of crustal movement is not high enough for detecting earthquake precursors.

7.7.3. American examples

Arrays of tiltmeters have been set up over the San Francisco Bay region by the NCER, the Earthquake Mechanism Laboratory (now attached to the USGS) and the University of California, Berkeley. It has often been noticed that a change occurs in the rate of tilt shortly before earthquakes which have magnitudes of about 4 (Healy et al., 1972).

Three earthquakes of $M > 4$ occurred within 50 seconds' time at Danville, California, 40 km east of San Francisco on June 12, 1970. In association with the swarm, tiltmeters at the University of California, Berkeley, seismological vault and at the Presidio of San Francisco, respectively at epicentral distances of about 30 and 40 km, indicated interesting changes. The tiltmeters consist of two interconnected pots of mercury, and the tilt is detected by means of the changes in capacity. Pre-earthquake tilts at both the stations are characterized by an almost linear rate of change of 8×10^{-10} radian/hour which seem to have lasted for a 1-month period. These changes can be clearly seen after removing tidal tilts from the original records. Just prior to the earthquakes an accelerated tilt change, which put the instrument off scale, was observed at Berkeley. The pre- and post-earth-

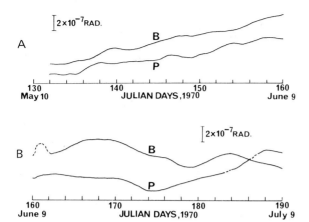

Fig. 7-14. Anomalous changes in ground tilt preceding swarm earthquakes at Danville, California. Pre- (A) and post- (B) tilting curves at Berkeley and the Presidio of San Francisco, respectively denoted by B and P, indicate a change in the long-term trend and a short-term signal just prior to the swarm activity on June 12, 1970 (Wood and Allen, 1971).

quake records are reproduced in Fig. 7-14 (Wood and Allen, 1971).

Sylvester and Pollard (1972) observed an anomalous deviation of a level bubble of a Wild T-2 theodolite when they were carrying out surveys over a quadrilateral near the Sylmar fault segment, which appeared in association with the February 9, 1971 San Fernando earthquake (see subsection 5.7.5). The location of their observation point is somewhere around point e in Fig. 5-67. Such an apparent tilt event occurred between 00.40 and 01.35 GMT, February 21, 1971. The apparent tilt, downward toward the fault, amounted to 2 minutes of arc which is so large that it is hard to believe its connection with seismic activity, but no other plausible explanation could be found. Two large aftershocks of magnitudes 4.7 and 4.5 occurred about 10 km north of the observation point respectively at 05.50 and 07.15 GMT. Should the tilt event be a precursor, the precursor time amounts to 4 hours or so.

K.L. Cook and J.M. Anderson (Kisslinger and Rikitake, 1974) reported that a number of precursory tilts and strains were observed in association with local earthquakes at epicentral distances of a few tens of kilometers from the Granite Mountain Observatory located near the Wasatch fault about 25 km south of Salt Lake City, Utah. The magnitude of the earthquakes ranged from 2 to 3.

When an earthquake of magnitude 6.0 occurred near Pt. Mugu, California, on February 21, 1973, nine tiltmeters were operating at seven stations in southern California (Alewine and Heaton, 1973). The epicentral distances ranged from 50 to 90 km. Although unusually large coseismic tilts were observed, no precursory effects were found. According to the experiences in

Japan, this is not surprising. There were many instances for which no precursors were observed in association with an earthquake of magnitude 6 or so, provided the epicentral distances exceeded 40—50 km.

An array of fourteen borehole tiltmeters has recently been installed along 60 km of the San Andreas fault around Hollister (Johnston and Mortensen, 1974). The interval between neighboring tiltmeters is about 6 km. The depth of the instruments is only 2 m. However, they are set up at carefully selected sites having approximately radially symmetric topography 1—4 km from the fault.

No indication of a rapid tilt change just prior to earthquakes was observed for scores of earthquakes of magnitudes, 2.5—4.3. However, it turns out that a steady tilting in a fixed direction seems to change its direction prior to local earthquakes, and that another steady tilting again occurs in a new fixed direction after the earthquake. Such an effect was observed for ten cases by the middle of 1974, and no similar effect has been seen yet without an earthquake. For instance, such an effect was observed at a site just southwest of Hollister 15 days before an earthquake of magnitude 4.3 that occurred at an epicentral distance of 17 km to the northwest on December 26, 1973. According to Johnston and Mortensen (1974), the precursor time T in days is generally correlated to magnitude M by the relation:

$$\log_{10} T = 0.8M - 1.9 \qquad\qquad\qquad\qquad [7\text{-}2]$$

as derived by Whitcomb et al. (1973). At the moment, detection of precursors by arrays of borehole tiltmeters looks highly promising.

7.7.4. Other examples

Caloi and Spadea (1955) reported on tilt precursors observed in Italy. Ostrovskiy (1972) pointed out, however, that the tilt in these Italian examples is extremely large. As the background noise is also large, these precursors, if any, must be handled with great caution.

Summarizing the reports on precursors presented in this section, it may be noted that there are two kinds of precursors. One that is characterized by a precursor time counted in hours (type 1), while the other is counted in days, months and even years (type 2). Detailed discussion of these two types of precursor will be presented in section 15.5.

7.8. EARTH TIDES

Nishimura (1950) analyzed the 1942—1946 tiltmeter records taken at the Makimine Crustal Movement Observatory, Kyoto University, which is situated near the central part of the east coast of Kyushu, Japan; the distance from the nearest sea is 28 km. The observation was made in a copper mine at a depth of 165 m. The country rock is Paleozoic clay slate.

Nishimura's analysis brought out striking fluctuations in the amplitude of the tidal constituents denoted by M_2, O_1 and S_2. These tides are largely controlled by crustal deformation due to ocean loading rather than the tidal deformation of the solid earth purely due to the attraction of the moon and sun. The fluctuations of the M_2 tide are so large that the ratio of the maximum amplitude to the minimum one amounts to 4 or thereabouts.

According to Nishimura, there is some correlation between changes in tidal amplitude and secular variations in ground tilt. It is likely that the increase in inclination of the ground toward the nearest sea corresponds to the increase in the amplitude of tidal variation. Although no definite correlation was found between changes in tidal amplitude and earthquake occurrences beneath the sea east of Kyushu, where the seismic activity is fairly high, Nishimura speculated that there might be some relation between the changes in tidal amplitude and the general seismic activity.

Should the changes in tidal amplitude as observed at Makimine be real, it must be considered that the elastic properties in the crust around the observatory change to a large extent, although in the early 1950s it was very difficult to think of a physical reason for such an extraordinary change. The observation at Makimine during a later period revealed smaller fluctuations in the tidal amplitude (T. Tanaka, personal communication, 1974). Meanwhile the seismic activity also became low.

In the light of the recent development of the dilatancy theory (see Chapter 14), however, it would not be impossible to have an earth crust in which the elastic properties can change by a considerable fraction of the original values. It might be that Nishimura's pioneering work has something to do with dilatancy developed near the observatory although there is nothing to prove such a speculation.

At the U.S.–Japan Conference on Earthquake Prediction held in Boulder, Colorado, in 1973, P.R. Roming, M.W. Major and D. Butler (Kisslinger and Rikitake, 1974) pointed out the importance of the observation of tides in relation to earthquake prediction. They referred to the work by Suh (1973) who made tidal analyses of strainmeter records of five observatories within a 25-km radius area centering on Denver, Colorado. It has been shown that the amplitude of the M_2 tide varies by a factor of two between stations 5 km apart and this is likely to be caused by the difference in rock type and thus in the elastic properties near the station. Nishimura (1950) suggested such a site effect many years ago.

According to Pan (1973), however, the data analyzed by Suh is so strongly contaminated by noise that Suh's conclusion may not be valid.

Wood (1973) reported that the amplitude of the M_2 tilt at a site within 10 km of the San Andreas fault is anomalously large and dominated by ocean loading at this frequency.

By 1973—1974 it has become well understood that the earth tides should be largely influenced by local irregularities in the elastic properties of the earth's crust. Of particular interest is the time variation of the elastic properties which may possibly be caused by dilatancy related to an earthquake. Beaumont and Berger (1974) theoretically studied modification of the M_2 tide near an annular dilatant zone superimposed on a spherical earth. A significant increase in earth-tide tilt and strain is to be observed near the border between the dilatant and non-dilatant zones. It is estimated that tilt and strain can be amplified by scores of percent corresponding to a V_p / V_s change amounting to 15%. Should dilatancy develop prior to an earthquake, it would readily be detected by an earth-tide observation. At an observatory near the coast, Tanaka and Kato (1974) also suggested the possibility of detecting changes in earth tides caused by dilatancy off the Pacific coast of Central Japan on the basis of a simplified calculation of earth tides.

Chapter 8

SEISMIC ACTIVITY

Most important and fundamental to earthquake prediction is to see where and how earthquakes occur. This is also one of the most basic problems of modern seismology, and a number of excellent texts on the subject are available (e.g. Gutenberg and Richter, 1954; Richter, 1958; Lomnitz, 1974).

In the light of what has been given in detail in the above texts, the author feels that it is quite useless to repeat a detailed discussion of world seismicity in this book, which is particularly aimed at the study of earthquake prediction. At this point, he would only like to point out that almost all earthquakes occur along the Circum-Pacific and Alpide-Asiatic Belts. Actually, the percentages of earthquake energy released have been estimated by Gutenberg and Richter (1954) as 75.6 and 22.1 respectively for the two belts.

8.1. IMPLICATION OF PLATE TECTONICS

Much of the world's distribution of earthquake epicenters has been found in standard text books on geophysics and seismology (e.g. Garland, 1971), so that no illustration of epicentral maps will be reproduced here. The author should like to point out, however, that the accuracy of locating earthquake epicenters was dramatically improved in the 1960s mostly because of the construction by the U.S. Coast and Geodetic Survey (now NOAA) of more than 125 seismological observatories equipped with standard seismographs in many countries.

One of the most remarkable aspects of the inferred distribution of epicenters throughout the world is an almost linear alignment of epicenters underneath the middle parts of large oceans. The alignment of epicenters running from north to south in the Atlantic Ocean turns around the tip of South Africa and enters the Indian Ocean, where it is divided into two branches. One runs up to the Red Sea where it makes a sharp turn ending at the East African Rift. The other runs around the south of Australia going as far as the sea off South America, and finally enters the Gulf of California. No extremely large earthquakes occur along these belts.

Seismic energy, which is 40 times or a little larger than that released at the oceanic belts, is released along a belt running along the periphery of the Pacific Ocean connecting New Zealand, Kermadec, Tonga, Samoa, Fiji, Solomon, North New Guinea, the Philippines, Formosa, Ryukyu, Japan, Kurile, East Kamchatka, the Aleutians, Alaska, and the west coasts of North, Central and South America.

Another marked seismic belt runs through Italy, the Balkans, Turkey, Middle Asia, Iran, Afghanistan, Pamirs, Himalaya, Tibet and West China.

Great earthquakes, for which the magnitude exceeds 8, occur frequently along the seismic belts mentioned in the last two paragraphs. Most of the earthquakes having a focal depth larger than 100 km occur along the island arcs surrounding the Pacific Ocean, although there are some beneath the Aegean Sea, Himalaya and Burma. No earthquakes of focal depth greater than 700 km have been reported.

8.1.1. Extrusion

The focal depths of earthquakes occurring underneath the middle of the Pacific, Atlantic and Indian Oceans are shallow. The linear alignment of epicenters underneath these oceans coincides with the submarine ridges, i.e. the Mid-Atlantic Ridge, East Pacific Rise and so on.

According to the modern idea of geophysics and geology (e.g. Holmes, 1944; Hess, 1962), these oceanic ridges are large-scale fissures of the earth where high-temperature materials are ascending from the interior of the earth. The portion of the earth beneath the crust that has a thickness of 30—50 km and 5—10 km respectively under continents and oceans is called the mantle. In contrast to the fact that the crust is composed mostly of basaltic and granitic layers, there is evidence to believe that the mantle immediately below the crust is composed of a heavier substance such as peridotite. The mantle extends down to a depth of 2,900 km where it contacts the core which is believed to be composed mostly of molten iron.

8.1.2. Mantle convection

The earth is believed to have been created by accretion of meteor-like materials, several billions of years ago. The heat, that is generated in association with the natural disintegration of radioactive materials, is accumulated within the earth which, having a radius as large as about 6,400 km, does not allow a quick heat radiation from its surface. Accordingly, it is not unreasonable to suppose a temperature difference amounting to a few thousand degrees centigrade between the surface and the core/mantle interface of the earth.

The situation is much the same as the water in a kettle heated from below. A convective motion may therefore occur in the mantle. Although the mantle material reacts as a solid to a rapidly varying mechanical force such as due to seismic waves, it is believed that it behaves as a viscoelastic medium when it is subjected to a force having a time scale of tens or hundreds of thousands of years.

The idea of mantle convection has been put forward by Holmes (1944) although only very little geophysical evidence supporting the hypothesis was available at that time. In the 1960s, however, many observations supporting the mantle convection hypothesis were found.

8.1.3. Creation of sea bottom

Let us suppose that the mantle material is rising up at oceanic ridges owing to mantle convection. If it is so, it may well be understood why the uplifted topography is formed on the ocean floor there. As the material that comes up from the earth's interior cannot pile up indefinitely, it tends to spread out from the ridges, so that a tensional force would predominate, sometimes producing a rift such as the one on the top of the Mid-Atlantic Ridge.

The recent development of geothermal studies made it clear that terrestrial heat flow, which comes out from the earth's interior, is high at oceanic ridges, so that high-temperature material must lie beneath there close to the earth's surface.

The speculation that a new sea bottom is formed at oceanic ridges and, as a consequence, that the newly solidified sea bottom must spread from there becomes almost certain by the geomagnetic findings to be mentioned in the following subsection.

8.1.4. Magnetic lineation observed at sea

The technique for measuring the geomagnetic field at sea made great progress in the late 1950s and early 1960s especially by the introduction of a proton precession magnetometer that can be towed behind a ship. Intensive magnetic surveys at sea brought unexpected anomalies of the geomagnetic field to light (e.g. Vacquier, 1972).

It is now known that most parts of oceans are covered with magnetic anomalies of several hundred gammas in amplitude and several tens of kilometers in wavelength. No such large-scale anomalies are usually found on continents. The anomalies in fact vanish as continental shelves are approached. As marine surveys progressed, it became clear that the anomalies are remarkably parallel to the axes of the oceanic ridge. If one connects the highs or lows of anomaly profiles, lineations parallel to the axes are observed. The symmetric feature of the anomaly about the axes of the oceanic ridge is so marked that it is hard to make a distinction between a profile of the magnetic anomaly across a ridge and its mirror image about the ridge axis.

8.1.5. Reversals of the geomagnetic field

It was difficult to account for marine magnetic anomalies on the basis of existing knowledge about rock magnetism because an incredibly strong intensity as well as contrast of magnetization must be assumed. In order to reach a plausible interpretation of marine anomalies, one must be familiar with palaeomagnetism which brings out the direction and intensity of the geomagnetic field in prehistoric and geological times.

Although the author cannot spare pages for a detailed discussion about outstanding outcomes of palaeomagnetic studies in recent years, it should be mentioned here that frequent reversals of the geomagnetic field during geologic time have been confirmed through intensive studies in palaeomagnetism. Palaeomagnetic studies on volcanic rocks combined with age determination by radioactive isotopes made it clear that the earth's magnetic field changed its polarity at least nine times during the last 3.6 million years (Cox et al., 1964). Such field reversals are also strongly supported by the magnetization of deep-sea and lake sediments. Existing models of the origin of geomagnetism suggest possible reversals as brought out by palaeomagnetic studies (e.g. Rikitake, 1958, 1966c).

8.1.6. Ocean-floor spreading

Vine and Matthews (1963) put forward a theory that may possibly account for marine magnetic anomalies by combining the mantle convection with geomagnetic reversals. When the mantle material extruding from the earth's interior is solidified beneath the axes of oceanic ridges, the newly formed sea bottom acquires a magnetization in the direction of the geomagnetic field at that time. Supposing that the field direction agrees with that of the present one, i.e. normal direction, we say that the magnetization is normal (N). After some time the geomagnetic field will be in a reversed state, so that the sea bottom formed during that period will have a reverse (R) magnetization. As the sea floor spreads out from the ridge axis, we have a sea floor having an alternating magnetic polarity, N and R. The difficulty in accounting for an incredibly large contrast of magnetization has thus been overcome by the introduction of magnetization in the N and R directions.

As the periods for the N and R magnetizations are known from palaeomagnetic studies of volcanic rocks, it is possible to estimate the speed of sea-floor spreading by dividing the distance of a particular anomaly lineation from the ridge axis by the time required for the lineation to reach there. It is thus obtained that the speed of ocean-floor spreading amounts to 2—5 cm/year.

Application of the ocean-floor hypothesis to much older magnetic lineations also seems possible. Heirtzler et al. (1968) concluded that there must have been 171 reversals during 76 million years in the past. It thus becomes possible to draw isochrons over parts of the world's oceans.

8.1.7. Plate tectonics

Close examination of ocean-floor spreading suggests that the motions of the ocean floor seem to be approximated by rotation of rigid plates covering the surface of the earth. A model showing that the earth is covered by a number of major plates each rotating about its own axis has now become widely accepted. There are also a number of subsidiary plates. It appears that only few important geophysical and geological phenomena are taking place within a plate. However, various phenomena of geophysical and geological importance such as mountain building, volcanic eruption, earthquake generation and the like are mostly correlated to the boundaries of plates.

Called plate tectonics, the above model is likely to account for many phenomena observed geophysically and geologically from a unified point of view (e.g. Isacks et al., 1968).

8.1.8. Subduction

Let us pay special attention to the East Pacific Rise, for instance. The newly extruded mantle material forms two plates of which the thickness is estimated as about 100 km. The plate that moves eastwards tends to come down beneath the South American continent. Meanwhile the plate moving westwards reaches as far as the Aleutian, Kamchatka, Kurile and Japan arcs where it tends to come down beneath the continental plate.

Many earthquakes including the great ones for which the magnitude exceeds 8 occur in association with such a subduction of the oceanic plate. The above process of plate tectonics is schematically illustrated in Fig. 8-1 (Uyeda, 1971). The downgoing plates seem to reach a depth of 700 km or so where they are consumed. Many deep-focus earthquakes are located within

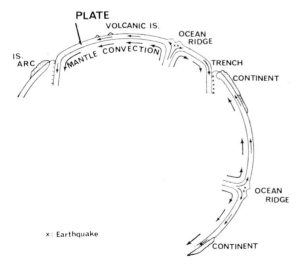

Fig. 8-1. Schematic view of the generation and consumption of the lithospheric plates (Uyeda, 1971).

the dipping plate. Friction at the interface between continental and oceanic plates may give rise to excess heating, and so molten magma may be produced there. The magma thus produced may in turn rise up to the earth's surface forming volcanoes. High heat flows observed on the bottom of marginal seas may also be accounted for by such a process.

The idea of ocean-floor spreading and plate tectonics was originally introduced mostly on the basis of data taken around oceanic ridges, so that the interpretation of what is happening around island arcs is by no means complete. What is the driving force of a plate? Why does the Pacific plate go down beneath the Asian one? Why do the Atlantic plates move together with the American and African continents in contrast to the Pacific plate? There still remain many questions to be answered.

8.1.9. Compression and rebound

According to the current theory of plate tectonics, an island arc such as the Japan arc is compressed by a spreading oceanic plate. At the same time, it is pulled down by the plate as is schematically shown in Fig. 8-2, this being the reason why a deep trench is formed in front of the arc. That the Japan arc is generally subjected to a state of compression has been proved by precise traverse surveys as has already been mentioned in subsection 5.4.3.

Fig. 8-2A illustrates the compressed state of the arc. The Pacific side of the Japan Islands tends to be displaced landwards and, at the same time, to subside. Since the strength of the earth's crust is finite, however, the crust must come to a rupture probably at the interface between the continental and oceanic plates, as shown in Fig. 8-2B, when the compression exceeds a certain limit. At that moment the strained crust would rebound giving rise to

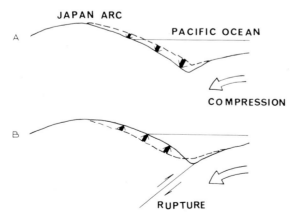

Fig. 8-2. Compression and rebound of an island arc. A. Compressed state. B. State of rebound.

an oceanward shift along with an uplift as is also shown in Fig. 8-2B. The strain energy, that has accumulated in the crust, would be released and converted into that of seismic waves to be radiated from the ruptured zone; and a huge mass of seawater, which is pushed up in association with the rebound, would tumble down giving rise to tsunami waves.

A crude model of extremely large earthquakes off the Pacific coast of Japan, Kurile, Kamchatka, the Aleutians and Alaska may be something like the one described above. As the plate motion would last over a time span of geological scale, the above supposed cycle of compression and rebound would last over a period of comparable length. It is feared, therefore, that there is no way for an island arc like Japan to be free of large earthquakes.

When the above idea is accepted, it is subsequently seen why an earthquake prediction program puts much stress on monitoring the accumulation of crustal strain by repeating geodetic surveys. It is possible to have a rough idea about the probability of earthquake occurrence on the basis of strain accumulation because the ultimate value of crustal strain is statistically known (see section 15.3). The spatial extent of crustal deformation may well suggest the zone of a coming earthquake and possibly even its magnitude. Anderson (1975), who takes into account the coupling and decoupling between a stressed lithospheric plate and a viscous asthenosphere, proposed a realistic model of large earthquakes at island arcs.

Considering earthquakes which are not directly correlated to major plate motions, however, the above compression and rebound model seems to be so simple that it does not explain all aspects of earthquake occurrence. For instance, moderately large earthquakes of magnitude 7 or so sometimes occur inland and along the coast of the Japan Sea in Japan. The physical mechanism for these earthquakes has not as yet been worked out.

8.1.10. Transcursion

There are boundaries where two plates slide past one another. An oceanic ridge is not a smooth range of uplifted sea floor. Many fracture zones cut the ridge in such a way that the overall ridge is formed by many segments being displaced along the fracture zones. On both sides of the portion of a fracture zone connecting one segment to another, the motion of the sea floor or plate occurs in an opposite direction with one another. Wilson (1965) called that portion of the fracture zone a transform fault. A source-mechanism study by Sykes (1967) confirmed that earthquakes occurring there are in fact caused by the horizontal shear stress expected from such a relative motion.

The San Andreas fault in California, the Alpine fault in New Zealand and so forth are also located at borders where two plates pass each other. These faults are characterized by creep and fault (strike-slip) movements. Fairly large earthquakes sometimes occur in association with the latter movement. Some of these faults are believed to be transform faults.

8.2. REGIONAL SEISMICITY AND MICROEARTHQUAKES

8.2.1. Gutenberg-Richter formula

It is well known that the smaller the earthquake magnitude is, the larger is the number of occurrences (Ishimoto and Iida, 1939; Gutenberg and Richter, 1944). The number of occurrence (N) for earthquakes of magnitude M in a region during a certain period is correlated to M as:

$$\log_{10} N = a - bM \tag{8-1}$$

where a and b are constants. Equation [8-1], which has been obtained empirically, is usually called the Gutenberg-Richter formula.

Constant b generally assumes a value of approximately 1, so that the frequency of earthquakes having a magnitude of $M - 1$ is approximately ten times as large as that of earthquakes having a magnitude of M. It seems likely that equation [8-1] can be applicable even to extremely small earthquakes for which the magnitude is smaller than 0.

Present-day technique makes it easy to detect earthquake motion with a magnification factor of 1 million or so for a certain frequency range. Most seismographs are nowadays electromagnetic with an appropriate recording system. It becomes possible, therefore, to follow the seismicity in a region within a relatively short period by observing the microearthquakes ($3 > M \geqslant 1$) and the ultra-microearthquakes ($1 > M$).

8.2.2. Microearthquake studies in Japan

Much about observation networks for seismic study in Japan was given in subsection 4.2.5. As a result of intensive observations by a network of micro-earthquake observatories as shown in Fig. 4-6, an enormous set of seismicity data has been accumulated, and consequently the distribution of seismically active and inactive areas is brought to light. Fig. 8-3A—C gives the distributions of microearthquake epicenters respectively for North, Central and South Japan as monitored by the network; it was compiled by Oike (1973) and Matsumura and Oike (1973).

It is apparent from the figures that the epicenters are sometimes distributed along a nearly straight line in highly seismic areas. Many of such lineations seem to be closely correlated to active faults (see subsection 11.2.2 and Fig. 11-1). In the Kinki—Chugoku district, i.e. an area around Kyoto and Osaka in Central Japan, such correlations have been made with a dense array of microearthquake observatories operating over a fairly long period (e.g. Huzita et al., 1973).

That a fair number of microearthquakes are still occurring along the seismic faults which appeared in association with the 1927 Tango (see subsec-

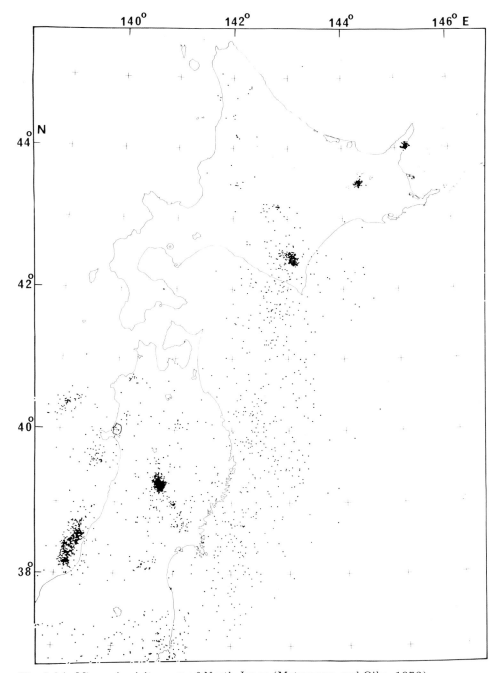

Fig. 8-3A. Microseismicity map of North Japan (Matsumura and Oike, 1973).

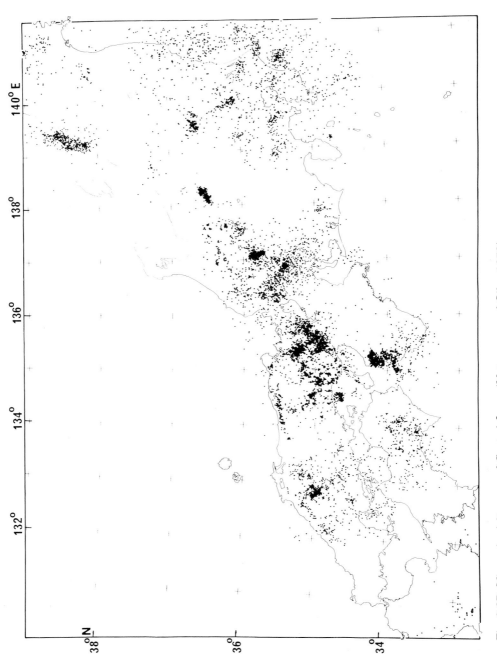

Fig. 8-3B. Microseismicity map of Central Japan (Matsumura and Oike, 1973).

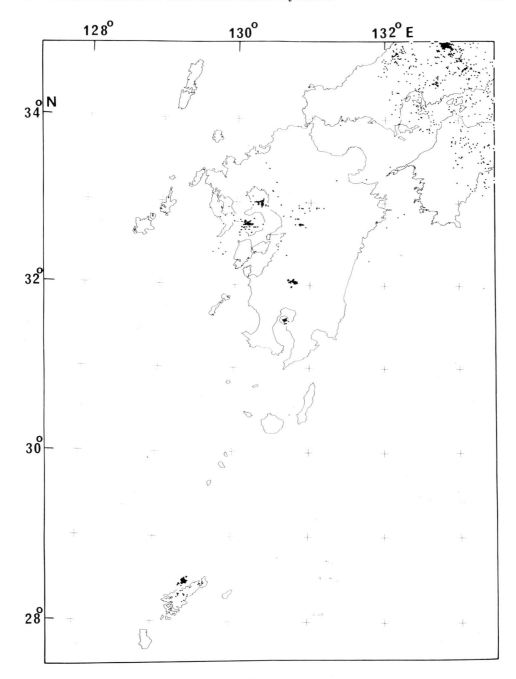

Fig. 8-3C. Microseismicity map of South Japan (Matsumura and Oike, 1973).

tions 5.3.2 and 5.6.5) and the 1943 Tottori (see subsections 5.3.4 and 5.6.9) earthquakes is thus brought out. Although it is supposed that an E—W compressional force is predominating almost uniformly within the earth's crust in Central Japan (Ichikawa, 1971), microearthquake occurrence is not quite as uniform in its mode.

There are many microearthquakes occurring underneath a zone south of the Median tectonic line (see subsection 11.2.2), an active strike-slip fault running through Shikoku and Kii Peninsula and another zone in the Chugoku district, the western part of Honshu, at a depth of 3—15 km. On the other hand, the number of earthquakes is markedly small underneath the Setonaikai Sea, an inland sea lying between the above two zones. It has been suggested that such a distinction may be caused by the difference in physical properties within the crust between those zones; a low-temperature and high-pressure metamorphism prevails for the high-seismicity zones, while the crust of the low-seismicity zone has been subjected to a high-temperature and low-pressure metamorphism. It might be supposed that the former crust is brittle while the latter one has some viscous property.

Turning to the Hokkaido—Tohoku area, the northernmost part of Japan, an extremely large number of microearthquakes are occurring along and off the Pacific coast. Extremely large earthquakes also occur frequently along this zone. Meanwhile, microseismicity is very low in the interior of Hokkaido.

In the Tohoku region, the northernmost part of Honshu, many microearthquakes occur along a tectonic line running in a N—S direction. Microseismic aftershock activity associated with fairly large earthquakes of magnitudes 6—7, that occur inland and along the Japan Sea coast from time to time, are also seen in Fig. 8-3A. Many microearthquakes also occur along the surface of the downgoing lithospheric plate. The Pacific plate, which is believed to dip beneath the Japan arc at the Japan Trench, seems to reach a depth of 100—150 km beneath that portion of Japan.

The mode of microearthquake occurrence is complicated in the Kanto area around Tokyo where the Japan arc meets with the Izu—Mariana arc. Although no regularity of epicentral distribution can be seen at first glance, close examination of the hypocentral distribution brought to light that many microearthquakes occur along a plane dipping landward from east to west (Tsumura, 1973). Tsumura pointed out a similarity between the vertical distribution of earthquake foci as obtained by microseismic observations over a period of 10 months and that for earthquakes of magnitude 4 or larger from the routine network of JMA over a 10-year period. It is demonstrated that an overall seismicity may well be brought to light by microearthquake observations over a short period.

Fig. 8-4 shows how the epicenters of conspicuous and moderately conspicuous earthquakes are distributed in and around Japan during 1900—1950 (Tsuboi, 1958). According to the JMA, an earthquake is nominated to be

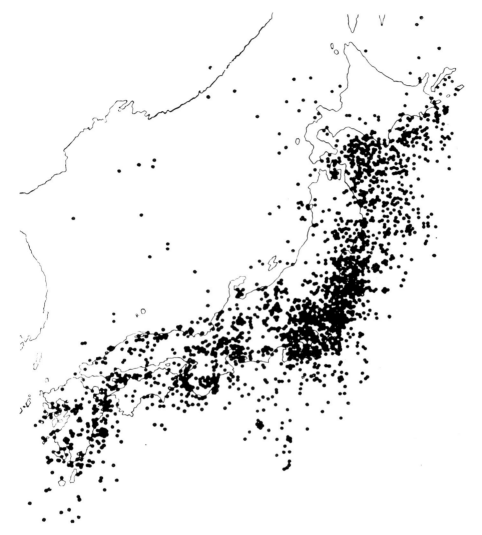

Fig. 8-4. Epicenters of 3,147 conspicuous and moderately conspicuous earthquakes during the period 1900—1950, as plotted by Tsuboi (1958).

conspicuous when it is felt over an area having an epicentral distance of 300 km or larger. Similarly, a moderately conspicuous earthquake is defined for an epicentral distance of 200 km or larger. On comparing Fig. 8-4 to Fig. 8-3A—C we see that the pattern of epicenter distribution for microearthquakes is more or less the same as that for larger earthquakes. The only noticeable differences between them are the distributions in the area off eastern Hokkaido, the Tokai area in Central Japan and the western Shikoku—Kyushu area where the coverage by the microearthquake observation network has as yet been incomplete.

8.2.3. Microearthquake studies in the U.S.A.

A major effort in monitoring microearthquakes has been made over the San Andreas and associated faults in the U.S.A. (e.g. Healy et al., 1972). J.P.

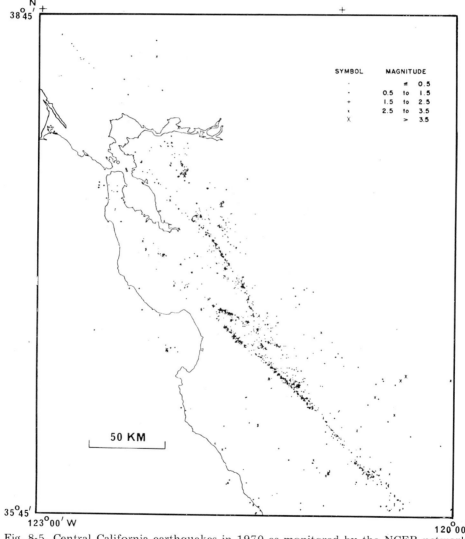

Fig. 8-5. Central California earthquakes in 1970 as monitored by the NCER network of seismographs (Healy et al., 1972).

Eaton (Kisslinger and Rikitake, 1974) reported on microearthquake observations carried out by the NCER. An extensive array of 102 seismometers covering an area of 350 km × 50 km over the northern part of the San Andreas fault is now operating. Seismic signals are telemetered to the NCER in Menlo Park, California, where they are recorded and, at the same time, subjected to a real-time processing including hypocenter determination.

Countless epicenters have been determined as can be seen in Fig. 8-5 for 1970, for example. One of the most striking features of this microearthquake distribution is certainly its coincidence with the San Andreas fault around the Hollister area, south of San Francisco, and furhter south where the fault is creeping. However, the lineation of microseismicity does not seem to reach San Francisco Peninsula. The activity follows rather the Hayward and Calaveras faults east of San Francisco Bay. Creep has also been observed at these faults.

Not many microearthquakes occur on the San Francisco Peninsula which was the seat of the 1906 San Francisco earthquake. The fault seems to be locked now. Healy et al. (1972) suspect that microearthquakes there may be foreshocks that reflect regional strain buildup.

Seismicity in southern California is monitored by a seismographic network of the California Institute of Technology. Microseismic surveys by mobile parties have often been carried out there. An extremely low microseismicity has been reported over an area about 100 km northwest of Los Angeles (Allen et al., 1965; Brune and Allen, 1967). The area is identified as that portion of the San Andreas fault where the 1857 Fort Tejon earthquake, which shook a widespread area comparable to that of the 1906 San Francisco earthquake, took place.

8.2.4. Microearthquake studies in other countries

Intensive studies of earthquake phenomena in general have been underway in Garm, Tadjik S.S.R., Central Asia, over a period of many years. Changes in microseismicity for earthquakes of magnitude 1—3 have been studied there resulting in findings of long- and short-range precursory effects (Sadovsky et al., 1972; Sadovsky and Nersesov, 1974; Nersesov et al., 1974b) as will be presented in subsection 8.3.4.

Bolt (1974) reported on a seismographic network around Peking, the People's Republic of China (see section 4.6). According to Coe (1971), Chinese seismologists found a systematic change in microseismicity around Peking preceding earthquakes of magnitude 5—6. Reyes et al. (1975) reported on a microearthquake survey in Baja California, Mexico.

Unfortunately, the author has no information about microearthquake studies in other nations.

8.3. FORESHOCK

8.3.1. Small shocks or rumblings forerunning a main shock

That many small shocks occur before a large earthquake was often reported in the classical literature in Japan. For example, such foreshocks were
felt by local inhabitants 2 days prior to the 1854 Iga earthquake (M = 6.9;
34.8°N, 136.2°E), 8 days prior to the 1896 Rikuu earthquake (M = 7.5;
39.5°N, 140.7°E) and 19 days prior to the 1930 North Izu earthquake
(M = 7.0; 35.1°N, 139.0°E; see subsections 5.3.3 and 5.6.7). As was mentioned in subsection 6.1.3, it was reported that local people had noticed
rumblings of the ground several days before the 1872 Hamada earthquake
(M = 7.1, 34.8°N, 132.0°E).

An interesting report on foreshocks prior to the 1855 Edo earthquake
(M = 6.9) can be found in Musha (1951). A workman was digging a well in
downtown Edo (now Tokyo) on the very day of the earthquake. As he felt
many detonation-like sounds coming from the deep bottom of the earth, the
workman could not help feeling uneasy and so went back home around
midday. About 10 hours later, the main shock struck Edo. Many small
foreshocks must have been taking place there at least 10 hours preceding the
main shock.

Richter (1958, p. 37) described a typical example of a sequence of the
foreshock—main shock—aftershock event in connection with the 1929 Whittier earthquake (M = 4.7; 34°N, 118°W) in east Los Angeles, California. In
this case a moderately strong earthquake occurred 64 days before the main
shock.

8.3.2. Nature of foreshocks

The physical nature of foreshocks is not at all clear. This is mainly because
of the fact, according to Mogi (1963), that not many instances of earthquake
foreshocks have been observed. Mogi analyzed about 1,500 earthquakes of
magnitude 4, or over, which occurred in and around Japan during 1926—
1961. But he found only 60 earthquakes that were accompanied by foreshocks. If a precursor time T is defined by the time interval between the first
shock observed and the main one, T ranges from a few minutes to a few
hundreds of days (see Table 15-XIII). Richter (1958, p. 67) in fact pointed
out ". . ., foreshocks seldom afford any opportunity for warning or prediction of major earthquakes, since there is nothing to distinguish foreshocks
from ordinary small shocks".

Spatial distribution of earthquakes preceded by foreshocks

Mogi (1963) found, however, that there are zones in Japan where earthquakes with foreshocks tend to occur frequently. They are:

(1) Izu—Nagano zone: the zone crossing Central Honshu.

(2) Miyoshi—Hamada zone: Northern Hiroshima Prefecture and Shimane Prefecture in the Chugoku district, Western Honshu.

(3) Oita—Kumamoto—Nagasaki zone in Northern Kyushu.

(4) Hyuganada zone: the sea east of Kyushu.

The tendency that earthquakes preceded by foreshocks occur in rather limited zones such as those above may have an important bearing on earthquake prediction studies.

According to Mogi's experiment on rock breaking (see subsections 4.2.9 and 13.1.1), it is suggested that the crustal structure under the zones, where earthquakes associated with foreshocks tend to occur, might be moderately fractured by faulting, volcanic action and some other processes although such results of a laboratory experiment should be applied to the actual earth's crust with much caution.

Two types of foreshock occurrence

Mogi (1966) claimed that there are two different patterns of foreshock sequences that were observed in laboratory experiments on rock specimens.

Type 1: foreshocks increase continuously up to the time of a main shock. This type is common in many heterogeneous brittle rocks.

Type 2: foreshocks occur more discontinuously and decrease before a main shock. This type seems to occur more frequently than the former type for more uniform rock specimens.

These two different types of foreshock sequences are also the cases for natural earthquakes.

Reservoir-associated foreshocks

A large earthquake sometimes occurs in association with the impounding of water in a man-made lake (e.g. Rothé, 1970). Such a reservoir-associated earthquake is often preceded by numerous foreshocks. Papazachos (1973), who studied the 1966 Kremasta Lake earthquake ($M = 6.2$) in Greece, showed that the frequency of foreshocks increased until the instant of the main shock, i.e. a typical example of the type-1 foreshock sequence.

An empirical formula that gives the number of foreshocks (n) on the tth day after the commencement of the sequence is suggested as:

$$n(t) = 4736 \, (159 - t)^{-1.99} \quad t \leqslant 154 \text{ days} \qquad [8\text{-}2]$$

Similar formulas are obtained for the 1963 Kariba Lake earthquake ($M = 6.1$) in Zambia—Rhodesia and the 1967 Koyna Reservoir earthquakes ($M = 5.0, 6.4$) in India.

Mogi (1969) pointed out that the pattern of increase in the number of foreshocks as reported in the case of the Kremasta Lake earthquake is similar to that for a granite specimen under a stress increasing with a constant rate. He believes that the precursor time of foreshocks depends not only on the crustal structure but also on the way in which stresses are applied. This may be the reason why the precursor times for foreshocks are widely scattered in the actual examples. It is almost impossible to foresee the time when a main shock occurs only from the time variation of foreshock occurrence.

Microearthquake work over the Matsushiro area

That many small shocks had occurred at a number of places where a moderately large earthquake occurred during the 1965—1967 Matsushiro earthquake swarm was already mentioned in subsection 4.2.1. As can be seen in Fig. 5-55, earthquakes of magnitude 5 or thereabouts often occurred at the margins of the seismic area. Observations of ultra-microearthquakes at fixed stations and by mobile parties made it clear that very small shocks had been occurring, almost without exception, in the epicentral areas of the main shock a few months earlier.

In a village named Sakai at the southwestern corner of the seismic area, for example, numerous ultra-microearthquakes were first observed around August, 1966. After some time, many felt earthquakes started to occur there eventually resulting in earthquakes of magnitudes 5.0 and 4.8 on January 16 and February 3, 1967, respectively. In Table 15-XIII are listed six examples of this kind of forerunning activity.

It is also interesting to note that microseismicity indicated no increase, or rather seemed to decrease to some extent, immediately before the main shocks.

8.3.3. Foreshocks in a broad sense

The definition of foreshocks is somewhat arbitrary not only in time distribution but also in spatial distribution. It appears to the author that most seismologists talk about foreshocks by selecting earthquakes occurring in the immediate neighborhood of the main shock or, more strictly speaking, in the region where the associated aftershock activity takes place.

However, there are instances which indicate premonitory seismic activity in an area a few hundred kilometers away from the location of main shock.

Earthquake swarm activity and great earthquakes

Kanamori (1972c) pointed out an outstanding relationship between occurrences of large earthquakes off the Pacific coast in Central Japan and the temporal variations of earthquake swarm activity in the Wakayama area on Kii Peninsula. Referring to Fig. 5-31, the large earthquakes concerned here and other earlier ones are shown in the figure, the peninsula in the lefthand corner is Kii Peninsula. An enormous increase in the number of felt earthquakes, from a few tens to a few hundreds or more a year was found in the

Wakayama area, where the number of felt earthquakes had been recorded since 1880, respectively starting about 1,500 and 2,200 days prior to the 1923 Kanto ($M = 7.9$) and the 1953 Boso-oki ($M = 7.5$) earthquakes (Table 15-XIII). The epicenter of the Kanto earthquake is shown in Fig. 5-31. The epicenter of the Boso-oki earthquake is located in the vicinity of the junction of the Sagami Trough and the Japan Trench though it is not shown in the figure.

The current theory of plate tectonics stresses that these earthquakes occurred along the northeastern edge of the Philippine Sea plate, which tends to move in a northwest direction as inferred from the source mechanisms of the 1944 Tonankai ($M = 8.0$) and the 1946 Nankai ($M = 8.1$) earthquakes (Kanamori, 1972b). These earthquakes occurred off Kii Peninsula where the Philippine Sea plate is believed to interact with the continental lithosphere.

Kanamori (1972c) pointed out that the motion of the Philippine Sea plate would be propelled by a rebound at the interface between this plate and the neighboring plates. At the time of the Kanto and the Boso-oki earthquakes, therefore, the stresses within a continental block involving the Wakayama area would become strengthened, stimulating an increase in swarm activity. If a creep-like deformation at depths preceding a main rupture is assumed at the plate boundary, the increase in swarm activity forerunning the large earthquakes may be explained.

The Wakayama earthquake swarm indicated a sudden decrease immediately after the Tonankai earthquake. This is compatible with the drop of compressional stress associated with the rebound, which is responsible for the earthquake, resulting in a decrease in the swarm activity.

The interesting point of the above consideration is the fact that the relation between earthquake swarms and great earthquakes, whose locations are separated by 500 km, can be accounted for on the basis of plate tectonics. A violent eruption of an active volcano on Oshima Island (see Figs. 5-29 and 5-31), about 100 km south of Tokyo, always seems to be associated with the rise of the swarm activity. It may be speculated that magma is pushed up by an increase in the internal compressive stress in the crust. Should the rise of swarm activity always be correlated to the occurrence of a great earthquake in the vicinity of the Kanto area in the way mentioned above, monitoring of earthquakes in the Wakayama area would provide a means of predicting large earthquakes along the Sagami Trough.

General increase in seismicity in a wide area forerunning a large earthquake

The author has been informed by senior colleagues, who had experienced the 1923 Kanto earthquake, that the seismic activity around the Kanto area was unusually high before the earthquake. In 1915, scores of moderately strong earthquakes occurred immediately off the Pacific coast of Chiba Prefecture to the southeast of Tokyo. Earthquakes having magnitudes 7.1 and 6.9 occurred beneath the northern part of Chiba Prefecture on December 8,

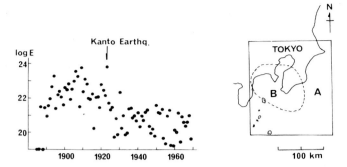

Fig. 8-6. Annual energy release in units of ergs in region A before and after the 1923 Kanto earthquake (Suyehiro and Sekiya, 1972).

1921, and Tokyo Bay on April 26, 1922, respectively. On January 14, 1923, an earthquake of magnitude 6.3 occurred beneath the southwestern corner of Ibaragi Prefecture to the northeast of Tokyo. It should especially be mentioned that scores of felt earthquakes, including the one of magnitude 7.5 on June 2, occurred off the Pacific coast underneath the Kashimanada Sea to the northeast of Tokyo in May and June, 1923. All these earthquakes occurred within an epicentral distance of 250 km or less from Tokyo.

The yearly values of seismic energy released from area A bounded by the 34--36°N parallels and 139--141°E meridians, which is shown in the right-hand map of Fig. 8-6, were estimated (Sekiya, 1971; Suyehiro and Sekiya, 1972) for the period 1885--1965 as shown in Fig. 8-6. It is noticeable that the yearly energy released from region A during the period before the Kanto earthquake is on the average two orders of magnitude larger than that after the earthquake. Area B, indicated by the dashed line in Fig. 8-6, is the seat of substantial aftershock activity and crustal deformation associated with the main shock. The yearly seismic energy released from region B was of the order of 10^{20} erg during a few years prior to 1922, but it exceeded 10^{22} erg in 1922. The ratios of energy from B to that from A are estimated as 0.0016 and 0.95 respectively for 1921 and 1922.

It may be concluded, therefore, that the general seismicity of the broad region surrounding the area, which later became the epicentral area of the major earthquake, was high during a period of a few tens of years before the Kanto earthquake. No remarkable seismic activity took place within the area in which substantial crustal deformation and aftershock activity were observed associated with the earthquake, until about 1.5 years before the main shock. The increase in seismic activity in the area concerned tremendously accelerated from that point in time, eventually reaching the catastrophe. Should an earthquake of a similar kind be repeated in the future, the pre-earthquake activities mentioned above would doubtless be monitored by the observation network provided by the earthquake prediction program in Japan.

Kelleher and Savino (1975) examined the distribution of seismicity before large earthquakes along the northwestern, northern and eastern margins of the Pacific.

Deep-focus earthquakes forerunning a large shallow earthquake

Mogi (1973a) pointed out the tendency that deep-focus earthquake activity sometimes increases preceding a large shallow earthquake occuring along the Kamchatka—Kurile—Japan arcs. An earthquake of magnitude 8.3, called the Sanriku earthquake, occurred off northeastern Japan. Its epicenter was located at 39.1°N and 144.7°E. Three deep-focus earthquakes of large magnitude occurred beneath Sikhote-Alin, U.S.S.R., a couple of years prior to the Sanriku earthquake. They are the ones of magnitude $M = 7.25$—7.5 with a focal depth $H = 350$ km on February 20, 1931, $M = 7$ and $H = 350$ km on September 23, 1932, and $M = 7$—7.25 and $H = 300$ km on November 13, 1932, respectively. The epicenters of these deep-focus earthquakes were about 900 km distant from the epicenter of the Sanriku earthquake in a northwest direction which, according to Mogi (1973a), coincided with the direction of motion of the Pacific plate.

Prior to the 1952 Tokachi-oki earthquake ($M = 8.1$) that occurred off Hokkaido, an enhancement of deep-focus earthquake activity was observed beneath northern Hokkaido and southern Sakhalin, including the occurrence of a large earthquake of $M = 7.75$ and $H = 320$ km. A few deep-focus earthquakes of magnitude 7 or so occurred beneath Central Japan in 1952 and 1953 before the 1953 Boso-oki earthquake ($M = 7.5$) which is believed to be associated with the Sagami Trough (see the earlier part of this subsection).

A line connecting the epicenters of these premonitory deep-focus earthquakes to that of the shallow large earthquake concerned seems to be approximately perpendicular to the depth contours of deep-focus earthquakes. Mogi (1973a) speculated that a rupture at depth in a downgoing oceanic plate might have accelerated its motion leading to a major break in the upper part. He presented a few more examples associated with the 1923 Kamchatka ($M = 8.4$), the 1968 Tokachi-oki ($M = 7.9$) and the 1969 East Hokkaido-oki ($M = 7.8$) earthquakes.

8.3.4. Characteristics of foreshocks pertinent to earthquake prediction

b-value

A small earthquake of magnitude 3.3 occurred at a location 16 km distant from the Matsushiro Seismological Observatory in Central Japan in January, 1964. It happened that a special high-sensitivity seismographic observation was in progress at the observatory on that occasion, so that 25 foreshocks and 173 aftershocks were recorded (Suyehiro et al., 1964). When the Gutenberg-Richter formula as given in [8-1] is applied to the two groups of shocks, the constant b is determined as 0.35 and 0.76 respectively for foreshocks and aftershocks. Such a small b-value for foreshocks, which is unusually low in this case, indicates that the number of smaller shocks is lower than that for ordinary seismic activity during the sequence concerned.

Suyehiro (1966), who analyzed 45 foreshocks and 250 aftershocks of the 1960 Chilean earthquake (M = 8.3), obtained b-values amounting to 0.55 and 1.13 respectively for foreshocks and aftershocks. On the occasion of an earthquake of magnitude 5.1 in 1967 that took place at almost the same location as the 1964 one mentioned in the last paragraph, Suyehiro (1969) obtained b-values amounting to 0.59 and 0.89 for the foreshocks and aftershocks, respectively.

Frequency vs. magnitude relationship can also be studied by rock-breaking experiments. Mogi (1962a,b, 1967, 1969, 1973b) and Scholz (1968b) found that the b-value for foreshocks is smaller than that for aftershocks in the case of small shocks before and after a main rupture of nonuniform rock specimens. The reason why a high b-value is obtained for aftershocks seems likely due to the fact that the specimen becomes highly nonuniform because of the main rupture. If it is established that a b-value of foreshocks is always smaller than that for ordinary seismic activity in a certain region, b-value investigation may have an important bearing on earthquake prediction.

In association with the 1970 Danville earthquake swarm in California, Bufe (1970) found decreases in the b-value prior to moderately large earthquakes, i.e. the b-value decreased from 1.2 to 0.8 and 1.05 to 0.6 respectively 1 and 1.2 days prior to earthquakes of magnitudes 4.3 and 4.0. Wyss and Lee (1973) analyzed seismic activities in California and reported on a b-value decrease prior to a number of earthquakes of which the magnitudes ranged from 3.6 to 5.0 as listed in Table 15-XIII.

L. Gedney and J. van Wormer reported on decreases in the b-value before earthquakes near Fairbanks in Alaska (Scholz et al., 1973; Kisslinger and Rikitake, 1974). Fiedler (1974) found that the local b-value decreased from 1.3 to 0.7 about 900 days prior to the 1967 Caracas earthquake (M = 6.5) in Venezuela.

The reason why the b-value of small shocks tends to decrease preceding an earthquake is believed to have something to do with the stress state around the focal region. An interpretation of the b-value decrease prior to an earthquake in terms of a dilatancy model will be presented in section 14.1. If a premonitory decrease in b-value as described here is confirmed for most earthquakes, it would certainly provide a promising means of earthquake prediction.

Seismicity
Changes in the seismicity level prior to a strong earthquake have been

reported by Sadovsky et al. (1972), Nersesov et al. (1974b), Sadovsky and Nersesov (1974) on the basis of an extensive seismographic observation in Garm, Central Asia. From the data taken by a dense array of seismographs (see Fig. 8-8), it is possible to estimate the density of earthquake occurrence as defined by the yearly earthquake number per square kilometer. Fig. 8-7 indicates the seismic background activity thus calculated for I (northern), II (central) and III (southern) zones in the Garm region. Thick lines are the 3-year running averages which may indicate long-term changes in the activity. These estimates are made for small earthquakes of K = 7—9 (M = 1.5—2.8).

It is customary for Soviet seismology to use the index K instead of M. K is defined by a common logarithm of the earthquake energy measured in units of joules. A conversion table of K into M is provided in Table 8-I for convenience.

A decrease of background seismicity can be seen in the very active central area (II) after a group of strong earthquakes in 1955—1959. After that the seismicity level tends to rise over a 7-to 8-year period ending up with an earthquake of K = 14 (M = 6.1) in 1969.

It may be that the long-term increase in background seismic activity over several years or longer has something to do with stress buildup culminating in a strong earthquake some time later.

Close examination of the background seismicity curves enables us to notice short-term drops of the seismicity level immediately prior to strong earthquakes. For example, the 1969 earthquake was preceded by a temporary decrease in seismicity starting approximately 1.5 years before the shock.

A decrease in microseismicity immediately prior to a main shock was also

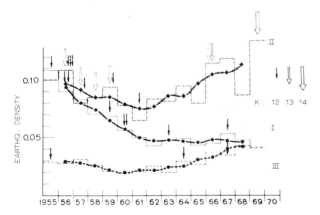

Fig. 8-7. Secular changes in earthquake density as defined by earthquake numbers per km² year in three zones in the Garm region. Thick lines indicate the 3-year running averages (Sadovsky et al., 1972).

TABLE 8-I

Conversion table of energy class K into magnitude M

K	M	K	M	K	M
6.0	0.8	10.0	3.5	14.0	6.1
6.5	1.1	10.5	3.8	14.5	6.5
7.0	1.5	11.0	4.1	15.0	6.8
7.5	1.8	11.5	4.5	15.5	7.1
8.0	2.1	12.0	4.8	16.0	7.5
8.5	2.5	12.5	5.1	16.5	7.8
9.0	2.8	13.0	5.5	17.0	8.1
9.5	3.1	13.5	5.8	17.5	8.5

detected in Alaska by L. Gedney and J. van Wormer (Scholz et al., 1973; Kisslinger and Rikitake, 1974). A decrease in the daily frequency of microearthquake from 80 to 40 was observed 7 days prior to an earthquake of magnitude 3.0 that occurred near Fairbanks. Similar decreases in the microseismicity level were reported in association with moderately large earthquakes during the 1965—1967 Matsushiro earthquake swarm (see subsection 8.3.2).

Such decreases in seismicity may be interpreted in terms of dilatancy hardening (see section 14.1), although many more data are certainly needed in order to establish precursory changes of this kind.

Focal mechanism

Probably one of the most convincing premonitory effects in the Garm region is provided by the rotation of the compressional axes as obtained from fault-plane solutions of small shocks (Sadovsky et al., 1972; Nersesov et al., 1974b; Sadovsky and Nersesov, 1974). Fig. 8-8 shows the epicenter and the compressional axis of the April 14, 1966, earthquake ($M = 5.4$) with double circles and thick arrows. The axes of compression for small shocks occurring in the region surrounded by the dashed lines took no constant direction until the beginning of 1965. The direction of the compressional axes tended to point ESE or ES for the period January—December, 1965, as can be seen in Fig. 8-8A. Starting in January of the following year, however, the mean direction of compressional axes suddenly shifted in an ENE direction as shown in Fig. 8-8B. After the April earthquake, the tendency for compression axes to take a preferred direction vanished.

In the beginning of 1968, the compressional axes tended to take an ES direction again. The direction shifted to an east direction in December eventually ending up with an earthquake of magnitude 6.1 a few months later.

Fig. 8-9A shows the time variation of the direction of compressional axes just mentioned. Sudden shifts of azimuth are clearly demonstrated in the figure. Fig. 8-9B shows three histograms, expressed in an arbitrary unit, of

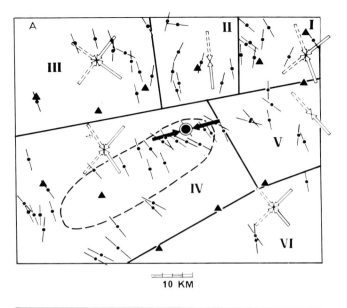

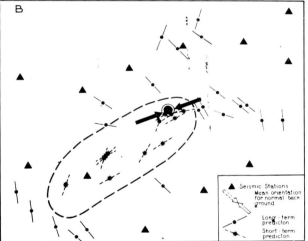

Fig. 8-8. Reorientation of compressional axes of small earthquakes with time in the Garm region. A. Directions of compressional axes prior to the April 14 earthquake in 1966, i.e. for the period January—December, 1965. B. Directions of compressional axes immediately before the earthquake, i.e. for the period January—April, 1966 (Sadovsky et al., 1972).

the azimuth of compressional axes for the periods 1964, 1965 and January—April, 1966, respectively. They also indicate very clearly the two-stage shifts of the direction of compressional axes.

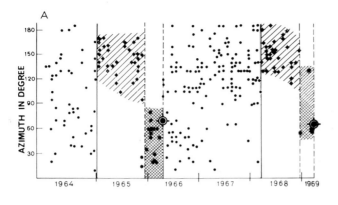

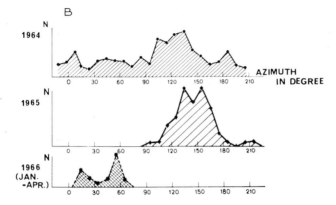

Fig. 8-9. Changes in the azimuth of compressional axes with time. A. This figure clearly shows that the axis azimuth changed twice preceding the 1966 and 1969 earthquakes which are indicated with large circles. B. Histograms of axis azimuth in an arbitrary unit for the three stages prior to the 1966 earthquake (Sadovsky et al., 1972).

The precursor times are determined for long- and short-range precursory effects in this case. They are 470 and 130 days for the 1966 earthquake and 360 and 110 days for the 1969 one, respectively (Table 15-XIII).

No clear-cut explanation has been given for the physical cause of the reorientation of compressional axes such as presented here. It has been supposed (e.g. Kisslinger, 1974; Wyss, 1975b), however, that some kind of stress concentration, possibly accompanied by production of very strong dilatancy in the immediate neighborhood of the incipient fracture (Brady, 1974; Mogi, 1974; see section 14.2), may be responsible for the rotation of the compressional axes. Gupta (1975) proposed an explanation based on the vertical migration of seismic activity.

Simbireva (1973) also reported a similar rotation of the compressional axes in relation to two earthquakes each having a magnitude 4.8 in the Naryn region, Central Asia.

Energy ratio of high- to low-frequency waves

Nersesov et al. (1974b) and Sadovsky and Nersesov (1974) reported an increase in the energy of high-frequency seismic waves prior to a major shock. From the observed amplitude of S waves, the energies for high- and low-frequency waves are determined, and the time variation of the logarithm of the energy ratio is studied. When an earthquake of $K = 12$ occurred at Khait near Garm in April 1966, a sharp rise of the logarithmic ratio was observed about 4 months prior to the main shock.

On the other hand Fedotov et al. (1972) reported a stable decrease of P- and S-wave frequencies for earthquakes of $M = 3$—3.5 preceding earthquakes of $M \geqslant 6$ on the basis of an observation on Iturup Island, one of the southern Kurile Islands. This seems to conflict with the tendency as observed in the Garm region.

At the moment it is hard to say that the study of frequency composition of small earthquakes in relation to earthquake prediction has been well developed.

It is interesting to note, however, that ground motions of very high frequency sometimes forerun an earthquake. Probably one of the most outstanding reports would be the one presented by Antsyferov (1969) who made observations with a geophone in a frequency range from 20—30 to 400—500 Hz in Garm. On October 5, 1950, for example, a fairly intense shock was observed at 22.45 GMT with an epicentral distance of about 15 km and a focal depth of the order of 15 km. Outstanding acoustic activity that lasted scores of minutes took place about 2 hours prior to the main shock. It might be useful for earthquake prediction to study the vibrations in acoustic ranges because such high-frequency waves may possibly be associated with rock fracture.

8.4. SEISMICITY GAP

8.4.1. San Francisco and Fort Tejon areas, California, U.S.A.

That the seismicity is very low over portions of the San Andreas fault, where the 1857 Fort Tejon and the 1906 San Francisco earthquakes took place, was stated in subsection 8.2.3. A zone, in which seismicity is considerably lower than that in surrounding areas, is called a seismicity gap.

8.4.2. South Kanto area, Japan

Fig. 8-10 (Shimazaki, 1971b) shows the epicenters of 678 earthquakes, of

Fig. 8-10. Epicenters of earthquakes, the foci of which are shallower than 60 km, in the South Kanto area from 1926 to 1967 (Shimazaki, 1971b).

which the focal depth is shallower than 60 km, as determined by the JMA for the South Kanto region in Japan during the period 1926—1967. The magnitudes of these earthquakes are larger than 3 with a few exceptions. It is noticeable in the figure that very few earthquakes occurred in an approxi-́mately elliptic area elongated in a NW direction which covers the southern part of Miura and Boso Peninsulas and eastern Sagami Bay, the low-seismicity area coinciding with the trend of the Sagami Trough (see Figs. 5-31 and 5-32). The earthquake located approximately at the center of the elliptic area occurred on August 19, 1930, and it may possibly be regarded as one of the aftershocks of the 1923 Kanto earthquake. A microearthquake observation over the South Kanto region in recent years (Ishibashi and Tsumura, 1971) also indicated a low microseismicity over the area in question.

    Fig. 8-11 shows the distribution of epicenters of large earthquakes that occurred in the South Kanto region in historical time. Although the locations of epicenters of early years may be subjected to a considerable error, it can be seen that many of the great earthquakes of magnitudes greater than 7

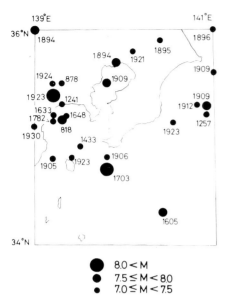

Fig. 8-11. Epicenters of large earthquakes ($M \geqslant 7$) which occurred in historical time (Shimazaki, 1971b).

originated from the now quiescent area. It should also be pointed out that many of the major aftershocks of the 1923 Kanto earthquake occurred there.

It is apparent from Figs. 5-29, 5-30 and 5-32, on the other hand, that the low-seismicity area has been considerably strained probably by plate motion. Yet, no ruptures have taken place there over a period of 50 years or so after the 1923 earthquake and associated aftershock activity. There is every reason to believe, therefore, that an enormous strain accumulation has been in progress around the seismicity gap in the South Kanto region, so that it is highly likely that a major earthquake would eventually recur there.

8.4.3. Eastern Hokkaido area, Japan

Utsu (1972a,b) summarized the recurrence pattern of large earthquakes off the Kurile—Hokkaido arc along the deep trench. As is reproduced in Fig. 8-12, a tendency that large earthquakes originate repeatedly from a source region every 100 years or so has been noticed off Hokkaido and the Kurile Islands. In spite of the fact that large earthquakes of magnitude 8 or thereabouts occurred in most of the regions noted by A, B, C, ... in the figure in 1950s and 1960s, no such repetition of a major earthquake took place in region C, where an earthquake of magnitude 7.9 had occurred in 1894, until 1973. It has been pointed out by Japanese seismologists that region C must

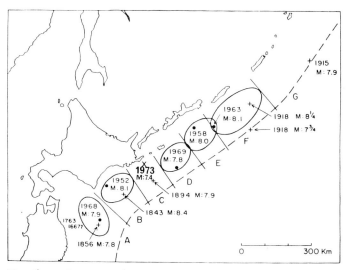

Fig. 8-12. Source regions of large earthquake off Hokkaido and the southern Kurile Islands (Utsu, 1972a, 1972b).

be a seismicity gap although no special mention was made of this gap by Kelleher et al. (1973) who undertook an extensive study of seismicity gaps along plate boundaries of the Pacific and the Caribbean. Utsu (1974) further studied the space—time pattern of large earthquakes occurring off the Pacific coast of the Japanese Islands.

The tectonics in eastern Hokkaido were summarized by Shimazaki (1972b). A horizontal contraction of the earth's crust in eastern Hokkaido in a direction approximately perpendicular to the trench axis was detected by a precise traverse survey as shown in Fig. 5-35 (Geographical Survey Institute, 1973) and by a recent triangulation survey (Harada and Kassai, 1971), both surveys having been compared to a triangulation survey carried out in 1903–1908, although the amount of strain accumulation is considerably different for the two estimates. In any case, however, it seems likely that a contraction amounting to 10^{-6} multiplied by a factor took place there during the period of several tens of years.

Repetitions of a levelling survey along a route running in a NW—SE direction in eastern Hokkaido (Geographical Survey Institute, 1972a) made it clear that a bench mark on the Pacific coast has subsided by 64 cm relative to that near the Okhotsk Sea during 1903—1970, so that the tilting rate along the route of 60 km in length amounts to 0.016×10^{-5}/year on the average. Shimazaki (1974a) discussed quantitatively the crustal movements in eastern Hokkaido in relation to their probable cause, i.e. the drag by a downgoing oceanic plate.

If the crustal deformation on land is extrapolated to that near the trench axis, an enormous strain accumulation is suggested off eastern Hokkaido. On the basis of the probability of earthquake occurrence estimated from such an extrapolation of crustal deformation, the present author testified at a committee of the National Diet about the possibility of having a large earthquake in region C (see subsection 4.2.1).

An earthquake of magnitude 7.4 according to the JMA estimate actually took place at a location, which is noted by a thick cross in Fig. 8-12, on June 17, 1973. The earthquake is thus noted as a predicted one on the basis of crustal deformation and the seismicity gap concept.

Attention should be drawn to the fact, however, that the coseismic deformation of the crust does not quite fit the rebound which is suggested by the model illustrated in Fig. 8-2. The magnitude of the 1973 earthquake was also not quite as large as had been expected. It is surmised that rebound occurred only along the upper half of the interface of the underthrusting lithosphere.

A number of Japanese seismologists, notably Shimazaki (1974b) and Kasahara (1975), speculated on the possibility of aseismic faulting at the lower half of the plate boundary although the possibility of having a sudden break there cannot be ruled out. One of the data that supports such an aseismic post-earthquake faulting is the land uplift observed at a tide-gauge station on the coast of eastern Hokkaido after the 1894 earthquake followed by an enormous subsidence which persisted over several decades. The tide-gauge data indicated a land subsidence amounting to several centimeters at the time of the 1973 earthquake. There is yet-to-be-confirmed evidence that a land uplift started in the beginning of 1974. As was pointed out in subsection 6.2.1, the accuracy of land movement measurement relative to sea level is so low that an uplift or subsidence amounting to 10 cm or so may possibly be masked by noise of meteorological and oceanographical origins. Should such a tendency of land uplift be taken for granted, however, possible growth of an aseismic fault, which would finally reach a depth of 50—100 km immediately underneath the coast line, could be imagined.

8.4.4. Tokai area, Japan

An earthquake of magnitude 8.4 occurred off the Tokai region facing the Pacific Ocean including Aichi and Shizuoka Prefectures in Central Japan in 1854. Its epicenter is shown in Fig. 5-31 along with those of many other great earthquakes that occurred off the Kanto—Tokai region since 1600. Going back to the earlier history of Japan, we see that a number of great earthquakes originated from almost the same epicentral area, with time intervals amounting to 100 years or so, off Central Japan as shown in Fig. 5-31. It was reported that an earthquake of magnitude 8.6 occurred at a location, which is believed to be about the same as that for the 1854 one, in 1498, accompanied by such a violent tsunami that Lake Hamanako near Hamamatsu City along the Tokai coast was connected to the open sea because land was washed away by the high waves. Although the epicenter of the 1707 earthquake of magnitude 8.4 is located off Kii Peninsula (see Fig. 5-31), it would not be unreasonable from analyses of historical documents to believe that another large earthquake occurred off the Tokai region almost at the same time. There is a tendency for large earthquakes off Central Japan to occur in pairs. As can be seen in Fig. 5-31, another earthquake of magnitude 8.4 in fact took place off Kii Peninsula, 32 hours after the 1854 earthquake off the Tokai region. Twin epicenters are also supposed for the 1605 earthquake ($M = 7.9$). In spite of the 1944 Tonankai ($M = 8.0$) and the 1946 Nankai ($M = 8.1$) earthquakes in recent years, however, no large earthquake occurred off the Tokai region.

Since 120 years, the mean interval of repetition of great earthquakes off Central Japan, have past since the last large earthquake in 1854, Japanese seismologists fear that the occurrence of another catastrophe might be approaching. A tremendous contraction of land, probably caused by the motion of the Philippine Sea plate in a NW direction, was made clear by a traverse survey across Central Japan (see Fig. 5-38). The land along the Pacific coast in Shizuoka Prefecture has been subjected to enormous subsidence ever since the first levelling survey was carried out several decades ago. There is every reason to believe, therefore, that a tremendous amount of strain has been accumulating in the earth's crust around the Nankai Trough where the oceanic plate is believed to be subducted into the earth.

Fig. 8-13 shows the epicenters of earthquakes which occurred off the Pacific coast of Central Japan during 1926--1972 (Sekiya and Tokunaga,

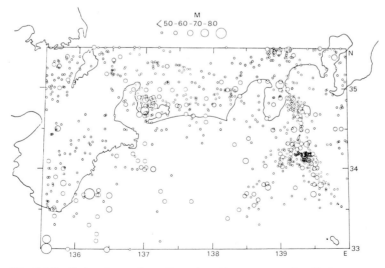

Fig. 8-13. Epicenters of earthquakes that occurred off the Tokai area, Central Japan during 1926--1972 (Sekiya and Tokunaga, 1974).

1974). It is clearly observed from the figure that a seismicity gap exists over the epicentral area of the 1854 earthquake. Many Japanese seismologists (e.g. Rikitake, 1974b; Ando, 1975) consider the area as one of the likely places where a great earthquake will originate sooner or later.

To the west of the area discussed above, the 1944 Tonankai earthquake (M = 8.0) occurred. A recent study by Sekiya and Tokunaga (1974) indicates that an extensive seismicity gap existed around the epicentral zone of the earthquake before its occurrence.

8.4.5. Kurile—Kamchatka—Aleutian—Alaska zone

The concept of a seismicity gap was first put forward by Fedotov et al. (1970), Kelleher (1970), Sykes (1971), Kelleher et al. (1973) and others. It is said that Fedotov was successful in predicting the location of the 1968 Tokachi-oki earthquake (M = 7.9). He also pinpointed two seismicity gaps of immediate danger; they are the one off Boso Peninsula in the South Kanto area, Japan, and another around Kamchatka Gulf. As shown in Fig. 5-31, an earthquake of magnitude 8.2 occurred off Boso Peninsula in 1703. The possibility of recurrence of a large earthquake there has been seriously considered by Japanese seismologists although no effective way of conducting prediction-oriented studies can readily be provided over such an area so far away from the coast line.

Along the Kurile—Kamchatka—Aleutian—Alaska arcs, we recently had large earthquakes such as the Kamchatka (November 1952, M = 8.3), Andreanof Islands (March 1957, M = 8.3), Kurile Islands (October 1963, M = 8.1), Alaska (March 1964, M = 8.4) and Rat Islands (February 1965, M = 7.8) earthquakes. These earthquakes are characterized by associated aftershock zones which are elongated along the trend of the arcs sometimes having a length of several hundred kilometers. These aftershock zones are regarded as those in which major fracture of the earth's crust takes place at the time of the main shock. It is remarkable that they hardly overlap.

A close examination of the above-mentioned aftershock zones brings to light gaps in the Alaska Peninsula (155—165°W), Commander Islands (165—170°E) and North Kurile Islands. These areas may be likely sites for a large earthquake to occur in the future.

8.4.6. Central and South Americas

Kelleher et al. (1973) studied the seismicity gaps along the Pacific coast of Central and South Americas. Extensive gaps such as those along the Ecuador—Peru coast (0—10°S) and along northern Chile and southeastern Peru (18—25°S) were pointed out.

8.4.7. A paradox

On summarizing what is stated in sections 8.3 and 8.4, we now encounter two different views on the relationship between preseismic activity and occurrence of the main shock. The Matsushiro experience indicates that the higher the microseismicity is, the greater is the danger of having a strong earthquake. On the other hand, a major earthquake may some day occur in the area of a seismicity gap, where very low seismicity is at present, because of the accumulation of crustal stresses. Aki (1968) pointed out that the response of the crust to regional tectonic stress differs from place to place even in the same general tectonic area, resulting in a complex pattern of strain concentration and microearthquake activity.

In reference to Mogi's work (Mogi, 1962a; see subsections 4.2.9 and 13.1.1), the author is inclined to think that such a paradox may be resolved by taking the difference in the crustal conditions into account. When a heterogeneous crust is subjected to a stress, no large strain accumulation is achieved because the overall strength is not high. Instead, many small ruptures would take place. When microearthquakes begin to occur in a region having such crustal characteristics, it may be supposed that either an increase in crustal stresses or weakening of the crust for some reason such as occurrence of dilatancy is developing there. In this case microearthquake activity may well culminate in a moderately strong shock, but never in an extremely large one having magnitude 8 or so.

In the case of a major seismicity gap, it is supposed that the crustal strength is high there, so that very few microfractures occur even though the stress becomes fairly high. A fault that was associated with a former major shock usually seems to be locked by a not-clearly-understood mechanism. The situation is much the same as a fairly uniform rock specimen under a breaking test as demonstrated by Mogi (1962a). If the crust is highly uniform, the experimental results suggest a sudden break. But an actual crust would not be as uniform as that, so that there may be some hope that seismicity starts to increase around a seismicity gap when the crustal strain approaches its ultimate value.

A case history related to the 1923 Kanto earthquake (see subsection 8.3.3) in fact indicates such an increase in general seismicity in the broad zone surrounding the area that later became the focal region. In spite of such a well-documented example, however, it is still hard to say that the relationship between the forerunning seismicity and main shock is well understood. In view of the recent development of microearthquake observations, some more clues to this intricate problem will hopefully be established in the near future.

8.5. DEEP-WELL OBSERVATION OF MICROEARTHQUAKES

Microearthquake observation over the Tokyo area in Japan relies on an array of seismographs, whose signals are telemetered to the ERI in the central area of Tokyo. As the Kanto plain around Tokyo is covered with thick alluvium of several kilometers in depth, observations at extremely high sensitivity are difficult to carry out because of the high background noise of natural and artificial origins. All the high-sensitivity seismometers of the array are set up on solid ground composed of hard rocks where the noise level is very low. It cannot be helped, therefore, that all the observation sites are outside the plain area.

Although the array is so sensitive that it often monitors microearthquakes occurring off Boso Peninsula, where the recurrence of the 1703 earthquake (M = 8.2) is seriously feared (see subsection 8.4.5 and Fig. 5-31), it is hardly likely that microearthquakes that occur immediately beneath the Tokyo area can be fully monitored by the array because the distance between Tokyo and the seismographic stations is as large as several tens of kilometers.

As was mentioned in subsection 4.2.5, the National Research Center for Disaster Prevention undertook microearthquake observations by installing high-sensitivity seismometers at the bottom of a borehole drilled through the soft sediments. A borehole having a depth of 3,510 m and a diameter of 15.9 cm was completed near Iwatsuki City (35°55′N, 139°44′E) located 28 km north of Tokyo. The hole is fully cased and cemented. H. Takahashi (e.g. Kisslinger and Rikitake, 1974) reported on the special care taken to make the observation system work under the high temperature and pressure prevailing at the bottom of the borehole, the temperature being 86°C and the pressure 350 atmospheres. Details of the observation system can be found in Takahashi and Hamada (1975).

Three-component seismometers for measuring the acceleration and velocity of ground motion were placed in a stainless-steel container of 9 m in length and 14 cm in diameter together with tiltmeters, thermometers and other accessories. The output signals from these instruments are sent by means of FM multiplex transmission to a recording system at the ground surface through a cable of 2.6 cm in diameter, which contains nineteen soft-copper wires plated with silver.

The seismometers were placed in a pre-Tertiary layer composed of metamorphic rocks, and it turned out that the noise level was very low there, so that microearthquake observations, with a magnification amounting to 10^5–10^6, can be carried out for a frequency range of 10–20 Hz. The sensitivity is about 10^3 times higher than that for an observation made at the ground surface.

Combining the deep-well observation with the ERI array, it now becomes possible to detect and locate many microearthquakes occurring beneath the Tokyo area. For instance, a number of shocks (M < 3) having a focal depth of 30 km or thereabouts were located beneath the northern part of Tokyo Bay in April and May, 1974 (National Research Center for Disaster Prevention, 1974). Earthquakes occurring in that area usually have deeper hypocenters although a destructive shock of magnitude 6.9 occurred at almost the same location as that of the 1974 small shocks on April 26, 1922.

There is evidence that small foreshocks had occurred prior to the 1855 Edo (now Tokyo) earthquake (M = 6.9) which occurred at a shallow depth in eastern Tokyo (see subsection 8.3.1). Should such foreshock activity repeat before a large earthquake strikes the Tokyo area, the borehole seismographs would doubtless monitor it.

After the 1855 earthquake, an earthquake of magnitude 7.0 occurred immediately beneath Tokyo in 1894 although the damage was not as large as that of the former earthquake because its hypocenter was somewhat deeper. Since that time no earthquake of this kind has hit Tokyo. Because of the incredibly heavy damage caused by the 1923 Kanto earthquake, most Japanese people are afraid of great earthquakes originating from the Sagami Bay in association with the crustal activity of the Sagami Trough such as the 1923 and 1703 ones (see Fig. 5-31). However, much attention should also be drawn to the potential risk of earthquakes of the 1855 and 1894 type. Earthquakes of this kind occurring immediately underneath a densely populated city could give rise to tremendous damage as was the case of the 1971 San Fernando (M = 6.4) and the 1972 Managua (M = 6.3) earthquakes even though their magnitudes were not very large.

In view of the success of the Iwatsuki deep-well microearthquake observations, the Japanese national program on earthquake prediction has been urging the Japanese government to provide a few more stations of this kind around the Tokyo area so as to make it possible to locate microearthquake hypocenters by an array of deep-well seismographs. It is no easy matter, however, to construct such a system because of the high expense for digging deep boreholes. It is said that a sum of 600 million yen (ca. 2 million U.S. dollars) or more was spent for establishing the Iwatsuki observation system. After much debate, however, it was decided in the end to construct two more deep-well stations around the Tokyo area starting in 1975.

8.6. SUBMARINE SEISMOLOGY

Most of the extremely large earthquakes that strike Japan occur along or off the Pacific coast of the Japan Islands. There is no doubt about the importance, therefore, of monitoring seismic activity on the sea bottom immediately above the focal zones of these earthquakes.

Nothing was mentioned in the "blueprint" (see section 4.1) about sea-bottom seismic observations. This is simply because no submarine seismograph was developed to a level of practical use by that time. In recent years, however, submarine seismographs of anchored-buoy type have become widely used for actual observations (Nagumo, 1973). A submarine seismograph of this type, operating off northeastern Honshu, in fact recorded the foreshocks before the 1968 Tokachi-oki earthquake ($M = 7.9$).

No real-time monitoring is possible, however, for an anchored-buoy-type seismograph. A container, in which the seismograph is set up, is sunk down to the sea bottom together with a recording system. After a certain period, the container is recovered with the aid of a radio-buoy to which the observing system is connected. Although such a submarine seismograph is useful for monitoring seismicity in a certain submarine area, no continuous observation can be conducted. A submarine seismograph of a self-falling and self-rising type has also been developed. It is often difficult, however, to recover a seismograph which is floating on the sea surface. This type of seismograph is also incapable of making a real-time observation.

In association with the proposed intensification of the earthquake prediction program in Japan in 1973, the development of a sea-bottom seismograph connected to an observatory on land by submarine cables is stressed. As techniques for the sea-bottom seismograph as well as submarine cables for telecommunication have already been fully developed, there should not be any essential difficulties in developing such a system. It is proposed to set up a group of sensors, not only seismographs but also magnetometers, tsunami-meters and the like, over a submarine area immediately above the expected focal zone of a large earthquake off the Pacific coast of Japan. The data taken by these sensors are to be sent by submarine cables to a near-coast station, and further to a central data center by commercial telephone lines.

It would be ideal if such submarine monitoring systems were set up over areas some 200 km off Hokkaido, northeastern Honshu, Boso Peninsula, Tokai and Shikoku regions. It is difficult, however, to have such a complete array of submarine seismographs at the moment because the expense expected for completing the array would be so large that it would exceed the whole budget of the national program on earthquake prediction. However, preliminary work on setting up a small-scale array of submarine seismographs over the sea bottom immediately off the Tokai area, Central Japan, was begun in the 1974 fiscal year.

Chapter 9

CHANGE IN SEISMIC WAVE VELOCITIES

Seismologists have long suspected that the velocity of seismic waves passing through the focal region of a forthcoming large earthquake may be modified because of strain accumulation there. Imamura (1928) was probably the first who stated such an idea very clearly in his speech at the Japanese House of Peers. However, there was no way to verify the idea in these earlier years because of the low accuracy of seismometric observation.

Sassa (1948) later called attention to the same topic again, and Hayakawa (1950) actually tried to detect changes in seismic wave velocities on the basis of then available data of natural earthquakes. It is regrettable, however, that this work was perhaps too early to reach any established conclusion judging from the accuracy of seismic observation at that date.

As the author briefly wrote in subsection 4.2.6, the Japanese national program on earthquake prediction took up a project of measuring arrival times of seismic waves from man-made explosions. It is hoped to detect changes in seismic wave velocities, if any, by the highly developed techniques of explosion seismology. Detonations of about 500 kg of explosives have been made at the northernmost part of Oshima Island (see Fig. 5-29), roughly at 1-year intervals since 1968. Seismic waves from the origin are observed at a number of stations scattered on the Izu–Kanto area to the southwest of Tokyo. Although the P-wave velocity crossing the Sagami Bay seemed to increase by about 1 part in 10^3 or a little less for a period during 1968–1969, no marked changes in velocity were observed over a period of several years (Iizuka, 1971; Geological Survey of Japan, 1972).

Eisler (1967, 1969) performed explosion experiments of a similar kind over the San Andreas fault at Salinas in the Gabilan Range, California. The arrival times of P waves were measured at a point 42 km distant from the shot point. Repetition of explosions with 100-kg explosives led to the conclusion that the error of arrival-time measurement is smaller than ±1 millisecond. However, no significant change was revealed by the experiments over a period of a year. It seems that the collapse of boreholes due to the repeated explosions implies a certain limit on the accuracy of measurement.

A much more sophisticated experiment on the changes in seismic wave velocity was carried out by Aki et al. (1970) and Defazio et al. (1973). In contrast to the shot experiments like the above, continuous sinusoidal waves from a hydrodynamic shaker were used, and the phase difference between the source and receiver was measured. In connection with a series of measurements along a 300-m mine shaft in Ogdenburg, New Jersey, U.S.A., a velocity change with a marked correlation with the strain due to the earth tide was observed. The in-situ stress dependence seems by 1–2 orders of magnitude larger than that obtained from experiments on rock specimens in the laboratory.

In contrast to rather indeterminate or comparatively small changes in seismic wave velocities as mentioned above, surprisingly large changes in the ratio of P-wave velocity V_p to S-wave velocity V_s were reported in recent years, first in Garm, U.S.S.R., and followed by similar findings in other countries.

9.1. CHANGES IN THE V_p/V_s RATIO

It is possible to obtain the V_p/V_s ratio from seismometric observation even though V_p and V_s are not determined separately. Changes in the V_p/V_s ratio that will be dealt with in this section are usually obtained from an analysis of the travel times of P- and S-waves. Denoting the arrival times of P- and S-waves, reckoned from the origin time, by t_p and t_s respectively, the $S - P$ time vs. t_p relation can be approximately expressed by a straight line on the $(t_s - t_p) - t_p$ plane. The inclination (k) of the line is given as:

$$k = (t_s - t_p)/t_p \qquad\qquad\qquad [9\text{-}1]$$

If the propagation path for both waves is assumed to be identical, we obtain:

$$V_p t_p = V_s t_s \qquad\qquad\qquad [9\text{-}2]$$

so that we have:

$$k = V_p/V_s - 1 \qquad\qquad\qquad [9\text{-}3]$$

or:

$$V_p/V_s = 1 + k \qquad\qquad\qquad [9\text{-}4]$$

It is therefore seen that the V_p/V_s ratio is readily obtained from k calculated on the basis of travel-time analysis.

9.1.1. Findings in the U.S.S.R.

At a symposium on earthquake prediction in Zürich in 1967, Savarensky (1968) reported on Soviet work on changes in the V_p/V_s ratio preceding a moderately large earthquake. Although a few papers had been published earlier, this was practically the first disclosure of Soviet work of this kind to seismologists in western countries.

Kondratenko and Nersesov (1962) examined travel-time curves of relatively small earthquakes before and after moderately large earthquakes, originating in the region between Garm and Djirgital in Tadjikistan in southern

Central Asia during the period 1958–1961. The data for more than 800 shocks were used for the study. In the statistical travel-time curves of the P-wave passing through the epicentral area, a systematic difference was found between the P-wave travel times before and after the main shocks. The P-wave velocity amounts to 5.3 km/s before strong earthquakes, while it becomes as high as 6.3 km/s after the shocks, so that a 15% increase in the P-wave velocity is associated with seismic events.

If such a change is interpreted in terms of a change in elasticity of the earth's crust, some 30% change must be assumed. It has therefore been hard to believe in such a change in seismic wave velocity unless a very special mechanism of some kind is taken for granted.

In the meantime an English translation of a paper by Semyenov (1969) appeared in the succeeding year. As many examples of the V_p/V_s change prior to an earthquake were described in the paper, earth scientists became inclined to believe in such phenomena. In 1972 Sadovsky et al. (1972) published a paper in a well-distributed journal summarizing the various phenomena preceding a strong earthquake in the Garm region. As the examples of the decrease and recovery of the V_p/V_s ratio were clearly presented, it appeared that most geophysicists began to believe in the Soviet results. After that some more papers related to the topic were published (Nersesov et al., 1973, 1974b; Sadovsky and Nersesov, 1974).

Fig. 9-1 shows examples of the change in velocity ratio V_p/V_s for a few earthquakes as redrawn from illustrations originally given by Semyenov (1969) and presented by Kisslinger (1974). It is observed in the figure that the V_p/V_s ratio which usually fluctuates around its normal value of 1.75 tends to decrease very remarkably some time before an earthquake. The

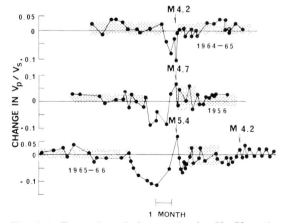

Fig. 9-1. Examples of changes in the V_p/V_s ratio in the Garm region (Semyenov, 1969; Kisslinger, 1974; reproduced from *Physics Today* with the permission of the American Institute of Physics).

drop of the ratio comes to an end after some time perhaps with a small overshoot. An earthquake occurs around that time.

It appears that the larger the magnitude of the impending earthquake is, the longer is the period of the decrease of V_p/V_s. The amplitude of the decrease has nothing to do with the earthquake magnitude. The exact time of earthquake occurrence is not known. It seems likely, however, that the main shock occurs within a time span, which amounts to 10% of the anomaly duration, after the recovery of the ratio.

Although no physical cause of the decrease and rise of V_p/V_s ratio was given by Soviet colleagues, there was little doubt about the importance of the Soviet finding to earthquake prediction.

9.1.2. U.S. work

Investigations into possible premonitory changes in the V_p/V_s ratio similar to the Soviet work were taken up by American seismologists in 1972. The first report along this line came from observations at Blue Mountain Lake, Adirondack Mountains, New York State. Aggarwal et al. (1973) reported that they had found decreases and recoveries of V_p/V_s prior to earthquakes of magnitude 3 or so. Whitcomb et al. (1973), who examined seismograms taken at observatories in California, found a sharp drop of V_p/V_s about 3.5 years before the 1971 San Fernando earthquake ($M = 6.4$). It was also shown that the reduction of the ratio was mostly due to decreases in V_p.

The above findings were followed by many similar investigations in the following years. Kisslinger and Engdahl (1974) reported a 5% decrease in V_p/V_s about 50 days prior to an earthquake of magnitde 3.8 that occurred on Windy Island, Aleutian Islands in 1971. Brown (1973), who analyzed the seismograms for two earthquakes each having a magnitude of 5.0, that occurred in the Chugoku—Kinki district in Japan, an area west of Kyoto on Honshu, found decreases of the ratio 50 and 52 days preceding the shocks.

There are a few reports, however, that no significant changes in the V_p/V_s ratio were observed before a moderately large earthquake. Bakun et al. (1973) showed that premonitory V_p/V_s variations are not apparent for the 1972 earthquakes of magnitude 4—5 that occurred near Bear Valley, south of Hollister on the San Andreas fault. McEvilly and Johnson (1973) also pointed out on the basis of observations of seismic waves from quarry explosions in Central California that the V_p/V_s ratios are fairly constant assuming values around 1.75 over 10 years or so.

Nur et al. (1973) suspected on the basis of these results that no changes in the V_p/V_s ratio might take place in association with earthquakes of the strike-slip type in contrast to those of the thrust-fault type as observed in Garm, Blue Mountain Lake and the Traverse Ranges in southern California. However, Robinson et al. (1974) reported a clear premonitory variation of the P-wave velocity before the Bear Valley earthquake of magnitude 5.0 on

February 24, 1972. It does not seem hopeless, therefore, to apply the method of earthquake prediction to earthquakes on the San Andreas fault which is predominantly of strike-slip type.

Aggarwal et al. (1975) reported on a successful prediction of an earthquake that occurred in the Blue Mountain Lake area. On the basis of an observed drop of the $V_\mathrm{p}/V_\mathrm{s}$ ratio from 1.73 on July 30, 1973, to about 1.5 over the next few days, a prediction was made on August 1 that an earthquake of magnitude 2.5—3 would occur in a few days. An earthquake of magnitude 2.6 in fact occurred on August 3. Upper limits of the magnitude and the time of occurrence of the expected earthquake were inferred from the spatial extent of the seismic anomaly.

9.1.3. Japanese work

In spite of earlier attention to the problem of possible changes in seismic wave velocities forerunning an earthquake (Imamura, 1928; Sassa, 1948; Hayakawa, 1950), no instances of changes in the $V_\mathrm{p}/V_\mathrm{s}$ ratio has been reported from Japan until recently, as Smith (1974) commented in a review on earthquake prediction. He wrote "But it is ironic that, in spite of this success (the successful warnings during the Matsushiro activity*) and in spite of Japan's long-term commitment to earthquake studies, the current wave of prediction stems from a phenomenon to which they gave comparatively little attention."

As soon as Japanese seismologists began to take up the study of changes in seismic wave velocity since 1973, premonitory changes in the $V_\mathrm{p}/V_\mathrm{s}$ ratio were found for a number of earthquakes in the past (Table 15-XIII). Ohtake (1973) reported on decreases in $V_\mathrm{p}/V_\mathrm{s}$ about 360 and 110 days prior to the 1962 North Miyagi ($M = 6.5$) and the 1968 North Nagano ($M = 5.3$) earthquakes. Meanwhile similar effects were found by the Research Group for Microearthquakes, Tohoku University (1974), for the 1964 Niigata ($M = 7.5$) and the 1970 Southeast Akita ($M = 6.2$) earthquakes with precursor times respectively amounting to 3,450 and 730 days. Mizutani et al. (1973), who made use of many shocks of the Matsushiro swarm activity, found that the ratio $V_\mathrm{p}/V_\mathrm{s}$ decreased around the Gifu seismological station in Central Japan about 2 years prior to the 1969 Central Gifu earthquake ($M = 6.6$).

9.1.4. Chinese work

Feng et al. (1974) found that the $V_\mathrm{p}/V_\mathrm{s}$ ratio decreased from 1.73 to 1.63 about 300 days prior to the Sichi earthquake ($M = 5.7$) in Ningsia Province, China, on December 3, 1970. The curve shown in Fig. 9-2 is obtained by

---

* The sentence in the parentheses is added by the present author.

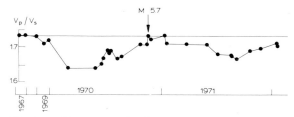

Fig. 9-2. Changes in the V_p/V_s ratio associated with the 1970 Sichi earthquake, Ningsia Province, China (Feng et al., 1974).

averaging the observed results at Sichi and two other neighboring stations within a distance of 60—70 km.

9.2. CHANGES IN SEISMIC WAVE VELOCITIES AND RESIDUAL TIMES

When a high-quality observation is available, it is possible to determine V_p and V_s separately by means of the ordinary techniques of seismometry. Whitcomb et al. (1973) pointed out that changes in the V_p/V_s ratio prior to the 1971 San Fernando earthquake were largely due to changes in V_p. It seems likely that V_p decreased by 20% about 1,100 days prior to the earthquake as shown in Fig. 9-3.

Changes in V_p can usually be detected by two methods; one is to calculate local apparent V_p by dividing the difference in epicentral distance from the station by the difference in arrival time between the stations, while the other relies on teleseismic P-wave delay. For the latter case, the delay or P residual may be obtained in reference either to the arrival time at a nearby standard station or to the travel time for a standard earth model. We may call the former method the V_p anomaly method and the latter the P residual method.

Stewart (1973) found a 20% decrease in V_p 380 days prior to the 1973 Pt. Mugu earthquake ($M = 6.0$), California, by the V_p anomaly method. He

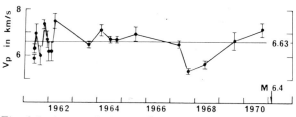

Fig. 9-3. Averaged changes in V_p associated with the 1971 San Fernando earthquake as observed at Pasadena and Riverside in California within a distance of 120 km from the epicenter (Whitcomb et al., 1973, *Science*, Vol. 180, pp. 632—635, fig. 1b. Copyright 1973 by the American Association for the Advancement of Science).

also analyzed teleseismic signals from the South and Middle Americas, Fiji and Kermadec—Tonga, and the Aleutian—Kurile—Japan Islands and found a delay of 1.0 second which seemed likely to have occurred about 180 days preceding the earthquake. This kind of study requires an average of many data.

Kanamori and Chung (1974) paid attention to a P-delay amounting to 0.8 second or thereabouts at Riverside, southern California, as obtained from analyses of seismic waves from nuclear explosions in the Aleutian Islands and deep-focus earthquakes in the Marianas. As no explanation was possible on the basis of the seismic activity in the past, they suggested that the anomaly may have something to do with future activity.

A decrease in V_p by 18% was observed by Feng et al. (1974) about 300 days prior to the 1970 Sichi earthquake ($M = 5.7$) in China.

Whitcomb et al. (1974) indicated that a decrease in V_p had been taking place around Riverside, California, since the middle of 1972. As the anomaly seemed to terminate in the later half of 1973, they suggested in an abstract of a paper read at the 1974 Annual Meeting of American Geophysical Union (AGU) that an earthquake of magnitude 5.5 is expected to occur in the near future. Indeed an earthquake took place there in February 1974, but the magnitude was only 4.1.

In contrast to the examples of earthquakes associated with a V_p anomaly as mentioned above, Allen and Helmberger (1973) and McEvelly and Johnson (1973), who analyzed seismic waves from quarry explosions in California, could not find any V_p anomaly for earthquakes, including the 1968 Borrego Mountain earthquake ($M = 6.4$), in central and southern California. McGarr (1974) showed that a magnitude 3.8 mining tremor in South Africa in March 1973 was not preceded by a V_p anomaly.

Myachkin et al. (1972) reported that they found some change in V_p observed at two stations in Kamchatka. Seismic signals were sent from explosions at sea at a number of shot points located along an extension of the straight line connecting the two stations.

The P-residual method has been extensively applied to various data by M. Wyss and his associates. Wyss and Holcomb (1973) analyzed arrival times of seismic waves from the Aleutian and Tonga earthquakes observed at the Matsushiro Seismological Observatory, Japan. It turned out that a delay amounting to 0.5 second developed about 1.5 years before the 1965—1966 swarm activity for which the cumulative magnitude was estimated as 6.3. The observed P-residual can be accounted for by assuming a 20% decrease in V_p in a source region having a radius of 16 km underneath the Matsushiro area.

Wyss and Johnston (1974) reported on similar increases in the P-residual, each amounting to 0.4 second, approximately 360 and 550 days preceding the 1966 Seddon ($M = 6.1$) and the 1966 Gisborne ($M = 6.2$) earthquakes in New Zealand. Sutton (1974), who independently analyzed data relevant to the Gisborne earthquake, found a 0.5-second increase in the P-residual 480 days prior to the earthquake. Wyss (1974), who analyzed P-residuals at observatories in Central California, concluded that no earthquakes of magnitude 7 would occur within 7 to 8 years' time from 1974 and of magnitude 8 within 20 years' time because no anomalous P-delay has been found at present. He further looked into P-residuals at Garm (Wyss, 1975b), where premonitory effects such as changes in the V_p/V_s ratio, reorientation of compressional axis, changes in electric resistivity and the like had been found, and actually found a 0.4-second increase in the P-delay approximately 440 days prior to an earthquake of magnitude 5.7 in 1969.

The Research Group for Microearthquakes, Tohoku University (1974), reported on a 10-second increase in the P-residual at near distances about 10 years preceding the 1964 Niigata earthquake ($M = 7.5$) in Japan. There is a possibility, however, that the readings of P-waves on the seismograms are not accurate enough (A. Hasegawa, personal communication, 1975). Temporal variations in the P-residual at the Matsushiro Seismological Observatory and the Kamikineusu Microearthquake Observatory were examined by Utsu (1973), from data relevant to underground nuclear explosions in Nevada, U.S.A. The latter observatory is located about 20 km southwest of the epicenter of the Hidaka, Hokkaido, earthquake ($M = 6.7$) of January 20, 1970. No significant changes in the P-delay were found.

9.3. V_s ANISOTROPY

It is known that rocks indicate a velocity anisotropy under nonhydrostatic stresses giving rise to the splitting of S-waves into SV- and SH-waves. Particle motions for these waves are in the vertical and horizontal planes, respectively. The SH-phase usually arrives slightly earlier than the SV-phase.

Gupta (1973a,b) found that $V_{SH} - V_{SV}$ increased by 2.3 and 2.5% about 38 and 10 days prior to two events of magnitudes 4.0 and 3.9 with epicenters in the Slate Mountain (near Fairview Peak) and Mina regions, Nevada, respectively. Such a result seems likely to be caused by anisotropic properties of dilatancy (Gupta, 1973c).

The logarithmic precursor time of changes in seismic wave velocities studied in this chapter seems to be correlated to earthquake magnitude in a linear fashion. The point at which the V_p/V_s ratio and P-residual return to the pre-anomaly level just before the main shock has an important bearing on prediction of the occurrence time of earthquakes and may well provide a deterministic approach to earthquake prediction rather than a probabilistic one.

Chapter 10

GEOMAGNETIC AND GEOELECTRIC EFFECTS

10.1. CLASSICAL OBSERVATIONS OF CHANGES IN THE GEOMAGNETIC FIELD ASSOCIATED WITH AN EARTHQUAKE

In section 2.4 a story was told about a huge horseshoe magnet which lost its attracting power just before the 1855 Edo (now Tokyo) earthquake. According to the present knowledge of geomagnetism, the intensity of the geomagnetic field amounts to only 0.5 gauss or so. Meanwhile even a magnet used for a toy produces a magnetic field amounting to several hundred gauss. It is therefore out of the question to suppose that the geomagnetic field changed to such an extent before the 1855 earthquake to nullify the attracting force of the magnet. Even if the geomagnetic field vanished completely, there should be practically no effect on nails and iron pieces which were attracted to the magnet because the geomagnetic field is very much smaller than that produced by the magnet. The falling of nails and iron pieces from the magnet must therefore be attributed to some other cause.

Extraordinarily large changes in the geomagnetic field were often reported in relation to earthquakes, even from scientific measurements of the geomagnetic field in earlier years. For example, A. von Humboldt (Milne, 1890) reported a large change in the geomagnetic dip angle (the angle between the horizontal plane and a magnetic needle when it is supported in such a way that it can rotate freely around a horizontal axis in the magnetic meridian) associated with a large earthquake in Cumana, Venezuela, that occurred on November 4, 1799. On the basis of measurements of the dip angle on November 1 and 7, he found a change in dip angle amounting to 48 minutes of arc.

Before and after the 1891 Nobi earthquake ($M = 7.9$) in Japan, measurements of the geomagnetic field were made near the epicenter with an apparent earthquake-associated change as large as 920 gammas (Tanakadate and Nagaoka, 1893; Kato, 1939). A gamma is equal to 10^{-5} gauss, while a gauss is the unit intensity of geomagnetic field measured in electromagnetic units (e.m.u.) and is equal to 10^{-4} tesla (T) in SI units which will be widely used in the future.

Changes in the geomagnetic field associated with an earthquake have been pursued by geomagneticians, notably by Kato (1939, 1966) and others in Japan since the 1891 earthquake. In Table 10-I are summarized the reported seismomagnetic effects (changes in the geomagnetic field associated with an earthquake) as found in various articles in the literature. As demonstrated by the author (Rikitake, 1968c) and Johnston et al. (1973), it is interesting to plot the amount of seismomagnetic effect against the years during which the change was obtained. The outstanding feature of such a plot as shown in Fig.

TABLE 10-I

Changes in the geomagnetic field reported to be caused by earthquakes

Earthquake	Year	M	Max. change (gamma)	Component[1]	Reference
Nobi, Japan	1891	7.9	902	H	Kato (1939)
Sakata, Japan	1894	7.3	289	H	Kato (1939)
Rikuu, Japan	1896	7.5	228	F	Kato (1939)
Susaka, Japan	1897	6.3	607	F	Kato (1939)
Hiroshima, Japan	1905	7.6	118	I	Kato (1939)
San Francisco, U.S.A.	1906	8.3	182	I	Kato (1939)
North Izu, Japan	1930	7.0	114	I	Kato (1939)
Sanriku, Japan	1933	8.3	181	I	Kato (1939)
Shizuoka, Japan	1935	6.3	315	I	Kato (1939)
Osaka, Japan	1936	6.4	75	I	Kato (1939)
Nankai, Japan	1946	8.1	35	D	Kato (1966)
Imaichi, Japan	1949	6.4	182	I	Kato (1966)
Tokachi-oki, Japan	1952	8.1	159	I	Kato (1966)
North Miyagi, Japan	1962	6.5	78	I	Kato (1966)
Tanabe, Japan	1962	6.1, 6.4	7	H	Tazima (1968)
Fairview Peak, U.S.A.	1962	2.1	1	F	Breiner (1964)
Niigata, Japan	1964	7.5	48	I	Kato (1966)
Niigata, Japan	1964	7.5	20	H	Fujita (1965)
Alaska, U.S.A.	1964	8.4	100	F	Moore (1964)
Shizuoka, Japan	1965	6.1	5	H	Tazima (1968)
Matsushiro, Japan	1965	5.7[2]	12	Z	Yanagihara (1966)
Ethiopia	1965	4.3	1?	F	Gouin (1965)
Matsushiro, Japan	1966	6.1[2]	7	F	Rikitake et al. (1966a,b,c,d, 1967a,b)
Northwest Turkey	1970	5.3	2	F	Ispir and Uyar (1971)
U.S.S.R.[3]	1970	several	0—8	F	Abdullabekov et al. (1972)
Southeast Akita, Japan	1970	6.2	0	F	Earthquake research Institute (1971)

[1] H, Z, F, D and I denote horizontal intensity, vertical intensity, total intensity, magnetic declination and inclination, respectively.
[2] Cumulative magnitude.
[3] Garm and Tashkent regions.

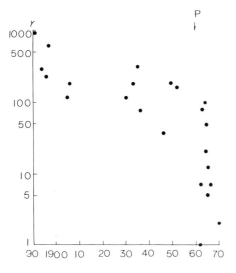

Fig. 10-1. Geomagnetic changes reported that are associated with earthquake occurrences as plotted against the year. *P* denotes the epoch when the proton precession magnetometer was introduced to geomagnetic work.

10-1 is certainly the steep drop of the magnitude of seismomagnetic effect as years advanced.

Most likely, such an apparent decrease in seismomagnetic effect does not witness the existence of a real secular diminution, but it reveals the secular improvements of the field measuring techniques with time. The sharp drop of the plots around 1960 in the figure coincides with the period when use of the proton precession magnetometer became popular. As earlier magnetometers are not as stable as the proton precession magnetometer, as will be explained in the following section, it is possible that earlier results were affected by instrumental drift.

It should also be emphasized that the magnetic survey techniques have very much improved in these two decades. In earlier days no mark was placed at a magnetic station. Many magnetic stations with a monument buried in the ground are now provided, so that it becomes possible to repeat magnetic measurements at exactly the same place.

Very little attention was paid to the influence of temporal geomagnetic variations which also had nothing to do with a seismomagnetic effect in earlier days. Techniques for eliminating noise fields arising from outside the earth and those produced by electric currents induced in the earth by time variations of the former fields have now been developed.

10.2. MODERN MAGNETOMETERS AND PRESENT-DAY MAGNETIC SURVEY

The classical magnetometers are extensively described in any standard text book of geomagnetism (e.g. Chapman and Bartels, 1940). However, it has long been difficult to measure an absolute value of the magnetic field intensity with an accuracy of ±1 gamma because no stable standard for reference had been available. A geomagnetic observation of such high accuracy over a long period could be carried out only at a first-class magnetic observatory.

Packard and Varian (1954) devised a method of measuring the absolute intensity of the geomagnetic field by counting the frequency of free precession of protons in water. The measuring device is called the proton precession magnetometer, and it differs from classical magnetometers in the fact that it relies on an atomistic constant, i.e. the magnetic moment of a proton or hydrogen nucleus. Accordingly, a proton precession magnetometer is free from instrumental drift and is not affected by environmental factors such as temperature, humidity and so on. Introduction of the proton precession magnetometer to monitoring seismomagnetic effects dramatically improved the reliability of observed values.

Optical pumping magnetometers working on the principle of quantum electronics (e.g. Alldredge, 1967) are now available, too. The magnetometer is especially useful for continuous observations of high sensitivity of the geomagnetic field although the reliability of a magnetometer of this class is not as high as that of a proton precession magnetometer.

For monitoring changes in the geomagnetic field by repetition of magnetic survey, it is extremely important to occupy an observation point which is exactly the same as that which was occupied before. In a volcanic area, it is not unusual to observe a geomagnetic field intensity which differs by 1,000 gammas or more from that observed at a point only 1 m apart because of irregular distribution of highly magnetized rocks. In view of this, the GSI, which is responsible for land magnetic surveys in Japan, provided 97 first-order and about 800 second-order magnetic stations all over Japan. A stone monument is buried in the ground in order to indicate the precise location of a magnetic station in a fashion similar to a triangulation station. Care must also be taken for adjusting the height of a tripod on which the sensor of a magnetometer is mounted in such a way that the sensor occupies exactly the same space for each survey.

A local anomalous change such as seismomagnetic effect is customarily detected by comparing an observed value to that at a standard magnetic observatory far away from the earthquake area, e.g. 100 km or more.

10.3. PROBLEMS OF NOISE ELIMINATION

The geomagnetic field always undergoes fluctuations which are not related to earthquakes. First of all, the geomagnetic field is ever changing with a time scale of several tens and hundreds of years. Called the geomagnetic secular variation, such variations in the geomagnetic field are believed to be caused mostly by magnetohydrodynamic processes within the earth's core which occupies the part of the earth at a depth of 2,900 km or more. It is therefore necessary to eliminate geomagnetic variations of this kind in order to pick up a seismomagnetic effect. For that purpose, the geomagnetic field observed at a particular observation point is compared to that at a standard magnetic observatory and corrected by making use of an isoporic magnetic chart on which the distribution of the secular variation as obtained by nationwide magnetic surveys is shown. Even in a narrow country like Japan, the geomagnetic secular variation is not uniform all over the country, so that it is necessary to repeat magnetic surveys every 5 years or so in order to trace the geomagnetic secular variation very accurately.

The next task necessary for detecting a seismomagnetic effect is to eliminate geomagnetic changes arising from outside the earth such as the daily geomagnetic variations and magnetic storms caused by electromagnetic processes in the earth's ionosphere and magnetosphere under the control of solar wind, a plasma stream coming from the sun. If the magnetic field of these variations is uniform over a wide area, the noise field can be eliminated by differencing the simultaneously observed field between a magnetic station and the standard observatory.

In an actual usage, at least in Japan, however, it has been shown that such a simple difference method is not accurate enough for eliminating the noise field to an extent sufficient for picking up a local geomagnetic change with an accuracy of ± 1 gamma. Rikitake (1966b) compared the total intensity values of the geomagnetic field observed at Matsushiro (F_M), where a violent earthquake swarm occurred in 1965—1967, to those simultaneously observed at Kanozan (F_K), the latter observatory, located several tens of kilometers southeast of Tokyo, about 200 km distant from Matsushiro. If it is assumed that fluctuations of the geomagnetic field are the same for both observation points, $F_M - F_K$ should take a constant value for the total period of comparison which is so short that the influence of secular variation can be ignored when no local changes occur. It appeared, however, that $F_M - F_K$ scattered around a mean value with a standard deviation amounting to 3.7 and 2.6 gammas respectively for daytime and nighttime data.

Close examination of the data revealed that changes in F_K are always slightly larger than those in F_M. Accordingly, a weighted difference technique for noise elimination, which makes use of $F_M - cF_K$ instead of $F_M - F_K$ where c is a constant empirically determined, is proposed. However, it seems difficult to make the standard deviation smaller than 2 gammas even if such a technique is introduced.

Stacey and Westcott (1965) compared a set of geomagnetic total intensity data taken by a proton precession magnetometer to that simultaneously observed at a station 25 km distant in England and obtained a standard deviation amounting to 0.85 gamma, a value substantially smaller than the Japanese one.

The reason why a geomagnetic variation field of short period differs markedly from place to place even over a narrow country such as Japan can only be understood by taking into account the magnetic field produced by electric currents, which are induced within the earth by changes in the primary field of external origin. It has now become clear (e.g. Rikitake, 1969c) that there is an anomalous distribution of electric conductivity underneath Japan, so that the induced magnetic field, especially the vertical one, differs from place to place. Such an influence of induced field is demonstrated most clearly by an observation on an island which is surrounded by the highly conducting sea. Rikitake et al. (1968) analyzed a set of 1,440 total intensity data taken by synchronized observations with 1-minute intervals on a certain day at two stations on Oshima Island about 100 km south of Tokyo (see Fig. 5-29). As the stations were located on the west and east coasts of the island, which has a diameter of about 10 km, the distance between the stations amounted to only 7 km. The differences in total intensity between the stations are distributed around a mean value with standard deviations amounting to 1.9 and 5.7 gammas on geomagnetically quiet and disturbed days, respectively. For the disturbed day, the range of scatter was as large as 31 gammas. It is really surprising that local geomagnetic variations are different from one another to such a large extent between two stations whose distance apart amounts to only several kilometers. Such an extremely large anomaly in geomagnetic variation field is certainly caused by induced electric currents flowing around the island. Judging from the above example, it is almost hopeless to look for a local geomagnetic change of the order of a few gammas on an island.

The Japanese national program on earthquake prediction (see subsection 4.2.8) stressed accurate observations of geomagnetic secular variation over Japan by an array of proton precession magnetometers whose distribution is shown in Fig. 4-7. The array also serves to check the natural noise level by comparison of a synchronized observation between each station. Let us denote the total intensity values simultaneously observed at the ith and jth station by F_i and F_j. On the basis of an organized observation in July, 1968, Mori and Yoshino (1970) calculated the differences in total intensity between the ith and jth stations, i.e. $F_i - F_j$, for various combinations of i and j observed every minute for a period during 00.00 and 01.00 local time. The standard deviations of $F_i - F_j$ for various combinations of stations increase with the distance between the stations as can be seen in Fig. 10-2. For a combination of the most distant stations for which the distance amounts to 1,815 km, the standard deviation amounts to 3.0 gammas. For a combination of stations a few hundred kilometers apart, the standard deviation amounts to 2 gammas or so.

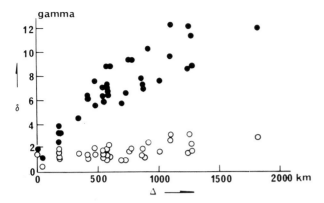

Fig. 10-2. Standard deviations of the statistical distribution of differences in the geomagnetic total intensity value between two stations in Japan as plotted against the distance between them for hourly mean values from 00.00 to 01.00 local time (open circles) and from 09.00 to 10.00 (solid circles) (Mori and Yoshino, 1970).

When similar estimates of standard deviation are made for daytime data between 09.00 and 10.00 local time, the standard deviation becomes very large, exceeding 12 gammas at most, as can also be seen in Fig. 10-2. It should therefore be emphasized that data taken in a midnight period (or at least nighttime data) be used for comparison of the geomagnetic field values. It may be concluded that in Japan a comparison of instantaneous geomagnetic field values with a standard deviation of 1—2 gammas for stations whose distance is smaller than 200 km seems possible, provided midnight data are used. In order to make the accuracy of comparison higher, it would be necessary to have a number of reference stations operating continuously over parts of Japan. It would also be helpful to make observations by means of an array of proton precession magnetometers around an observation point, where the noise level would be lessened by mixing signals from a number of sensors.

It may be that the situation of noise elimination problem is different for other countries. In vast areas like Siberia, China, Canada, the U.S.A. and so on where the underground structure is less complicated than that beneath Japan, comparisons could be made with a much higher accuracy. It is not utterly hopeless, therefore, to detect a seismomagnetic effect in those countries although highly sophisticated techniques would be required for Japan and other countries having a complex underground structure.

In a highly industrialized country like Japan, to make the matter worse, magnetic fields arising from stray electric currents leaking from d.c.-operated railways and other artificial sources tend to mask natural geomagnetic variations. The author is afraid that it is becoming difficult to use the magnetic method to search for earthquake forerunners as industrialization develops.

10.4. SEISMOMAGNETIC EFFECT

10.4.1. Matsushiro earthquakes

Probably the most intensive effort toward monitoring a seismomagnetic effect was made at the time of the Matsushiro earthquake swarm in 1965—1967 (Rikitake et al., 1966a,b,c,d, 1967a,b). On that occasion six proton precession magnetometers were set up over an area having a 20-km width and a 50-km length covering the earthquake area as shown in Fig. 5-55. Fig. 10-3 shows the changes in the difference in 5-day means of the total intensity value between Matsushiro (F_M) and Kanozan (F_K) for 1965—1970 although there was an interruption of about 3 years. Around August and September in 1966, an increase in $F_M - F_K$ amounting to 10 gammas or so is observed in the figure. This period coincides with one of the most active periods of swarm activity associated with enormous land uplift and water exudation. Judging from the accuracy of observation as discussed in the last section, the change in Fig. 10-3 must have actually taken place. When the increase in F_M relative to F_K reached its maximum, a decrease in total intensity amounting to 5 gammas or thereabout was observed at another station about 6 km north of the Matsushiro observation point. It may be that the crustal magnetization around the Matsushiro area slightly increased at that time although nothing definite was known about the cause of the geomagnetic changes.

The holder of the magnetometer sensor had been left there for about

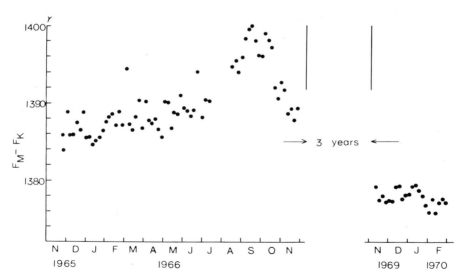

Fig. 10-3. Changes in 5-day means of $F_M - F_K$ during 1965—1970 (Yamazaki and Rikitake, 1970).

3 years, and an observation was resumed when an experiment of injecting water in a borehole having a depth of 1,800 m was undertaken in 1970 (Yamazaki and Rikitake, 1970). The aim of the experiment was to see whether there would be any increase in seismicity in association with water injection in a borehole drilled in the central area of the swarm activity a few years before (see section 16.2). Although no marked changes in the geomagnetic field were observed in relation to the experiment, it was ascertained that an anomalous decrease in total intensity of the geomagnetic field amounting to some 10 gammas relative to Kanozan Observatory had taken place during the period of 3 years.

10.4.2. Southeast Akita earthquake

An earthquake of magnitude 6.2 occurred in the southeast corner of Akita Prefecture, North Honshu, Japan on October 16, 1970. It happened that a magnetic survey by a portable proton magnetometer had been carried out over the earthquake area on September 7—9 (Earthquake Research Institute, 1971). As this provided a good opportunity for checking possible seismomagnetic effects, a resurvey was immediately made on October 19—21. The survey data were corrected referring to the observations at the Mizusawa Geodetic Observatory about 50 km southeast of the epicenter. The differences in total intensity value between the two surveys were found to be so small at all the stations, however, that no significant effect exceeding the overall accuracy of observation could be found. At the station closest to the epicenter, the difference amounted to only 0.2 gammas, the epicentral distance being about 10 km. It was thus concluded that no marked seismomagnetic effect was associated with the earthquake.

10.4.3. Work related to the faults in California

An array of optical-pumping rubidium magnetometers for detecting local changes in the geomagnetic field was set up by Breiner (1967) on the San Andreas fault notably over the Hollister area, California. It was reported that a geomagnetic change of the order of a few gammas or a little less seemed likely to be associated with the intermittent creep motion of the fault.

Johnston et al. (1973) set up magnetic stations amounting to 70 in number along the San Andreas and Sierra faults (see Fig. 5-17) with 10—15 km intervals. Differences in total intensity between neighboring stations were observed by a differential proton precession magnetometer synchronized by radio signals. Taking an average of 75 measurements, the standard deviation was estimated as 0.5 gammas. At a certain station, the total intensity of the geomagnetic field seems to be always decreasing amounting to 3 gammas during a period of 9 months. It seems likely that many earthquakes of mag-

nitude 3—4 are occurring around stations where large changes in the geomagnetic field intensity were found.

Johnston (1974) recently reported that a geomagnetic change amounting
to about 4 gammas was found in association with earthquakes of magnitudes
3.8 and 4.2 that occurred near the Garlock fault (see Fig. 5-17) in June,
1974. As a survey had been conducted over the epicentral area in May, it was
certain that the change occurred within one month's time. A few more
examples of a similar kind were also reported by him.

Seismomagnetic effects are also reported from other parts of the U.S.A.
(Moore, 1964; Breiner, 1964), Ethiopia (Gouin, 1965), Turkey (Ispir and
Uyar, 1971) and the U.S.S.R. (Abdullabekov et al., 1972) in recent years as
can be seen in Table 10-I.

10.5. GEOMAGNETIC CHANGES ASSOCIATED WITH WATER IMPOUNDED IN A MAN-MADE LAKE AND EXPLOSION

As a seismomagnetic effect seems likely to be caused by stress-induced
changes in the magnetization of rocks composing the earth's crust (see section 10.6), either impounding of water in a large man-made lake or detonation of conventional and/or nuclear explosives would be capable of producing some magnetic effects.

When a reservoir formed by the Talbingo Dam (35.6°S, 148.3°E) in the
Snowy Mountains, Australia, was filled, systematic magnetic surveys with a
proton precession magnetometer were conducted at fifteen magnetic stations
around the reservoir having a length and width respectively amounting to 3
and 1 km. The maximum depth was 150 m (Davis and Stacey, 1972). As a
result of a comparison of the data to the geomagnetic total intensity values
at a fixed station 3.5 km north of the dam wall, it was made clear that
decreases in total intensity of the geomagnetic field amounting to 2—8 gammas occurred at the magnetic stations in connection with the filling.

An underground nuclear explosion equivalent to that of TNT explosives
amounting to 5×10^6 tons was made on Amchitka Island, Aleutian Islands,
on November 6, 1971 (Hasbrouck and Allen, 1972). Among many geophysical observations in relation to the explosion which was called the CANNI-
KIN experiment, it was shown that the magnetic field at a point several
kilometers distant from the epicenter changed permanently. Within 30 seconds after the detonation, a proton magnetometer placed at an epicentral
distance of 3 km recorded a stepwise increase of 9 gammas. A magnetic
survey made over the shot-point area revealed that a change in the geomagnetic total intensity amounting to the order of 10 gammas took place there.

It was reported (Abdullabekov et al., 1972) that a blast at Medeo in
Kazakhstan, U.S.S.R., gave rise to an increase in the geomagnetic total intensity of 9 gammas at a station 0.7 km distant from the shot point. Unlike the

CANNIKIN blast, the change decreased to the pre-explosion level within a few hours.

According to an experiment over a magnetite ore (Undzendov and Shapiro, 1967), an irreversible change in the geomagnetic field of the order of 10 gammas, which is induced by gunpowder explosions near the ore, was observed.

When an underground chamber of natural gas near Tashkent, U.S.S.R., was filled with gas at a pressure of 30 atmospheres, a change in the geomagnetic total intensity amounting to 20 gammas was observed along a distance of a few kilometers over the chamber (Abdullabekov et al., 1972).

10.6. PRECURSORY GEOMAGNETIC CHANGE

10.6.1. Japanese examples

Whereas much stress is nowadays put on monitoring changes in the geomagnetic total intensity by proton precession magnetometers, it is also important to know the changes in the three components of the geomagnetic field in order to maintain accurate knowledge about the geomagnetic field over a country. Repetition of magnetic surveys for the three components by the GSI over Japan sometimes disclosed anomalous geomagnetic changes.

Fig. 10-4 shows the secular variation of horizontal intensity of the geomagnetic field at Tanabe and neighboring first-order magnetic stations in Kii Peninsula (see Fig. 5-14), Central Japan, as disclosed by first-order magnetic surveys (Tazima, 1968). The accuracy of measurement by the GSI-type magnetometer used for the first-order magnetic survey has been estimated as ±0.1 minute of arc for measuring the magnetic declination (the angle between the true north and the magnetic meridian) and dip angles, and ±1 gamma for measuring the intensities. However, the overall accuracy after

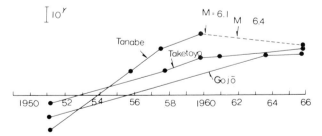

Fig. 10-4. Anomalously large secular variation in the geomagnetic horizontal intensity at Tanabe on Kii Peninsula, Central Japan. The changes at neighboring stations, a few tens of kilometers distant from Tanabe, are also shown. Occurrences of the two earthquakes in the vicinity of Tanabe are indicated in the figure along with their magnitudes (Tazima, 1968).

performing epoch reduction and noise elimination becomes ±0.3 minute of arc for angular observations and ±4 gammas for intensity observations (Tazima, 1968).

Even if we take the overall accuracy of the survey into consideration, it is apparent that the change in horizontal intensity at Tanabe was anomalous compared to those at neighboring stations which are several tens of kilometers distant from Tanabe. It is interesting to note that the anomalous change seemed to vanish after the earthquakes of magnitudes 6.1 and 6.4 that occurred near Tanabe respectively in 1960 and 1961. An anomalously large rate of secular variation in horizontal intensity as observed at Tanabe in the 1950s might be a precursory change in the geomagnetic field.

Fujita (1965) reported on an anomalous change in the geomagnetic field amounting to 15—20 gammas that occurred around Niigata, Japan, during a 10-year period preceding the 1964 Niigata earthquake ($M = 7.5$; see subsection 5.7.3). It is remarkable that the anomalous change seems likely to be almost compensated by a change following the earthquake within a 1-year period.

It is somewhat ironic that, despite a long history of pursuing premonitory geomagnetic effects relevant to an earthquake in Japan, only the two examples as stated above seem to be reliable.

10.6.2. U.S. examples

Probably the most reliable geomagnetic precursor so far reported would be the one that occurred about 2 months prior to the Thanksgiving Day earthquake ($M = 5.3$) near Hollister, California, on November 28, 1974 (Smith et al., 1974; Johnston, 1974). The NCER has been operating a proton precession magnetometer array of seven stations along an 80-km section of the San Andreas fault near Hollister. In the beginning of October, 1974, an increase of 2 gammas was observed at a station several kilometers south of Hollister. The change lasted for some time, and the geomagnetic field recovered its previous level in the beginning of November. On November 6, a tilt step amounting to 5 microradians was observed by a tiltmeter installed in a borehole nearby. The tiltmeter was already recording a tilt in an anomalous direction which started about the middle of October. An anomalous change in the rate of creep motion of the San Andreas fault as well as a P-delay of 0.3 second were also recognized prior to the earthquake. The epicentral distance from the magnetometer site was 10 km.

A search for a geomagnetic precursor was made by Wyss (1975a) in relation to the 1972 earthquake ($M = 7.1$) off Sitka, Alaska. He found a decrease in the horizontal intensity of the geomagnetic field of 20 gammas starting 7.5 years before the earthquake and returning to normal during the year after the event. The anomaly was discussed in reference to the observations at College, Alaska, and Victoria, British Columbia, both observatories at a distance of 1,200 km or so from Sitka. The epicenter was located at a distance of 200 km from Sitka.

10.6.3. Chinese examples

Much stress seems likely to be put on searching possible geomagnetic precursors in the People's Republic of China. Coe (1971; see section 4.6) reported that the difference in the vertical intensity between Peking and Hongshan near Hsingtai sometimes decreased by 2 gammas 4—5 days before an earthquake of magnitude 3 or larger near Hongshan. The decrease appears to recover 2 days prior to the earthquake. The distance between the two observation points is about 300 km. No more details about the Chinese work on precursory geomagnetic changes are known by the author at this stage.

10.6.4. Soviet examples

Efforts toward searching for precursory geomagnetic changes have been made in the Garm and Tashkent areas, U.S.S.R. Skovorodkin et al. (1973) reported on an anomalous decrease in the geomagnetic total intensity of 15 gammas on July 24, 1967, starting 4 hours preceding an earthquake of $K = 7$ (see Table 8-I) in the Garm region. The epicentral distance was 24 km. The geomagnetic field recovered to a normal level several hours after the shock. The change was observed in reference to two fixed stations at Garm and Chusal which are several tens of kilometers away from the observation point. There are some other reports on geomagnetic precursors from the U.S.S.R. although the author cannot follow their details.

10.7. THEORY OF TECTONOMAGNETISM

10.7.1. Piezo-remanent magnetism

Rocks composing the earth's crust are more or less magnetic. Magnetization of rocks generally consists of two parts, i.e. magnetic induction and remanent magnetization. On defining a magnetic susceptibility by χ, the magnetic induction of a rock specimen in a magnetic field having an intensity F_0 is given by χF_0. The natural remanent magnetization (NRM) can be formed by various processes. One of the most common processes is cooling of volcanic rocks, as is the case for molten lavas, from a temperature as high as several hundred degrees centigrade. In that case the rock acquires a highly stable magnetization called the thermoremanent magnetization (TRM). NRM is larger than magnetic induction for most volcanic rocks.

According to the recent results of a uniaxial compression experiment on a rock specimen (e.g. Nagata and Kinoshita, 1965; Nagata, 1970), susceptibility χ in a direction of compression σ is given by:

$$\chi = \chi_0 /(1 + \beta\sigma) \hspace{6cm} [10\text{-}1]$$

in which χ_0 is the susceptibility at zero pressure. β is a positive constant of the order of 10^{-4}/bar. It is therefore seen that the magnetization in the direction of compression decreases. On the contrary the magnetization in a direction perpendicular to that of the compression increases.

Pressure effect on a remanent magnetization such as TRM seems likely to be expressed by an equation similar to [10-1] with a β of the same order of magnitude (e.g. Ohnaka and Kinoshita, 1968; Nagata, 1970). The magnetization that is acquired by a rock under the influence of pressure is called the piezo-remanent magnetization (PRM) although it is beyond the scope of this book to deal with its physical mechanism.

Nagata (1969) presented a review on the geomagnetic changes possibly caused by pressure effects in the earth's crust with a physical interpretation based on experiments on PRM. It can by now be said that a subfield of geophysics called "tectonomagnetism" as named by Nagata (1969) has been established.

10.7.2. Interpretation of seismomagnetic effect

Let us suppose that the magnetization of an underground spherical volume having a radius r undergoes a change ΔJ due to a pressure effect. If it is assumed that the volume is magnetized in a vertical direction, the change in the magnetic field in the same direction immediately on top of the spherical volume is given by:

$$\Delta H = 2\Delta M/r^3 \hspace{6cm} [10\text{-}2]$$

where ΔM is the change in the magnetic moment of a dipole that represents the magnetization of the sphere as a whole and is given by:

$$\Delta M = (4/3)\pi r^3 \,\Delta J \hspace{6cm} [10\text{-}3]$$

so that we have:

$$\Delta H = 2(4/3)\pi\Delta J \hspace{6cm} [10\text{-}4]$$
$$\doteqdot 8\Delta J$$

When the magnetization of rock is assumed as 10^{-3} e.m.u./cm^3, a typical value for an andesitic rock, the rate of change in magnetization due to pressure given as 10^{-4}/bar and the pressure as 100 bars, the change in magnetization becomes:

$$\Delta J = (10^{-3} \times 10^{-4} \times 10^2) = 10^{-5} \text{ e.m.u.} \hspace{4cm} [10\text{-}5]$$

We therefore obtain from [10-4] that:

$$\Delta H \doteq 8 \text{ gammas} \tag{10-6}$$

The simple order-of-magnitude estimation in the above tells us that a possible magnetic change related to an earthquake would be of the order of 10 gammas. The magnetization for a basaltic rock may be several to ten times as large as the present value adopted. However, the stress value assumed here may be larger by a certain factor than that for most earthquakes. It does not seem likely, therefore, that a seismomagnetic effect is much larger than the order of 10 gammas.

It is possible to estimate the magnetic changes to be associated with a more realistic model of seismic source. Stacey (1963, 1964) estimated magnetic changes associated with a strike-slip fault. Yukutake and Tachinaka (1967) estimated similar changes caused by an underground cylindrical volume subjected to a hydrostatic pressure from inside. This study may possibly be applied to magnetic changes caused by a local dilatancy. All these models resulted in magnetic changes of which the maximum value is more or less the same as that derived by a simple calculation in this subsection. Shamsi and Stacey (1969) presented a similar study on the 1906 San Francisco and the 1964 Alaska earthquakes.

On the basis of what has recently been observed and also the model estimates, it is concluded that a seismomagnetic effect, if any, would be of the order of 10 gammas, and a precursory change may well be a little smaller. Much care should be taken in eliminating the noise to these effects as was discussed in section 10.3 in order to acquire a real magnetic effect associated with an earthquake.

10.8 ANOMALOUS CHANGES IN EARTH CURRENTS

Many examples of anomalous changes in earth currents preceding or accompanying an earthquake have been reported in the classical literature (e.g. Milne, 1890; Yoshimatsu, 1957). Earth currents or telluric currents are always flowing in the earth's crust, and most of their fluctuations are caused by electromagnetic induction in the earth by temporal geomagnetic variations of primarily external origin. It is therefore difficult to correlate fluctuations in earth currents to an earthquake occurrence because those induced currents cannot be completely eliminated.

Nevertheless there were many instances for which observers claimed that they had detected earthquake-associated earth-current signals. The author had a number of experiences of observing earth currents over an earthquake area mostly in relation to aftershock activity of a large earthquake, but he has never observed anomalous changes in earth currents associated with an earthquake except a coseismic change on the occasion of a magnitude 5.0 shock in the Matsushiro area on November 23, 1965 (Rikitake et al., 1966a). Not that the author does not believe in classical reports, therefore, it cannot be helped that he feels pessimistic about earthquake-correlated earth currents of anomalous character.

There are a number of reports, however, that may appear reliable. Anomalous earth-current changes as reported by Hatai et al. (1932; see subsection 2.1.1) in connection with catfish behavior and those reported by Nagata (1944) on the occasion of aftershock observation of the 1943 Tottori earthquake (see subsection 5.3.4) doubtless induce us to believe in precursory earth-current signals preceding earthquakes. Only these reports are somewhat fragmentary, so to speak, so that we really could not say when, where and under what conditions such signals are observed.

It appears to the author that much effort has recently been made toward monitoring anomalous earth-current changes forerunning earthquakes in Kamchatka notably by Sobolev and his colleagues (Fedotov et al., 1970; Sobolev and Morozov, 1972; Sobolev, 1974). Although they reported a number of anomalous earth-current changes, their precursory behaviors are not quite clear. Precursor times of anomalous earth-current signals do not seem to fit those of any other elements as can be seen in subsections 15.5.1 and 15.5.2.

Coe (1971) reported on Chinese earth-current measurements. They monitored small changes in the electric field of 2 mV/km about 5 hours before an earthquake of magnitude 3 near Hsingtai. Despite Coe's report, it is regrettable that no detailed results of earth-current observation in China have been accessible to the author.

Earth-current observation is now becoming very difficult to carry out in an industrialized country like Japan because of stray electric currents from d.c.-operated railways, factories and so on. It would seem that earthquake prediction based on earth-current observation is going to become increasingly difficult, at least in industrialized areas.

10.9. CHANGES IN EARTH RESISTIVITY

Whereas earth-current signals of precursory character are still not quite clear in spite of observations over many years, it appears that precursory and coseismic changes in earth resistivity seem to be brought out very clearly in some cases in the U.S.S.R., Japan, the U.S.A. and China. This is probably because of the fact that a powerful filtration technique against natural and artificial noise can be applied to resistivity measurement while no such technique is utilized for the measurement of earth currents.

10.9.1. Soviet observation

Intensive observations of changes in earth resistivity have been conducted in the Garm region, U.S.S.R. (Barsukov, 1972, 1973, 1974; Al'tgauzen and Barsukov, 1972; Barsukov and Sorokin, 1973; Barsukov et al., 1974). Electric pulses of about 100 amperes are sent into the ground, and the electric fields excited by the pulses are picked up at an observation point 6 km distant from the source. The changes in the electric field are thus made proportional to those in earth resistivity.

As can be seen in Fig. 10-5, the resistivity observed fluctuates in a wide range. It is apparent from the figure that the resistivity decreases by 10—15% prior to moderately large earthquakes. The larger the magnitude of an impending earthquake is, the longer is the precursor time for these changes.

Although the reason why such large changes in earth resistivity forerun earthquakes is not well understood, it seems likely that those changes have something to do with those revealed by laboratory experiments on rock specimens saturated with water. Brace et al. (1965) and Brace and Orange (1966, 1968a,b) showed that the resistivity of a water-saturated granite specimen increases by a factor of 1,000 or so under a hydrostatic pressure of 10 kbars. This is interpreted to be caused by closure of the conducting paths due to pores filled with water. When a stress is further applied to the specimen under the confining pressure, a sudden decrease in resistivity begins at a stress, which is equal to $\frac{1}{3}-\frac{2}{3}$ of that for rupture. The resistivity seems likely to become only one-half or so immediately before rupture. Brace and others claimed that such a decrease in resistivity is caused by generation of new microcracks due to the stress, so that paths of electric conduction are formed anew (see subsections 13.2.1 and 13.2.3). It is thus surmised that precursory resistivity change is closely connected with dilatancy (Chapter 14).

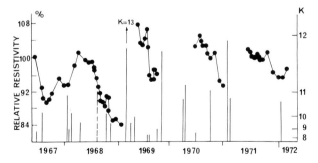

Fig. 10-5. Secular changes in electric resistivity in the Garm region and occurrences of local earthquakes (Barsukov, 1974).

10.9.2. U.S. observation

Since around 1972, observations of changes in earth resistivity have commenced by a number of U.S. institutes near Hollister, California, on the San Andreas fault.

Bufe et al. (1973) reported on stepwise changes that occur associated with strain steps which are caused by moderately large earthquakes occurring nearby. They pointed out that the rate of resistivity change is as large as 10^4 times or more than the strain observed.

Mazzella and Morrison (1974) reported on decreases in earth resistivity by 10—20% 60 and 30 days preceding earthquakes of magnitudes 3.9 and 3.5 (cumulative value for a swarm) which occurred on June 22 and October 8—13, 1973, respectively. It seems likely, therefore, that precursory changes in resistivity do sometimes take place on the San Andreas fault as is the case in the Garm area.

10.9.3. Chinese observation

A fantastic report of premonitory changes in earth resistivity came from the People's Republic of China (Geoelectric Division, Lanchou Seismology Brigade, 1974). It appears that monitoring of changes in resistivity forerunning an earthquake is becoming very popular in China. For example, a

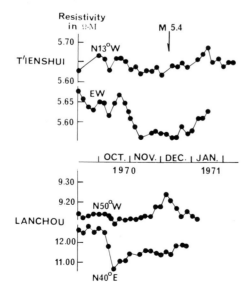

Fig. 10-6. Changes in electric resistivity for two directions as noted in the figure at T'ienshui and Lanchou in association with the 1970 Sichi earthquake. As for locations of stations, see text (Geoelectric Division, Lanchou Seismology Brigade, 1974).

marked decrease in resistivity of 14% was observed at T'ienshui, Kansu Province, 40 days preceding an earthquake of magnitude 5.4* occurred at Sichi, Ningsia Province on December 3, 1970. The observation point is about 140 km south of the epicenter. The resistivity anomaly lasted 80 days or a little longer. On the same occasion a similar change in resistivity amounting to 16% as shown in Fig. 10-6 was observed at Lanchou, Kansu Province, about 150 km west of the epicenter, about 60 days prior to the earthquake.

More than 30 examples of resistivity change of this character have been reported in connection with earthquakes having magnitudes ranging from 3.8 to 7.9. It sounds almost incredible that a resistivity change is observed at a point as distant as 800 km or more from the epicenter of an earthquake of magnitude 7.9 which occurred at Luho (31.4°N, 100.6°E), Szechwan Province, on February 6, 1973. Unlike the Soviet and American examples, the Chinese premonitory changes in resistivity sometimes exhibit an increase. Believe the Chinese examples or not, it seems likely that the precursor times of these resistivity changes increase as the magnitude of an impending earthquake becomes large in a manner concordant with an empirical law for earthquake precursors suggested by Scholz et al. (1973) and others.

10.9.4. Japanese observation

At the suggestion of the author, I. Yokoyama (1952, unpublished) observed time variations in earth resistivity at the Aburatsubo Crustal Movement Observatory, 60 km south of Tokyo, and found that the resistivity changes in accordance with the crustal extension and contraction due to oceanic tidal load. It was pointed out that the rate of change in resistivity is 300 times larger than the mechanical strain, which is of the order of 10^{-6} for tidal deformation. It was difficult, however, to develop the study to a much more advanced degree because of underdeveloped electronics at that time.

From 1965 on, intensive studies of in-situ measurements as well as laboratory experiments on the resistivity of rocks at Aburatsubo was resumed by the ERI (Yamazaki, 1965, 1966, 1967, 1968, 1974; Rikitake and Yamazaki, 1967, 1969, 1970). Yamazaki (1967, 1968) constructed an unusually sensitive variometer for measuring the changes in resistivity. The principle of the variometer is essentially the same as that of the four-pole method which is widely used for geophysical prospecting of underground electrical structures.

An a.c. electric current of 67 Hz is sent into the ground from a pair of electrodes, the intensity of the current being usually 100 mA. Between these two electrodes, there are two inner electrodes buried in the ground; the

---

* In Feng et al. (1974), the magnitude of this earthquake was reported as 5.7 (see subsection 9.1.4).

distance between these electrodes arranged along a straight line is 1.6 m for the present variometer.

Denoting the distance between the electrodes by a, the resistivity ρ is then given by:

$$\rho = 2\pi a V/I \qquad\qquad\qquad\qquad [10\text{-}7]$$

where V and I are the voltage between the inner two electrodes and the intensity of electric current sent into the ground, respectively. It is designed to cancel V for this particular measuring system by a voltage taken from the source generator through a transformer. In practice a variable resistor is driven by a servo-motor in such a way as to keep the system in balance all the time, i.e. V is always cancelled by the voltage through the transformer. For that purpose a small deviation ΔV from an equilibrium state is amplified and supplied to the servo-motor which works on the principle of phase detection. A filter having an extremely narrow band is used, otherwise noise from the commercial power line of 50 Hz and other artificial origins is enormous even though an odd frequency such as 67 Hz is used for the source.

Rotations of the servo-motor are converted into voltage changes which are recorded by a recorder of multi-channel plotting. Usually, the resistivity change is recorded by high- and low-sensitivity channels. It appears that a change in resistivity of the order of 10^{-4} with an amplitude of 1 cm or so, can be stably recorded on the recording paper.

The resistivity variometer usually records changes accompanied by extension and contraction of the ground due to the tidal loading in the sea nearby. A crustal deformation of this kind amounting to 10^{-6} in strain is now observed in terms of a resistivity change with a rate of 10^{-4} multiplied by a factor. It is therefore concluded that some sort of amplification mechanism for monitoring earth strain must be working in the formation where the electrodes are buried.

The ground, where the variometer is set up, is composed of lapilli tuff, a highly porous and permeable rock. Compression tests of rock specimens taken from there made it clear that the rate of resistivity change $\Delta\rho/\rho$ is much larger than the linear strain $\Delta L/L$. The $(\Delta\rho/\rho)/(\Delta L/L)$ value amounts to 300 or thereabouts for a strain of the order of 10^{-6}, which is compatible with the results of in-situ tidal observation. It seems also likely that the $(\Delta\rho/\rho)/(\Delta L/L)$ value further increases for smaller strains although no experimental proof in a laboratory is possible because of the limited sensitivity of strain-gauges available. The reason why the rock reveals such a behavior is not known. There must be a particular mechanism of electric conduction probably through many pores filled with water. It is speculated that the contact area between neighboring pores would be considerably increased by compression. Such a mechanism might be responsible for the rather peculiar dependence of resistivity on strain.

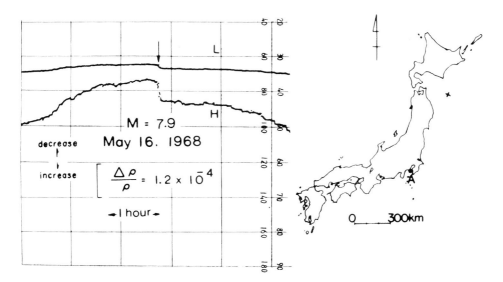

Fig. 10-7. Resistivity step at the time of the Tokachi-oki earthquake (M = 7.9) as recorded by high (H) and low (L) sensitivity channels. The observation point (A) and epicenter are indicated on the map with a small circle and a cross, respectively (Rikitake and Yamazaki, 1970).

The variometer happened to record quite unexpectedly a stepwise change at the time of the Tokachi-oki earthquake (M = 7.9) that occurred on May 16, 1968, at an epicentral distance amounting to more than 700 km. After that similar steps in resistivity have been recorded by the variometer whenever comparatively large earthquakes occur in and around Japan.

Fig. 10-7 shows the change in resistivity at the time of the Tokachi-oki earthquake. The step is not quite instantaneous. As changes in resistivity are recorded by a multi-channel recorder having a plotting interval of 30 seconds, it is seen from the figure that the time, which is hereafter called the rise-time, required for the step to be completed exceeds a few minutes.

About 30 examples of resistivity step have been observed during an observation period of several years. Even an earthquake of magnitude 7.8 that occurred off East Hokkaido at a distance exceeding 1,000 km gave rise to a step. A few deep-focus earthquakes having a focal depth of 300—500 km also caused steps. Meanwhile, steps were also observed for earthquakes of which the magnitude is smaller than 5, provided the shocks occurred underneath the Tokyo area.

It is possible to convert a step into $(\text{step})_{100\,\text{km}}$, a hypothetical step that should have been observed at an epicentral distance (Δ) of 100 km on the assumption that the step decreases proportionally to $\Delta^{-3/2}$ as was proposed for strain steps by Wideman and Major (1967; see section 7.5). It is striking that $\log_{10}(\text{step})_{100 \text{km}}$ thus obtained for each step is very well correlated linearly with earthquake magnitude.

It now appears that these resistivity steps are nothing but strain steps which are picked up by an unusually highly sensitive device. Comparing the observed steps to what is expected from the dislocation theory (Yamazaki, 1974), it is concluded that the magnification factor or $(\Delta\rho/\rho)/(\Delta L/L)$ value amounts to 10^4 or thereabouts for strains of the order of 10^{-9}.

It is interesting to see the limit of detectability of the resistivity step on an $M-\log_{10}\Delta$ plane. It is found that earthquakes plotted on the upper half of the plane bounded by the straight line:

$$M = -12.5 + 2.5 \log_{10}\Delta \qquad\qquad [10\text{-}8]$$

where Δ is measured in units of centimeters, seem likely to give rise to an observable resistivity step at Aburatsubo. The line as indicated by [10-8] roughly agrees with those along which strain steps of the order of 10^{-8} to 10^{-9} should be observed (Wideman and Major, 1967), so that it may be concluded that the resistivity variometer can detect a strain change of the order of 10^{-9} or thereabouts.

The rise-time of a step or the time required for completing a resistivity step seems to increase for earthquakes of larger magnitude. It is speculated that the larger the energy released by an earthquake is, the longer becomes the time needed for completing such a release.

It is of particular interest to look closely at the resistivity step as shown in Fig. 10-7. One can clearly see that a change in resistivity started a few hours prior to the step. There are a number of examples of precursory changes of this character. Yamazaki (1975) applied a numerical high-pass filter to the records observed, and he could show very clearly that these precursors start a few hours preceding an earthquake (see Table 15-XIII).

Although the nature of resistivity precursors thus detected is not entirely clear at the present stage of investigation, it appears that the precursor time seems to have nothing to do with earthquake magnitude. It may well be that these resistivity precursors reflect a creep-like rupture immediately before a main rupture in the earth's crust. Resistivity precursors of this character may have an important bearing on short-range earthquake prediction.

A resistivity measurement was made by Kawada (1966) over the epicentral area of the 1965—1967 Matsushiro earthquake swarm. Because of much rainfall, no reliable change in resistivity which is closely correlated with the earthquake activity was found although some anomalous decrease seemed likely to be monitored preceding marked seismic activities.

10.10. CHANGES IN GEOMAGNETIC VARIATION ANOMALY

It has been observed at the Kakioka Magnetic Observatory, a standard magnetic observatory in Japan located at a distance of 60 km north of

Tokyo, that the ratio of the vertical field (ΔZ) to the horizontal one (ΔH), $\Delta Z/\Delta H$, for geomagnetic bays, sudden storm commencement and similar variations seems to undergo a secular variation (Yanagihara, 1972a,b). $\Delta Z/\Delta H$ assumed a value of about 0.65 in the early 1900s decreasing to a value amounting to 0.50 or so around 1920. After that it increased steeply reaching 0.75 or thereabouts around 1940. A steady decrease seems to have continued since then, arriving at a value of 0.65 or so in 1975. It is interesting to note that the great Kanto earthquake ($M = 7.9$; see section 3.3) occurred to the southwest of Tokyo in 1923 when the $\Delta Z/\Delta H$ ratio reached its minimum value.

The reason why the $\Delta Z/\Delta H$ ratio at Kakioka undergoes such a secular change is not known. Yanagihara (1972a,b) suggested, however, that some change in the slope of the underground conductor's surface of the Rikitake model (Rikitake, 1969c; see section 10.3), which accounts for the geomagnetic variation anomaly as observed not only at Kakioka but also in Central Japan on the basis of a depression of the surface of a highly conducting layer in the mantle, might be able to explain the secular change in question although no immediately acceptable cause of such a large-scale change in the configuration of the underground conductor is available.

Whether the suggestion is true or not, it is of interest to study to what extent local geomagnetic variations of short period will be modified by a change in conductivity in an underground volume. The current theory of dilatancy (e.g. Scholz et al., 1973; see Chapter 14) claims a change in the electrical conductivity in the focal zone of a forthcoming earthquake. Changes in earth resistivity amounting to a few tens of percent have in fact been observed in the U.S.S.R., the U.S.A. and China as presented in the last section.

Hughes (1973, 1974a,b) showed that geomagnetic micropulsations could be largely modified by a local conductivity anomaly on the basis of his study on electromagnetic induction by an external field expressed by a plane wave. Although no actual observation of the modification of geomagnetic variation anomaly has as yet been reported except the one from Kakioka, it would be worthwhile to check such an effect in connection with earthquake occurrence. The situation is much the same as that for earth-tide tilts and strains to be modified by local dilatancy (Beaumont and Berger, 1974; see section 7.8). Rikitake (1975d) studied electromagnetic induction in a conducting volume embedded in a less-conducting medium. As an enhancement of the horizontal component of short-period geomagnetic variations by a factor of 3 or so takes place in conceivable cases, it may well be possible to monitor an underground dilatant zone by observing the short-period geomagnetic variations.

Miyakoshi (1975) also showed that the geomagnetic variation anomaly in Tashkent underwent a secular change which seems likely to have something to do with the 1966 earthquake there.

Chapter 11

ACTIVE FAULTS AND FOLDING

11.1. CREEP OF FAULT

11.1.1. San Andreas fault

It has been known that portions of the San Andreas fault and its branches such as the Hayward and Calaveras faults are continually creeping without accompanying large earthquakes (e.g. Steinbrugge and Zacher, 1960; see subsections 5.4.4 and 8.2.3; also see Figs. 5-17 and 5-39). Several years after its construction, a winery building built in the early 1950s near Hollister, some 150 km south of San Francisco, suffered from cracks that broke its walls and floors. The crack generation appeared to continue further although the walls and floors had been mended. It has finally turned out that the building is built directly on the San Andreas fault, which undergoes a right-lateral creep movement with a speed of a few centimeters per year. This is the reason why the winery building is damaged.

Fig. 11-1 shows the crack, that is seen at a ditch outside the winery building. The crack was formed within a period of several years. Even in the city of Hollister, shifts of pavement, cracks on house walls, relative displacements of meadow fences and the like have recently been noticed along the San Andreas fault running through the city. Hollister has by now become famous for the fault creep which is taking place continuously.

Much effort has recently been made toward measuring the creep movement by setting up creepmeters (e.g. Tocher, 1960; Nason, 1973) and repeating geodimeter surveys (e.g. Hofmann, 1968). The creep rate obtained through these observations amounts to a few centimeters per year. It may be said that the San Andreas fault is active because it is creeping at present. The portions of the San Andreas fault, which are creeping today, are associated with microseismic activity in contrast to the very low activity at portions of the fault, for instance the San Francisco and Fort Tejon areas, where the fault is apparently locked at present.

Nason (1973) described an anomalous increase in the creep rate from 12 to 20 mm/year at Hollister about 800 days preceding earthquakes of magnitudes 5.6 and 5.5 on April 9, 1961. It appears that the high creep rate was terminated by the earthquakes. No creep was observed for 1.5 years following the earthquakes when the creep resumed with a low rate.

Fresh cracks were found in the ground 1.5 km southeast of Parkfield on the San Andreas fault 2 weeks prior to the 1966 Parkfield earthquake (M = 5.3; see section 4.3). It was suggested by Allen and Smith (1966) that creeping at a high rate might have taken place about that time.

Since 1968, more than forty creepmeters have been at work on the San

Fig. 11-1. A crack at a ditch outside the winery building near Hollister caused by the creep motion of the San Andreas fault. The photo was taken by the author in 1966.

Andreas, Hayward and Calaveras faults. Measurements at closely spaced instruments show that creep events propagate along the faults with a speed amounting to 1–10 km/day.

11.1.2. Anatolian fault

Many earthquakes occur in Anatolia (Asia Minor). Probably the worst one was the 1939 Erzincan earthquake (M = 8.0; 39.5° N, 39.5° E; Richter, 1958, p. 612) which killed about 30,000 people and destroyed more than 30,000 houses. A right-lateral earthquake fault with a maximum offset of 4.2 m appeared over a length of 350 km.

Most of the large earthquakes in Turkey occurred along a geological fault running in an E—W direction on the southern foot of the North Anatolian mountain range parallel to its strike. It was remarkable that the seismic activity of magnitude 7 and over migrated from east to west after 1939 (e.g. Mogi, 1968).

Ambraseys (1970), who paid special attention to Turkish earthquakes, found that the railroad tracks crossing a fault that had appeared at the time of the 1944 Hamamli earthquake (M = 7.6), which occurred at a distance of about 100 km north of Ankara, showed an offset of 30 cm during 6 years without an earthquake. When an earthquake of magnitude 6.5 occurred in 1951, the tracks were offset again. In 1957 a masonry wall was built near the location of the 1951 offset. Ambraseys found that the wall facing east had sheared off and displaced in a right-lateral sense by 24 cm in 1969. Although it is not known whether or not such an offset appeared in a slow movement, it seems highly probable that that portion of the Anatolian fault is creeping in a fashion similar to that of the San Andreas fault.

11.2. FAULTS THAT OFTEN MOVED IN THE PAST

11.2.1. Movement of the Tanna fault

In subsection 5.3.3 the author described the Tanna fault that appeared at the time of the 1930 North Izu earthquake (M = 7.0) with an almost left-lateral strike-slip displacement amounting to 2--3 m as shown in Fig. 5-8. An earthquake with an estimated magnitude of 7.0 occurred in the same district in 841. Kuno (1936), who had been studying the geology of volcanoes in the Izu area, an area about 100 km southwest of Tokyo, found out that ravines on the slopes of the volcanoes there do not cross over the Tanna fault. Instead, the ravines can be nicely connected to those on the other side of the fault provided a left-lateral offset amounting to about 1 km was assumed. It turned out that geologically dated formations around there also underwent similar displacements. Kuno came to the conclusion that such topography around the Tanna fault must have been caused by continual movements of the fault amounting to about 1 km during a period of 5×10^5 years. The rate of movement is therefore estimated as 2 m/1,000 years.

A fault that must have moved intermittently with a time interval of several hundred to thousands of years is also called an active fault by Japanese geologists and geographers.

11.2.2. Active faults in Japan

Intensive field studies supplemented by use of aerophotographs led Japanese geologists and geographers to the discovery of many active faults (National Research Center for Disaster Prevention, 1969, 1973; Geological Survey of Japan, 1973). Probably active faults are most extensively studied in the Kinki--Chubu district, Central Japan. As can be seen in Fig. 11-2 in which the main active faults in the district are shown, faults are classified into two classes, i.e. the right-lateral faults having a strike in a NE—SW direction and the left-lateral ones in a NW—SE direction. The mode of movement of these faults is concordant with an E—W compressional force prevailing in the earth's crust of that portion of Japan (Ichikawa, 1971; see subsection 8.2.2).

Fig. 11-2. Main active faults in Central Japan (Matsuda, 1972). 1 = Itoigawa—Shizuoka tectonic line, 2 = Atera fault, 3 = Neo valley fault, 4 = Atotsugawa fault, 5 = Yanagase fault, 6 = Hanaore fault, 7 = Gomura fault, 8 = Yamazaki fault, 9 = Median tectonic line.

The Atera (Sugimura and Matsuda, 1965) and Atotsugawa (Matsuda, 1966) faults provide evidence that the total offset amounts to several kilometers and the mean rate of movement is estimated as several meters per 1,000 years. It is suspected that the earthquakes that occurred in Central Japan in 1586 ($M = 7.9$) and 1858 ($M = 6.9$) might be caused by movements of the Atotsugawa fault. The Atera fault runs parallel to the Neodani fault, which appeared in association with the 1891 Nobi earthquake (see section 3.2 and subsection 5.6.2), at a distance of 60 km to the east although there is no historical document that suggests possible movements of the fault. It is feared that a movement of the fault might cause a large earthquake in the future.

It now appears that the Median tectonic line and the Itoigawa—Shizuoka line, the most remarkable tectonic lines in Japan, are identified as active faults (e.g. Kaneko, 1966). No movement of the central portion of the Median tectonic line, that extends more than 800 km running through Shikoku and Kii areas, has been reported in history. Should this portion of the fault move, an earthquake of magnitude 8 or so could be generated. Much of the neotectonics of the Median tectonic line was presented by Huzita et al. (1973) in relation to the microseismicity in Southwest Japan (see subsection 8.2.2).

Matsuda (1972) presented the ranking of main active faults in Japan on the basis of the mean rate of movement. When the rate of a fault is 1–10 m/1,000 years, it is ranked to class A. The rate for classes B and C is 0.1–1 and less than 0.1 m/1,000 years, respectively, Strictly speaking, the rate of movement obtained geomorphologically does not tell anything about the amount of displacement when a fault moves next time, if it moves at all. It seems likely, however, that a fault having a high rate may give rise to a large movement. Table 11-I indicates the ranking of main active faults in Japan as prepared by Matsuda (1972).

It is interesting to note that a fault at the extremity of Izu Peninsula, that had been designated as an active one (see Fig. 5-4), was offset by 45 cm at

TABLE 11-I

Main active faults in Japan (Matsuda, 1972)

Location	Name of fault	Type	Length (km)	Class
Akita Pref.	Rikuu	reverse fault	60	B
Iwate Pref.	Morioka	reverse fault	40	B
Fukushima Pref.	Fukushima basin	reverse fault	50	B
Fukushima Pref.	Aizu basin	reverse fault	40	B
Niigata Pref.	Nagaoka plain	reverse fault	30	B
Nagano Pref.	Zenkoji basin	reverse fault	70	B
Nagano Pref.	Itoigawa—Shizuoka	left-lateral	80	A
Shizuoka Pref.	North Izu	left-lateral	30	A
Toyama and Gifu Pref.	Atotsugawa	right-lateral	60	A
Gifu Pref.	Atera	left-lateral	70	A
Gifu Pref.	Neo valley	left-lateral	70	A
Aichi Pref.	Fukozu	reverse fault	10	C
Kyoto Pref.	Tango	left-lateral	20	C
Hyogo Pref.	Rokko	reverse fault	50	B
Hyogo Pref.	Yamazaki	left-lateral	50	A
Tottori Pref.	Tottori	right-lateral	15	C
Southwest Japan	Median tectonic line	right-lateral	800	A

the time of the Izu Peninsula earthquake (M = 6.9; 34.6°N, 138.8°E) on May 9, 1974 (Murai and Kaneko, 1973, 1974).

11.3. ACTIVE FOLDING

There are places where folding in geological time is still going on, notably in northeastern Honshu, Japan. By repeated levelling surveys along a route perpendicular to a folding axis, Miyamura et al. (1968) found a number of bench marks uplifted by 1 cm or so during 1958—1967. Moderately large earthquakes of magnitudes 5—6 sometimes occur in areas of active folding in Japan.

11.4. COASTAL TERRACES

At the time of the 1923 Kanto earthquake (M = 7.9) the extremities of Boso and Miura Peninsulas uplifted by 1 to 2 m (see section 3.3 and Fig. 5-45). An uplift of the Boso Peninsula was also reported in historical documents in association with the 1703 earthquake (M = 8.2) that occurred off the Pacific coast. The location of the epicenter is shown in Fig. 5-31.

It is apparent that the 1707 and 1854 earthquakes, each having a magnitude of 8.4, which occurred off the Pacific coast of Central Japan (see Fig. 5-31), gave rise to uplift of 1 m or so at Pt. Omaezaki (see Fig. 5-63) where an uplift of the order of 10 cm was also observed associated with the 1944 Tonankai earthquake (M = 8.0; see Fig. 5-31 and subsection 5.7.2). It is well known that the extremity of Kii Peninsula and Muroto Promontory, Shikoku, jumped up when large earthquakes occurred off the coast of these areas, e.g. the 1946 Nankai earthquake (M = 8.1; see subsection 5.6.11, Figs. 5-31 and 5-53). Such coseismic uplifts of promontories can be approximately accounted for by a rebound as shown in Fig. 8-2. Uplifts of these promontories have often been reported in connection with large earthquakes in the history of Japan.

Land uplifts of this kind can be traced back to prehistoric time because they have been left as coastal terraces. Geomorphological studies (e.g. Sugimura and Naruse, 1954, 1955; Yoshikawa et al., 1964) led to the conclusions: (1) that the Boso Peninsula experienced about 55 large earthquakes in the past 6,000 years and that 80% of uplift was recovered by aseismic subsidence, and (2) that large earthquakes must have been occurring off Shikoku in the past 10^5 years with a time interval of 100 years or so.

These investigations have nothing to do with the immediate prediction of earthquakes, but they have an important bearing on studies of the mechanism of large earthquakes occuring off the Pacific coast of Japan.

Chapter 12

OTHER ELEMENTS FOR EARTHQUAKE PREDICTION

12.1 GRAVITY

The gravity of the earth consists of the attractive force of the earth's mass and the centrifugal force due to the earth's rotation. No large change in gravity can be expected because a large-scale increase or decrease in density within the earth does not seem likely to occur except for the case of transfer of large amounts of mass, such as magma movement in a volcano. The measurement of gravity changes has therefore been almost ignored in relation to earthquake occurrence until recent years.

The gravity value at a gravity station changes when the height of the station changes, so that a crustal deformation may cause some gravity change which can readily be corrected by taking the measured change in height into account. Such a procedure of correction is called the free-air correction.

The acceleration of gravity at the surface of the earth amounts to about 980 gal (= cm/s^2). A present-day gravimeter can detect a change of 0.01 mgal, an amount as small as 10^{-8} times the absolute value of gravity. However, the overall accuracy of an actual gravity survey becomes as low as ±0.02 mgal due to various causes.

The GSI and ERI have been conducting gravity surveys over the South Kanto area including Boso and Miura Peninsulas which are shown in Fig. 5-29. Hagiwara and Tajima (1973) reported on secular increases in gravity value amounting to about 0.02 mgal/year near the extremities of these peninsulas. A cyclic change having a period of about 3 years seems to superpose on a linear one. The amplitude of this change on the west coast of Miura Peninsula amounts to as much as 0.04 mgal.

The cause of such large changes in gravity is not entirely clear. Comparisons of the gravity value at Tokyo, which is used as a gravity survey datum by the ERI, to that at Kakioka, a station 60 km north of Tokyo, suggested some correlation between the fluctuations in gravity value and the level of underground water measured in a deep well in Tokyo although some more observations are certainly necessary for establishing such a correlation.

Modern gravimeters are of the spring-balance type. It is therefore required for gravity surveys to calibrate the spring constant very precisely all the time. Such a difficulty would be eliminated when devices for an absolute measurement of gravity, as have been under development in France, the U.S.A., Japan and other countries, could be completed.

One of the most remarkable examples of gravity change related to seismic activity is certainly the one that was observed in association with the 1965—1967 Matsushiro earthquake swarm (I. Tsubokawa and Y. Hagiwara, personal communication, 1974; see subsection 5.6.14). Changes in the gravity

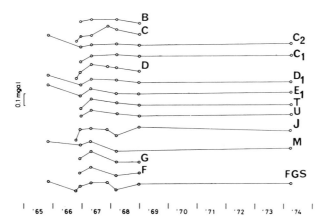

Fig. 12-1. Changes in gravity at stations around Mt. Minakami in the Matsushiro area. The locations of the stations are shown in Fig. 5-56 (I. Tsubokawa and Y. Hagiwara, personal communication, 1974).

value as measured by the ERI at a number of gravity stations set up around Mt. Minakami, the center of the seismic activity (see Figs. 5-55 and 5-56), are shown in Fig. 12-1, the location of these stations has been shown in Fig. 5-56. At the typical station FGS, i.e. the first-order gravity station at the Matsushiro Seismological Observatory, the gravity value decreases by almost 0.1 mgal during the period from November, 1965 to December, 1966.

Gravity surveys over the Matsushiro area were also made by the GSI in addition to those made by the ERI although the GSI survey covered an area much wider than that of the ERI with a less dense distribution of stations. Kisslinger (1975), who combined the two series of gravity measurements, presented an overall view of the changes in gravity in the Matsushiro area. It is apparent that, following the aforementioned remarkable decrease, the gravity value seemed to indicate a steep increase for a certain period of time. After that a gradual change that recovered to the pre-activity level of gravity value seems to occur as can be seen in Fig. 12-2.

It is surmised by Kisslinger (1975) that the initial decrease of gravity during a period of land uplift, which changed with a rate not largely different from the free-air rate, can be interpreted by a decrease in density in the crust immediately under the gravity station probably due to generation of dilatancy (see Chapter 14). Even though possible inflow of water in newly created void space is taken into consideration, it seems possible to interpret the observed gravity change in terms of dilatancy generation.

The increase in gravity with a surprisingly high rate following the initial decrease cannot be interpreted only by a density increase due to crack closure.

Nur (1974a) also presented an interpretation of the Matsushiro activity on

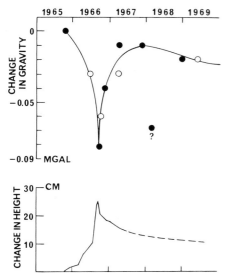

Fig. 12-2. Changes in gravity at station FGS (Matsushiro Seismological Observatory) as compared to those in land uplift there. Solid and open circles indicate measurements by the ERI and GSI, respectively (Kisslinger, 1975; the permission of reproduction from *Geology* was given by the Geological Society of America).

the basis of the dilatancy theory. Fujita and Fujii (1974), who analyzed the GSI gravity data, also independently proposed the possible occurrence of dilatancy.

12.2. UNDERGROUND WATER

A few legends of premonitory changes in underground water selected from historical documents in Japan were presented in section 2.3. However, not many reports of a reliable change in level and/or temperature of underground water are available from modern studies.

Changes in the level of underground water and the flow rate of springs are often reported on the occasion of a large earthquake. For instance, the gush of a hot spring at Dogo, Matsuyama City, Shikoku, Japan, was suspended at the time of the 1946 Nankai earthquake ($M = 8.1$) in spite of the large epicentral distance which exceeded 250 km. As the spring is famous for its long history, occurrences of similar events have been reported at the times of large earthquakes in 684 ($M = 8.4$), 1605 ($M = 7.9$), 1707 ($M = 8.4$) and 1854 ($M = 8.4$). However, the spring always recovered within several months' time. The present author (Rikitake, 1947), who analyzed the change in water level and temperature of the hot spring, concluded that the paths of shallow underground water had been suddenly closed probably by the strong

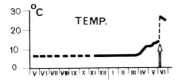

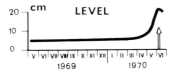

1969   1970

Fig. 12-3. Changes in temperature and water level of underground water preceding an earthquake that occurred at Przhevalsk, U.S.S.R., in June, 1970 (Sadovsky et al., 1972).

ground motion of the earthquake, but nothing seemed to occur at the deep-seated origin of the hot spring. Most of the coseismic changes in underground water are of this class, so that no precursory effect is usually observed.

Recent work by Wakita (1975), who examined coseismic changes in the water level at 95 observation wells in the Tokai and Kanto areas, Japan, at the time of an earthquake of magnitude 6.9 that occurred off Izu Peninsula on May 9, 1974, suggests, however, that the rise and fall of the groundwater level are closely correlated to the tectonic strain due to the earthquake.

Sadovsky et al. (1972) quoted changes in water head and temperature preceding an earthquake that occurred at Przhevalsk ($42.5°$ N, $78.4°$ E), U.S.S.R., in June, 1970, as reproduced in Fig. 12-3. The magnitude of the earthquake was not reported. The epicentral distance was 30 km.

Gordon (1970) reported on an anomalous change in water level at a well 110 km distant from the epicenter 1.5 hours prior to the 1968 Meckering earthquake (M = 6.9; see subsection 5.6.20). The water level increased by 2.9 cm on that occasion.

Johnson and Kovach (1973) monitored water level at a few wells drilled along the San Andreas fault in the Hollister area. The deepest well has a depth of 152 m. They observed a large anomaly in water level starting on September 7, 1972. As it appeared that the anomaly recovered after 296 days, the occurrence of an earthquake of magnitude 5.8 some time in July, 1974, was suggested on the assumption that the anomaly was caused by dilatancy generation (see Chapter 14), but nothing happened. Johnson et al. (1974), however, found pore-pressure changes associated with the progress of fault creep from water level data. Kovach et al. (1975) reported on short-term changes in water level forerunning an earthquake of magnitude 5 or thereabouts.

Coe (1971) wrote that monitoring of underground water level is one of the important tools of earthquake prediction in China. Around Hongshan area near Hsingtai, Hopei Province, there are 175 wells having depths of 50—150 m. Changes in water level are automatically recorded at eight deep wells of 150 m or so in depth. Peasant volunteers measure the water level at other shallow wells. Chinese seismologists are trying to establish criteria for predicting the earthquake magnitude and occurrence time on the basis of the data. It appears that the longer the anomalous period of water level is, the larger is the impending earthquake. It seems also likely that the wider the anomalous area is, the larger is the earthquake.

Kuo et al. (1974) showed that water level in an elliptic area, of which the major axis coincides with a tectonic line running in a NEN direction approximately parallel to a line connecting Hantan to Shihchiachung via Hsingtai, indicated an increase preceding the 1966 Hsingtai earthquake ($M = 6.8$). The lengths of the major and minor axes are respectively about 150 and 50 km. Outside the elliptic area, decreases in water level were observed.

A table of precursor times for 11 earthquakes is provided by Kuo et al. (1974). Table 12-I is an English translation of that table. It seems to the author that the precursor times are not correlated with earthquake magnitude in a definite way.

TABLE 12-I

Precursor times of the changes in underground water level in China (Kuo et al. 1974)

Earthquake	Year	M	Location	Precursor time
Boundary between Hanfung County, Hopei Province, and Tsinchiang County, Szechuan Province	1856	6.0		several days
Haiyuen, Ningsia Prov.	1920	8.5	36.5°N,105.7°E	3 days
Taichung, Sinchu, Taiwan Prov.	1935	7.0	24.5°N,120.8°E	14 hours
Hanlungchi, Taiwan Prov.	1935	6.0	24.3°N,121.3°E	14 hours
Luenyuen, Hopei Prov.	1945	6.3	39.7°N,118.7°E	1 day
Hangting, Szechuan Prov.	1955	7.5	30.0°N,101.8°E	2 days
Tingchung, Yunan Prov.	1961	5.8		1 day
Hsingtai, Hopei Prov.	1966	6.8	37.2°N,114.8°E	1—2 and 5—10 days
Tsunghai, Yunan Prov.	1970	7.7	24.2°N,102.7°E	a few to more than 10 days
Sichi, Ningsia Prov.	1970	5.5[1]	36.0°N,105.8°E	1—5 days
Donan, Tsinghai Prov.	1971	6.3	35.5°N,98.1°E	more than 10 days

[1] Feng et al. (1974) reported that the magnitude of this earthquake is 5.7 (see subsection 9.1.4).

As was also written by Coe (1971), the water level seems likely to be affected by the weather and irrigation. Hence, the interpretation of the changes in water level is not always straightforward. Nevertheless, monitoring of water level, especially that of deep wells, would be worth carrying out for earthquake prediction studies in the future.

12.3. OIL FLOW

Arieh and Merzer (1974) reported on anomalous fluctuations of oil flow from wells in the Gulf of Suez preceding earthquake which occurred at a distance of 100 km. The precursor times are 330, 120 and 150 days for earthquakes of magnitudes 6.1, 4.8 and 5.1, respectively. It is speculated that these fluctuations of oil flow may have something to do with pre-earthquake deformations of the earth's crust.

12.4. RADON CONTENT

It was reported that the content of radon, a radioactive gas having a half-life of 3.5 days, in the mineral water of the Tashkent Basin increased from 5 to 15 emans (Curie/litre) during 1961—1965 (Ulomov, 1968; Sadovsky et al., 1972). The increased state lasted about 6 months until the time of the main shock of the Tashkent earthquakes in April, 1966. After the shock the radon content decreased rapidly.

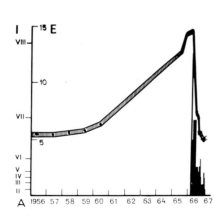 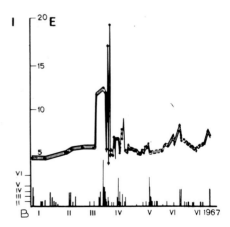

Fig. 12-4. Changes in radon emission of mineral water from a deep well in Tashkent associated with the 1966 main shock (A) and the aftershocks (B). The radon content is measured in units of emans (Curie/litre) while the intensity of shocks is shown in the modified Mercalli scale (Sadovsky et al., 1972).

The shape of the time-variation curve of the radon content as reproduced in the graph of Fig. 12-4A resembles that of the land uplift in the case of the Niigata earthquake in 1964 as shown in Fig. 5-64. Should dilatancy occur preceding an earthquake and water flows through newly created cracks, various substances would melt into the water from the fresh surface of cracks. Because of its short half-life, radon is most suitable for tracing such underground water coming through new cracks. Mineral water in the Tash-kent area is taken from deep wells having a depth larger than several hundred meters.

Observations during the aftershock activity in Tashkent provided a number of precursory increases of the radon content as shown in the graph of Fig. 12-4B; a few of them have been used by Scholz et al. (1973) for forming their theory of earthquake prediction. Monitoring of the radon content has also been in progress in Ferganda (40.4°N, 71.3°E), U.S.S.R., where a finding of a similar precursory effect was reported in association with a local earthquake in 1969 (T. Hagiwara, personal communication, 1974).

Chapter 13

LABORATORY EXPERIMENTS

Many earthquake prediction studies have been developed mostly on the basis of observational experiences over many years. It could not be helped to trudge along such an empirical approach because no realistic model of an earthquake mechanism was put forward until recently. Very little effort has thus been made toward theorizing the physical mechanism of various effects, described in the foregoing chapters, which are forerunners of earthquakes.

Since the early 1960s, however, an approach to simulate an earthquake by laboratory experiments was begun by a number of researchers, resulting in many discoveries that may possibly provide a physical basis of earthquake prediction. As one can handle only rock specimens of limited size in a laboratory, it should be borne in mind that what is found in the laboratory may be applied to actual phenomena of crustal scale with certain limitations. Nevertheless it is true that laboratory tests provide something useful for promoting earthquake prediction studies. It may be said that much of the physical background of earthquake prediction theory can be put forth from studies on "laboratory earthquakes".

Nur (1974b) presented a comprehensive review on the applications of laboratory experiments to the actual earth.

13.1. ROCK-BREAKING EXPERIMENTS

13.1.1. Microfracture and main rupture

Probably Mogi (1962a) was the first who paid attention to the importance of microfracturing of brittle substance under stress. He made experiments on rock specimens which are cut in a rectangular shape and polished. An axial pressure is applied to the specimen until it ruptures eventually. Small shocks that are caused by occurrences of microfractures are recorded by a small pickup microphone attached to the specimen. Such generation of microfractures is known to start when the strain exceeds the limit of elastic deformation entering into the so-called plastic deformation state. Shocks of this kind are often called the acoustic emission or simply AE in similar studies on metals.

A very important fact resulted from Mogi's experiment. It became clear from experiments with a constant stress rate that many microshocks occur before the main rupture when the specimen is heterogeneous. For a very uniform specimen, however, no microshocks occur before the rupture. On the contrary, many microshocks occur for an extremely heterogeneous specimen without having a conspicuous rupture.

Mogi's results provided a basis to interpret the relationship between fore-shocks and main shock in actual earthquakes (subsection 8.3.2). As the author discussed in subsection 8.4.7, it is really important to take the characteristics of the earth's crust into account in order to understand the mode of earthquake occurrence in a certain region.

13.1.2. Experiments under a confining pressure

Mogi's experiments were extended to those under a pressure which is likely to prevail in the earth's crust, notably by Brace (1968) and his associates (e.g. Scholz, 1967, 1968a). An enormous increase in the occurrence numbers of microfracturing is found above 95% of the fracture stress as shown for a granite specimen in Fig. 13-1.

It was also found that fractured rock can support a high stress (Byerlee, 1967) under a high confining pressure. In contrast to brittle fracture, it appears that frictional sliding provides another mechanism of earthquakes

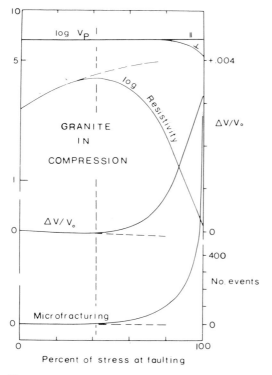

Fig. 13-1. Changes in the physical properties of granite with compressive stress. Data are for Westerly granite under several kilobars confining pressure (Brace, 1968). Microfracturing data are from Scholz (1967).

characterized by stick-slips. That many of the earthquake faults, which appeared at the time of the earthquake, seem to be locked in a short while might have something to do with frictional sliding of this kind.

Brittle fracture would tend not to occur in deeper parts of the earth's crust because the rocks composing the crust would lose brittleness and become ductile under the high pressure and temperature prevailing there. In spite of such supposition, we know that earthquakes do occur even in the mantle at a depth of several hundred kilometers. The reason why an earthquake can occur in such a deep part of the earth is not quite clear although sudden transition of phase from solid to liquid or of a crystal structure is sometimes suggested (e.g. Evison, 1970). It is pointed out by Raleigh and Paterson (1965), however, that brittleness of serpentine recovers under high pressures and temperatures due to dehydration.

It is known that there are many pores in the rocks composing the earth's crust. These pores are filled with water in many cases. The shear stress τ for rupture at a high pressure is given by:

$$\tau = \tau_0 + \mu\sigma \qquad\qquad [13\text{-}1]$$

where σ is the normal stress acting at fracture plane, μ the friction coefficient and τ_0 is the shear stress for rupture at zero pressure. [13-1] indicates that the frictional force $\mu\sigma$ increases the stress which gives rise to a fracture. **Hubbert and Rubey (1959)** showed that equation [13-1] can be modified as:

$$\tau = \tau_0 + \mu(\sigma - P) \qquad\qquad [13\text{-}2]$$

where P is the pore pressure that is acting on the fracture plane. If $\sigma = P$, the strength for shear fracture would become the same as that for zero pressure.

It is therefore shown that brittle fracture can take place even in a deep part of the earth's crust provided the pore pressure is high enough there. The unexpected occurrence of many earthquakes in Denver, Colorado, U.S.A., beginning in 1962 was associated with the injection of waste fluid in a deep well and may well be understood by the above-stated mechanism (Evans, 1966; Pakiser et al., 1969; see section 16.1).

13.1.3. Further developments in rock-breaking experiments

Mogi (1969) made an experiment in which a granite specimen was ruptured by bending. With the aid of pickups attached to the specimen, the locations of microfractures were determined in a manner similar to determining hypocenters of natural earthquakes. It was then found that microfractures occur almost uniformly all over the specimen under increasing stress. In a following stage under a more increased stress, microfractures tend to concentrate at a certain portion of the specimen with a decrease in the occurrence numbers of microfracture at other portions. Finally, the main rupture takes place at the portion where the concentration of microfractures was observed. Scholz (1968a), who made a uniaxial compression experiment on a granite specimen, also found a similar tendency of microfracture occurrences.

The fact that microfractures, which occur fairly uniformly over an area under stress, tend to concentrate at a location where the main rupture would occur has an important bearing on the pattern of occurrence of foreshocks and main shock, provided that the experiments are assumed to simulate natural earthquakes.

Studies of the b-value of microshocks from rock-breaking experiments brought to light the marked similarity of laboratory results to those of natural earthquakes as discussed in subsection 8.3.4.

13.2. PHYSICAL PROPERTIES OF HIGHLY STRESSED ROCKS

Physical properties of rocks in a state just before rupture are of special interest in relation to the precursory effect of an earthquake that may possibly be monitored by various geophysical techniques.

13.2.1. Dilatancy

Generation of microcracks as decribed in the last section necessarily results in an increase in volume as is shown by the $\Delta V/V_0$ curve in Fig. 13-1. Such a volume increase is called the dilatancy (Reynolds, 1886), and special attention has been paid to it notably by Brace et al. (1966). It is understood that the volume increase is caused by the formation of microcracks oriented parallel to the axis of maximal compression and opening up in the direction of least compression. As can be seen in Fig. 13-1, the generation of dilatancy seems to start at a stress about one-half of the rupture stress.

The dilatancy seems likely to play a vital role in the effects of various disciplines forerunning an earthquake as will be seen in the following chapter.

13.2.2. Change in elastic wave velocities

In connection with changes in seismic wave velocities which play an important role in earthquake prediction as summarized in Chapter 9, it is important to see how elastic wave velocities change under stress (e.g. Matsushima, 1960). A typical example of such experiments is to measure the velocity of P-waves in directions parallel and perpendicular to the compressional force applied to a rock specimen.

When the compression is not large, an increase in wave velocity in both directions is observed, and this is attributed to closures of pores and cracks in the specimen. Under a confining pressure of 1 kbar or higher, the wave velocity in the direction of compression does not change or rather decreases a few percent before rupture as the compressional force increases. On the other hand, a sharp drop in the wave velocity in a direction perpendicular to the compression is observed at a load roughly half or more that required for the specimen to rupture. According to Matsushima (1960), the drop of the wave velocity of a granite specimen at rupture amounts to 38 and 20% for confining pressures of 400 bars and 3.5 kbars. These pressures correspond to those at depths of 1 and 10 km in the earth's crust, respectively.

Gupta (1973c,d) extended the earlier experiments to those under triaxial compression. He found that the change in V_s is significantly smaller than that of V_p as the specimen approaches rupture. He also found that a large decrease in V_p/V_s amounting to 10—20% occurs in the direction of minimal compressive stress. The decrease in the direction of intermediate stress is only a few percent, while the decrease of maximal stress hardly shows any change.

Gupta's results may throw some light on understanding why a decrease in V_p and V_p/V_s is not always observed. Wang (1974) claimed that changes in V_p and V_p/V_s are observed when seismic waves are propagating in a direction perpendicular to the orientation of cracks. In most cases the cracks are presumed to be parallel to the earth's surface, so that waves coming from an origin at some depth are likely to be more susceptible to cracks than those from an origin near the surface. Anderson et al. (1974), who studied the effect of oriented cracks theoretically, showed a similar anisotropy of the V_p/V_s ratio.

13.2.3. Change in electric resistivity

Brace and Orange (1966, 1968a,b) measured electric resistivity of rocks saturated by water. An increase in resistivity with increasing pressure is observed for a low-pressure range, and this is understood by taking the effect of the closure of pores into account. An enormous decrease in resistivity then follows as can be seen in Fig. 13-1 when the compressional stress exceeds a certain value. This seems to be caused by generation of conducting paths associated with newly produced microfractures.

What the author summarized in this chapter seems to provide a physical basis of applying various premonitory effects to earthquake prediction studies. It is certainly of importance and interest to strengthen laboratory experiments, especially those under pressures and temperatures which are likely to prevail in the earth's crust.

Chapter 14

DILATANCY MODELS

The reality of a decrease in the V_p/V_s ratio forerunning an earthquake is now believed by many seismologists (see Chapter 9). Meanwhile, laboratory experiments on rocks have achieved some success in accounting for the V_p/V_s change before rupture (see section 13.2) on the basis of the production of cracks or dilatancy under the action of compressional stress.

Against such a background, a theory, which may possibly account for changes in seismic wave velocities preceding an earthquake, was proposed by Nur (1972) and Aggarwal et al. (1973) on the basis of dilatancy generated in rocks saturated by water.

14.1. WET MODEL

Scholz et al. (1973) put forward a more advanced model based on the dilatancy in saturated rocks, and attempted to account for not only changes in the V_p/V_s ratio or V_p but also other precursors such as land uplift, decrease in electric resistivity, increase in radon emission and so on. Major points of a dilatancy model in saturated rocks may be summarized as follows.

When the earth's crust is subjected to a tectonic stress caused by a plate motion or some other causes, it is expected that dilatancy occurs in the rocks composing the crust, provided that the stress exceeds a certain limit. In that case many microcracks probably oriented parallel to the axis of maximal compression would be produced.

The velocity of a P-wave or compressional wave propagating through such a medium including many pores is known to be smaller than that through a medium containing no pores (e.g. O'Connell and Budiansky, 1974). On the other hand, the S-wave or torsional wave is affected very little by the pores. It is thus understood why a decrease in the V_p/V_s ratio takes place under a crustal stress which is not quite as large as that which causes the main rupture but enough for generating dilatancy.

Scholz et al. (1973) demonstrated how V_p and V_s of wet and dry rocks change with the increase in effective stress, i.e. a stress equal to the difference between total stress and pore pressure, as is shown in Fig. 14-1. Stage I along AB for the V_p curve of saturated rock indicates a slight increase in V_p due to simple accumulation of tectonic stress. As microcracks are produced for stage II along BC, V_p becomes smaller because the rock is no longer saturated.

At the same time, inflow of water into newly created pores from existing pores would result in a decrease in pore pressure giving rise to the so-called

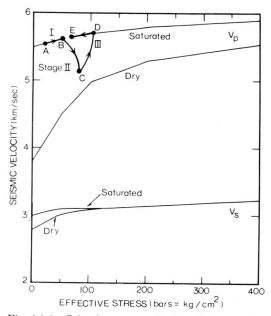

Fig. 14-1. Seismic wave velocities V_p and V_s as a function of the effective confining pressure for wet and dry Westerly granite (see text for various notations) (Scholz et al., 1973, *Science*, Vol. 181, pp. 803—810, fig. 1. Copyright 1973 by the American Association for the Advancement of Science).

dilatancy hardening which prevents further generation of microcracks. As influx of water keeps up and overcomes crack generation, V_p tends to increase along CD which is designated to stage III.

When point D is reached, the rock is saturated again and V_p recovers its normal value. The pore pressure increases a little more accompanying a V_p change along DE. As the tectonic stress is also increasing, the main rupture or an earthquake occurs at E.

In contrast to the fact that V_p, once decreased, returns to the previous level as the above-stated process indicates, no recovery of electric resistivity would be expected until the earthquake occurrence because the water content is even increasing until point E is reached. Also, radon emission that is probably connected with the rate of water flow would not decrease until the earthquake occurs. That is also the case for land uplift and precursory tilt caused by the volume increase. On the contrary, microshock activity and b-values would decrease during the period of dilatancy hardening. Scholz et al. (1973) presented a figure in which idealized behavior of these elements is schematically summarized.

Another important point of the work by Scholz et al. is that precursor times of the elements treated are closely correlated with the magnitude of an impending earthquake as will be discussed in section 15.5. It appears that the logarithmic precursor time is linearly correlated with earthquake magnitude. Such a correlation is also pointed out for the precursory V_p/V_s change by Semyenov (1969) and Whitcomb et al. (1973), the b-value by Wyss and Lee (1973), tilting of the ground by Johnston and Mortensen (1974) and crustal deformation by Tsubokawa (1969, 1973). These precursory effects will be discussed in a summarized form in subsection 15.5.4.

The logarithm of a typical linear dimension of crustal movement associated with an earthquake is linearly correlated with earthquake magnitude as given in [5-11] (Dambara, 1966). It is also the case for that of the aftershock area (Utsu, 1969; Utsu and Seki, 1955). An analysis of these empirical facts along with the above precursor time vs. magnitude relationship strongly suggests that a typical length L of the focal region such as fault length is correlated with precursor time τ in the manner:

$$\tau \propto L^2 \tag{14-1}$$

Relation [14-1] indicates that the whole process is a kind of diffusion one which is governed by the differential equation:

$$\partial P/\partial t = c\nabla^2 P \tag{14-2}$$

where P, t and c are the pore pressure, time and diffusion coefficient, respectively.

The dilatancy model has been widely discussed on the basis of water diffusion into newly created pores (Scholz et al., 1973; Whitcomb et al., 1973; Anderson and Whitcomb, 1973; Rikitake, 1975b) with general success. Rikitake (1975b) claimed that the Dambara-Utsu formula for the relationship between the dimension of the focal region and earthquake magnitude can be approximately accounted for by the dilatancy model discussed in this section. However, Scholz et al. (1973), Whitcomb et al. (1973) and Anderson and Whitcomb (1973) argued that a dilatant zone must be much wider than the focal zone in contrast to the author's view that both the zones are more or less the same in dimension. At this point, it is interesting to note that Griggs et al. (1975) proved that an observable V_p/V_s change can occur even though the anomalous region is small compared to the dimensions of the seismic array.

14.2. DRY MODEL

Mogi (1974), Stuart (1974) and Brady (1974) claimed that a dilatancy model without water diffusion may be capable of accounting for the various precursory effects just as the wet dilatancy model discussed in the last section.

According to Mogi (1974), the first and second stages, i.e. the strain accumulation by a tectonic process (stage I) and the generation of dilatancy (stage II) may be the same as those postulated in the wet model. During the following stage (stage III), however, the dilatancy and associated stress would concentrate in a very limited zone, so that a decrease of stress would occur except for that limited zone where a fault would eventually appear.

The present model is characterized by a very strong dilatancy in the immediate neighborhood of incipient fracture (Brady, 1974; Mogi, 1974) for stage III. The dilatancy that once occurred in a wide area surrounding the focal region should vanish because of stress decrease for stage III, so that closure of cracks must take place.

The very localized dilatancy which is required for the model might be able to account for premonitory reorientation of the compression axis of small earthquakes (see subsection 8.3.4). The present model suggests that the time variation of the V_p/V_s ratio and land uplift for the focal zone may be a little different from that around it. Electric resistivity outside the focal zone would rather increase for stage II although it would decrease for stage III due to crack closure.

The dry model seems to account for the point that a dilatant zone is wider than the focal zone as suggested by Whitcomb et al. (1973), Scholz et al. (1973) and Anderson and Whitcomb (1973). The author does not quite understand how the precursor time vs. earthquake magnitude relationship can be accounted for by a dry model because a factor such as water diffusion does not play an explicit role in the model.

In conclusion it may be said that both models of dilatancy are fascinating in that they provide a physical basis of interpreting possible premonitory effects preceding an earthquake. However, arguments so far put forward are not quite quantitative, especially for the dry model. It is hoped to refine the dilatancy theory to an extent which enables us to develop a highly quantitative discussion.

Chapter 15

THEORY OF EARTHQUAKE PREDICTION

We are now in a position to systematize what has been discussed in the foregoing chapters. In other words, a theory of earthquake prediction should be set out from the achievements by studies of the various disciplines relevant to earthquake prediction, although they are by no means complete.

One may think that it would be premature to work on a theory of earthquake prediction because we still do not know whether an earthquake is predictable and data necessary for prediction have not been acquired to a satisfactory extent. The author does not deny such a view. Nevertheless, he believes that it is an urgent matter to try to work out a theory of earthquake prediction as much as is possible even at this point. Such a theory, however unripe it is at the moment, would doubtless stimulate further development and would suggest a direction in which earthquake prediction studies may proceed.

It is the author's belief that earthquake prediction should be achieved from a physical standpoint or actually observed effects having a physical background. Statistics of earthquakes are of course invaluable for promoting earthquake science. Typical achievements of earthquake statistics are the relationship between the frequency of earthquake occurrence and earthquake magnitude (see subsection 8.2.1), the law of the decreasing rate of aftershocks and the like. These findings doubtless play an important role in understanding earthquake phenomena. Even so, prediction based only on statistics, without paying attention to the present physical conditions within the earth's crust, could sometimes be misleading.

As many non-professional people still rely on statistical prediction, however, the author would like to discuss briefly the usefulness and limitations of this type of prediction before dealing with the prediction based on physical forerunners.

15.1. STATISTICAL PREDICTION OF EARTHQUAKES

Much of the statistical prediction of earthquakes has been reviewed by Aki (1956), Lomnitz (1966, 1974) and others. It had been of special interest to see whether or not earthquake occurrence has a periodicity. Aki (1956) pointed out that many periodicities in earthquake occurrence such as 42 minutes, 1 day, 14.8 days, 29.6 days, 6 months, 1 year, 11 years, 100 years, 200 years, 240 years, 284 years and so on have been proposed. Should all these periodicities really exist, they would almost compose a white noise. Schuster (1897) presented a method for testing the significance of a periodicity. Applying Schuster's test to obtained periodicities, it turns out that many of the periodicities proposed do not seem significant, although periodicities having a stable amplitude and phase have been found in some cases. Even so, it is in many ways doubtful that a periodicity study can be applied to earthquake prediction. It may be that a statistical study of large earthquakes possibly enables us to estimate, to a degree of approximation, a probable return period of large earthquakes in a certain region. Such a study on earthquake risk is certainly useful for planning urban and industrial development, dam construction, earthquake insurance and the like. But such a study is quite useless for foretelling the occurrence of a particular earthquake that will strike a certain region next time because the conclusion from the statistics is valid only for the mean state of the set of earthquakes analyzed.

15.1.1. 69-year period recurrence of large earthquakes in the Tokyo area

Kawasumi (1970) claimed that he found a 69-year periodicity for strong earthquakes that hit the Tokyo area on the basis of his statistics of strong earthquakes experienced at Kamakura, a city about 50 km south of Tokyo. Kamakura was once the nation's capital of Japan around 1200, so that the earthquake records taken there in earlier years must be fairly reliable.

Kawasumi applied a periodgram analysis to the earthquake data taken at Kamakura. He considered earthquakes that gave rise to an intensity V or larger in the JMA scale (about intensity VIII or larger in the modified Mercalli scale). After making a Fourier analysis, he found a fairly large amplitude for a 69-year period constituent. Applying Schuster's test of significance to the result, he insisted that the probability of the existence of a 69-year period is estimated to be as high as 99.94%. He also calculated the standard deviation of the period obtaining a value of 13.2 years. The author is afraid that Kawasumi used a rather tricky terminology; the period of ±13.2 years centering the year of the maximum amplitude of the 69-year period harmonic constituent was referred to as the "dangerous period".

As Kawasumi was working as chairman of a committee for preventing earthquake hazards of the Tokyo Metropolitan area, his idea of a 69-year period of occurrence of strong earthquakes attracted much attention of journalists as well as administrative officials of the local government of Tokyo who, as amateurs of earthquake study, did not fully understand the correct meaning of Kawasumi's statistics. As 50 years have already past since the horrible 1923 Kanto earthquake (see section 3.3), Kawasumi's warning about a possible occurrence of a strong earthquake in the near future stimulated planning, though insufficient, by local government in the Tokyo—Yokohama area for prevention of earthquake hazards. Whether or not Kawasumi's statistics are scientifically correct, it should be appreciated that his work stimulated planning for earthquake hazard reduction in one of the most highly populated areas in the world.

The understanding of an average Tokyoite about Kawasumi's warning would be something like the following. "As 50 years have past since the 1923 Kanto earthquake, a large earthquake should occur within a period of 19 years from now. The period of earthquake danger as it is called by the authorities begins within 5 years' time". There are some people who believe that, if the year 1992 (= 1923 + 69) would pass without having a strong earthquake, there would be no danger of an earthquake after all. The author thinks that such a misleading and confusing understanding must be put aside. The terminology "dangerous period" as adopted by Kawasumi does not seem adequate for popular use by non-professional people.

There are a number of objections to Kawasumi's argument. First of all, Shimazaki (1971a, 1972c) pointed out that Kawasumi's test of significance is not rigorous enough. Schuster's criterion may be applied to an arbitrarily chosen harmonic constituent, but not to a particular one such as that having the maximum power. The significance test devised by Fisher (1950), for instance, must be applied to such a particular case. It is shown by Shimazaki that the periodicity of 69 years is not statistically significant at a significance level of 0.1.

Kawasumi also argued that there are a number of instances where no earthquakes occurred within the time range of the standard deviation. He claimed that this is likely to be caused by the fact that earthquake records are missing for those periods because of civil wars or other social unrest in historic time. The author feels that Kawasumi speculated too much.

The author would here like to repeat that, even if a periodicity is obtained from a set of earthquake data in the past, the periodicity obtained is valid only for an average of the set as a whole. It would be another matter to predict the occurrence of a specified earthquake which will next occur in an area concerned.

Usami and Hisamoto (1970, 1971) analyzed the earthquake data in Tokyo and Kyoto by means of a method similar to Kawasumi's. Although they found that there are periodicities of 36 and 38 years respectively for Tokyo and Kyoto, they pointed out that such periodicities can be obtained even if earthquakes are occurring randomly and stationarily.

The author, together with many seismologists, fully agrees with the view that strong earthquakes have a tendency to recur, but he rather doubts that there is a periodicity. It may be that the return period of large earthquakes occurring along and off the Pacific coast of Japan could fluctuate in a wide range although it would seem possible to determine it with an accuracy of decades. It is therefore important to look very carefully into the forerunners of various disciplines when a year of mean return period of earthquake occurrence approaches. The earthquake prediction program that is underway in Japan is, in fact, planned from such a standpoint.

15.1.2. Earthquake statistics and their limitation

Simple statistics of earthquake magnitude

What can be said about the magnitude and occurrence time of a forth-coming earthquake on the condition that an observation of earthquakes over a fairly long period has been carried out in a certain region?

In subsection 8.2.1 the Gutenberg-Richter formula which is given by equation [8-1] was discussed. On the other hand, it is known that the following relation approximately holds between energy E released by an earthquake and its magnitude M (Gutenberg and Richter, 1956):

$$\log_{10} E = \alpha + \beta M \qquad\qquad [15\text{-}1]$$

where the constants α and β respectively are 11.8 and 1.5 if E is measured in units of ergs.

From [8-1] and [15-1], the earthquake frequency as a function of E is given by:

$$N(E) = cE^{-b/\beta - 1} \qquad\qquad [15\text{-}2]$$

where:

$$c = 10^{a + \alpha b/\beta}/(\beta \log_e 10) \qquad\qquad [15\text{-}3]$$

as obtained by Utsu and Hirota (1968) and Utsu (1971).

Accordingly, the number of earthquakes whose energy falls in a range between E_S and E_T ($E_T > E_S$) is obtained as:

$$N_0 = \int_{E_S}^{E_T} N(E)\mathrm{d}E = \frac{c\beta}{b}(E_S^{-b/\beta} - E_T^{-b/\beta}) \qquad\qquad [15\text{-}4]$$

If it is assumed that E has a value in a range $E_S \leqslant E \leqslant E_T$, the probability $p(E)$ for an earthquake energy to assume a value between E and $E + \mathrm{d}E$ is estimated as:

$$p(E) = \begin{cases} 0 & \text{for } E < E_S \\ N(E)/N_0 & \text{for } E_S \leqslant E \leqslant E_T \\ 0 & \text{for } E_T < E \end{cases} \qquad\qquad [15\text{-}5]$$

The probability for $E_S \leqslant E \leqslant E_T$ is thus given by:

$$p(E) = \frac{b}{\beta} \frac{E^{-b/\beta - 1}}{E_S^{-b/\beta} - E_T^{-b/\beta}} . \qquad\qquad [15\text{-}6]$$

Hence, the probability for an earthquake to assume a magnitude between

M_1 and M_2 is obtained as:

$$P(M_1,M_2) = \int_{E_1}^{E_2} p(E)\mathrm{d}E \qquad\qquad [15\text{-}7]$$

where E_1 and E_2 are the energies corresponding to M_1 and M_2, respectively. On performing the integration, we obtain:

$$P(M_1,M_2) = [(E_1/E_S)^{-\gamma} - (E_2/E_S)^{-\gamma}]/[1 - (E_T/E_S)^{-\gamma}] \qquad [15\text{-}8]$$

where:

$$\gamma = b/\beta \qquad\qquad [15\text{-}9]$$

As the strain energy, which can be stored in the earth's crust in a certain region, is finite, E_T cannot be assumed as infinity. Tsuboi (1964) estimated E_T for the crust in and around Japan by making a difference between the energies supplied and released. The rate of energy supply was estimated by Tsuboi as 2.24×10^{23} ergs/year.

An actual estimate of $P(M_1, M_2)$ as defined by [15-8] was demonstrated by Rikitake (1969a, 1969b) for the Kanto area around Tokyo, Japan, bounded by $34.5°\text{N} \leqslant \phi \leqslant 36.5°\text{N}$ and $139°\text{E} \leqslant \lambda \leqslant 141°\text{E}$, where ϕ and λ are latitude and longitude, respectively. The frequencies of the earthquakes classified according to their magnitudes in the Kanto area during 1926—1960 are given in Table 15-I, constants a and b in equation [8-1] being estimated as:

$$a = 5.48, \quad b = 0.803 \qquad\qquad [15\text{-}10]$$

by means of the least-squares method.

Following a technique by Tsuboi (1964), E_T is obtained as:

$$E_T = 9.2 \times 10^{23} \text{ ergs} \qquad\qquad [15\text{-}11]$$

TABLE 15-I

Frequency of earthquake occurrence in the Kanto area during 1926—1960 as classified according to magnitude (Rikitake, 1969a)

M	Frequency	M	Frequency	M	Frequency
5.0	37	5.7	3	6.4	0
5.1	21	5.8	5	6.5	2
5.2	25	5.9	5	6.6	1
5.3	20	6.0	5	6.7	0
5.4	9	6.1	6	6.8	0
5.5	13	6.2	3	6.9	0
5.6	16	6.3	3	7.0	2

TABLE 15-II

Probabilities of an earthquake occurring in the Kanto area to fall in a magnitude range between M_1 and M_2 (Rikitake, 1969a)

M_1	M_2	$P(M_1, M_2)$
5.0	5.5	0.599
5.5	6.0	0.245
6.0	6.5	0.097
6.5	7.0	0.038
7.0	7.5	0.015
7.5	8.0	0.006

for 1968. On the other hand E_S is defined by the energy corresponding to magnitude 5, so that we obtain:

$$E_S = 2.0 \times 10^{19} \text{ ergs} \tag{15-12}$$

It is now possible from [15-8], together with [15-9], [15-10], [15-11] and [15-12], to estimate the probabilities of an earthquake to fall in a magnitude range, having an interval of, for instance, 0.5, as given in Table 15-II.

We thus see that it is possible to say something about the probability of an earthquake, should it occur, to fall in a certain magnitude range on the basis of simple statistics as presented here. Nothing more can be said from such studies without adding some elements for earthquake prediction such as geodetic, geomagnetic, geoelectric and other precursors. The probability estimated here provides what the author calls the "preliminary probability" in his theory of earthquake prediction (Rikitake, 1969a,b; see subsection 15.2.1).

Simple statistics of occurrence time of earthquakes

If earthquake occurrence is assumed to be stationary and random in the time domain, the occurrence frequency is governed by a Poisson distribution (e.g. Aki, 1956; Lomnitz, 1966). Denoting the mean frequency of earthquakes per unit time by k, the probability of having n earthquakes during a time interval T is given by $(kT)^n e^{-kT}/n!$. If $n \to 0$, the probability of having no earthquake during a time period T is obtained as e^{-kT}. Accordingly, the probability of having at least an earthquake between t_1 and t_2 ($t_2 > t_1$) becomes:

$$P(t_1, t_2) = 1 - e^{-k(t_2 - t_1)} \tag{15-13}$$

The yearly frequencies of occurrence of an earthquake in the Kanto area of which the magnitude is larger than 5 are given in Table 15-III for the period 1926—1960. We have earthquakes amounting to 159 in number for

TABLE 15-III

Yearly frequency of earthquake occurrence in the Kanto area ($M \geqslant 5$) (Rikitake, 1969a)

Year	Frequency	Year	Frequency	Year	Frequency
1926	4	1938	4	1950	6
1927	4	1939	6	1951	5
1928	8	1940	5	1952	7
1929	4	1941	6	1953	7
1930	8	1942	2	1954	3
1931	8	1943	8	1955	2
1932	2	1944	7	1956	3
1933	4	1945	4	1957	1
1934	5	1946	8	1958	2
1935	13	1947	6	1959	1
1936	3	1948	7	1960	2
1937	7	1949	4		
				Total	176

$5.0 \leqslant M \leqslant 6.0$ and 17 for $6.0 < M$. It may be that the data set is large enough for obtaining the mean number k for $5.0 \leqslant M \leqslant 6.0$. The probabilities for an earthquake falling in this magnitude range to occur within a period of t at least one time are calculated from [15-13] putting $t_1 = 0$ and $t_2 = t$ and given in Table 15-IV.

For earthquakes having a magnitude larger than 6, the data are too few to say something. We therefore go back to 1600 and select earthquakes of

TABLE 15-IV

Probabilities of having at least one earthquake in the Kanto area during the period $0-t$ (Rikitake, 1969a)

t	$P_s(0,t)$	$P_l(0,t)$
10 days	0.128	0.003
30 days	0.337	0.008
90 days	0.709	0.025
0.5 year	0.915	0.048
1 year	0.994	0.095
2 years	1.000	0.181
5 years	1.000	0.423
10 years	1.000	0.632
20 years	1.000	0.865
30 years	1.000	0.950
40 years	1.000	0.982
50 years	1.000	0.993
60 years	1.000	0.998

P_s and P_l are defined in the text.

$M > 6$, amounting to 35 in number during the 360-year period. It is believed that historical records for such large earthquakes have been well preserved. In that case we obtain $k = 0.10$/year for the occurrence of earthquakes of this magnitude class. Adopting this value for k, the probabilities of having at least one earthquake of $M > 6$ between 0 and t are calculated as also given in Table 15-IV.

When the distributions of magnitude and time of occurrence are assumed to be independent from one another, the probability of having at least one earthquake, of which the magnitude falls in an interval between M_1 and M_2, within the period from 0 to t is given by:

$$P(0,t; M_1, M_2) = P_i(0,t) P(M_1, M_2) \qquad\qquad [15\text{-}14]$$

where:

$$i = s \qquad \text{for } 5.0 \leqslant M \leqslant 6.0$$
$$i = l \qquad \text{for } 6.0 < M \qquad\qquad\qquad [15\text{-}15]$$

$P(0,t; M_1, M_2)$'s for the Kanto area as calculated from Tables 15-II and 15-IV for various combinations of magnitude and time are given in Table 15-V. We now see that something can be said about probability of earthquake occurrence even though no special observations other than seismological ones, such as given in Tables 15-I and 15-III, are available. The probabilities, such as those tabulated in Tables 15-II, 15-IV and 15-V, may be of some value to see the general tendency of earthquake occurrence in a certain region. The author thinks, however, that the probabilities thus obtained from simple earthquake statistics are of no practical use for estimating the risk of a large earthquake that would hit the region concerned. Probabilities for a large earthquake to occur within a short period from a certain epoch are always small as can be seen in the above tables, so that we would estimate a small probability today even if an earthquake of magnitude 8 will occur tomorrow. The probabilities estimated here must be dramatically

TABLE 15-V

Probabilities of having at least one earthquake of a magnitude falling in the interval between M_1 and M_2 in the Kanto area within the period $0-t$ (Rikitake, 1969a).

M_1	M_2	$t = 10$ days	$t = 30$ days	$t = 90$ days	$t = 0.5$ year	$t = 1$ year	$t = 2$ years	$t = 5$ years	$t = 10$ years	$t = 20$ years
5.0	5.5	0.077	0.201	0.424	0.548	0.595	0.599	0.599	0.599	0.599
5.5	6.0	0.031	0.083	0.174	0.224	0.243	0.245	0.245	0.245	0.245
6.0	6.5	0.000	0.001	0.002	0.005	0.009	0.018	0.041	0.061	0.084
6.5	7.0	0.000	0.000	0.001	0.002	0.004	0.007	0.016	0.024	0.033
7.0	7.5	0.000	0.000	0.000	0.001	0.001	0.003	0.006	0.010	0.013
7.5	8.0	0.000	0.000	0.000	0.000	0.001	0.001	0.003	0.004	0.005

modified when some premonitory effects closely connected with earthquake occurrence are actually observed.

15.1.3. Statistics based on the theory of extreme values

Although the author has no intention of presenting a detailed account of earthquake statistics, it would perhaps be better to deal briefly with a statistical approach that is particularly useful for studying the general pattern of occurrence of large earthquakes. When one makes statistics of the maximum magnitude of earthquakes that occurred in a certain region during a certain period, it is possible to obtain an empirical law that governs the fluctuation of the maximum magnitude. Once such a law is obtained, mean return period and related probabilities with respect to earthquake occurrences there can be estimated.

Being called the extreme value theory, such a theory has been developed by Gumbel (1958). Applications of the theory to earthquakes were tried by Nordquist (1945), Epstein and Lomnitz (1966), Shakal and Willis (1972), Chen and Lin (1973) and others.

Shakal and Willis (1972) concluded that the area of the Aleutian—Alaska arc between about $155°W$ and $167°W$ has an 80% probability of occurrence of an event of $M \geqslant 8$ by 1980. This portion of the arc has been known as one of the marked seismicity gaps (see subsection 8.4.5). Observed data during 1930—1971 were used for their analysis.

Chen and Lin (1973) made extreme value statistics for 13 seismic zones in China. The periods analyzed are different from zone to zone. The longest period covers 270 years. In their analysis, a return period for earthquakes of various magnitudes was first obtained statistically. They then calculated the probable occurrence frequency (N_p) of earthquakes with a certain magnitude for a certain period in the future. They assumed that the risk of having an earthquake of a certain magnitude is high provided that N_p is larger than the actually observed frequency. The author does not really know if such an assumption is correct.

Chen and Lin (1973) indicated a number of zones where the probability of having a large earthquake is high. The zones are reproduced in Table 15-VI together with the expected earthquake magnitude and the probability of occurrence.

Similar statistics were applied to earthquakes in California (Epstein and Lomnitz, 1966; Lomnitz, 1974). The conclusions derived from the statistics are as follows (Lomnitz, 1974, p. 106):

(1) The probability of occurrence of event of magnitude 8 or over in any given year is about 1%.

(2) The probability of at least one such event occurring in a century is 63.3%.

(3) The probability of at least two such events occurring in a century is

TABLE 15-VI

Probabilities of earthquake occurrence in major seismic zones in China within 5 years' time from 1971 (Chen and Lin, 1973)

Seismic zone	Expected magnitude	Probability
North Tien-shen	6	0.8
South Tien-shen	6—6.5	0.7
Tsinghai plateau	6—6.5	0.75
Lanchou area	7	0.6
West Yunan	6.5	0.75
Chengtu area	6	0.6

26.6%. This will occur in one out of four centuries, approximately.

(4) The probability of an interval of less than 50 years is 39% while the probability of an interval of more than 50 years is 61%.

(5) The median return period is 70 years. Half of all intervals will be above 70 years and half will be below it.

(6) The earthquake risk in California for an earthquake of magnitude 8 or larger is about 9% in a decade, and about 39% in a 50-year period.

It is shown in this subsection that extreme value statistics are useful for estimating a mean return period of earthquake occurrence. The return period thus estimated for large earthquakes sometimes exceeds the length of period during which the data have been taken. It appears that we should not put too much stress on a return period. It indicates only a time interval of earthquake repetition averaged for the whole set of data. The actual time of occurrence of the next earthquake can largely deviate from such a mean value.

15.1.4. Correlation between earthquake occurrence and other phenomena

Correlations between earthquake occurrences and other phenomena such as atmospheric pressure and its gradient, temperature, positions of celestial bodies, sunspot numbers, latitude changes, thunderstorms, droughts, fish and animal behavior and so on have long been targets of statisticians. Many literature references of this kind of study can be found in Aki (1956).

A very high correlation has sometimes been reported from these studies. For instance, the correlation coefficient between the catch of horse mackerel and the daily frequency of earthquakes in the Izu area was surprisingly large in 1930 as can be seen in Fig. 2-1 (Terada, 1932; see subsection 2.1.1).

A high correlation between earthquake occurrence and some other phenomena may well be true in some cases. According to the author's experience, the correlation between geomagnetic storm and earthquake occurrence was unbelievably high during a certain period of the 1965—1967 Matsushiro earthquake swarm. However, such a high correlation did not last a long period (see section 2.5).

As frequency of earthquake occurrence is ever fluctuating, it is not surprising that some correlation between earthquake occurrence and other phenomena, which are also fluctuating all the time, apparently can be obtained. The correlation could sometimes be fairly high by chance. The author thinks that it is sometimes possible to have a high correlation between earthquake occurrence and some phenomena even though there is no physical causality. It is therefore dangerous to conclude at once that there is a causal relationship between them.

In any case, a correlation study as discussed in this subsection would be difficult to apply to the actual prediction of an earthquake.

15.2. EMPIRICAL APPROACH TO EARTHQUAKE PREDICTION BASED ON ACTUALLY OBSERVED PREMONITORY EFFECTS

In the last section the author emphasized that statistics of earthquake occurrence are useful for having an idea about the mean return period of a large earthquake and its expected magnitude although no exact time or magnitude of a particular earthquake which will strike a certain region next time can be given from such a statistical study. It is therefore important to develop a theory of earthquake prediction on the basis of actually observed premonitory effects such as geodetic, geomagnetic, geoelectric and other symptoms, which are believed to forerun an earthquake, on the empirical basis.

15.2.1. Prediction of magnitude

Rikitake (1969a,b) proposed a method that can be applied to reestimate a probability for an earthquake to fall in a certain magnitude range or to occur in a certain interval of time from the preliminary probability that has been statistically obtained in a manner as discussed in subsection 15.1.2.

Let us specify an area over which statistics of seismicity are available. Dividing the whole magnitude range into n intervals, the probabilities for an earthquake to fall in respective magnitude ranges are denoted by $W_0(1)$, $W_0(2)$, ... $W_0(n)$. These probabilities, which the author calls the preliminary probabilities, may be derived by some other means in some cases (see subsection 15.3.2).

Let us assume that we observe a geophysical element A_1, which is believed to be a premonitory effect of an earthquake occurrence. As a result of such monitoring of A_1, the probabilities for the magnitude of an impending earthquake to fall in the respective ranges as defined in the last paragraph can

sometimes be estimated as will be shown later in this subsection. Let us write
such probabilities as $W_1(1)$, $W_1(2)$, ... $W_1(n)$.

We now see that Bayes' theorem (e.g. Freiberger, 1960, p. 70), which is
well known in the probability theory, leads to a synthesized probability
given by:

$$W(s) = \frac{W_0(s)W_1(s)}{W_0(1)W_1(1) + W_0(2)W_1(2) + \cdots + W_0(n)W_1(n)} \qquad [15\text{-}16]$$

where $W(s)$ is the "a posteriori" probability of an earthquake, when it should
occur, falling in a magnitude range specified by s. The "a priori" probability
$W_0(s)$ is now converted into $W(s)$ by the fact that a prediction element A_1 is
observed.

It is readily proved that the synthesized probability for successively introduced elements A_1, A_2, ... A_k becomes:

$$W(s) = \frac{W_0(s)W_1(s)W_2(s) \cdots W_k(s)}{\sum\limits_{s=1}^{n} W_0(s)W_1(s)W_2(s) \cdots W_k(s)} \qquad [15\text{-}17]$$

which does not depend on the order of introducing these elements.

The discussion presented here resembles how a preliminary probability
changes when a witness testifies. In order to have a high value of synthesized
probability, the witnesses should be highly reliable.

Precursory land deformation as a prediction element

In section 5.7 were summarized precursory land uplifts so far reported. It
was suggested in that section, relations [5-7] or [5-11] between earthquake
magnitude M and mean radius of the crustal deformation area associated
with that earthquake may be approximately applied even to precursory land
deformations.

Let us now suppose that an anomalous crustal deformation is observed in
a certain area and that the mean radius of the area is determined. In that case
a probable magnitude M_0 of the coming earthquake can be estimated from
equation [5-11]. Due to the scatter of $\log_{10} r^3$ vs. M plots as can be seen in
Fig. 5-68, M_0 cannot be obtained deterministically. If we assume that the
difference between the actual magnitude M and M_0 follows a Gaussian distribution, the probability for the magnitude to take on a value between M and
$M + dM$ is obtained as:

$$W_{GM}(M)dM = \frac{h_M}{\sqrt{\pi}} e^{-h_M^2(M-M_0)^2} dM \qquad [15\text{-}18]$$

in which h_M is determined by the standard deviation (σ_M) of M_0 as:

$$h_M = 1/(\sqrt{2}\sigma_M)$$ [15-19]

Strictly speaking, the assumption that a Gaussian distribution holds good is not true because we have no M's which are larger than 8.8 or so. Nevertheless, the present discussion may be approximately applicable to an estimate of probability.

The probability for the magnitude to fall in a range between M_1 and M_2 is accordingly given by:

$$W_{GM}(M_1,M_2) = \frac{h_M}{\sqrt{2}} \int_{M_1}^{M_2} e^{-h_M^2(M-M_0)^2} \, dM$$ [15-20]

Defining an error function Φ by:

$$\Phi(\gamma) = \frac{2}{\sqrt{\pi}} \int_0^\gamma e^{-u^2} \, du$$ [15-21]

the probability is then calculated as:

$$W_{GM}(M_1,M_2) = \tfrac{1}{2}\{\Phi[h_M(M_2-M_0)] - \Phi[h_M(M_1-M_0)]\}$$ [15-22]

Dambara (1966) obtained $\sigma_M = 0.8$ for the data set of 19 earthquakes. Although the scatter for earthquakes having a large magnitude is considerably large as can be seen in Fig. 5-68, a fairly small standard deviation can be expected for the data for earthquakes of which the magnitude amounts to 6.6 or under. The following estimate of W_{GM}, which is given in Table 15-VII for $r = 10$ and 50 km respectively, is made assuming $\sigma_M = 0.2$.

The preliminary probabilities for respective magnitude ranges in the Kanto area are given in Table 15-II. In the case when a precursory land deformation having 10 and 50 km mean radii in the area occurs, the synthesized probabilities are immediately calculated from [15-16] as given in Table 15-VIII. The

TABLE 15-VII

$W_{GM}(M_1,M_2)$ for $r = 10$ and 50 km (Rikitake, 1969a)

M_1	M_2	$r = 10$ km	$r = 50$ km
5.0	5.5	0.000	0.000
5.5	6.0	0.023	0.000
6.0	6.5	0.668	0.000
6.5	7.0	0.308	0.000
7.0	7.5	0.002	0.067
7.5	8.0	0.000	0.775
8.0	8.5	0.000	0.158

TABLE 15-VIII

The synthesized probability when an anomalous crustal deformation is assumed to be observed in the Kanto area (Rikitake, 1969a)

M_1	M_2	$r = 10$ km	$r = 50$ km
5.0	5.5	0.000	0.000
5.5	6.0	0.069	0.000
6.0	6.5	0.789	0.000
6.5	7.0	0.142	0.000
7.0	7.5	0.000	0.178
7.5	8.0	0.000	0.822

probabilities thus obtained play an important role in guessing the magnitude of an impending earthquake.

Other prediction elements

Some other precursory changes for which the spatial extent can be observed may possibly be used as prediction elements about which something can be said regarding the magnitude of an expected earthquake. Rikitake (1969a,b) attempted to make use of the mean radius of a geomagnetically anomalous area and that of a foreshock area as well without much success because of scanty data. He demonstrated, however, that a very accurate anticipation of magnitude can be effected by estimating synthesized probabilities provided we could have sufficient data of this kind.

In some cases, the spatial extent of the V_p/V_s anomaly (e.g. Feng et al., 1974; see subsection 9.1.4), a focal mechanism anomaly (e.g. Sadovsky et al., 1972; see subsection 8.3.4), a seismicity gap (see section 8.4), an underground water anomaly (Kuo et al., 1974; see section 12.2) and the like may be used for the purpose raised in this section although it requires a much more complete set of data.

15.2.2. Prediction of occurrence time

The method of estimating synthesized probabilities from preliminary ones can also be applied to prediction of occurrence time of an earthquake provided reliable prediction elements are available. We may use probabilities as obtained from [15-13] as the preliminary ones. As for a possible prediction element, Rikitake (1969a,b) proposed to make use of anomalous land deformation.

Tsubokawa (1969, 1973) was the first who pointed out a linear relation between the logarithmic precursor time T of an anomalous land deformation and earthquake magnitude M. A typical relationship between them is expressed as:

$$\log_{10} T = 0.79M - 1.88 \tag{15-23}$$

in which T is measured in units of days. The coefficients involved have been revised a few times. The validity of equation [15-23] will further be discussed in subsection 15.5.4.

In a fashion similar to the theory developed in the last subsection, we may obtain the probability for an earthquake occurring during a time interval $t_1 - t_2$ as:

$$W_{Gt}(t_1,t_2) = \frac{h_\xi}{\sqrt{\pi}} \int_{\xi_1}^{\xi_2} e^{-h_\xi^2(\xi-\xi_0)^2} \, d\xi \qquad [15\text{-}24]$$

where:

$$\xi = \log_{10} T \qquad [15\text{-}25]$$

and ξ_0 is the logarithmic precursor time as obtained from [15-23]. M, which is involved in [15-23], is to be estimated from [5-11].

h_ξ is defined by:

$$h_\xi = 1/(\sqrt{2}\sigma_\xi) \qquad [15\text{-}26]$$

in which $\sigma_\xi = 0.2$ is tentatively assumed in the following calculation.

The probability for an earthquake to occur during $0 - t$ ($\xi = -\infty \sim \xi$) is obtained as:

$$W_{Gt}(0,t) = \tfrac{1}{2}\{1 + \Phi[h_\xi(\xi - \xi_0)]\} \qquad [15\text{-}27]$$

In the above derivation, it is of course assumed that $\xi - \xi_0$ follows the Gaussian distribution.

$W_{Gt}(0,t)$'s for various t's are then calculated taking r as a parameter as shown in Table 15-IX. The preliminary probability for at least one earthquake to occur during the period $0-t$ is given by [15-13] by putting $t_1 = 0$

TABLE 15-IX

$W_{Gt}(0,t)$ for $r = 10$ and 50 km (Rikitake, 1969a)

$r = 10$ km		$r = 50$ km	
t	$W_{Gt}(0,t)$	t	$W_{Gt}(0,t)$
10 days	0.000	1 year	0.000
30 days	0.000	2 years	0.000
90 days	0.000	5 years	0.000
0.5 year	0.000	10 years	0.002
1 year	0.004	20 years	0.088
2 years	0.114	30 years	0.321
5 years	0.784	40 years	0.568
10 years	0.989	50 years	0.739
20 years	1.000	60 years	0.850

TABLE 15-X

The synthesized probability for earthquake occurrence time when an anomalous crustal deformation is assumed to be observed in the Kanto area (Rikitake, 1969a)

r = 10 km		r = 50 km	
t	$W(0,t)$	t	$W(0,t)$
10 days	0.000	1 year	0.000
30 days	0.000	2 years	0.000
90 days	0.000	5 years	0.000
0.5 year	0.000	10 years	0.003
1 year	0.000	20 years	0.382
2 years	0.028	30 years	0.900
5 years	0.727	40 years	0.986
10 years	0.994	50 years	0.998
20 years	1.000	60 years	1.000

and $t_2 = t$. With the aid of an equation similar to [15-16], we may then be able to calculate synthesized probabilities for earthquake occurrence time. In this case, the whole time range is divided into two divisions, i.e. $0-t$ and $t-\infty$. Actual estimates of synthesized probability are made for the Kanto area on the basis of Table 15-IV combined with Table 15-IX as given in Table 15-X which is of some use in estimating the occurrence time of an earthquake.

If we further combine Table 15-VIII with Table 15-X on the assumption that equation [15-14] holds good, the probabilities of having at least one earthquake, of which the magnitude falls in an interval between M_1 and M_2, in the Kanto area during the period 0 (the epoch at which the anomalous crustal movement is observed) to t are calculated as given in Table 15-XI respectively for r = 10 and 50 km.

Effort to take into account other prediction elements such as foreshocks was made by Rikitake (1969a,b) without much success in improving the probabilities obtained here because the nature of these elements as a precursor are not known very clearly. In view of now-developing precursor time statistics (see section 15.5), however, a better estimate of probabilities of occurrence time of an earthquake will be effected in the near future.

15.2.3. Rating of earthquake risk based on probabilities

In subsection 4.2.1 the strategy of earthquake prediction proposed by the CCEP was briefly mentioned. Whenever the CCEP confirms that something anomalous is taking place in a certain area, the area is designated as an *area of intensified observation*. The area will then be under the special observation of various disciplines. In case these intensified observations lead to a

TABLE 15-XI

The probability for at least one earthquake of magnitude falling in the interval M_1-M_2 to occur in the period $0-t$ as estimated on the assumption that an anomalous crustal deformation is observed in the Kanto area (Rikitake, 1969a)

M_1	M_2	$t=10$ days	$t=30$ days	$t=90$ days	$t=0.5$ year	$t=1$ year	$t=2$ years	$t=5$ years	$t=10$ years	$t=20$ years	$t=30$ years	$t=40$ years	$t=50$ years	$t=60$ years
r = 10 km														
5.0	5.5	0.000	0.000	0.000	0.000	0.000	0.000	0.000	0.000	0.000				
5.5	6.0	0.000	0.000	0.000	0.000	0.000	0.002	0.050	0.069	0.069				
6.0	6.5	0.000	0.000	0.000	0.000	0.000	0.022	0.574	0.784	0.789				
6.5	7.0	0.000	0.000	0.000	0.000	0.000	0.004	0.103	0.141	0.142				
7.0	7.5	0.000	0.000	0.000	0.000	0.000	0.000	0.000	0.000	0.000				
7.5	8.0	0.000	0.000	0.000	0.000	0.000	0.000	0.000	0.000	0.000				
r = 50 km														
5.0	5.5					0.000	0.000	0.000	0.000	0.000	0.000	0.000	0.000	0.000
5.5	6.0					0.000	0.000	0.000	0.000	0.000	0.000	0.000	0.000	0.000
6.0	6.5					0.000	0.000	0.000	0.000	0.000	0.000	0.000	0.000	0.000
6.5	7.0					0.000	0.000	0.000	0.000	0.000	0.000	0.000	0.000	0.000
7.0	7.5					0.000	0.000	0.000	0.000	0.068	0.160	0.175	0.178	0.178
7.5	8.0					0.000	0.000	0.000	0.002	0.314	0.740	0.810	0.820	0.822

conclusion that the anomaly seems likely to be correlated with an earth-quake, the area will be designated to an *area of concentrated observation*. Every effort will then be made toward possible earthquake prediction by concentrating all kinds of observation there.

It should be borne in mind, however, that the sentences such as "some-thing anomalous is taking place" and "a conclusion that the anomaly seems likely to be correlated with an earthquake" are not quite quantitative. How can we define "something anomalous"? What is the measure to think that "the anomaly seems likely to be correlated with an earthquake"?

Rikitake (1969a,b) proposed to make use of the probabilities as estimated in this section for nominating an area to one of intensified observation and/or concentrated observation in order to avoid a subjective-minded deter-mination, although actual estimation of probabilities must be improved in many ways.

The synthesized probabilities in the Kanto area as given in Table 15-XI can be expressed on a $t-M$ plane as can be seen in Fig. 15-1. A point defined by (t, M) on the plane indicates the probability of having at least one earthquake, of which the magnitude falls in the interval between $M -0.25$ and $M +0.25$, occurring between 0 and t.

We may assume that an area is designated as an area of intensified observa-tion when the probability of an earthquake having a magnitude M_α or over to occur exceeds P_α. An area of concentrated observation may be similarly specified by P_β. If:

$$M_\alpha = 6, \quad P_\alpha = 0.2 \qquad\qquad\qquad [15\text{-}28]$$

are tentatively assumed, it is seen that the Kanto area would be designated as an area of intensified observation respectively 2.6 and 15 years after an

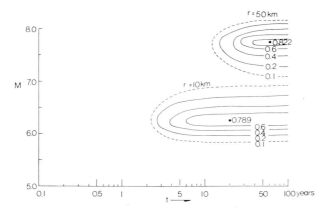

Fig. 15-1. Distribution of the synthesized probability when an anomalous crustal defor-mation having a mean radius r is assumed to be observed in the Kanto area (Rikitake, 1969a,b).

anomalous crustal deformation having a mean radius of 10 and 50 km is observed.

It is not at all clear what values should be taken for P_α and P_β at the present stage of investigation. Their most suitable values must be decided by future experience.

15.3. ULTIMATE STRAIN AND PROBABILITY OF EARTHQUAKE OCCURRENCE

Whereas the probability theory developed in the last section is almost based on empirical facts, a little more physically realistic approach of estimating a probability of the earthquake occurrence time may be possible in some cases.

Let us go back to the working hypothesis on the mechanism of an earthquake based on plate tectonics (see subsections 8.1.7, 8.1.8, and 8.1.9). If it is accepted that the earth's crust is compressed or sheared by a plate motion and that it finally ruptures causing a large earthquake, one may be led to the idea that something can be said about an earthquake occurrence provided that the earth strain is monitored constantly. The most important point of this idea is to assess when the rupture would take place or, in other words, what value the ultimate strain would assume.

15.3.1. Statistics of ultimate strain

Tsuboi (1933), who analyzed the triangulation data of crustal deformation associated with the 1927 Tango earthquake, concluded that the earth's crust ruptures when the crustal strain exceeds 10^{-4} or so (see subsection 5.3.2). This important conclusion was also confirmed by an analysis of the crustal deformation associated with the 1930 North Izu earthquake (Tsuboi, 1933; see subsection 5.3.3).

As data for earthquake-associated crustal movements have accumulated considerably since Tsuboi's analyses, Rikitake (1974b, 1975a) derived statis-

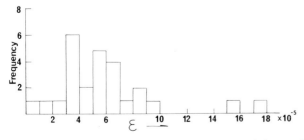

Fig. 15-2. Histogram of the ultimate strain of the earth's crust as deduced from levellings and triangulations over earthquake areas (Rikitake, 1975c).

TABLE 15-XII

Crustal strain associated with an earthquake in the immediate vicinity of the epicenter (Rikitake, 1974b, 1975a)

Earthquake	Year	M	Location	Strain $\times 10^{-5}$	Remarks
Levelling survey					
Nobi	1891	7.9	35.6°N, 136.6°E	5.9	route 1
Nobi	1891	7.9	35.6°N, 136.6°E	5.8	route 2
Ugosen	1914	6.4	39.5°N, 140.4°E	6.2	
Omachi	1918	6.1,6.1	36.5°N, 137.8°E	3.0	two shocks
Kanto	1923	7.9	35.2°N, 139.3°E	5.8	Sagami Bay coast
Tango	1927	7.5	35.6°N, 135.1°E	3.2	Gomura fault
Tango	1927	7.5	35.6°N, 135.1°E	3.5	Yamada fault
South Bulgaria	1928	6.7,6.7	42° N, 25° E	15.0	two shocks
North Izu	1930	7.0	35.1°N, 139.0°E	4.0	
Noto	1933	6.0	37.1°N, 137.0°E	0.5	
Nagano	1941	6.2	36.7°N, 138.3°E	2.8	
Tottori	1943	7.4	35.5°N, 134.2°E	1.7	
Fukui	1948	7.3	36.1°N, 136.2°E	3.6	
Kern County	1952	7.7	35.0°N, 119.0°W	6.0	
North Miyagi	1962	6.5	38.7°N, 141.1°E	3.5	
Matsushiro	1965	6.3	36.5°N, 138.2°E	6.3	swarm activity;
	− 1966				cumulative magnitude
Triangulation survey					
San Francisco	1906	8.3	38° N, 123° W	17.0	San Andreas fault
Kanto	1923	7.9	35.2°N, 139.3°E	7.5	submarine fault
Tango	1927	7.5	35.6°N, 135.1°E	3.5	Gomura fault
North Izu	1930	7.0	35.1°N, 139.0°E	9.0	Tanna fault
Imperial Valley	1940	7.1	32.8°N, 115.5°W	8.5	
Tottori	1943	7.4	35.5°N, 134.2°E	5.0	
Fukui	1948	7.3	36.1°N, 136.2°E	5.6	subsurface fault
Kern County	1952	7.7	35.0°N, 119.0°W	4.3	
Fairview Peak	1954	7.1	39.5°N, 118.5°E	6.2	
Alaska	1964	8.4	61.1°N, 147.6°E	8.4	

tics of the ultimate strain on the basis of the now-available data as shown in Table 15-XII. A histogram of the ultimate strain of the earth's crust is then drawn as shown in Fig. 15-2. The mean strain to rupture E and the standard deviation of the rupture strain σ are obtained as:

$$E = 4.7 \times 10^{-5}, \quad \sigma = 1.9 \times 10^{-5} \tag{15-29}$$

15.3.2. Probability of earthquake occurrence as estimated from crustal strain

On assuming that $\epsilon - E$, where ϵ is the crustal strain in a certain region, obeys the law of Gaussian distribution and that $d\epsilon/dt$ or accumulation rate of strain is given there, Rikitake (1974b) calculated probabilities for a large earthquake to recur in areas such as the Kanto area, off eastern Hokkaido and off the Pacific coast of Central Japan. As no observation of crustal deformation is available off the coast, crustal strains in the crust under the sea are estimated by extrapolating those on land on the basis of the subduction plate model (Shimazaki, 1974a, b). It is interesting to note that an earthquake of magnitude 7.4 actually occurred off eastern Hokkaido on June 17, 1973. The cumulative probability of recurrence there since the time of the 1894 earthquake ($M = 7.9$) has been estimated as 80% or so (Rikitake, 1974b; see Fig. 8-12, subsections 4.2.1 and 8.4.3).

Weibull distribution analysis

The assumption that $\epsilon - E$ is governed by a Gaussian distribution is obviously inadequate because ϵ is to be defined over a range for which $\epsilon < 0$. In order to improve this point, Hagiwara (1974b) proposed to apply a Weibull distribution (Weibull, 1951), which has been widely used in quality control research, to the present analysis of probability. It has been proved that the distribution is very useful for analyses of the failure time of buildings, factory products and so on.

Let us denote a small time interval by Δt. The probability for crustal rupture to occur between t and $t + \Delta t$ is given by $\lambda(t)\Delta t$ on the condition that the rupture did not occur prior to t. $\lambda(t)$, called the hazard rate, is distributed in a Weibull distribution as:

$$\lambda(t) = Kt^m \tag{15-30}$$

where $K > 0$ and $m > -1$.

The cumulative failure rate is given as:

$$F(t) = 1 - R(t) \tag{15-31}$$

where $R(t)$ is called the reliability and defined by:

$$R(t) = \exp\left[-\int_0^t \lambda(t)dt\right] = \exp\left(-\frac{Kt^{m+1}}{m+1}\right) \tag{15-32}$$

Failure density function $f(t)$ is then obtained as:

$$f(t) = -\frac{dR(t)}{dt} = Kt^m \exp\left(-\frac{Kt^{m+1}}{m+1}\right) \tag{15-33}$$

The mean time to rupture, or mean life so called in quality control research, is given as:

$$E[t] = \int_0^\infty t f(t)dt = \left(\frac{K}{m+1}\right)^{-1/(m+1)} \Gamma\left(\frac{m+2}{m+1}\right) \tag{15-34}$$

where Γ denotes a gamma function. In a similar fashion, the mean square of the time to rupture is obtained as:

$$E[t^2] = \int_0^\infty t^2 f(t)dt = \left(\frac{K}{m+1}\right)^{-2/(m+1)} \Gamma\left(\frac{m+3}{m+1}\right) \tag{15-35}$$

The standard deviation of the rupture time is defined by $(E[t^2] - E^2[t])^{\frac{1}{2}}$ which is obtained as:

$$(E[t^2] - E^2[t])^{\frac{1}{2}} = E[t] \left[\Gamma\left(\frac{m+3}{m+1}\right) - \Gamma^2\left(\frac{m+2}{m+1}\right)\right]^{\frac{1}{2}} \bigg/ \Gamma\left(\frac{m+2}{m+1}\right) \tag{15-36}$$

When the double logarithm of $1/R$ is taken, we obtain:

$$\log_e \log_e \left(\frac{1}{R}\right) = \log_e \left(\frac{K}{m+1}\right) + (m+1) \log_e t \tag{15-37}$$

The above discussion has been developed in terms of t. It may be approximately assumed, however, that strain accumulation due to a plate motion proceeds with a constant strain rate u. The time origin is taken at the occurrence time of a large earthquake when most of the strain energy accumulated is released. In that case, we assume:

$$\epsilon = ut \tag{15-38}$$

and so the entire discussion above can be made in terms of ϵ. For instance, [15-37] can be rewritten as:

$$\log_e \log_e \left(\frac{1}{R(\epsilon)}\right) = \log_e \left(\frac{Ku^{-m-1}}{m+1}\right) + (m+1) \log_e \epsilon \tag{15-39}$$

which indicates that $\log_e \log_e (1/R)$ is linearly correlated with $\log_e \epsilon$.

In order to determine m and K from actual data, we usually proceed in the following way. Counting frequency of earthquake occurrence n_i for each strain range having an interval $\Delta\epsilon$, probability density for a range between $i\Delta\epsilon$ and $(i+1)\Delta\epsilon$ $(i = 0, 1, 2, ...)$ can be obtained from:

$$f_i \Delta\epsilon = n_i/N \tag{15-40}$$

where N is the total number of the data. Accordingly, the cumulative probability is obtained as:

$$F = \Delta\epsilon \sum_{i=0}^{i} f_i = \sum_{i=0}^{i} n_i/N \tag{15-41}$$

so that R can readily be calculated from [15-31].

The above-mentioned procedure is applied to the data of ultimate strain which are given in Table 15-XII. Omitting extreme values of ultimate strain such as those for the 1906 San Francisco, 1928 South Bulgaria and the 1933

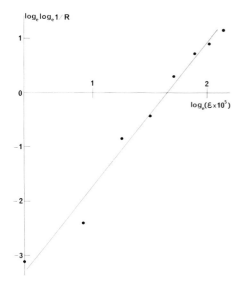

Fig. 15-3. $\log_e \log_e (1/R)$ vs. $\log_e \epsilon$ fit for a Weibull distribution (Rikitake, 1975a).

Noto earthquakes, a straight line fitting the $\log_e \log_e (1/R)$ vs. $\log_e \epsilon$ plots is made as can be seen in Fig. 15-3. $m = 1.6$ and $Ku^{-m-1} = 0.0337$ are thus obtained when ϵ is measured in units of 10^{-5}.

On the condition that no crustal rupture occurs in the strain range $0—\epsilon$, the probability for the crust to break for the strain range $\epsilon—(\epsilon + \epsilon_s)$ is given by:

$$F_s(\epsilon_s | \epsilon) = [F(\epsilon + \epsilon_s) - F(\epsilon)]/[1 - F(\epsilon)] \qquad [15\text{-}42]$$

which is nothing but a hazard rate for the strain range in question.

South Kanto area

Much of the crustal deformation currently in progress in the South Kanto area near Tokyo, Japan, was presented in subsection 5.4.1. The mean rate of maximum shearing strain was estimated as 0.0568×10^{-5}/year.

With the aid of parameters m and K, determined above, and the strain rate, it is possible to calculate various quantities related to the Weibull distribution analysis. In Figs. 15-4 and 15-5 are shown how the cumulative probability for a major earthquake to recur and the hazard rate for 10 years (probability of having a crustal rupture within 10 years' time) change with the year, the time origin being taken at 1923 when the Kanto earthquake ($M = 7.9$) occurred. The probability of having an earthquake during the period 1923—1974 is 20%. The probability will reach 50 and 90% by 2000 and 2050, respectively.

The statistics of the ultimate strain made in subsection 15.3.1 are only for

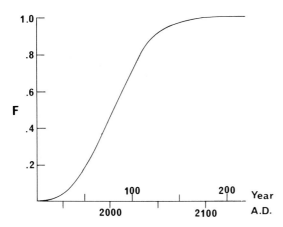

Fig. 15-4. Cumulative probability for an earthquake to recur in the South Kanto area (Rikitake, 1975a).

crustal movement associated with a major earthquake having a magnitude 6 or over, it is implicitly assumed that the probabilities estimated in this subsection are for major earthquakes only. The probability estimated here may be used for the preliminary probability of earthquake occurrence as argued in subsection 15.2.2. It would in fact be more realistic to rely on a probability derived from physically observed facts than only to make use of statistical data from the past.

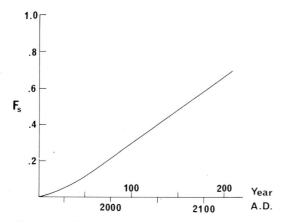

Fig. 15-5. Conditional probability for an earthquake occurring in the South Kanto area within 10 years' time from a certain epoch indicated on the abscissa. No earthquake is assumed to occur before the epoch (Rikitake, 1975a).

North Izu area

In subsection 5.4.2 we obtained a current shearing strain rate of 0.096×10^{-5}/year in the North Izu area, about 100 km southwest of Tokyo, where the North Izu earthquake ($M = 7.0$) occurred in 1930. The probability for an earthquake recurring there in these 45 years is estimated as 40%. The probability will reach 85% by the end of this century.

San Andreas fault area

Scholz and Fitch (1969, 1970; see subsection 5.4.4) studied strain accumulation over the San Andreas fault. For an area including San Francisco, they obtained a strain rate for the maximum shear of 0.05×10^{-5}/year. Assuming that this value can be taken for the strain rate and that all the strain hitherto accumulated was released at the time of the 1906 San Francisco earthquake, the cumulative probability is calculated as shown in Fig. 15-6. It is seen from the figure that the probability of an earthquake recurring there during 1906—1975 amounts to some 30%. The probability will reach 50% by the end of this century.

Similar estimate of probability can be made for the Fort Tejon area where a great earthquake occurred in 1857. If the strain rate amounting to 0.06×10^{-5}/year (Scholz and Fitch, 1969) is true, the cumulative probability of having an earthquake there has already reached 80% in 1975.

In view of the objections by Savage and Burford (1970, 1971) that the strain accumulation estimated by Scholz and Fitch (1969, 1971) may be an overestimate because the crustal movements seem to be accounted for largely by creeping at the fault, the probabilities obtained here may contain some uncertainties.

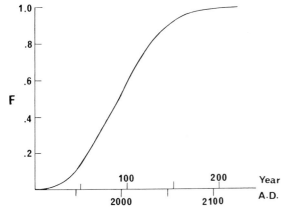

Fig. 15-6. Cumulative probability for an earthquake to recur in the San Francisco area (Rikitake, 1975a).

15.4. PREDICTION BASED ON A DILATANCY MODEL

What the author presented in the last two sections may be considered to be a kind of long-term prediction of earthquake magnitude and occurrence time in terms of probability.

Field observations resulted in various premonitory effects that may possibly be applicable to earthquake prediction. They are the anomalous land uplift, the change in electric resistivity, the change in underground water, the change in radon content, the change in the V_p/V_s ratio or V_p and the like as presented in the foregoing chapters. Laboratory experiments (see Chapter 13) generally seem to support these premonitory effects revealed by field observations when rock samples are in a state close to rupture.

Most of these premonitory effects seem to be accounted for by dilatancy generation (see Chapter 14) when the earth's crust is stressed to a strain close to its ultimate one. The fact that the crust does not break all of sudden, but that it undergoes premonitory changes of various kinds is especially important for earthquake prediction.

The logarithmic precursor time seems to be correlated with earthquake magnitude as already argued in section 14.1 and will be supplemented by the extensive statistics of precursors in section 15.5. It is therefore possible to foresee the magnitude of a coming earthquake to some extent provided a precursor time is known. The trouble is that a precursor time is only obtained after an earthquake occurs. Reversing the logic, the time of earthquake occurrence may be obtained provided the magnitude can be guessed, at least probabilistically, by some other means such as the spatial extent of the precursory effect. This is what was presented in subsection 15.2.2.

Precursors of a few particular kinds such as the V_p/V_s ratio tend to recover their pre-anomaly level prior to the earthquake occurrence. In this case, it seems possible to define the approximate precursor time and consequently the earthquake magnitude. Although the exact time of earthquake occurrence is not known, it seems likely that the main shock occurs within a time span amounting to 10% of anomaly duration after the recovery of the V_p/V_s ratio.

In such lucky cases as mentioned in the last paragraph, the prediction can be said to be semi-deterministic, so that much stress should be put on studying precursors which indicate a pre-earthquake recovery in the future study of earthquake prediction.

15.5. STATISTICS OF EARTHQUAKE PRECURSORS

The linear relationship between the logarithmic precursor time and earthquake magnitude, as first pointed out by Tsubokawa (1969, 1973) and extended by Scholz et al. (1973), Whitcomb et al. (1973) and others, has an important bearing on earthquake prediction. It is obvious from these empirical laws that the longer the precursor time is, the larger is the magnitude. For example, the precursor time for a magnitude 7 earthquake amounts to several years, while that for a magnitude 4 one amounts to a few tens of days. In contrast to these magnitude-dependent precursors, we sometimes observe precursors of another kind which appear immediately prior to, say a few hours, a comparatively large earthquake.

In order to see when, how and by what kind of measurement precursors of these two kinds are observed, the author (Rikitake, 1975c) developed statistics of earthquake precursors on the basis of as many data as he could collect. Although the collection is by no means complete, he could analyze 282 precursors. Some more data were added later although they became available too late to be included in the statistics. Many of the data are of Japanese and American origins because they are readily accessible to the author, but fairly many Soviet data were also made use of from literature published or translated either in Japanese or English. The author thinks that many data may be available from the People's Republic of China, New Zealand, Italy, Turkey and other seismic countries although no great effort was made to include them in the statistics.

After completing the statistics, the author discovered a paper by Myachkin and Zubkov (1973) on the statistics of earthquake precursors. This paper does not seem to indicate the various natures of precursors of different kinds in great detail.

15.5.1. Classification of precursors

The precursors are classified into 15 disciplines according to observational methods, and are given in Table 15-XIII which is supplemented with the data in Table 15-XIV although they became known to the author after completing the present statistics.

In Table 15-XV are given the numbers of data assigned to the 15 disciplines along with their abbreviations.

Brief descriptions of each discipline will be given below:

Land deformation (l)
Most of data of this discipline were taken by means of levelling surveys (section 5.7). A few data were taken from geodimeter surveys (subsection 5.4.4) and the measurement of a 100-m base line of rhombic shape near Tokyo (subsection 5.3.13). Precursory land uplifts revealed as anomalous sea retreats (section 6.1) and those observed by a tide-gauge observation (subsection 6.2.2) were also included.

Tilt and strain (t)
Many changes in ground tilt and strain have been reported from observa-

TABLE 15-XIII

Precursor data (Rikitake, 1975c)

Earthquake	Year	M	Epicenter	Amount	Precursor time (days)	Epicentral distance (km)	Remarks
Discipline 1: land deformation							
Rhombus base-line							
Kanto, Japan	1923	7.9	35.2°N, 139.3°E	1×10^{-5} in strain	1,500	70	Tsuboi (1933)
Geodimeter							
Hollister, U.S.A.	1960	5.0	36.8°N, 121.4°W	4×10^{-6}	0.0125	10	California, Hofmann (1968)
Corralitos	1964	5.2	37.0°N, 121.7°W	3×10^{-6}	400	10	California, Hofmann (1968)
Levelling							
Sekihara, Japan	1927	5.3	37.5°N, 138.8°E	1.5×10^{-5}	90	0	Tsuboi (1933)
Tonankai	1944	8.0	33.7°N, 136.2°E	—	3,600	150	sudden change in secular movement; Geographical Survey Institute (1969b)
				5×10^{-6}	0.15		Geographical Survey Institute (1969b)
Nagaoka	1961	5.2	37.5°N, 138.8°E	3×10^{-6}	1,000	4	Kaminuma et al. (1973)
North Mino	1961	7.0	36.0°N, 136.8°E	7×10^{-6}	4,300	15	Tsubokawa (1973)
Niigata	1964	7.5	38.4°N, 139.2°E	3×10^{-6}	3,600	40	Dambara (1973)
Omi	1967	5.0	36.5°N, 138.0°E	5×10^{-6}	120	3	Tsubokawa (1973)
Dunaharaszti, Hungary	1956	6	near Budapest	—	290	—	5.5 cm subsidence a few days before the shock; Bendefy (1966)

Location	Year	Magnitude	Coordinates	Precursor			Reference
Tashkent, U.S.S.R.	1966	5.5	41.3°N, 69.3°E	—	7,000	—	sudden change in secular movement; Mescherikov (1968)
Garm	1969	5.7	39.0°N, 70.3°E	—	620	—	sudden change in secular movement; Sadovsky and Nersesov (1974)
San Fernando, U.S.A.	1971	6.4	34.4°N, 118.4°W	1.2×10^{-5} in strain	2,500	15	Castle et al. (1974)
Sea retreat							
Ajikazawa, Japan	1793	6.9	40.7°N, 140.0°E	1 – 2 m in land uplift	0.17	—	
Sado	1802	6.6	37.8°N, 138.4°E	1 m	0.21	—	
Hamada	1872	7.1	34.8°N, 132.0°E	2–3 m	0.008	—	
Tango	1927	7.5	35.6°N, 135.1°E	1 m	0.10	—	Data taken from Imamura (1937)
Tide-gauge							
Niigata, Japan	1964	7.5	38.4°N, 139.2°E	2 cm in subsidence	360	40	Tsubokawa et al. (1964)
Discipline t: tilt and strain							
Horizontal pendulum tiltmeter							
Kanto, Japan	1923	7.9	35.2°N, 139.3°E	1.5×10^{-5} in tilt	0.33	80	Tokyo Univ. Obs., Imamura (1928)
Tottori	1943	7.4	35.5°N, 134.2°E	5×10^{-7}	0.25	60	Ikuno Obs., Sassa and Nishimura (1951)
Tonankai	1944	8.0	33.7°N, 136.2°E	2×10^{-7}	0.24	160	Kamigamo Obs., Sassa and Nishimura (1951)
Nanki	1950	6.7	33.9°N, 135.8°E	7.5×10^{-7}	0.29	80	Tamamizu Obs.
				2×10^{-7}	0.28	120	Kamigamo Obs.
				1×10^{-7}	0.23	200	Kochi Obs., Sassa and Nishimura (1951)

TABLE 15-XIII (continued)

Earthquake	Year	M	Epicenter	Amount	Precursor time (days)	Epicentral distance (km)	Remarks
Discipline t: tilt and strain (continued)							
Daishoji-oki	1952	6.8	36.5°N, 136.2°E	3×10^{-4} in tilt	90	40	Ogoya Obs.
				1×10^{-4}	10		Ogoya Obs., Nishimura and Hosoyama (1953)
Yoshino	1952	7.0	34.5°N, 135.8°E	—	400	80	change in tilt direction; Kamigamo Obs.
				3×10^{-6}	15		Kamigamo Obs.
				1×10^{-5}	15	60	Kishu Obs.
				1×10^{-5}	15	80	Yura Obs., Tanaka (1965)
Odaigahara	1960	6.0	34.5°N, 136.0°E	3×10^{-6}	200	40	Kishu Obs.
				5×10^{-6}	100		Kishu Obs.
				3×10^{-6}	10		Kishu Obs.
				1.5×10^{-5}	120	90	Shionomisaki Obs.
				2×10^{-6}	20		Shionomisaki Obs.
				3.3×10^{-5}	200	90	Yura Obs.
				4×10^{-6}	110		Yura Obs.
				3×10^{-6}	20	90	Yura Obs.
				—	30	90	change in tilt direction; Akibasan Obs.
				—	5		change in tilt direction; Akibasan Obs.
				1.5×10^{-5}	30	90	Oura Obs.
				3×10^{-6}	5		Oura Obs.
				6×10^{-6}	30	100	Kamigamo Obs.
				1×10^{-6}	5		Kamigamo Obs., Tanaka (1965)

Region	Year	M	Coordinates				Observatory / Reference
Hyuganada	1961	7.0	31.6°N, 131.9°E	5×10^{-7}	12	120	Makimine Obs.
				5×10^{-7}	4		Makimine Obs., Tanaka (1965)
North Mino	1961	7.0	36.0°N, 136.8°E	2.5×10^{-5}	50	40	Ogoya Obs.
				5×10^{-6}	15		Ogoya Obs.
				1×10^{-5}	50	60	Kamioka Obs.
				5×10^{-7}	15		Kamioka Obs., Tanaka (1965)
Shirahama-oki	1962	6.4	33.6°N, 135.2°E	1×10^{-6}	20	35	Yura Obs.
				5×10^{-7}	7		Yura Obs.
				1×10^{-5}	40	65	Kishu Obs.
				1×10^{-6}	3		Kishu Obs., Tanaka (1965)
Echizenmisaki-oki	1963	6.9	35.8°N, 135.8°E	1.8×10^{-5}	180	80	Kamigamo Obs.
				5×10^{-6}	60		Kamigamo Obs.
				3×10^{-6}	15		Kamigamo Obs.
				5×10^{-6}	180	90	Ogoya Obs.
				7×10^{-6}	70		Ogoya Obs.
				4×10^{-6}	15		Ogoya Obs.
				2×10^{-6}	180	110	Ikuno Obs.
				2×10^{-6}	60		Ikuno Obs.
				1×10^{-6}	10		Ikuno Obs., Tanaka (1965)
Ashkhabad, U.S.S.R.	1957	4	—	5×10^{-7}	0.042	25	Ashkhabad Obs., Ostrovskiy (1972, 1974)
Alma Ata	1958	4.0 4.7	—	3×10^{-7}	0.125	250	Alma Ata Obs., Ostrovskiy (1972, 1974)
Afghanistan	1959	5.0	—	3×10^{-6}	0.5	245	Kondara Obs., Ostrovskiy (1972, 1974)
Afghanistan	1959	3.5	—	3×10^{-6}	0.5	300	Kondara Obs., Ostrovskiy (1972, 1974)

TABLE 15-XIII (continued)

Earthquake	Year	M	Epicenter	Amount	Precursor time (days)	Epicentral distance (km)	Remarks
Discipline t: tilt and strain (continued)							
Bubble level							
San Fernando, U.S.A. (aftershock)	1971	4.7	34.4°N, 118.4°W	6×10^{-4} in tilt	0.17	10	observed by a level attached to a theodolite; Sylvester and Pollard (1972)
Water-tube tiltmeter							
Fukui, Japan (aftershock)	1948	ca. 5	36.2°N, 136.2°E	1×10^{-6}	0.008	20	Bandojima Obs., Hagiwara et al. (1949a)
Niigata	1964	7.5	38.4°N, 139.2°E	1.5×10^{-5}	3,000	80	Maze Obs., Kasahara (1973)
Matsushiro	1966	4.5 4.5 4.5	36°N, 138°E	1.5×10^{-7}	0.083	2.4 4.2 2.4	Matsushiro Obs., Yamada (1973)
Matsushiro	1966	4.6	36°N, 138°E	3×10^{-7}	0.042	6.7	Matsushiro Obs., Yamada (1973)
Matsushiro	1966	4.7	36°N, 138°E	8×10^{-7}	0.042	8.1	Matsushiro Obs., Yamada (1973)
Matsushiro	1966	4.4 4.4	36°N, 138°E	6×10^{-7}	0.042	4.5 4.1	Matsushiro Obs., Yamada (1973)
Matsushiro	1966	4.6	36°N, 138°E	5×10^{-7}	0.050	4.9	Matsushiro Obs., Yamada (1973)
Central Gifu	1969	6.6	35.8°N, 137.1°E	5×10^{-7}/year 5×10^{-7}/year	250 250	48 60	Inuyama Obs., Kamitakara Obs., Shichi (1973)
Atsumi Peninsula	1971	6.1	34.5°N, 137.1°E	5×10^{-7}/year	250	90	Inuyama Obs., Shichi (1973)
Danville, U.S.A.	1970	4.3 4.3 4.1 4.0	37.8°N, 121.9°W	3×10^{-7}	30 1.0	30	Berkeley Obs., Wood and Allen

Borehole tiltmeter

Location	Year						Reference
Hollister area, U.S.A.	1973	3.0	ranging from 36.5–37.0°N to 121.1–121.7°W		7	3	Nutting Obs.
Hollister area	1973	2.8			5	7	Nutting Obs.
Hollister area	1973	2.7			5	6	Nutting Obs.
Hollister area	1973	2.9			5	7	Nutting Obs.
Hollister area	1974	4.3			15	17	Nutting Obs.
Hollister area	1973	2.8			7	8	Libby Obs.
Hollister area	1973	2.6			33	5	Libby Obs.
Hollister area	1974	2.7			30	10	Libby Obs.
Hollister area	1973	2.9			15	6	Sage Obs.
Hollister area	1973	2.8		sudden change in tilt direction	10	7	Sage Obs.
Hollister area	1974	2.7			15	4	Sage Obs.
						Data taken from Johnston and Mortensen (1974)	

Strainmeter

Location	Year						Reference
Yoshino, Japan	1952	7.0	34.5°N, 135.8°E	2.5×10^{-6} in strain	300	50	Osakayama Obs., Sassa and Nishimura (1955)
				1.5×10^{-6}	120	72	Ide Obs.
				3×10^{-6}	60		Ide Obs.
				1×10^{-6}	11		Ide Obs., Takada (1959)
Central Gifu	1969	6.6	35.8°N, 137.1°E	5×10^{-7}/year	250	48	Inuyama Obs., Shichi (1973)
South Tien Shan, U.S.S.R.	1965	6.0	41.8°N, 79.4°E	9×10^{-8}	15	250	Talgar Obs.
				5×10^{-8}	4		Talgar Obs., Latynina and Karmaleyeva (1970)

TABLE 15-XIII (continued)

Earthquake	Year	M	Epicenter	Amount	Precursor time (days)	Epicentral distance (km)	Remarks
Discipline t: tilt and strain (continued)							
Hindu Kushu	1965	7.5	36.3° N, 70.7° E	change in strain rate	4	300	Kondara Obs., Latynina and Karmaleyeva (1972)
Dushambe	1965	4.5		change in strain rate	3	100	Kondara Obs., Latynina and Karmaleyeva (1972)
Djungarskoie Ala-Tau	1967	5.0	45.4° N, 80.4° E	5×10^{-8} in strain	10	320	Talgar Obs., Latynina and Karmaleyeva (1970)
Pamirs	1969	3.0	39.0° N, 70.3° E	3×10^{-8}	2	5	Garm Obs., Latynina and Karmaleyeva (1970)
Discipline f: foreshock							
Hachinohe-oki, Japan	1763	7.4	40.7° N, 142.0° E		30		Utsu (1972a)
Tokachi-oki	1843	8.4	41.8° N, 144.8° E		15		Utsu (1972a)
Iga	1854	6.9	34.8° N, 136.2° E		2		Musha (1951)
Edo	1855	6.9	35.8° N, 139.8° E		0.42		Musha (1951)
Hachinohe-oki	1856	7.8	40.5° N, 143.5° E		4		Utsu (1972a)
Hamada	1872	7.1	34.8° N, 132.0° E		5		Kaminuma et al. (1973)
Nemuro-oki	1894	7.9	42.4° N, 146.3° E		0.21		Utsu (1972a)
Rikuu	1896	7.5	39.5° N, 140.7° E		8		Kaminuma et al. (1973)
Kamitakai	1897	6.3	36.6° N, 138.2° E		0.35		Kaminuma et al. (1973)

Location	Year	Magnitude	Coordinates	Value	Reference
Omachi	1918	6.1 6.1	36.5°N, 137.8°E	0.42	Kaminuma et al. (1973)
Shimabara	1922	6.5 5.9	32.7°N, 130.1°E	0.46	Kaminuma et al. (1973)
Kanto	1923	7.9	35.2°N, 139.3°E	1,500	activity in Wakayama Pref.; Kanamori (1972c)
North Gifu	1927	4.6	36.1°N, 137.0°E	40	Mogi (1963)
North Hiro-shima	1927	6.0	35.0°N, 132.8°E	70	Mogi (1963)
Sekihara	1927	5.3	37.5°N, 138.8°E	0.029	Kaminuma et al. (1973)
Central Kuma-moto	1929	4.9	32.9°N, 130.8°E	11	Mogi (1963)
North Izu	1930	7.0	35.1°N, 139.0°E	19	Mogi (1963)
North Hiro-shima	1930	6.0	35.0°N, 132.9°E	60	Mogi (1963)
East Yamanashi	1931	6.0	35.4°N, 138.9°E	14	Mogi (1963)
Hyuganada	1931	6.6	32.2°N, 132.1°E	8	Mogi (1963)
Sanriku	1933	8.3	39.1°N, 144.7°E	60	Kaminuma et al. (1973)
North Kuma-moto	1933	5.0	33.0°N, 130.9°E	15	Mogi (1963)
West Oita	1935	4.8	33.1°N, 131.1°E	1	Mogi (1963)
Central Kyoto	1936	4.5	35.1°N, 135.8°E	21	Mogi (1963)
Central Kuma-moto	1937	5.0	32.8°N, 130.8°E	174	Mogi (1963)
South Nagasaki	1937	5.0	32.8°N, 130.0°E	76	Mogi (1963)
Central Yama-nashi	1940	5.0	35.6°N, 138.5°E	12	Mogi (1963)
Nagano	1941	6.2	36.7°N, 138.3°E	56	Mogi (1963)
Mikawa	1945	7.1	34.7°N, 137.0°E	2	Kaminuma et al. (1973)
East Kumamoto	1946	5.1	32.7°N, 130.6°E	2	Mogi (1963)
Imaichi	1949	6.4 6.7	36.7°N, 139.7°E	1	Kaminuma et al. (1973)
Tokachi-oki	1952	8.1	42.3°N, 143.9°E	2	Kaminuma et al. (1973)

TABLE 15-XIII (continued)

Discipline f: foreshock (continued)

Earthquake	Year	M	Epicenter	Amount	Precursor time (days)	Epicentral distance (km)	Remarks
Oshima Peninsula	1953	5.4	42.2°N, 139.9°E		66		Mogi (1963)
Boso-oki	1953	7.5	34.3°N, 141.8°E		2,200		activity in Wakayama Pref.; Kanamori (1972c)
Amami-oshima	1954	6.1	29.3°N, 131.3°E		0.33		Mogi (1963)
Niijima Is.	1957	6.3	34.3°N, 139.4°E		12		Mogi (1963)
Kamikochi	1963	4.8	36.2°N, 137.6°E		5		Mogi (1963)
Matsushiro	1964	3.3	36°N, 138°E		0.17		Suyehiro et al. (1964)
Matsushiro	1967	ca. 5	36°N, 138°E		180		Sakai Village; Hagiwara (1973)
Matsushiro	1967	ca. 5	36°N, 138°E		210		Azuma Village; Hagiwara (1973)
Matsushiro	1967	ca. 5	36°N, 138°E		120		Koshoku City; Hagiwara (1973)
Matsushiro	1967	ca. 5	36°N, 138°E		120		Togura Town; Hagiwara (1973)
Matsushiro	1967	ca. 5	36°N, 138°E		120		Kamiyamada Town; Hagiwara (1973)
Matsushiro	1967	ca. 5	36°N, 138°E		150		Sanada Town; Hagiwara (1973)
Tokachi-oki	1968	7.9	40.7°N, 143.6°E		14		Kaminuma et al. (1973)
Off Kii Peninsula	1968	4.9	33.0°N, 135.6°E		5		Tsumura (1973)
Wachi	1968	5.6	35.2°N, 135.4°E		180		Kyoto Pref.; Okano and Hirano (1970)
Southeast Akita	1970	6.2	39.2°N, 140.8°E		100		Res. Group Microearthq. (1971)
Chizu	1970	4.3	35.3°N, 134.2°E		0.21		Tottori Pref.; Kijimuto und

Location	Year	Magnitude	Coordinates	Value	Reference
sula Hachijojima Is.-oki	1972	7.3	33.3°N, 141.0°E	2.3	Kasahara et al. (1973)
Off Itrup, Kuril Islands	1958	8.0	44.3°N, 148.5°E	120	Utsu (1972a)
Off Urup	1963	8.1	43.8°N, 150.0°E	1	Utsu (1972a)
Off Shikotan	1969	7.8	40.1°N, 142.5°E	1	Utsu (1972a)
Off South California, U.S.A.	1812	—	34°N, 120°W	0.021	NOAA (1973)
Soccoro	1906	—	34.0°N, 107.0°W	10	New Mexico; NOAA (1973)
Northeast Arizona	1910	—	36.0°N, 111.1°W	13	NOAA (1973)
Plesant Valley	1915	7.6	40.5°N, 117.5°W	0.8	Nevada; NOAA (1973)
Elsimore	1921	6.1	38.8°N, 112.2°W	17	Utah; NOAA (1973)
Whittier	1929	4.7	34°N, 118°W	64	California; Richter (1958) NOAA (1973)
Ellensburg	1934	—	47°N, 121°W	4	NOAA (1973)
Montana	1935	6.3	46.6°N, 112.0°W	9	NOAA (1973)
	1935	6.0			
Belen	1935	—	34.7°N, 106.8°W	5	New Mexico; NOAA (1973)
Kern County	1952	7.7	35.0°N, 118.8°W	0.092	Richter (1958)
Hawthorne	1956	5.3	38.3°N, 119.0°W	0.0021	Nevada; NOAA (1973)
Rat Islands	1965	7.7	51.3°N, 178.6°E	4	K. Mogi (personal communication, 1968)
Parkfield	1966	5.3	35.9°N, 120.9°W	0.13	California; K. Mogi (personal communication, 1968)
Danville	1970	4.3 4.3 4.1 4.0	37.8°N, 121.9°W	16	California; Lee et al. (1971)
Bear Valley South	1972	4.6	36.5°N, 121.1°W	5	California; Wyss and Lee (1973)

TABLE 15-XIII (continued)

Earthquake	Year	M	Epicenter	Amount	Precursor time (days)	Epicentral distance (km)	Remarks
Discipline f: foreshock (continued)							
Off Chile, Chile	1960	8.3	39.5°S, 74.5°W		1.38		Suyehiro (1966)
Kremasta, Greece	1966	6.3	38.9°N, 21.5°E		60		Rothé (1970)
Managua, Nicaragua	1972	6.2	12.1°N, 86.2°W		0.125		Matumoto and Latham (1973)
Discipline b: b-value							
Fairbanks, U.S.A.	1970	3.0	—	1.3 → 0.8 decrease	7		Alaska; Scholz et al. (1973)
Fairbanks	1970	5.0	—	—	60		Alaska; Scholz et al. (1973)
Danville	1970	4.3	37.8°N, 121.9°W	1.2 → 0.8	1		California; Bufe (1970)
Danville	1970	4.0	37.8°N, 121.9°W	1.05 → 0.6	1.2		California; Bufe (1970)
Danville	1970	3.7 3.6	37.8°N, 121.9°W	1.2 → 0.9	155		California; Wyss and Lee (1973)
Hollister	1971	3.9	36.7°N, 121.3°W	0.8 → 0.6	40		California; Wyss and Lee (1973)
Hollister	1971	3.9	36.7°N, 121.3°W	0.8 → 0.4	9		California; Wyss and Lee (1973)
Bear Valley North	1972	5.0	36.6°N, 121.2°W	1.0 → 0.8	130		California; Wyss and Lee (1973)
Bear Valley South	1972	4.6	36.5°N, 121.1°W	1.2 → 0.9	120		California; Wyss and Lee (1973)
Bear Valley South	1972	4.6	36.5°N, 121.1°W	0.9 → 0.8	5		California; Wyss and Lee (1973)
Caracas, Venezuela	1967	6.5	10.6°N, 67.3°W	1.3 → 0.7	930		Fiedler (1974)

Region	Year	Magnitude	Coordinates	Anomaly	Value	Reference
Fairbanks, U.S.A.	1970	3.0	—		7	Alaska; Scholz et al. (1973)
Garm, U.S.S.R.	1969	5.7	39.0°N, 70.3°E	daily freq. 80 → 40 decrease	550	Central Asia; Sadovsky and Nersesov (1974)
Garm	1966	5.5 / 5.5	39.0°N, 70.3°E	—	550	Central Asia; Sadovsky and Nersesov (1974)

Discipline s: source mechanism

Region	Year	Magnitude	Coordinates	Anomaly	Value	Reference
Garm, U.S.S.R.	1966	5.4	39°N, 70°E		470 / 130	Central Asia
Garm	1969	6.2	39°N, 70°E		360 / 110	Central Asia
						Data taken from Sadovsky and Nersesov (1974)
Naryn	1963	4.8	41.4°N, 76.0°E		720	Central Asia
Naryn	1966	4.8	41.4°N, 76.0°E		45	Central Asia
						Data taken from Simbireva (1973)

Discipline c: fault creep anomaly

Region	Year	Magnitude	Coordinates	Anomaly	Value	Reference
Hollister, U.S.A.	1961	5.6 / 5.5	36.7°N, 121.3°W	creep-rate doubled	800	
Parkfield	1966	5.3	35.9°N, 120.9°W	—	14	fresh cracks; Data taken from Nason (1973)

Discipline v: V_p/V_s

Region	Year	Magnitude	Coordinates	Anomaly	Value
Garm, U.S.S.R.	1956	5.5	39°N, 70°E	10% decrease	90
Garm	1956	4.8	39°N, 70°E	12%	57
Garm	1957	4.1	39°N, 70°E	12%	33
Garm	1959	5.5	39°N, 70°E	10%	72
Garm	1961	4.1	39°N, 70°E	9%	51
Garm	1961	4.8	39°N, 70°E	12%	36
Garm	1962	4.5	39°N, 70°E	8%	48
Garm	1962	4.5	39°N, 70°E	10%	48
Garm	1963	4.1	39°N, 70°E	17%	30
Garm	1963	4.8	39°N, 70°E	9%	45
Garm	1964	4.1	39°N, 70°E	13%	30
Garm	1966	5.5	39°N, 70°E	12%	90

TABLE 15-XIII (continued)

Earthquake	Year	M	Epicenter	Amount	Precursor time (days)	Epicentral distance (km)	Remarks
Discipline v: V_p/V_s (continued)							
Garm	1967	4.8	39°N, 70°E	9% decrease	45		Data taken from Semyenov (1969)
BML, U.S.A.	1971	1.3	43.9°N, 74.4°W	12%	0.12		Blue Mountain Lake, New York
BML	1971	1.7	43.9°N, 74.4°W	—	0.12		
BML	1971	2.0	43.9°N, 74.4°W	—	0.40		
BML	1971	2.7	43.9°N, 74.4°W	12%	3.4		
BML	1971	3.1	43.9°N, 74.4°W	12%	6.0		
BML	1971	3.3	43.9°N, 74.4°W	15%	6.1		
							Data taken from Scholz et al. (1973)
San Fernando	1971	6.4	34.4°N, 118.4°W	10%	1,100		Whitcomb et al. (1973)
Windy Islands	1971	3.8	51.6°N, 178.8°E	5%	50		Aleutian, Kisslinger and Engdahl (1974)
North Miyagi, Japan	1962	6.5	38.7°N, 141.1°E	70%	360		Ohtake (1973)
Niigata	1964	7.5	38.4°N, 139.2°E	40%	3,540		Res. Group Microearthq. (1974)
Chugoku-Kinki	1967	5.0	35°N, 135°E	9%	50		Brown (1973)
Chugoku-Kinki	1968	5.0	35°N, 135°E	7%	52		Brown (1973)
North Nagano	1968	5.3	36.8°N, 138.3°E	30%	110		Ohtake (1973)
Southeast Akita	1970	6.2	39.2°N, 140.8°E	20%	730		Res. Group Microearthq. (1974)
Discipline w: V_p and V_s							
V_p anomaly							
San Fernando, U.S.A.	1971	6.4	34.4°N, 118.4°W	20% decrease	1,100		Whitcomb et al. (1973)
Pt. Mugu	1973	6.0	34.1°N, 119.0°W	20%	380		Stewart (1973)
Riverside	1974	4.1	34.0°N, 117.4°W	—	200		Whitcomb et al.

Location	Year	M	Coordinates	Precursor			Reference
…	…	…	…	0.4 s increase	25	440	Wyss (1973b)
Pt. Mugu, U.S.A.	1973	6.0	34.1°N, 119.0°W	1.0 s	10	180	Stewart (1973)
Niigata, Japan	1964	7.5	38.4°N, 139.2°E	10 s	100	3,600	Res. Group Microearthq. (1974)
Matsushiro	1965–1967	6.3 (cumulative)	36.5°N, 138.2°E	0.5 s	0	950	Wyss and Holcomb (1973)
Seddon, New Zealand	1966	6.1	41.6°S, 174.3°E	0.4 s	40	360	Wyss and Johnston (1974)
Gisborne	1966	6.2	38.6°S, 177.7°E	0.4 s	18	550	Wyss and Johnston (1974)
V_s anisotropy							
Slate Mt., U.S.A.	1971	4.0	39.1°N, 118.2°W	2.3% increase in $V_{SH}-V_{SV}$		38	Nevada; Gupta (1973b)
Mina	1971	3.9	38.4°N, 118.2°W	2.5 s		10	Nevada; Gupta (1973b)
Discipline g: geomagnetism							
Tanabe, Japan	1962	6.1 / 6.4	33.7°N, 135.4°E	7 gammas	70	3,200	Tazima (1968)
Niigata	1964	7.5	38.4°N, 139.2°E	10–15 gammas	40	3,600	Fujita (1965)
Discipline e: earth currents							
Kamchatka, U.S.S.R.	1959	7.8		150 mV/km		17	
Kamchatka	1965	5.8		80 mV/km		16	
Kamchatka	1968	5.0		120 mV/km		17	
Kamchatka	1969	5.5		100 mV/km		20	
Kamchatka	1969	5.5		90 mV/km		13	
Kamchatka	1969	4.5		70 mV/km		10	
Kamchatka	1969	4.5		50 mV/km		10	
Kamchatka	1969	4.5		50 mV/km		8	
Kamchatka	1966	4.5	Russian Bay	—		0.13	Kronoki Obs., Sobolev and Morozov (1972)

Data taken from Myachkin et al. (1972)

Epicentral distances are smaller than 150 km

Epicenters are off the eastern coast

TABLE 15-XIII (continued)

Earthquake	Year	M	Epicenter	Amount	Precursor time (days)	Epicentral distance (km)	Remarks
Discipline e: earth currents (continued)							
Kamchatka	1968	6.0	53°N, 160°E	300 mV/km	9	30	Fedotov et al. (1970)
Kamchatka	1971	5.0	Kronotskiy Gulf	40 mV/km	10	—	
Kamchatka	1971	5.0	Kronotskiy Gulf	30 mV/km	4	—	
Kamchatka	1971	7.7	Kronotskiy Gulf	40 mV/km	22	—	
							Data taken from Sobolev (1974)
Discipline r: resistivity							
Hollister area, U.S.A.	1973	3.9	36.6°N, 121.2°W	24% decrease	60		
Hollister area	1973	3.5	36.6°N, 121.2°W	6%	30		Data taken from Mazzella and Morrison (1974)
Garm, U.S.S.R.	1967	4.2	39.0°N, 70.3°E	12%	66		
Garm	1968	4.3	39.0°N, 70.3°E	3%	57		
Garm	1969	5.7	39.0°N, 70.3°E	18%	225		
Garm	1969	4.8	39.0°N, 70.3°E	14%	141		
Garm	1970	4.8	39.0°N, 70.3°E	12%	180		
Garm	1972	4.2	39.0°N, 70.3°E	8%	102		
							Data taken from Baruskov (1974)
Tokachi-oki, Japan	1968	7.9	44.7°N, 143.6°E	-7.2×10^{-5} in rate of change	0.096	712	
Central Saitama	1968	6.1	36.0°N, 139.4°E	1.1×10^{-4}	0.14	96	
Off East Hokkaido	1969	7.8	43.1°N, 148.2°E	1.0×10^{-4}	0.17	1,094	
Central Gifu	1969	6.6	35.8°N, 137.1°E	6.0×10^{-5}	0.050	205	
Erimozaki-oki	1971	7.0	41.2°N, 143.7°E	-3×10^{-5}	0.29	780	
Hachijojima Is.	1972	7.3	33.3°N, 141.0°E	1×10^{-5}	0.10	252	
Tokyo Bay	1973	4.9	35.5°N, 139.9°E	-3×10^{-5}	0.15	50	
Choshi-oki	1974	6.1	35.6°N, 140.8°E	-3×10^{-5}	0.14	119	
Izu Peninsula	1974	6.9	34.6°N, 138.8°E	-4×10^{-5}	0.17	100	
							Data taken from Yamazaki (1975). Observa-

Discipline i: radon

	Year		Coordinates				Reference
Tashkent, U.S.S.R.	1966	4	41.3°N, 69.3°E	14% increase		11	Scholz et al. (1973)
Tashkent	1966	5.2	41.3°N, 69.3°E	20%		250	Scholz et al. (1973)
Tashkent	1966	5.5	41.3°N, 69.3°E	200%		2,500	Sadovsky et al. (1972)
Tashkent	1967	—	41.3°N, 69.3°E	—		3	
Tashkent	1967	—	41.3°N, 69.3°E	—		3	
Tashkent	1967	—	41.3°N, 69.3°E	—		8	
Tashkent	1967	—	41.3°N, 69.3°E	—		7	
Tashkent	1967	—	41.3°N, 69.3°E	—		4	
Ferganda	1969	—	40.4°N, 71.3°E	—		13	Data taken from T. Hagiwara (personal communication, 1974)

Discipline u: underground water

	Year		Coordinates				Reference
Przhevalsk, U.S.S.R.	1970	—	42.5°N, 78.4°E	15°C rise in temp., 15 cm rise in water level		72	Sadovsky et al. (1972)
Meckering, Australia	1968	6.9	32°S, 117°E	2.9 cm rise	0.063	110	Gordon (1970)

Discipline o: oil flow

	Year		Coordinates				Reference
Gulf of Suez	1969	6.1	27.5°N, 33.9°E		330	100	
Gulf of Suez	1971	4.8	27.5°N, 33.9°E		120	100	
Gulf of Suez	1972	5.1	27.5°N, 33.9°E		150	100	Data taken from Arieh and Merzer (1974)

TABLE 15-XIV

Additional precursor data

Discipline	Earthquake	Year	M	Epicenter	Amount	Precursor time (days)	Epicentral distance (km)	Remarks
w	Bear Valley, Calif., U.S.A.	1972	5.0	36.6°N, 121.2°W	P-delay, 0.3 s increase	54	2	Robinson et al. (1974)
Seismic waves[1]	Khait near Garm, U.S.S.R.	1966	4.8	—		120		Nersesov et al. (1974b)
v	Central Gifu Pref., Japan	1969	6.6	35.8°N, 137.1°E	20% decrease	950	50	Mizutani et al. (1973)
w	Gisborne, New Zealand	1966	6.2	38.6°S, 177.7°E	P-delay, 0.5 s increase	480	20	Sutton (1974)
v	Sichi, Ningsia Prov., China	1970	5.7	36.0°N, 105.8°E	5% decrease	300		Feng et al. (1974)
w	Sichi	1970	5.7	36.0°N, 105.8°E	V_p decrease, 18%	300		Feng et al. (1974)
g	Sitka, Alaska, U.S.A.	1972	7.2	56.8°N, 135.7°W	20-gamma decrease in horizontal intensity	2740	50	Wyss (1975a)
w	Bear Valley	1974	5.3	36.6°N, 121.2°W	P-delay, 0.3 s increase	60		M.J.S. Johnston (personal communication, 1974)
t	Bear Valley	1974	5.3	36.6°N, 121.2°W	sudden change in tilt azimuth	60		Johnston (1974)
g	Bear Valley	1974	5.3	36.6°N, 121.2°W	2-gamma increase and decrease	60		Smith et al. (1974)
c	Bear Valley	1974	5.3	36.6°N, 121.2°W	sudden change	60		M.J.S. Johnston (personal communication, 1974)
g	Garm, U.S.S.R.	1974	1.5	39.0°N, 70.3°E	15 gammas	0.17		Skovorodkin et al. (1973)

TABLE 15-XV

Number of precursors (Rikitake, 1975c)

Discipline	Abbreviation	Number of data
Land deformation	l	19
Tilt and strain	t	84
Foreshock	f	73
b-value	b	11
Microseismicity	m	3
Source mechanism	s	6
Fault creep anomaly	c	2
V_p/V_s	v	27
V_p and V_s	w	11
Geomagnetism	g	2
Earth currents	e	13
Resistivity	r	17
Radon	i	9
Underground water	u	2
Oil flow	o	3
	Total	282

tions by horizontal pendulum tiltmeters, bubble levels, water-tube tiltmeters, borehole tiltmeters and strainmeters (section 7.7).

Foreshock (f)

That foreshocks occur prior to the main shock has often been reported since historical time when no instrumental observations were available. The precursor time so far reported for foreshocks ranges from a few minutes to a few hundreds of days (section 8.3). A precursor time is defined here by the time interval between the shock first noticed and the main shock.

b-value (b)

Decreases in the value of the constant b in the Gutenberg-Richter formula (8-1) are sometimes reported (subsection 8.3.4).

Microseismicity (m)

A decrease in the number of microearthquakes before a main shock has sometimes been reported (subsection 8.3.4).

Source mechanism (s)

Changes in the compression axis for small earthquakes have been observed in Garm, U.S.S.R. (subsection 8.3.4) preceding earthquakes having a moderately large magnitude.

Fault creep anomaly (c)

A couple of reports are available on a precursory change in the creep rate of the San Andreas fault (subsection 11.1.1).

V_p/V_s ratio (v)

The decrease and recovery of V_p/V_s ratio has been observed prior to an earthquake in a number of countries (section 9.1).

V_p and V_s (w)

Changes in V_p itself (section 9.2) and shear velocity anisotropy (section 9.3) have sometimes been reported.

Geomagnetic change (g)

In spite of many reports that the geomagnetic field undergoes a change preceding an earthquake, only a few data seem reliable (section 10.6).

Earth currents (e)

Earth-current data are taken from the observations in Kamchatka (section 10.8). They do not seem to match with data of different disciplines.

Resistivity (r)

Short-term resistivity precursors observed in Japan (subsection 10.9.4) and long-term ones in the U.S.S.R. (subsection 10.9.1) and the U.S.A. (subsection 10.9.2) are used. Although there are many data from China (subsection 10.9.3), they are not used for the present analysis because the author cannot see their details.

Radon emission (i)

Precursory changes in radon emission of underground water have been reported in the U.S.S.R. (subsection 12.4).

Underground water (u)

Only a few reliable reports are available (section 12.2). Chinese data such as given in Table 12-I became available too late for the present analysis.

Oil flow (o)

Precursory changes in the amount of oil flow from petroleum wells have been reported in the Gulf of Suez (section 12.3).

15.5.2. Histograms of the precursor time

As there are fairly many data for disciplines t (tilt and strain) and f (foreshock), 84 and 74 in number respectively, histograms of the logarithmic precursor time, $\log_{10} T$, are drawn for each discipline as can be seen in Figs.

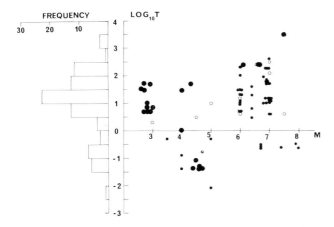

Fig. 15-7. Histogram of the data for discipline t (tilt and strain) combined with the logarithmic precursor time in days vs. magnitude plots. As the histogram includes the data for which the magnitude is not known, there is some discrepancy in number between the histogram and the plots. Large solid, small solid and open circles denote data taken by water-tube and borehole tiltmeters, horizontal pendulum tiltmeters and strainmeters, respectively (Rikitake, 1975c).

15-7 and 15-8 in which the dependency of the logarithmic precursor time on earthquake magnitude is also examined. The plots in the figures are so scattered that no dependency of precursor time on earthquake magnitude can be seen.

It seems likely, however, that there are two peaks in the histogram of tilt and strain around $\log_{10} T = 1$ and -1 where T is measured in units of days.

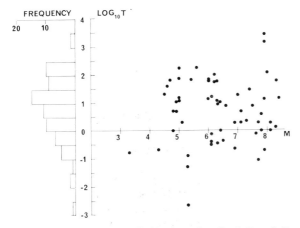

Fig. 15-8. Histogram of the data for discipline f (foreshock) combined with the logarithmic precursor time in days vs. magnitude plots (Rikitake, 1975c).

This might suggest that there are long- and short-range precursors. No such tendency can be seen for foreshock precursors.

In order to see whether there is any difference in nature between tilt and strain precursors observed by instruments of different kinds, the plots in Fig. 15-7 are made by making use of large solid circles, small solid circles and open circles respectively for data taken by water-tube or borehole tiltmeters, horizontal pendulum tiltmeters (including bubble levels) and strainmeters.

Whereas small solid circles or horizontal pendulum tiltmeter data scatter so largely that no relation between precursor time and magnitude can be seen, as in the case for foreshocks in Fig. 15-8, a close look at Fig. 15-7 suggests a tendency that the logarithmic precursor time becomes larger as the magnitude increases and, at the same time, that some isolated plots cluster around $\log_{10} T = -1$ for large solid circles. It might therefore be said that tilt precursors observed by tiltmeters other than horizontal pendulum ones are similar in nature to those for land deformation as detected by geodetic work, the change in the V_p / V_s ratio, resistivity change and the like (see Figs. 15-9 and 15-12). At the moment, the author is afraid that data taken by horizontal pendulum tiltmeters and strainmeters do not lead to any systematized results concerning the precursor time. This is also the case for foreshocks despite the fact that there are many foreshock data.

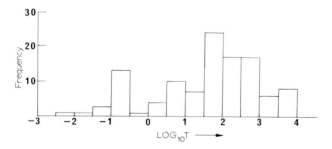

Fig. 15-9. Histogram of the data excluding those for disciplines t and f (Rikitake, 1975c).

Almost all earth-current precursor times assume a value around $\log_{10} T = 1.1$ regardless of the magnitude of the associated earthquakes. They are tentatively disregarded in the present statistics because they do not fit in with any other precursors.

Apart from the above precursors of disciplines t, f, and e, precursors of all other disciplines are put together. A histogram of the precursor times of these disciplines amounting to 112 in number is reproduced in Fig. 15-9. It is apparent in the figure that the precursor times indicate two maxima, one is around $\log_{10} T = 2$ and another is around $\log_{10} T = -1$.

15.5.3. Histograms for different magnitude ranges

In order to show the physical characteristics of precursors more clearly, histograms for different magnitude ranges are drawn for the entire set of data and the data except for those of disciplines t, f and e as shown in Figs. 15-10 and 15-11, respectively. Although it is hard to see any regularity in Fig. 15-10, it is clearly demonstrated in Fig. 15-11 that the maximum frequency for each magnitude range shifts to larger precursor times as the earthquake magnitude becomes larger. Another important point that should be pointed out in Fig. 15-11 is the fact that there is an isolated peak of precursor times around $\log_{10} T = -1$ regardless of the magnitude range. The

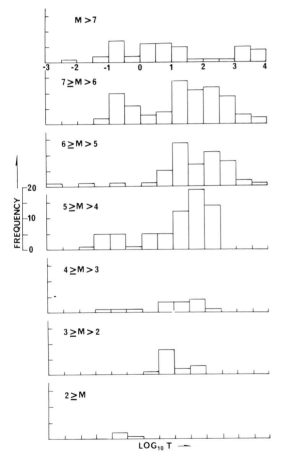

Fig. 15-10. Histograms of logarithmic precursor time in days for the whole set of data as classified into successive magnitude ranges (Rikitake, 1975c).

peak seems to become more marked as the magnitude increases.

It is therefore suggested that the precursors treated in Fig. 15-11 consist of two types, i.e. the one (A_1 type) characterized by a small precursor time amounting to $\log_{10} T = -1$ or so and the other (A_2 type) which has a magnitude-dependent precursor time. In contrast to the precursors of the A ($A_1 + A_2$) type, it is hard to see any regularity for precursor times for the precursors of disciplines t and f although the precursors observed by water-tube and borehole tiltmeters may in general be similar to those of the A-type. We may call precursors of disciplines t and f B-type precursors, if they are precursors at all.

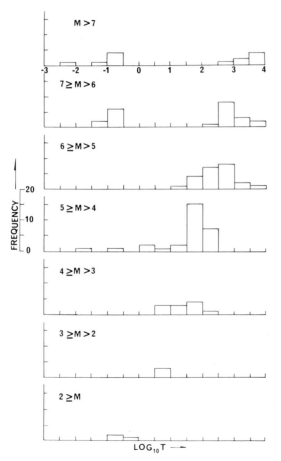

Fig. 15-11. Histograms of logarithmic precursor time in days for the data excluding those for disciplines t and f as classified into successive magnitude ranges (Rikitake, 1975c).

15.5.4. Characteristics of A-type precursors

Fig. 15-12 shows the logarithmic precursor time vs. magnitude plots for precursors of the A type. Each plot is made with a letter which is used for the discipline abbreviation (see Table 15-XV and subsection 15.5.1). As expected from Fig. 15-11, the plots are clearly separated into two groups.

The plots, which cluster around $\log_{10} T = -1$ for magnitudes larger than 5, belong to the A_1 type. The remaining plots, which are for the A_2-type precursors, are evidently magnitude-dependent. The best fitting by a straight line as obtained by the least-squares method leads to:

$$\log_{10} T = 0.76M - 1.83 \qquad\qquad\qquad\qquad [15\text{-}43]$$

It is interesting to note that relation [15-43] is compatible with similar relations obtained by a few authors, i.e.:

$$\log_{10} T = 0.685M - 1.57 \quad \text{(Scholz et al., 1973)} \qquad\qquad [15\text{-}44]$$

$$\log_{10} T = 0.80M - 1.92 \quad \text{(Whitcomb et al., 1973)} \qquad\qquad [15\text{-}45]$$

$$\log_{10} T = 0.79M - 1.88 \quad \text{(Tsubokawa, 1969, 1973; see [15-23])} \quad [15\text{-}46]$$

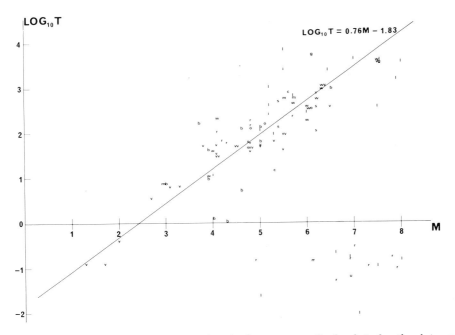

Fig. 15-12. Logarithmic precursor time in days vs. magnitude plots for the data excluding those for disciplines t and f (Rikitake, 1975c).

Despite the fact that these empirical relationships are deduced from data sets which are one order of magnitude smaller in number than those for the present analysis, agreement between coefficients is amazingly good. Equation [15-23], used for estimating the probabilities of occurrence time of an earthquake, should be replaced by [15-43] although numerical values of coefficients involved do not differ much from one another.

Analyses of A-type precursors by making use of the Weibull distribution (see subsection 15.3.2) were made by Rikitake (1975c). It is concluded that the probabilities for an earthquake to occur within 0.1, 0.5 and 0.7 days' time after observing an A_1-type precursor amount to 1, 25 and 70% respectively. A similar estimate indicates that the probabilities for an earthquake to occur within 10, 100 and 1,000 days' time after an A_2-type precursor is observed amount to 35, 68 and 91%, respectively.

The numbers of precursors of various disciplines as listed in Table 15-XV enable us to estimate the probabilities for an observed precursor to be assigned to the one of the A_1, A_2 and B types. The estimate is made for the following three cases:

(1) Data for discipline t (tilt and strain) and f (foreshock) are assigned to B.

(2) Data for discipline f are assigned to B.

(3) Similar to (2), but data taken by water-tube and borehole tiltmeters are transferred to the set of A-type data.

The probabilities for a precursory signal to be assigned to respective types of precursors are given in Table 15-XVI. Although it is certain that these probabilities will be modified by a better set of data to be taken in the future, it may tentatively be said that about one-half of the signals can be regarded as either short- or long-term precursors, namely those of the A_1 and A_2 types. Whenever we observe a precursor-like change of a certain prediction element, we may think that it indicates a precursory signal of the A_1, A_2 and B types with a probability as shown in Table 15-XVI.

It is highly important that A-type precursors are divided into long- and short-term signals. The A_2-type precursor is certainly caused by a crustal process such as dilatancy generation when the crustal strain approaches the ultimate one. The A_1 type, on the other hand, may be closely correlated

TABLE 15-XVI

Probabilities in percent for a precursory signal to be assigned to respective type precursors (Rikitake, 1975c)

	A_1	A_2	B
(1)	6	36	58
(2)	8	49	43
(3)	11	57	32

with creep-like rupture that would occur at the focal region immediately before the main rupture.

15.6. FOUR STAGES OF EARTHQUAKE PREDICTION

What we have learned in the foregoing sections of this chapter would suggest a possible procedure for achieving earthquake prediction as may be summarized in the following.

15.6.1. Statistical prediction — preliminary stage

When a region is specified, it is possible to carry out statistics of seismicity on the condition that a series of seismic observations over a period of several decades or longer is available there. In that case preliminary probabilities for an earthquake having a specified magnitude to occur in a specified time interval may be estimated as demonstrated in section 15.1.

Although not much can be said about the occurrence of a particular earthquake there in the future, what we learned in section 15.1 is useful to some extent for quantifying earthquake risk in a certain area.

15.6.2. Long-term prediction — strain accumulation stage

Geodetic surveys are frequently repeated over seismic areas in Japan and California and Nevada, U.S.A. In that case the accumulation of crustal strain, which was released at the time of the last large earthquake, can sometimes be monitored, so that a probability theory based on the ultimate strain statistics as developed in section 15.3 can afford a probability of the recurrence of a large earthquake.

This is a sort of long-term prediction covering a time span of several decades. If a dense geodimeter survey network such as planned in Japan (see subsection 4.2.2) is completed, a dramatic advancement of this kind of prediction may be possible. At the moment, however, strain accumulation and associated probability estimate can be applicable only to earthquakes of magnitude 7 or over because the geodetic network is not dense enough.

15.6.3. Medium- and short-term prediction — dilatancy generation stage

If it is possible to have intensive observations of various disciplines over a seismic area, especially an area for which the probability of earthquake occurrence as estimated by the method described in the last subsection is high, it would not be unreasonable to expect to observe an A_2-type precursor as defined in subsections 15.5.3 and 15.5.4 sooner or later.

When a precursor such as a change in the V_p/V_s ratio, which returns to its pre-anomaly level before the occurrence of main shock, is monitored, we may have an approximate value of the precursor time and consequently the magnitude of an impending earthquake. Strictly speaking, these values are given in terms of probability as studied in section 15.2. However, the prediction of occurrence time could be almost deterministic in favorable cases as claimed by Scholz et al. (1973).

Even if precursors such as a resistivity change, a land uplift and the like, which do not return to their pre-anomaly state before the occurrence of an earthquake, are observed, the magnitude of a coming earthquake can be assessed to some extent provided that the spatial extent of these precursors is known. Once the magnitude is guessed, the occurrence time of the main shock can be estimated, at least probabilistically (see subsection 15.2.2).

According to the logarithmic precursor time vs. magnitude relations as given by [15-43], [15-44], [15-45] or [15-46], the precursor times for magnitudes 7 and 6 seem to be 6—7 and 1—2 years, respectively, although a more rigorous estimate of risk can be put forward in terms of probability.

15.6.4. Prediction of extremely short range — stage immediately prior to main rupture

It has been most difficult to monitor an earthquake precursor immediately prior to the occurrence of an earthquake, yet a warning based on such an extremely short-range prediction could doubtless save at least many lives, if not all property. As is described in many of the foregoing chapters of this book, there are many instances of anomalous sea retreats, sudden changes in ground tilt and electric resistivity and the like which occur immediately preceding an earthquake of large magnitude. Only most of these reports are fragmentary, so to speak, and so even the present author has not been sure whether or not they can be used for prediction even if they do exist.

The situation seems to have changed very much by the statistics of precursors presented earlier in this section. As we can clearly see in Fig. 15-12, the author is quite convinced that we sometimes observe extremely short range precursors, called the A_1-type ones by the author, having a precursor time of a few hours or so. The precursor time does not seem to depend on the earthquake magnitude although, as can be seen in Fig. 15-11, it seems likely that frequencies of observing an A_1-type precursor increase as the earthquake magnitude becomes larger.

It is estimated that the probability of having an earthquake within several hours would be high if an A_1-type precursor should be observed. Although the reason why such a short-range precursor is observed is not clear, we simply suppose that a pre-earthquake creeping at the focal zone may well take place, especially for large earthquakes. It is therefore urgent for short-range prediction to make every effort towards detecting an A_1-type precursor in a region where an A_2-type precursor has already been observed. The author fears, however, that actual observation of such a precursory signal is difficult to carry out in many cases because of natural and artificial noise. It is therefore important to monitor precursors in various disciplines in order to make the signal-to-noise ratio high. As data of the A_1-type precursor are accumulating with an immense speed by observations made under the earthquake prediction programs in Japan, the U.S.A., the U.S.S.R., China and other countries, it would not be unreasonable to expect that we would shortly arrive at a more complete understanding of the A_1-type precursor and, consequently, a better application of it to short-range earthquake prediction.

15.7. OPERATIONS RESEARCH RELATED TO EARTHQUAKE PREDICTION

Earthquake prediction is different from ordinary research in geophysical phenomena in that it is necessary to say something about an earthquake occurrence even though there are not sufficient data which indicate a causal relation between precursory effects and earthquake occurrence. The situation is something like the operations in a battle field. A commander must decide how to use his forces even if he does not have sufficient information about the movements of his enemy.

Under the circumstances, the author has been stressing that much emphasis on operations research-type approach in earthquake prediction study, and even on a PPBS (Planning-Programming-Budgeting System) -type approach in planning an earthquake prediction program, is necessary. Only little success has so far been achieved in this type of approach in the Japanese program, perhaps because of difficulties in coordinating the budgets of the various organizations involved. However, a few studies of operations research relevant to earthquake prediction were accomplished by younger colleagues.

15.7.1. Most effective way of carrying out levelling surveys for earthquake prediction in Japan

Hagiwara (1971) presented an attempt based on operations research for seeking the most effective way of planning levelling surveys over Japan in order to monitor precursory crustal deformation. Assume that an anomalous land deformation, of mean radius r, takes place in an area A. Let ΔL be the length of a survey along a levelling route within the area concerned. Then the probability of detecting the deformation is estimated as $2r_e \Delta L/A$, where r_e is the effective radius of the deformed portion of the area. Since some finite length of levelling route is required for evaluating the result of a levelling survey, r_e must be smaller than r. As the area A is much larger than that of premonitory deformation, it may be assumed that $r_e \doteqdot r$. The probability is estimated from the consideration that an anomalous deformation must be detected when the deformation area is overlapped by an area $\Delta L \times r_e$, on both sides of ΔL.

We now assume that a survey is conducted along a levelling route of length L within A. The probability of detecting a premonitory deformation is then $2r_e L/A$. Dividing A into a number of sub-areas A_i (i = 1, 2, ... n) and denoting the length of the levelling route by L_i, we have:

$$\sum_{i=1}^{n} L_i = L \qquad\qquad\qquad\qquad\qquad\qquad [15\text{-}47]$$

The expectancy of the number of earthquakes that can be detected by levelling survey is:

$$\widetilde{N} = \sum_{i=1}^{n} \int_{r_S}^{r_T} N_i(r) \, (2 \, r_e L_i/A) \, dr \qquad\qquad\qquad\qquad [15\text{-}48]$$

where $N_i(r)$ is the frequency of earthquake occurrence as a function of r. The limits of integration r_S and r_T are the radii of deformation for the earthquakes of the minimum and maximum magnitudes considered, respectively. These can be estimated from the seismicity of the area and also from the Gutenberg-Richter formula as given by [8-1] along with equation [15-1]. The optimum proportion of levelling route length for the respective subareas is obtained by maximizing N under condition [15-47].

Hagiwara applied the theory to the Japan Islands, which are divided into seven districts of roughly equal area. It is striking that the conclusion was reached that levelling surveys should be concentrated mostly in the central part of Japan. For achieving effectiveness, it is of little use to carry out surveys in the northernmost and southernmost areas, i.e. Hokkaido and Kyushu. In forming the estimate, the seismicities in respective areas are determined from the catalog of earthquakes for $M > 6$ during the period 1800—1968.

The above conclusion seems quite reasonable, judging from the low seismicities in the Hokkaido and Kyushu Islands. Attention is drawn to the fact that no consideration is taken into account in the theory of the existing distribution of levelling routes, so that the actual capability of detecting a forerunning land deformation will be somewhat different from that estimated. It seems impractical to discuss further details of dividing Japan into many subareas of smaller extent because of insufficient seismic data.

Hagiwara and Tajima (1973) discussed an optimum distribution of gravity stations for earthquake prediction in a similar fashion.

15.7.2. Where should we set up a new crustal deformation observatory in Japan?

Shimazaki (1972a) estimated, on the basis of the present-day seismicity, the probability of observing three or more precursory strain changes within 5 years at a number of hypothetical observatories covering Japan. It is assumed that the precursory change is as large as one-tenth of the strain steps for the entire course of the earthquake event. It is striking that high-probability areas are located along the Pacific coast of northeastern Japan. The location of a crustal deformation observatory has been selected, thus far, without consideration of the resulting weight of an observation. However, the accumulation of data for earthquake prediction could be accelerated very much by selecting appropriate locations for the observation points. On the basis of this kind of operations research, it is recommended that the location of the crustal deformation observatory, which has been planned for a location about 190 km northeast of Tokyo, should be shifted about 50 km southward.

Chapter 16

EARTHQUAKE MODIFICATION AND CONTROL

In spite of the rapid advancement of seismology and related earth sciences in recent years, earthquake prediction is still in an unsatisfactory state, especially where foretelling the time of occurrence of a destructive earthquake is concerned. An attractive idea that we should not worry about the time of earthquake occurrence provided the earthquake energy accumulated in the earth's crust could somehow be gradually released without giving rise to a destructive earthquake was originated notably among seismologists in the U.S.A., although it is still an open question whether or not the energy of an extremely large earthquake occurring around island arcs can really be controlled.

As this book is planned to describe matters devoted mostly to earthquake prediction, only a brief account of earthquake modification and control will be given in the following.

16.1. DENVER EARTHQUAKES

Injection of waste water in a deep well was undertaken at the Rocky Mountain Arsenal near Denver, Colorado, U.S.A., in 1962. The depth of the well was 3,800 m. Quite unexpectedly, many earthquakes began to occur there 1 month or so after the commencement of injection. The area has long been aseismic. The volume of injected water amounted approximately to 2×10^4 m^3 per month.

The number of earthquakes markedly decreased when the injection was suspended, but the seismic activity tended to recover when the injection was resumed. In spite of a complete stop of injection in September, 1969, the occurrence of earthquakes continued. On the contrary, a number of comparatively large earthquakes began to occur. The series of earthquakes lasted for nearly 10 years. The total volume of injected water was 6×10^5 m^3 or so.

According to a seismographic observation during the period from December, 1965, to March, 1966, 10—20 microearthquakes were observed a day. Their magnitudes ranged from less than 0 to 3.7. The epicenters were distributed over an approximately elliptic area having a length of 8 km and a width of 3 km centering on the well in question. The focal depths were 4.5—5.5 km.

The Denver earthquakes became a target of investigation by many seismologists (e.g. Evans, 1966, 1967; Healy et al., 1968; Pakiser et al., 1969). Evans proposed a theory that these earthquakes are excited by the injected water. He claimed that the friction at the rupture planes in the earth's crust decreases by increased pore pressure eventually giving rise to slips as the theory of Hubbert and Rubey (1959; see subsection 13.1.2) suggested. As the cores taken from the borehole indicated that the well was drilled in a fractured zone, there were doubtless many cracks in the crust there. "The time—space correlation of seismic activity compared with the location and rates of injection into the disposal well clearly demonstrates a causative relation between the earthquakes and fluid injection" was the conclusion by Healy et al. (1972).

16.2. WATER-INJECTION EXPERIMENT AT MATSUSHIRO

Large amounts of mineral water, amounting to 10^7 m^3 or thereabouts in volume, came out of the ground towards the end of the most violent stage of the seismic swarm activity at Matsushiro in Central Japan (see subsection 5.6.14). There is no doubt about the fact that the water had something to do with the seismic activity.

The National Research Center for Disaster Prevention (Takahashi, 1970) drilled a well of 1,800 m in depth on the foot of Mt. Minakami, the center of the activity in its early stage, and performed experiments by injecting water into the well in January and February, 1970, when the activity had already become so low that only about 20 felt earthquakes were reported per month. The total volume of injected water was only 2,880 m^3. The pumping pressure was 50—14 bars.

According to a seismographic study (Ohtake, 1974), the daily frequency of microearthquakes suddenly increased by a factor of 10 or so 5—10 days after an injection. The epicenters of these small shocks are located about 4 km distant from the well coinciding with the trend of the fault which appeared during the swarm activity. The foci clustered at a shallow depth in the beginning and migrated to depths as time went on. It seems almost certain that these microshocks are induced by the water injection. It is speculated that no microearthquakes took place at the immediate vicinity of the well because the crust had already been almost completely fractured by the earlier swarm activity there.

16.3. MAN-MADE LAKES AND EARTHQUAKES

A number of occurrences of moderately large and sometimes destructive earthquakes have been reported in association with the impounding of water in man-made reservoirs. As already mentioned in subsection 8.3.2, a reservoir artificially formed by the *Kremasta Dam* in Greece became the seat of many foreshocks 5 months after the beginning of impounding eventually

TABLE 16.I

Man-made lakes and induced earthquakes

Dam	Location	Height (m)	Total volume ($10^6 \, m^3$)	Beginning of impounding	Earthquake of maximum magnitude	
					date	M
Hoover (U.S.A.)	36.0°N, 114.7°W	142	35,000	1935	May 4, 1939	5.0
Monteynard (France)	44.9°N, 5.7°E	130	275	Apr., 1962	Apr. 25, 1963	4.9
Kariba (Rhodesia)	16.5°S, 28.8°E	125	175,000	Dec., 1958	Sept. 23, 1963	6.1
Kremasta (Greece)	38.9°N, 21.5°E	147	4,750	July, 1965	Feb. 5, 1966	6.2
Koyna (India)	17.4°N, 73.7°E	103	2,780	1962	Dec. 10, 1967	6.4
Hsinfengkiang (China)	23.7°N, 114.7°E	105	11,500	Oct., 1959	Mar. 19, 1962	6.1

culminating with a shock of magnitude 6.2 in February, 1966 (Papazachos, 1973).

Similar reservoir-associated earthquakes have been reported for the *Hoover Dam*, U.S.A. (Carder, 1945), the *Monteynard Dam*, France (Rothé, 1968, 1970), the *Kariba Dam*, Rhodesia (Gough and Gough, 1970a,b), the *Koyna Dam*, India (Dutta, 1969; Gupta et al., 1969), the *Hsinfengkiang Dam*, China (Sheng et al., 1973) and other man-made reservoirs. Essentials of these events are summarized in Table 16-I.

Reservoir-associated earthquakes seem to be related to dams which have a height exceeding 100 m. It seems likely that the total volume of stored water has nothing to do with earthquake occurrence. Rather, the height of the dam seems to have something to do with the induced earthquakes. It seems highly probable that the water permeates the ground due to the water load and this results in earthquake generation as in the cases for the Denver and Matsushiro experiments.

According to a microearthquake observation by Hagiwara and Ohtake (1972) at the *Kurobe Dam* (36°34′N, 137°40′E) in Central Japan, a dam of 186 m in height and 148.8 × 10^6 m³ in total volume of water at maximum, a high correlation between the number of microearthquakes and the height of water level was found, although no destructive earthquake had occurred there.

Further references can be found in Rothé (1973), Gupta et al. (1973), Hofmann (1973) and Mickery (1973).

16.4. EXPERIMENTS AT RANGELY OIL FIELD

Experiences at Denver, Matsushiro and other man-made lakes suggest that we might control occurrences of earthquakes by injecting water into, or withdrawing it from the ground. The NCER (Healy et al., 1972) undertook an experiment on earthquake control and modification with the cooperation of the Chevron Oil Company in an oil field at Rangely, western Colorado, U.S.A.

Fig. 16-1 shows how the monthly frequency of microearthquakes monitored by 14 seismographs set up over the oil field, the signals of which are telemetered to the NCER at Menlo Park, California, changed with injection and withdrawal of water at the experimental well of about 2,000 m in depth. It becomes apparent that earthquakes tend to occur when the impounding pressure exceeds a certain value, for instance about 250 bars. The experimen-

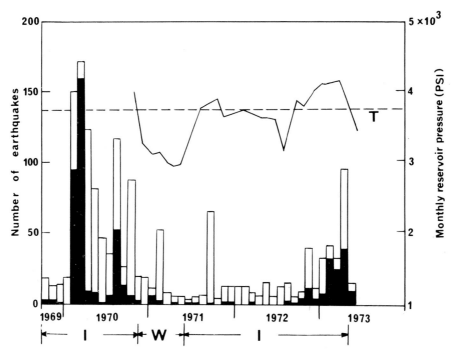

Fig. 16-1. Changes in monthly number of earthquakes in association with fluid injection and withdrawal at Rangely Oil Field. Open and solid columns show the monthly number of all earthquakes and that for earthquakes within 1 km of the bottom of experimental wells. The dashed line denoted by T indicates the threshold needed to initiate earthquakes. The reservoir pressure is shown by the curve around T with a scale in psi on the right side. The periods for fluid injection (I) and withdrawal (W) are indicated at the bottom (Wallace, 1974).

tal results at Rangely Oil Field strongly suggest the possibility of controlling and modifying earthquakes by water injection and withdrawal.

16.5. PROGRAM ON EARTHQUAKE MODIFICATION AND CONTROL

According to the EHRP (Wallace, 1974), the goals of earthquake modification and control are the following:

(1) Determine the feasibility of limiting the magnitude of earthquakes on active faults.

(2) Design subsurface waste-disposal operations and reservoir siting so as to prevent inadvertent triggering of earthquakes.

A possible approach is to make a test to generate an experimental fault having a length of several tens of meters at a site where an appropriately stressed fault in a well-exposed outcrop exists. It might be possible to control the length of a fault that would appear at the time of rupture by adjusting the distance between an injection point and withdrawal points. Such a test site must be remote enough from inhabited areas. At the moment, the Mina area of 8,000 km^2 in Nevada is regarded as one of the candidates. The area is characterized by a high seismicity although no extremely large earthquake has ever occurred there.

Should the above test of earthquake control ever be successful, a limited portion of the San Andreas fault would become the next target. Much care should be taken in that case not to induce a large earthquake.

It does not seem practicable to apply such techniques of controlling earthquakes to a subduction zone like Japan where, unlike the San Andreas fault, most of the large earthquakes occur beneath the sea and at depths beyond present-day drilling technique. But the feasibility of controlling inland earthquakes cannot be ruled out even in Japan, although it would be no easy matter to conduct an actual experiment in such a densely populated country.

A much more drastic method for releasing strain energy by nuclear explosions has been suggested. The 1968 underground nuclear explosion BENHAM (1.1 megatons) in Nevada triggered numerous aftershocks (e.g. Hamilton and Healy, 1969; Healy et al., 1970; Aki, 1972). These shocks occurred in an approximately 10 km × 10 km area with a maximum depth of 7 km. No aftershocks having a magnitude larger than 5 were observed. Compared to the magnitude of the BENHAM event, which was estimated as 6.3, these shocks were much smaller in magnitude. Many strike-slip faults appeared in association with the explosion. It is understood that some of the strain energy stored in the earth's crust was released by earthquakes which were triggered by the explosion. These earthquakes seem likely to be caused by an increase in pore pressure due to the movement of underground water associated with the explosion.

If nuclear explosions could be made at depths in a zone where the crust is believed to be stressed almost up to its ultimate strain, it might be possible to release the strain energy accumulated there, although a large earthquake, followed by aftershocks, would necessarily occur. However, people can prepare for the shock well beforehand because the exact time of the event is foretold. As no lives would be lost in such a case, it might be better to trigger an earthquake in such a way rather than waiting for its natural occurrence because the occurrence time of the artificially induced earthquake would be known.

At present, however, the above idea is too fantastic. There is no guarantee that things would go as exactly as we plan. We do not know what to do with radioactive substances that might leak out from the ground. In contrast to the use of a nuclear explosion, the possible control of earthquakes by water injection sounds very practicable. If we can develop techniques of earthquake control in this way, we might reach a better understanding of the earthquake mechanism which would some day lead us to a realistic way of controlling large earthquakes.

Chapter 17

WHAT TO DO WITH AN EARTHQUAKE WARNING?

In a guest editorial for the President's Page of the EOS (Transactions of the American Geophysical Union), Hamilton (1974) wrote "Within the last year, two earthquakes in the United States — one in New York and the other in California — have been successfully predicted on the basis of variations in seismic wave travel time. Recent studies revealed that two shocks in central California could have been predicted by similar methods. In addition, tiltmeters operating in central California since May 1973 have shown premonitory tilting for at least 10 earthquakes that occurred near an instrument . . . An earthquake prediction capability is apparently not far away."

When an (unsuccessful) earthquake forecast was announced by the USGS in 1973, according to Hamilton, what a city councilman in Hollister, where an occurrence of a magnitude 4 earthquake was foretold, first did was to put his bottle of bourbon a little further back on the shelf. Insofar as an earthquake, which is not damaging as is the case in Hollister, is forecast, nothing serious would happen among local inhabitants especially in an area where people are accustomed to frequent earthquakes of small or medium magnitude.

In contrast to such a forecast of non-damaging earthquakes, what should people do in case a credible forecast of a destructive earthquake was issued? Judging from the rapid development of earthquake prediction study in recent years as summarized in the foregoing chapters of this book, it would not be in the remote future that a realistic warning based on scientific observations of a hazardous earthquake will become possible, at least over areas such as parts of the U.S.A., Japan and so on where intensive work of monitoring earthquake precursors is in progress.

How shall we react against such a warning? This is certainly one of the most urgent matters to be seriously considered by administrators, legislators, earth scientists, mass media and even individuals living in the area of potential danger. The matter is very complicated because a prediction of occurrence time as well as magnitude must necessarily allow for some errors.

17.1. EXPERIENCE AT MATSUSHIRO

The 1965—1967 Matsushiro earthquake swarm (see subsections 4.2.1 and 5.6.14) provided a unique opportunity to issue earthquake warnings officially from a local office of the JMA on the basis of intensive observations by the ERI and other institutions. The warnings usually read "Such and such town will be hit by a moderately large and slightly damaging earthquake within a period of a few months".

The reaction of local people to such a warning varied very much depending upon their jobs and living circumstances. Local governments behaved properly by mending school buildings, old bridges and so on or by strengthening fire brigades, medical facilities and so on. However, those who run hotels and souvenir shops did not like such a warning because they were afraid of losing their clients. Local inhabitants never fell into a state of panic because the anticipated shock was not quite destructive, and, at the same time, they seemed to have already been accustomed to earthquakes through the swarm activity which at one time was so violent that they felt 600 earthquakes or more a day. The author really feels that it is important that people are trained for evaluating a warning of this kind. It should also be emphasized that the responsible organization for warning must choose the right timing.

17.2. HOW SHOULD AN EARTHQUAKE WARNING BE ISSUED TO THE PUBLIC?

Should a highly damaging earthquake having a magnitude 7, or over, be forecast by authorized experts to occur within a certain period of time, for instance a few years, what would the local inhabitants do? If it is going to happen in a densely populated area, great confusion will be anticipated. Those who take the warning seriously would like to run away from there, if they could, but others who have never experienced a severe earthquake would not take the warning seriously.

As many people are living near jobs which are closely connected with the locale, it would be difficult to evacuate them over a long period of time. If it should be required, for the sake of safety, to shut down nuclear power plants, blast furnaces, oil refineries and other heavy industries or to suspend public transportation, the financial losses would be tremendous. As an earthquake prediction must allow for an error in occurrence time probably ranging from a few months to a year for a magnitude 7 earthquake, it is almost impossible to materialize a complete shutdown of industries which are hazardous at the time of a strong earthquake.

No local government has legal power to control industries in the way mentioned in the last paragraph. Even if it becomes feasible to exercise such a control, those industries would ask the government to compensate for their losses. As a prediction in the foreseeable future would not be perfect, such a request for compensation would give rise to complicated disputes, especially when the prediction fails. It is almost certain that a prediction would often fail in the early period of enforcement, at least in the sense that it meets social demands, even though it is not quite a failure scientifically. In such a case the specialists involved would have to resign, so that there would soon be no earthquake prediction specialists.

Notwithstanding the defects pointed out above, the author thinks that an earthquake warning should be publicized whenever possible. As we experienced during the Matsushiro events, there are many things for national and local governments to prepare for an impending earthquake if it is ever foretold. It is most important to strengthen buildings of schools, hospitals and so on. Weak points of highways, waterworks and the like should be inspected. If there are water reservoirs nearby, special caution must be taken for their safety. Precaution for possible landslides is also a matter of top priority. Emergency foods must be stored in a safe place. Attention must be paid to insuring wired or wireless communication facilities. There are indeed many things for governments to do.

The situation is more or less the same for other private enterprises or even for individuals. They must prepare things for emergency needs such as food, water, clothes, fire extinguishers, portable radios, hand lamps and so on. They would also be able to repair their buildings and houses well beforehand if necessary.

The author is afraid that what is mentioned in this section is not systematized. They are only fragmentary suggestions which he can think of through his experiences related to damaging earthquakes in the past. The author would like to propose here that an intensive study on "Earthquake prediction and public reaction" be carried out. Socio-psychological studies of peoples' behavior at the time of a great earthquake have been conducted in Japan, but no research of the proposed character has ever been undertaken.

17.3. SOCIOECONOMIC AND POLITICAL STUDY OF RESPONSE TO EARTHQUAKE PREDICTION

The author gathered from Professor J.E. Haas (personal communication, 1974) at the University of Colorado that research on "A technology assessment of earthquake prediction" (Stanford Research Institute) and "Socioeconomic and political consequences of earthquake prediction" (University of Colorado) was about to start. These studies aim at preparing recommendations for legislative and administrative bodies about what to do in case a credible forecast of a destructive earthquake is issued. The author thinks that such studies are really timely and looks forward to seeing their outcomes.

In order to accomplish such studies, elaborate investigations of reactions against an earthquake prediction will be made by various organizations and individuals by making use of a Delphi technique.

On the assumption that a destructive earthquake equivalent to the 1971 San Fernando earthquake ($M = 6.4$) is predicted, the most probable responses of 100 or more public organizations and private enterprises in California will be sought. They are the city council, police, fire, hospital, water, sewer, streets, gas, electric, telephone, school, public works departments or organizations as well as manufacturing firms, retail establishments, real estate firms, banks and construction-development companies.

Investigations in the San Fernando area, where people experienced a damaging earthquake in 1971, would be of special importance for promoting this kind of study because replies to questionnaires from areas where no damaging earthquake has ever been experienced could sometimes be unrealistic.

Questions of the following types will be raised to organizations in the San Fernando area. If the 1971 event would have been predicted 9 months, 2 and 5 years prior to the actual occurrence, what would they have done in the prevention of earthquake damage? If a credible prediction of an earthquake, equivalent to the last one, would be issued at present, what would they do? How would they be affected by policies adopted by other organizations?

The probable response of citizens to an earthquake forecast will also be intensively examined at two areas in California which will be chosen according to the suggestions of seismologists. The author takes the liberty of quoting a mini-scenario for such a study as proposed by Professor Haas and his group in the following:

"After a very careful scientific appraisal and evaluation, a forecast has been made by experts that an earthquake of Richter magnitude 6.6 (comparable to the 1971 San Fernando earthquake) will occur in about 36 months from now (plus or minus one month). The center of the earthquake will be somewhere within the city limits of your town. Scientists say that 20% of the town will have heavy damage, 50% will have moderate damage, and the rest will have some minor damage.

Most of the radio, television and newspapers will give the forecast extensive coverage and make these damage estimates public very soon. What the Federal and State governments will do to help is still unclear.

Insurance companies have agreed to suspend the sale of all earthquake insurance in your area. The large banks and investment companies in the state (and those in your area) are close-mouth about their plans. They have said that they will invest their money with an eye to minimizing risk to them. The *Wall Street Journal* expects mortgage money for the area to dry up within 6 months. Builders plan on finishing the buildings and houses already under construction now but aren't planning on starting anything new. Most realtors in the city plan on encouraging their local clientele to look toward the surrounding counties for any moves they might have in mind.

Unemployment in your area is expected to increase. The branches of the major department stores in the area are considering a reduction in their personnel by converting to a self-service system.

The Governor's Office of Emergency Service is prepared to give your city technical assistance in getting ready. But the way things look now this will increase city taxes soon by about 6—7% to pay programs such as strengthening old public buildings, planning for the coordination of inter-county fire department services, and getting ready to bus students in the city schools to schools in surrounding areas as the time approaches.

The local Red Cross, Salvation Army and hospitals here and in other counties are revising their emergency plans.

Most local businessmen say they'll continue business as usual for now, but plan to close down as the time approaches (either for long vacations or to do things to protect their investments)."

Questions attached to the scenario may include:

(1) Do you anticipate a vacation out of the area about the time of the forecasted earthquake?

(2) Would you object to your children being bused to non-local schools?

(3) Would you make any structural changes to your house to try to cut down on possible loss?

Replies to questionnaires from organizations and individuals will be summarized. The results thus summarized will then be fed back to the organizations and individuals involved asking them further considerations about what they would most likely do when a forecast is issued. By repeating inquiries of this kind several times, replies will converge to realistic ones. The most probable response of local communities to earthquake forecasts will thus be brought out. Such information is certainly very useful for administrators and legislators in deciding their policies in case an earthquake warning is put into practice.

As the above studies will be finished within a few years' time, we could soon have a guideline for guessing peoples' reactions to an earthquake prediction. Such reactions could be different from country to country, and would largely depend on national traits, economic conditions and some other factors. The author hopes, therefore, that similar studies will be undertaken in as many seismic countries as possible.

REFERENCES

Abdullabekov, K.N., Bezuglaya, L.S., Golovkov, V.P. and Skovorodkin, Y.P., 1972. On the possibility of using magnetic methods to study tectonic processes. *Tectonophysics*, 14: 257—262.

Aggarwal, Y.P., Sykes, L.R., Armbruster, J. and Sbar, M.L., 1973. Premonitory changes in seismic velocities and prediction of earthquakes. *Nature*, 241: 101—104.

Aggarwal, Y.P., Sykes, L.R., Simpson, D.W. and Richards, P.G., 1975. Spatial and temporal variations in t_s/t_p and in P-wave residuals at Blue Mountain Lake, New York: application to earthquake prediction. *J. Geophys. Res.*, 80: 718—732.

Aki, K., 1956. Some problems in statistical seismology. *Zisin (J. Seismol. Soc. Japan)*, Ser. 2, 8: 205—228 (in Japanese).

Aki, K., 1968. Seismicity and seismological method. *Tectonophysics*, 6: 41—58.

Aki, K., 1972. Recent results on the mechanism of earthquakes with implications for the prediction and control program. *Tectonophysics*, 14: 227—243.

Aki, K., Defazio, T., Reasenberg, P. and Nur, A., 1970. An active experiment with earthquake faults for an estimation of the in situ stress. *Bull. Seismol. Soc. Am.*, 60: 1315—1336.

Alewine, III, R.W. and Heaton, T.H., 1973. Tilts associated with the Pt. Mugu earthquake. In: R.L. Kovach and A. Nur (Editors), *Proceedings of the Conference on Tectonic Problems on the San Andreas Fault System*. Stanford Univ. Publ., Geol. Sci., 13: 94—103.

Alldredge, L.R., 1967. Instuments and geomagnetic stations. In: S. Matsushita and W.H. Campbell (Editors), *Physics of Geomagnetic Phenomena*. Academic Press, New York, N.Y., 1: 29—66.

Allen, C.R., 1965. Transcurrent fault in continental areas. *Phil. Trans. R. Soc.*, Ser. A, 258: 82—89.

Allen, C.R. and Helmberger, D.V., 1973. Search for temporal changes in seismic velocities using large explosions in Southern California. In: R.L. Kovach and A. Nur (Editors), *Proceedings of the Conference on Tectonic Problems on the San Andreas Fault System*. Stanford Univ. Publ., Geol. Sci., 13: 436—445.

Allen, C.R. and Smith, S.W., 1966. Pre-earthquake and post-earthquake surficial displacements. *Bull. Seismol. Soc. Am.*, 56: 966—967.

Allen, C.R., Amand, P.S., Richter, C.F. and Nordquist, J.M., 1965. Relationship between seismicity and geologic structure in the southern California region. *Bull. Seismol. Soc. Am.*, 55: 753—798.

Alsop, L.E. and Oliver, J.E. (Editors), 1969. Joint U.S.—Japan conference: premonitory phenomena associated with several recent earthquakes and related problems. *EOS (Trans. Am. Geophys. Union)*, 50: 376—410.

Al'tgauzen, N.M. and Barsukov, O.M., 1972. On temporal variations in electrical conductivity. In: M.A. Sadovsky (Editor), *Physical Bases of Seeking Methods of Predicting Earthquakes*. Acad. Sci. U.S.S.R., Moscow, 1970, 152 pp. Translated in English from Russian by D.B. Vitaliano, U.S. Geological Survey.

Ambraseys, N.N., 1970. Some characteristic features of the Anatolian fault zone. *Tectonophysics*, 9: 143—165.

Anderson, D.L., 1975. Accelerated plate tectonics. *Science*, 187: 1077—1079.

Anderson, D.L. and Whitcomb, J.H., 1973. The dilatancy diffusion model of earthquake prediction. In: R.L. Kovach and A. Nur (Editors), *Proceedings of the Conference on Tectonic Problems on the San Andreas Fault System*. Stanford Univ. Publ., Geol. Sci., 13: 417—426.

Anderson, D.L., Minster, B. and Cole, D., 1974. The effect of oriented cracks on seismic velocities. *J. Geophys. Res.*, 79: 4011—4015.

Ando, M., 1971. A fault-origin model of the great Kanto earthquake of 1923 as deduced from geodetic data. *Bull. Earthquake Res. Inst., Univ. Tokyo*, 49: 19—32.

Ando, M., 1974a. Faulting in the Mikawa earthquake of 1945. *Tectonophysics*, 22: 173—186.

Ando, M., 1974b. Seismo-tectonics of the 1923 Kanto earthquake. *J. Phys. Earth*, 22: 263—277.

Ando, M., 1975. Possibility of a major earthquake in the Tokai district, Japan and its pre-estimated seismotectonic effects. *Tectonophysics*, 25: 69—85.

Antsyferov, M.S., 1969. On the possibilities of geoacoustic prediction of local earthquakes. *Acta 3rd All-Union Symp. Seismic Regime*, June 3—7, 1968. Science Press, Siberian Division. Translated into English from Russian by D.B. Vitaliano, U.S. Geological Survey.

Arieh, E. and Merzer, A.M., 1974. Fluctuations in oil flow before and after earthquakes, *Nature*, 247: 534—535.

Bakun, W.H., Steward, R.M. and Tocher, D., 1973. Variations in V_p/V_s in Bear Valley in 1972. In: R.L. Kovach and A. Nur (Editors), *Proceedings of the Conference on Tectonic Problems on the San Andreas Fault System*. Stanford Univ. Publ., Geol. Sci., 13: 453—462.

Barsukov, O.M., 1972. Variations of electric resistivity of mountain rocks connected with tectonic causes. *Tectonophysics*, 14: 273—277.

Barsukov, O.M., 1973. The search for electrical criteria for predicting earthquakes. In: M.A. Sadovsky (Editor), *Experimental Seismology*. Science Press, Moscow, 1971, 423 pp. Translated in English from Russian by D.B. Vitaliano, U.S. Geological Survey.

Barsukov, O.M., 1974. Variations in the electrical resistivity of rocks and earthquakes. In: M.A. Sadovsky, I.L. Nersesov and L.A. Latynina (Editors), *Earthquake Precursors*. Acad. Sci. U.S.S.R., Moscow, 1973, 216 pp. Translated in English from Russian by D.B. Vitaliano, U.S. Geological Survey.

Barsukov, O.M. and Sorokin, O.N., 1973. Variations in apparent resistivity of rocks in the seismically active Garm region. *Izv. Acad. Sci. U.S.S.R. (Phys. Solid Earth)*, 8: 685—687 (English edition).

Barsukov, O.M., Krasniuk, P.D., Listov, N.A. and Sorokin, O.N., 1974. Approximate estimation of the size of the zone of earthquake buildup from measurement of the electrical resistivity of a mountain massif. In: M.A. Sadovsky, I.L. Nersesov and L.A. Latynina (Editors), *Earthquake Precursors*. Acad. Sci. U.S.S.R., Moscow, 1973, 216 pp. Translated in English from Russian by D.B. Vitaliano, U.S. Geological Survey.

Bâth, M., 1966. Earthquake prediction. *Scientia (Milan)*, Mai-Juin: 1—10.

Beaumont, C. and Berger, J., 1974. Earthquake prediction: modification of the earth tide tilts and strains by dilatancy. *Geophys. J.*, 39: 111—121.

Bendefy, L., 1966. Elastic, plastic and permanent deformations of the earth's crust in connection with earthquake. *Proc. 2nd Int. Symp. on Recent Crustal Movements*. Helsinki, 1966, pp. 57—65.

Benioff, H., 1935. A linear strain seismograph. *Bull. Seismol. Soc. Am.*, 25: 238—309.

Benioff, H., 1959. Fuzed quartz extensometer for secular, tidal, and seismic strains. *Geol. Soc. Am. Bull.*, 70: 1019—1032.

Berger, J., 1971. Some observations of the San Fernando, California earthquake with a laser strain meter. The San Fernando, California, Earthquake of February 9, 1971. *U.S. Geol. Survey, Prof. Paper* No. 733, pp. 150—151.

Berger, J., 1973. Application of laser techniques to geodesy and geophysics. In: H.E. Landsberg and J. van Mieghem (Editors), *Advances in Geophysics*. Academic Press, New York, N.Y., 16: 1—56.

Bolt, B.A., 1974. Earthquake studies in the People's Republic of China. *EOS (Trans. Am. Geophys. Union)*, 55: 108—117.

Bouricius, G.M.B. and Earnshaw, K.B., 1974. Results of field testing a two-length optical distance-measuring instrument. *J. Geophys. Res.*, 79: 3015—3018.

Boyes, W.S., 1971. Horizontal and vertical crustal movement in the Inangahua earthquake of 1968. *Bull. R. Soc. New Zealand*, 9: 61—72.

Brace, W.F., 1968. Current laboratory studies pertaining to earthquake prediction. *Tectonophysics*, 6: 75—87.

Brace, W.F. and Orange, A.S., 1966. Electrical resistivity changes in saturated rock under stress. *Science*, 153: 1529—1531.

Brace, W.F. and Orange, A.S., 1968a. Electrical resistivity changes in saturated rocks during fracture and frictional sliding. *J. Geophys. Res.*, 73: 1433—1445.

Brace, W.F. and Orange, A.S., 1968b. Further studies of the effects of pressure on electrical resistivity of rocks. *J. Geophys. Res.*, 73: 5407—5420.

Brace, W.F., Orange, A.S. and Madden, T.R., 1965. The effect of pressure on the electrical resistivity of water-saturated crystalline rocks. *J. Geophys. Res.*, 70: 5669—5678.

Brace, W.F., Paulding, Jr., B.W. and Scholz, C.H., 1966. Dilatancy in the fracture of crystalline rocks. *J. Geophys. Res.*, 71: 3939—3953.

Brady, B.T., 1974. Theory of earthquakes, 1. A scale independent theory of rock failure. *Pure Appl. Geophys.*, 112: 701—725.

Breiner, S., 1964. Piezomagnetic effect at the time of local earthquakes. *Nature*, 202: 790—791.

Breiner, S., 1967. *The Piezomagnetic Effect in Seismically Active Areas*. Thesis, Stanford Univ., Stanford, Calif., 190 pp.

Bronson, W., 1971. *The Earth Shook, the Sky Burned*. Pocket Books, New York, N.Y., 368 pp.

Brown, R., 1973. Precursory changes in V_p/V_s before strike-slip events. In: R.L. Kovach and A. Nur (Editors), *Proceedings of the Conference on Tectonic Problems on the San Andreas Fault System*. Stanford Univ. Publ., Geol. Sci., 13: 463—472.

Brune, J.N. and Allen, C.R., 1967. A microearthquake survey of the San Andreas fault system in southern California. *Bull. Seismol. Soc. Am.*, 57: 277—296.

Bufe, C.G., 1970. Frequency—magnitude variations during the 1970 Danville earthquake swarm. *Earthquake Notes*, 41 (3): 3—7.

Bufe, C.G., Bakun, W.H. and Tocher, D., 1973. Geophysical studies in the San Andreas fault zone at the Stone Canyon Observatory, California. In: R.L. Kovach and A. Nur (Editors), *Proceedings of the Conference on Tectonic Problems on the San Andreas Fault System*. Stanford Univ. Publ., Geol. Sci., 13: 86—93.

Byerlee, J.D., 1967. Frictional characteristics of granite under high confining pressure. *J. Geophys. Res.*, 72: 3639—3648.

Caloi, P. and Spadea, M.C., 1955. Prime indicazioni di registrazioni clinografiche ottenute in zona ad elevata sismicita. *Ann. Geof.*, 8: 121—133.

Carder, D.S., 1945. Seismic investigations in the Boulder Dam area, 1940—1944, and the influence of reservoir loading and local activity. *Bull. Seismol. Soc. Am.*, 35: 175—192.

Castle, R.O., Alt, J.N., Savage, J.C. and Balazs, E.I., 1974. Elevation changes preceding the San Fernando earthquake of February 9, 1971. *Geology*, 2: 61—66.

Chapman, S. and Bartels, J., 1940. *Geomagnetism*. Oxford Univ. Press, London, 1049 pp.

Chen, P.S. and Lin, P.H., 1973. An application of statistical theory of extreme values to moderate and long interval earthquake prediction. *Acta Geophys. Sinica*, 16: 6—24 (in Chinese).

Chinnery, M.A., 1961. The deformation of the ground around surface faults. *Bull. Seismol. Soc. Am.*, 51: 355—372.

Coe, R.S., 1971. Earthquake prediction program in the People's Republic of China. *EOS (Trans. Am. Geophys. Union)*, 52: 940—943.

Cook, K.L., 1973. Granite Mountain records vault 15 miles south of Salt Lake City, Utah. Report presented to the 4th U.S.—Japan Conference on Earthquake Prediction.

Cox, A., Doell, R.R. and Dalrymple, G.B., 1964. Reversals of the earth's magnetic field. *Science*, 144: 1537—1543.

Dambara, T., 1966. Vertical movements of the earth's crust in relation to the Matsushiro earthquake. *J. Geod. Soc. Japan*, 12: 18—45 (in Japanese).

Dambara, T., 1973. Crustal movements before, at and after the Niigata earthquake. *Rep. Coord. Comm. Earthquake Prediction*, 9: 93—96 (in Japanese).

Dambara, T., 1975. A method of adjustment of the secondary geodetic net, and horizontal displacements in Tanna and Yamakita areas. *J. Geod. Soc. Japan*, in press (in Japanese).

Davis, P.M., 1975. The piezomagnetic computation of magnetic anomalies due to ground loading by a man-made lake. *Pure Appl. Geophys.*, in press.

Davis, P.M. and Stacey, F.D., 1972. Geomagnetic anomalies caused by a man-made lake. *Nature*, 240: 348—349.

Defazio, T.L., Aki, K. and Alba, J., 1973. Solid earth tide and observed change in the in-situ seismic velocity. *J. Geophys. Res.*, 78: 1319—1322.

Department of Geodesy and Geophysics, 1973. *Annual Report 1972—73*. Univ. of Cambridge, Cambridge, 8 pp.

Derr, J.S., 1973. Earthquake lights: a review of observations and present theories. *Bull. Seismol. Soc. Am.*, 63: 2177—2187.

Dutta, T.K., 1969. A note on the source parameter of the Koynanagar earthquake of 10th December 1967. *Bull. Seismol. Soc. Am.*, 59: 935—944.

Earthquake Research Institute, 1971. Changes in the total geomagnetic intensity before and after the Southeast Akita earthquake. *Rep. Coord. Comm. Earthquake Prediction*, 5: 22—23 (in Japanese).

Eisler, J.D., 1967. Investigation of a method for determining stress accumulation at depth, 1. *Bull. Seismol. Soc. Am.*, 57: 891—911.

Eisler, J.D., 1969. Investigation of a method for determining stress accumulation at depth, 2. *Bull. Seismol. Soc. Am.*, 59: 43—58.

Environmental Science Services Administration, 1966a. *E.S.S.A. Symposium on Earthquake Prediction*. U.S. Dept. of Commerce, Washington, D.C., 167 pp.

Environmental Science Services Administration, 1966b. *The Prince William Sound, Alaska, Earthquake of 1964 and Aftershocks*, Vol. 1. U.S. Government Printing Office, Washington, D.C., 263 pp.

Environmental Science Services Administration, 1969a. *The Prince William Sound, Alaska, Earthquake of 1964 and Aftershocks*, Vol. 2. U.S. Government Printing Office, Washington, D.C., 350 pp.

Environmental Science Services Administration, 1969b. *The Prince William Sound, Alaska, Earthquake of 1964 and Aftershocks*, Vol. 3. U.S. Government Printing Office, Washington, D.C., 161 pp.

Epstein, B. and Lomnitz, C., 1966. A model for the occurrence of large earthquakes. *Nature*, 211: 954—956.

Evans, D.M., 1966. Man-made earthquakes in Denver. *Geotimes*, 10 (9): 11—18.

Evans, D.M., 1967. Man-made earthquakes — a progress report. *Geotimes*, 12 (6): 19—20.

Evison, F.F., 1970. Seismogenesis. *Tectonophysics*, 9: 113—128.

Fedotov, S.A., Dolbilkina, N.A., Morozov, V.N., Myachkin, V.I., Preobrazensky, V.B. and Sobolev, G.A., 1970. Investigation on earthquake prediction in Kamchatka. *Tectonophysics*, 9: 249—258.

Fedotov, S.A., Gusev, A.A. and Boldyrev, S.A., 1972. Progress of earthquake prediction in Kamchatka. *Tectonophysics*, 14: 279—286.

Feng, T.Y., Tan, A.N. and Wang, K.F., 1974. Velocity anomalies of seismic waves from near earthquakes and earthquake prediction. *Acta Geophys. Sinica*, 17: 84—98 (in Chinese).

Fiedler, B.G., 1974. Local *b*-values related to seismicity. *Tectonophysics*, 23: 277—282.

Fisher, R.A., 1950. Tests of significance in harmonic analysis. In: R.A. Fisher (Editor), *Contribution to Mathematical Statistics*. Wiley and Sons, New York, N.Y., pp. 53—59.

Fitch, T.J. and Scholz, C.H., 1971. Mechanism of underthrusting in southwest Japan: a model of convergent plate interactions. *J. Geophys. Res.*, 76: 7260—7292.

Freiberger, W.F., 1960. *The International Dictionary of Applied Mathematics*. D. van Nostrand, Princeton, N.J., 1173 pp.

Fujita, N., 1965. The magnetic disturbances accompanying the Niigata earthquake. *J. Geod. Soc. Japan*, 11: 8—25 (in Japanese).

Fujita, N., 1971. Vertical movements of Miura Peninsula. *Rep. Coord. Comm. Earthquake Prediction*, 5: 36—37 (in Japanese).

Fujita, N. and Fujii, Y., 1974. Gravity change in Japan. *J. Geod. Soc. Japan*, 20: 77—79.

Garland, G.D., 1971. *Introduction to Geophysics — Mantle, Core and Crust*. W.B. Saunders, Philadelphia, Pa., 420 pp.

Geoelectric Division, Lanchou Seismology Brigade, 1974. *Changes of Strain-Resistivity before Earthquakes*. Publication of Lanchou Seismology Brigade, Lanchou, 12 pp.

Geographical Survey Institute, 1952. Resurvey of the southwestern part of Japan after the great Nankaido earthquake of 1946. *J. Geogr. Surv. Inst. Japan*, 3: 31—118.

Geographical Survey Institute, 1954. Resurvey of the southwestern part of Japan after the great Nankaido earthquake of 1946. *J. Geogr. Surv. Inst. Japan*, 4: 1—69.

Geographical Survey Institute, 1967. *Index Maps of Precise Leveling for Every Observation Year*. Tokyo.

Geographical Survey Institute, 1969a. Crustal activities in Boso and Miura Peninsula region. *Rep. Coord. Comm. Earthquake Prediction*, 1: 25—33 (in Japanese).

Geographical Survey Institute, 1969b. Vertical crustal movements in the Tokai district. *Rep. Coord. Comm. Earthquake Prediction*, 2: 49—53 (in Japanese).

Geographical Survey Institute, 1972a. Crustal movement in eastern part of Hokkaido district. *Rep. Coord. Comm. Earthquake Prediction*, 8: 1—6 (in Japanese).

Geographical Survey Institute, 1972b. Recent crustal movement in South Kanto district, 4. *Rep. Coord. Comm. Earthquake Prediction*, 8: 23—26 (in Japanese).

Geographical Survey Institute, 1972c. Deformations of Mitaka rhombus line. *Rep. Coord. Comm. Earthquake Prediction*, 8: 32—34 (in Japanese).

Geographical Survey Institute, 1973. G.D.P. traverse survey of high precision in eastern part of Hokkaido and Kanto—Hokuriku district. *Rep. Coord. Comm. Earthquake Prediction*, 9: 127—128 (in Japanese).

Geographical Survey Institute, 1974a. G.D.P. traverse survey of high precision in northeastern part of Japan. *Rep. Coord. Comm. Earthquake Prediction*, 11: 60—61 (in Japanese).

Geographical Survey Institute, 1974b. Precise strain measurements in Yamakita and Tanna regions. *Rep. Coord. Comm. Earthquake Prediction*, 11: 94—95 (in Japanese).

Geographical Survey Institute, 1974c. G.D.P. traverse survey of high precision in Chubu and Tokai districts. *Rep. Coord. Comm. Earthquake Prediction*, 11: 107—108 (in Japanese).

Geographical Survey Institute, 1974d. G.D.P. traverse survey of high precision in Kyushu district. *Rep. Coord. Comm. Earthquake Prediction*, 11: 123—124 (in Japanese).

Geological Survey of Japan, 1972. Measurements on the time variation of seismic wave velocities by explosion-seismic method (the results of the fifth experiment). *Rep. Coord. Comm. Earthquake Prediction*, 8: 46—53 (in Japanese).

Geological Survey of Japan, 1973. *Neotectonic Map Tokyo*. Tokyo, 5 sheets.

Gordon, F.R., 1970. Water level changes preceding the Meckering, Western Australia, earthquake of October 14, 1968. *Bull. Seismol. Soc. Am.*, 60: 1739—1740.

Gordon, F.R., 1971. Faulting during the earthquake at Meckering, Western Australia, 14 October 1968. *Bull. R. Soc. New Zealand*, 9: 85—93.

Gough, D.I. and Gough, W.I., 1970a. Stress and deflection in the lithosphere near Lake Kariba, 1. *Geophys. J.*, 21: 65—78.

Gough, D.I. and Gough, W.I., 1970b. Load-induced earthquakes at Lake Kariba, 2. *Geophys. J.*, 21: 79—101.

Gouin, P., 1965. Coincidence of magnetic disturbances with local earthquakes recorded from the Ethiopian rift system. *Nature*, 208: 541—543.

Greensfelder, R.W. and Bennett, J.H., 1973. Characteristics of strain variation along the San Andreas fault from geodimeter measurements. In: R.L. Kovach and A. Nur (Editors), *Proceedings of the Conference on Tectonic Problems on the San Andreas Fault System*. Stanford Univ. Publ., Geol. Sci., 13: 54—63.

Griggs, D.T., Jackson, D.D., Knopoff, L. and Shreve, R.L., 1975. Earthquake prediction: modeling the anomalous V_p/V_s source region. *Science*, 187: 537—540.

Gumbel, E.J., *Statistics of Extremes*. Columbia Univ. Press, New York, N.Y., 375 pp.

Gupta, H., Narain, H., Rastogi, B.K. and Mohan, I., 1969. A study of the Koyna earthquake of December 10, 1967. *Bull. Seismol. Soc. Am.*, 59: 1149—1162.

Gupta, H.K., Rastogi, B.K. and Narain, H., 1973. Earthquakes in the Koyna region and common features of the reservoir-associated seismicity. In: W.C. Ackermann, G.F. White and E.B. Worthington (Editors), *Man-Made Lakes: Their Problems and Environmental Effects*. Am. Geophys. Union, Geophys. Monogr. 17: 455—467.

Gupta, I.N., 1973a. Premonitory changes in shear velocity anisotropy in Nevada. In: R.L. Kovach and A. Nur (Editors), *Proceedings of the Conference on Tectonic Problems on the San Andreas Fault System*. Stanford Univ. Publ., Geol. Sci., 13: 479—488.

Gupta, I.N., 1973b. Premonitory variations in S-wave velocity anisotropy before earthquakes in Nevada. *Science*, 182: 1129—1132.

Gupta, I.N., 1973c. Dilatancy and premonitory variations of P, S travel times. *Bull. Seismol. Soc. Am.*, 63: 1157—1161.

Gupta, I.N., 1973d. Seismic velocities in rock subjected to axial loading up to shear fracture. *J. Geophys. Res.*, 78: 6936—6942.

Gupta, I.N., 1975. Precursory reorientation of stress axes due to vertical migration of seismic activity? *J. Geophys. Res.*, 80: 272—273.

Gutenberg, B. and Richter, C.F., 1944. Frequency of earthquakes in California. *Bull. Seismol. Soc. Am.*, 34: 185—188.

Gutenberg, B. and Richter, C.F., 1954. *Seismicity of the Earth and Associated Phenomena*. Princeton Univ. Press, Princeton, N.J., 2nd ed., 310 pp.

Gutenberg, B. and Richter, C.F., 1956. Magnitude and energy of earthquakes. *Ann. Geofis.*, 9: 1—15.

Hagiwara, T., 1947. Observation of changes in the inclination of the earth's surface at Mt. Tsukuba (3rd report). *Bull. Earthquake Res. Inst., Univ. Tokyo*, 25: 27—32.

Hagiwara, T., 1962. Earthquake prediction. *Kagaku*, 32: 367—371 (in Japanese).

Hagiwara, T. (Editor), 1964. *Proceedings of the United States—Japan Conference on Research Related to Earthquake Prediction Problems*. Earthquake Research. Institute, Univ. of Tokyo, Tokyo, 105 pp.

Hagiwara, T., 1969. Prediction of earthquakes. In: P.J. Hart (Editor), *The Earth's Crust and Upper Mantle*. Am. Geophys. Union, Geophys. Monogr., 13: 174—176.

Hagiwara, T., 1973. The development of earthquake prediction research. *Gakujitsu Geppo. Japan Soc. Promotion Sci.*, 26: 2—32 (in Japanese).

Hagiwara, T. and Ohtake, M., 1972. Seismic activity associated with the filling of the reservoir behind the Kurobe dam, Japan, 1963—1970. *Tectonophysics*, 15: 241—254.

Hagiwara, T. and Rikitake, T., 1967. Japanese program on earthquake prediction. *Science*, 157: 761—768.

Hagiwara, T. and Rikitake, T., 1969a. La previsione dei terremoti. *Enciclopedia della Scienza della Tecnica*, pp. 218—228.

Hagiwara, T. and Rikitake, T., 1969b. Neue Entwicklungen in der Erdbebenprognose. *Umschau*, 69: 56.

Hagiwara, T., Rikitake, T. and Yamada, J., 1948. Observations of the deformation of the earth's surface at Aburatsubo, Miura Peninsula, 1. *Bull. Earthquake Res. Inst., Univ. Tokyo*, 26: 23—26.

Hagiwara, T., Rikitake, T., Kasahara, K. and Yamada, J., 1949a. Observation of ground tilting and strain at Hokugo Village, Fukui Prefecture. *Rep. Spec. Comm. Investigation of Fukui earthquake*, Science Council Japan, Tokyo, pp. 61—64.

Hagiwara, T., Rikitake, T., Kasahara, K. and Yamada, J., 1949b. Observations of the deformation of the earth's surface at Aburatsubo, Miura Peninsula, 3. *Bull. Earthquake Res. Inst., Univ. Tokyo*, 27: 39—44.

Hagiwara, Y., 1971. Optimum project of leveling survey for earthquake prediction. *J. Geod. Soc. Japan*, 17: 38—40 (in Japanese).

Hagiwara, Y., 1974a. Geodesy in Japan. *Geophys. Surv.*, 1: 305—323.

Hagiwara, Y., 1974b. Probability of earthquake occurrence as obtained from a Weibull distribution analysis of crustal strain. *Tectonophysics*, 23: 313—318.

Hagiwara, Y. and Tajima, H., 1973. Secular changes in gravity. In: I. Tsubokawa (Editor), *Publ. 50th Anniv. Great Kanto Earthquake, 1923*. Earthquake Research Institute, Univ. of Tokyo, Tokyo, pp. 311—327 (in Japanese).

Hamilton, R.M., 1974. Earthquake prediction and public reaction. *EOS (Trans. Am. Geophys. Union)*, 55: 739, 742.

Hamilton, R.M. and Healy, J.H., 1969. Aftershocks of the Benham nuclear explosion. *Bull. Seismol. Soc. Am.*, 59: 2271—2282.

Harada, T. and Kassai, A., 1971. Horizontal strain of the crust in Japan for the last 60 years. *J. Geod. Soc. Japan*, 17: 4—7 (in Japanese).

Harada, Y., 1969. Investigation of active crust by means of geodetic surveys in Japan. In: L.E. Alsop and J.E. Oliver (Editors), *Joint U.S.—Japan Conference: Premonitory Phenomena Associated with Several Recent Earthquakes and Related Problems — EOS (Trans. Am. Geophys. Union)*, 50: 402.

Harrison, J.C., 1974. Tidal tilts in the Poorman Mine, Boulder, Colorado. *EOS (Trans. Am. Geophys. Union)*, 55: 221.

Hasbrouck, W.P. and Allen, J.H., 1972. Quasistatic magnetic field changes associated with the CANNIKIN nuclear explosion. *Bull. Seismol. Soc. Am.*, 62: 1479—1487.

Hatai, S. and Abe, N., 1932. The responses of the catfish, *Parasilurus Asotus*, to earthquakes. *Proc. Imp. Acad. Japan*, 8: 375—378.

Hatai, S., Kokubo, S. and Abe, N., 1932. The earth currents in relation to the responses of catfish. *Proc. Imp. Acad. Japan*, 8: 478—481.

Hayakawa, M., 1950. The variation of seismic wave velocity. *Rep. Geol. Surv. Japan*, Spec. Number, pp. 7—24.

Hayford, J.F. and Baldwin, A.L., 1907. The earth movements in the California earthquake of 1906. *U.S. Coast Geod. Surv. Rep.*, Appendix No. 3, pp. 69—99.

Healy, J.H., Rubey, W.W., Griggs, D.T. and Raleigh, C.B., 1968. The Denver earthquakes. *Science*, 161: 1301—1310.

Healy, J.H., Hamilton, R.M. and Raleigh, C.B., 1970. Earthquakes induced by fluid injection and explosion. *Tectonophysics*, 9: 205—214.

Healy, J.H., Lee, W.H.K., Pakiser, L.C., Raleigh, C.B. and Wood, M.D., 1972. Prospects of earthquake prediction and control. *Tectonophysics*, 14: 319—332.

Heirtzler, J.R., Dickson, G.O., Herron, E.M., Pitman III, W.C. and Le Pichon, X., 1968. Marine magnetic anomalies, geomagnetic field reversals, and motions of the ocean floor and continents. *J. Geophys. Res.*, 73: 2119—2136.

Hess, H.H., 1962. History of ocean basins. In: A.E.J. Engel, H.L. James and B.F. Leonard (Editors), *Petrological Studies*. Geological Society of America, New York, N.Y., pp. 599—620.

Hofmann, R.B., 1968. Geodimeter fault movement investigations in California. *Bull. Dept. Water Resour., State of Calif.*, No. 116-6, 183 pp.

Hofmann, R.B., 1973. Seismic activity and reservoir filling at Oroville and San Luis Dams, California. In: W.C. Ackermann, G.F. White and E.B. Worthington (Editors), *Man-Made Lakes: Their Problems and Environmental Effects*. Am. Geophys. Union, Geophys. Monogr., 17: 468—471.

Holmes, A., 1944. *Principles of Physical Geology*. Thomas Nelson and Sons, London-Edinburgh, 1288 pp.

Hosoyama, K., 1952. Characteristic tilt of the ground that preceded the occurrence of the strong earthquake of March 7, 1952. *J. Phys. Earth*, 1: 75—81.

Hubbert, M.K. and Rubey, W.W., 1959. Role of fluid pressure in mechanics of overthrust faulting, 1, 2. *Bull. Geol. Soc. Am.*, 70: 115—166.

Hughes, W.J., 1973. The effect of two periodic conductivity anomalies on geomagnetic micropulsation measurements. *Geophys. J.*, 31: 407—431.

Hughes, W.J., 1974a. The effect of micropulsations on a localized earth conductivity anomaly. *Geophys. J.*, 36: 641—649.

Hughes, W.J., 1974b. The polarization of micropulsations and geo-electric structure. *Geophys. J.*, 38: 95—117.

Huzita, K., Kisimoto, Y. and Shiono, K., 1973. Neotectonics and seismicity in the Kinki area, southwest Japan. *J. Geosci., Osaka Univ.*, 16, Art. 6: 93—124.

Ichikawa, M., 1971. Re-analyses of mechanism of earthquakes which occurred in and near Japan and statistical studies on the nodal plane solutions obtained. *Geophys. Mag.*, 35: 207—274.

Iida, K. and Shichi, R., 1972. Crustal deformation before the earthquakes of Sept. 9, 1969 (central part of Gifu Pref.) and Jan. 5, 1971 (off Atumi Peninsula). *Rep. Coord. Comm. Earthquake Prediction*, 7: 41—44 (in Japanese).

Iida, K., Shichi, R., Oida, T. and Yamada, K., 1971. Recent seismic activity, especially the Atsumi Peninsula earthquake on January 5, 1971. *Rep. Coord. Comm. Earthquake Prediction*, 5: 38—42 (in Japanese).

Iijima, H., 1969. Surface geology of Matsushiro area and disaster by the Matsushiro earthquake swarm. *Rep. Cooperative Res. Disaster Prevention*, 18: 103—115 (in Japanese).

Iizuka, S., 1971. Measurements on the time variations of seismic wave velocities by explosion-seismic method (preliminary report on the fourth experiment). *Rep. Coord. Comm. Earthquake Prediction*, 6: 15—24 (in Japanese).

Imamura, A., 1928. Present status of earthquake research. *Stenographic Records of Lunch-time Talks at the Japanese House of Peers*, No. 29, 45 pp. (in Japanese).

Imamura, A., 1937. *Theoretical and Applied Seismolgoy*. Maruzen, Tokyo, 358 pp.

Imperial Earthquake Investigation Committee, 1904 and 1973. *Dai Nihon Jishin Shiryo* (Japanese Historical Records Relevant to Earthquakes), Reprinted by Shibunkan, Kyoto, Part 1, 606 pp.; Part 2, 595 pp. (in Japanese).

Isacks, B., Oliver, J.E. and Sykes, L.R., 1968. Seismology and the new global tectonics. *J. Geophys. Res.*, 73: 5855—5899.

Ishibashi, K. and Tsumura, K., 1971. A microearthquake observation in the South Kanto region. *Bull. Earthquake Res. Inst., Univ. Tokyo*, 49: 97—113 (in Japanese).

Ishimoto, M., 1927. Observation sur les variations de l'inclination de la surface terrester (premier rapport). *Bull. Earthquake Res. Inst., Univ. Tokyo*, 2: 1—12.

Ishimoto, M. and Iida, K., 1939. Observations sur les séismes enregistrés par le micro-sismographe construit dernièrement, 1. *Bull. Earthquake Res. Inst., Univ. Tokyo*, 17: 443—478.

Ispir, Y. and Uyar, O., 1971. An attempt in determining the seismomagnetic effect in North West Turkey. *J. Geomagn. Geoelectr.*, 23: 295—305.

Japanese Network of Crustal Movement Observatories, 1970. Spatial distribution of strain-steps associated with the earthquake of the central part of Gifu Prefecture, September 9, 1969. *Bull. Earthquake Res. Inst., Univ. Tokyo*, 48: 1217—1233.

Johnson, A.G. and Kovach, R.L., 1973. Water level fluctuations on the San Andreas fault south of Hollister, California. In: R.L. Kovach and A. Nur (Editors), *Proceedings of the Conference on Tectonic Problems on the San Andreas Fault System*. Stanford Univ. Publ., Geol. Sci., 13: 489—494.

Johnson, A.G., Kovach, R.L. and Nur, A., 1974. Fluid-pressure variations and fault creep in Central California. *Tectonophysics*, 23: 257—266.

Johnston, M.J.S., 1974. Tectonomagnetic experiments in Western U.S.A. *EOS (Trans. Am. Geophys. Union)*, 56: 1113.

Johnston, M.J.S. and Mortensen, C.E., 1974. Tilt precursors before earthquakes on the San Andreas fault, California. *Science*, 186: 1031—1034.

Johnston, M.J.S., Smith, B.E., Johnston, J.R. and Williams, F.J., 1973. A search for tectonomagnetic effects in California and Western Nevada. In: R.L. Kovach and A. Nur (Editors), *Proceedings of the Conference on Tectonic Problems on the San Andreas Fault System*. Stanford Univ. Publ., Geol. Sci., 13: 225—238.

Johnston, M.J.S., Bakun, W.H., Pakiser, L.C. and Tarr, A.C., 1974. Earthquakes — can they be predicted or controlled? *Industr. Res.*, November 15: 30—37.

Jungels, P. and Anderson, D.L., 1971. Strains and tilts associated with the San Fernando earthquake. The San Fernando, California, Earthquake of February 9, 1971. *U.S. Geol. Surv., Prof. Paper* No. 733, pp. 77—79.

Kaminuma, K., Iwata, T., Kayano, I. and Ohtake, M., 1973. Summary of scientific data of major earthquakes in Japan, 1872—1972. *Spec. Rep. Earthquake Res. Inst., Univ. Tokyo*, 9: 1—136 (in Japanese).

Kanamori, H., 1970. Recent developments in earthquake prediction research in Japan. *Tectonophysics*, 9: 291—300.

Kanamori, H., 1971. Faulting of the great Kanto earthquake of 1923 as revealed by seismological data. *Bull. Earthquake Res. Inst., Univ. Tokyo*, 49: 13—18.

Kanamori, H., 1972a. Mode of strain release associated with major earthquakes in Japan. In: F.A. Donath (Editor), *Annual Review of Earth and Planetary Sciences*. Annual Reviews, Palo Alto, Calif., 1: 213—239.

Kanamori, H., 1972b. Tectonic implications of the 1944 Tonankai and the 1946 Nankai-do earthquakes. *Phys. Earth Planet. Inter.*, 5: 129—139.

Kanamori, H., 1972c. Relation between tectonic stress, great earthquakes and earthquake swarms. *Tectonophysics*, 14: 1—12.

Kanamori, H. and Chung, W.Y., 1974. Temporal changes in P-wave velocity in southern California. *Tectonophysics*, 23: 67—78.

Kanamori, H. and Miyamura, S., 1970. Seismometrical re-evaluation of the great Kanto earthquake of September 1, 1923. *Bull. Earthquake Res. Inst., Univ. Tokyo,* 48: 115—125.

Kaneko, S., 1966. Transcurrent displacement along the Median Line, southwestern Japan. *New Zealand J. Geol. Geophys.,* 9: 45—59.

Kasahara, J., Koresawa, S., Tsumura, K., Nakamura, I. and Nagumo, S., 1973. The earthquake of December 4, 1972 in the east off Hachijojima. *Rep. Coord. Comm. Earthquake Prediction,* 9: 51—62 (in Japanese).

Kasahara, K., 1957. The nature of seismic origins as inferred from seismological and geodetic observations, 1. *Bull. Earthquake Res. Inst., Univ. Tokyo,* 35: 473—532.

Kasahara, K., 1970. The source region of the Matsushiro swarm earthquake. *Bull. Earthquake Res. Inst., Univ. Tokyo,* 48: 581—602.

Kasahara, K., 1973. Tiltmeter observation in complement with precise levellings. *J. Geod. Soc. Japan,* 19: 93—99 (in Japanese).

Kasahara, K., 1975. Aseismic faulting following the 1973 Nemuro-oki earthquake, Hokkaido, Japan (a possibility). *Pure Appl. Geophys.,* in press.

Kasahara, K., Yamada, J., Takahashi, T. and Technical Division of the Earthquake Research Institute, 1973. The Odawara bore-hole station equipped with a buoy tiltmeter. *Rep. Coord. Comm. Earthquake Prediction,* 10: 51—56.

Kato, Y., 1939. Investigation of the changes in the earth's magnetic field accompanying earthquakes or volcanic eruptions. *Sci. Rep. Tohoku Imp. Univ.,* Ser. 1, 27: 1—100.

Kato, Y., 1966. Recent studies on geomagnetic changes accompanied by earthquakes. In: T. Nagata (Editor), *Proc. Symp. Geomagnetic Changes Associated with Earthquakes and Volcanic Activities.* Geophys. Institute, Univ. of Tokyo, Tokyo, pp. 1—20 (in Japanese).

Kawada, K., 1966. Electric resistivity measurement along and across a ground fissure in the Matsushiro area. *Bull. Earthquake Res. Inst., Univ. Tokyo,* 44: 1759—1769.

Kawasumi, H., 1970. Proofs of 69 years periodicity and imminence of destructive earthquake in southern Kwanto district and problems in the countermeasures thereof. *Chigaku Zasshi,* 79: 115—138 (in Japanese).

Kelleher, J., 1970. Space—time seismicity of Alaska—Aleutian seismic zone. *J. Geophys. Res.,* 75: 5745—5756.

Kelleher, J. and Savino, J., 1975. Distribution of seismicity before large strike slip and thrust-type earthquakes. *J. Geophys. Res.,* 80: 260—271.

Kelleher, J., Sykes, L. and Oliver, J., 1973. Possible criteria for predicting earthquake locations and their application to major plate boundaries of the Pacific and the Caribbean. *J. Geophys. Res.,* 78: 2547—2585.

King, G.C.P. and Bilham, R.G., 1973. Tidal tilt measurement in Europe. *Nature,* 243: 74—75.

Kisimoto, Y. and Nishida, R., 1971. Some properties of an earthquake sequence near Chizu, Tottori Pref., in April, 1970. *Rep. Coord. Comm. Earthquake Prediction,* 6: 60—65 (in Japanese).

Kisslinger, C., 1974. Earthquake prediction. *Phys. Today,* 27: 36—42.

Kisslinger, C., 1975. Processes during the Matsushiro earthquake swarm as revealed by levelling, gravity and spring-flow observations. *Geology,* 3: 57—62.

Kisslinger, C. and Engdahl, E.R., 1974. A test of the Semyenov prediction technique in the central Aleutian Islands. *Tectonophysics,* 23: 237—246.

Kisslinger, C. and Rikitake, T., 1974. U.S.—Japan seminar on earthquake prediction and control. *EOS (Trans. Am. Geophys. Union),* 55: 9—15.

Kondratenko, A.M. and Nersesov, I.L., 1962. Some results of a study of changes in the speeds of longitudinal waves and the ratio of the speeds of longitudinal and transverse waves in the focal zone. In: *Physics of Earthquakes and Explosion Seismology.* U.S.S.R., pp. 198—234 (English translation).

Kovach, R.L., Nur, A., Wesson, R.L. and Robinson, R., 1975. Water level fluctuations and earthquakes on the San Andreas fault zone. *Geology*, in press.

Kuno, H., 1936. On the displacement of the Tanna fault since the Pleistocene. *Bull. Earthquake Res. Inst., Univ. Tokyo*, 14: 619—631.

Kuo, T.K., Chin, P.Y. and Feng, H.T., 1974. Discussion on the change of groundwater level preceding a large earthquake from an earthquake source model. *Acta Geophys. Sinica*, 17: 99—105 (in Chinese).

Latynina, L.A. and Karmaleyeva, R.M., 1970. On certain anomalies in the variations of crustal strains before strong earthquakes. *Tectonophysics*, 9: 239—247.

Latynina, L.A. and Karmaleyeva, R.M., 1972. Measurement of slow movements in the earth's crust as a method of seeking forewarnings of earthquakes. In: M.A. Sadovsky (Editor), *Physical Bases of Seeking Methods of Predicting Earthquakes.* Acad. Sci. U.S.S.R., Moscow, 1970, 152 pp. Translated in English from Russian by D.B. Vitaliano, U.S. Geological Survey.

Lee, W.K.H., 1974. Earthquakes and China: a guide to some background materials. *U.S. Geol. Surv., Open File Rep.*, 88 pp.

Lee, W.H.K., Eaton, M.S. and Brabb, E.E., 1971. The earthquake sequence near Danville, California, 1970. *Bull. Seismol. Soc. Am.*, 61: 1771—1794.

Lensen, G.J., 1971. Phases, nature and rates of earth deformation. *Bull. R. Soc. New Zealand*, 9: 97—105.

Lensen, G.J. and Otway, P.M., 1971. Earthshift and post-earthshift deformation associated with the May 1968 Inangahua earthquake New Zealand. *Bull. R. Soc. New Zealand*, 9: 107—116.

Lomnitz, C., 1966. Statistical prediction of earthquakes. *Rev. Geophys.*, 4: 377—393.

Lomnitz, C., 1974. *Global Tectonics and Earthquake Risk.* Elsevier, Amsterdam, 320 pp.

Matsuda, T., 1966. Strike-slip faulting along the Atotsugawa fault, Japan. *Bull. Earthquake Res. Inst., Univ. Tokyo*, 44: 1179—1212 (in Japanese).

Matsuda, T., 1968. Active faults and active foldings. *Symp. Research on Earthquake Prediction*, Earthquake Research Institute, Univ. of Tokyo, Tokyo, pp. 46—49 (in Japanese).

Matsuda, T., 1972. Earthquakes and faults from geological standpoints. *Proc. 12th Conf. Earthquake Engineering*, Comm. Earthquake Engineering, Japan Society of Civil Engineers, Tokyo, 7 pp. (in Japanese).

Matsumura, K. and Oike, K., 1973. The microseismicities in and around Japan. *Annu. Rep. Disas. Prev. Res. Inst., Kyoto Univ.*, 16B: 77—87 (in Japanese).

Matsushima, S., 1960. Variation of the elastic wave velocities of rocks in the process of deformation and fracture under high pressure. *Bull. Disas. Prev. Res. Inst., Kyoto Univ.*, 32: 2—8.

Matumoto, T. and Latham, G., 1973. Aftershocks and intensity of the Managua earthquake of 23 December 1972. *Science*, 181: 545—547.

Mazzella, A. and Morrison, H.F., 1974. Electrical resistivity variations associated with earthquakes on the San Andreas fault. *Science*, 185: 855—857.

McEvilly, T.V. and Johnson, L.R., 1973. Earthquakes of strike-slip type in central California: evidence on the question of dilatancy. *Science*, 182: 581—583.

McGarr, A., 1974. Earthquake prediction: absence of a precursive change in seismic velocities before a tremor of magnitude 3.3/4. *Science*, 185: 1047—1049.

Meade, B.K., 1948. Earthquake investigation in the vicinity of El Centro, California; horizontal movement. *Trans. Am. Geophys. Union*, 29: 27—31.

Meade, B.K., 1969. Annual rate of slippage along the San Andreas fault. In: *Problems of Recent Crustal Movements.* 3rd Symp. on Recent Crustal Movement, IAG-IUGG, Leningrad, May 1968. Acad. Sci. U.S.S.R., Moscow, pp. 233—237.

Meade, B.K., 1971. Horizontal movement along the San Andreas fault system. *Bull. R. Soc. New Zealand*, 9: 175—179.

Mescherikov, J.A., 1968. Recent crustal movements in seismic regions: geodetic and geomorphic data. *Tectonophysics*, 6: 29—39.

Mickery, W.V., 1973. Reservoir seismic effects. In: W.C. Ackermann, G.F. White and E.B. Worthington (Editors), *Man-Made Lakes: Their Problems and Environmental Effects*. Am. Geophys. Union, Geophys. Monogr., 17: 472—479.

Milne, J., 1886. *Earthquakes and other Earth Movements*. D. Appleton, New York, N.Y., 363 pp.

Milne, J., 1890. Earthquakes in connection with electric and magnetic phenomena. *Trans. Seismol. Soc. Japan*, 15: 135—162.

Miyabe, N., 1931. On the vertical movement in Kanto districts. *Bull. Earthquake Res. Inst., Univ. Tokyo*, 9: 2—21.

Miyakoshi, J., 1975. Secular variation of Parkinson vectors in a seismically active region of Middle Asia. *J. Fac. General Education, Tottori Univ.*, 8: 209—218.

Miyamura, S., Okada, A., Izutuya, S. and Sugimura, A., 1968. Levelling resurvey along the River Oguni, Yamagata Prefecture. *Bull. Earthquake Res. Inst., Univ. Tokyo*, 46: 405—412 (in Japanese).

Mizutani, H., Ishido, T. and Matsui, T., 1973. Changes in V_p/V_s ratio in the Central Gifu earthquake (abstract). *Fall Meet. Seismol. Soc. Japan* (in Japanese).

Mogi, K., 1962a. Study of the elastic shocks caused by the fracture of heterogeneous materials and its relation to earthquake phenomena. *Bull. Earthquake Res. Inst., Univ. Tokyo*, 40: 125—173.

Mogi, K., 1962b. Magnitude-frequency relation for elastic shocks accompanying fractures of various materials and some related problems in earthquakes (2nd paper). *Bull. Earthquake Res. Inst., Univ. Tokyo*, 40: 831—853.

Mogi, K., 1963. Some discussions on aftershocks, foreshocks and earthquake swarms — the fracture of a semi-infinite body caused by an inner stress origin and its relation to the earthquake phenomena (3rd paper). *Bull. Earthquake Res. Inst., Univ. Tokyo*, 41: 615—658.

Mogi, K., 1966. Experiments on fracture of rocks. In: R. Page (Editor), *Proceedings of the Second United States—Japan Conference on Research Related to Earthquake Prediction Problems*. Lamont Geological Observatory, Columbia Univ., New York, N.Y., pp. 62—63.

Mogi, K., 1967. Earthquakes and fractures. *Tectonophysics*, 5: 35—55.

Mogi, K., 1968. Migration of seismic activity. *Bull. Earthquake Res. Inst., Univ. Tokyo*, 46: 53—74.

Mogi, K., 1969. Rock breaking tests. *Kagaku*, 39: 95—102 (in Japanese).

Mogi, K., 1973a. Relationship between shallow and deep seismicity in the western Pacific region. *Tectonophysics*, 17: 1—22.

Mogi, K., 1973b. Rock fracture, In: F.A. Donath (Editor), *Annual Review of Earth and Planetary Sciences*. Annual Reviews, Palo Alto, Calif., 1: 63—84.

Mogi, K., 1974. Rock fracture and earthquake prediction. *J. Soc. Materials Sci. Japan*, 23: 320—331 (in Japanese).

Moore, G.W., 1964. Magnetic disturbances preceding the 1964 Alaska earthquake. *Nature*, 203: 508—509.

Mori, T. and Yoshino, T., 1970. Local difference in variations of the geomagnetic total intensity in Japan. *Bull. Earthquake Res. Inst., Univ. Tokyo*, 48: 893—922.

Murai, I. and Kaneko, S., 1973. Notes on neotectonics of the South Kanto region. In: I. Tsubokawa (Editor), *Publication of the 50th Anniversary Great Kanto Earthquake, 1923*. Earthquake Research Institute, Univ. of Tokyo, Tokyo, pp. 125—145 (in Japanese).

Murai, I. and Kaneko, S., 1974. The Izu—Hanto-oki earthquake of 1974 and the earthquake faults, especially, the relationships between the earthquake faults, the active faults, and the fracture systems in the earthquake area. *Spec. Bull. Earthquake Res. Inst., Univ. Tokyo*, 14: 159—203 (in Japanese).

Musha, K., 1951. *Nihon Jishin Shiryo* (Japanese historical records relevant to earthquakes). Mainichi Press, Tokyo, 1019 pp. (in Japanese).

Musha, K., 1957. *Jishin Namazu* (Earthquake and catfish). Toyotosho, Tokyo, 208 pp. (in Japanese).

Muto, K., 1932. A study of displacements of triangulation points. *Bull. Earthquake Res. Inst., Univ. Tokyo*, 10: 384—391.

Muto, K., Okuda, T. and Harada, Y., 1950. The land deformation accompanying the Fukui earthquake of June 28, 1948. *Bull. Geogr. Surv. Inst.*, 2: 27—36.

Myachkin, V.I. and Zubkov. S.I., 1973. Compound curve of earthquake forerunner. *Izv. Acad. Sci. U.S.S.R. (Phys. Solid Earth)*, 8: 363—365 (English edition).

Myachkin, V.I., Sobolev, G.A., Dolbilkina, N.A., Morozow, V.N. and Preobrazensky, V.B., 1972. The study of variations in geophysical fields near focal zones of Kamchatka. *Tectonophysics*, 14: 287—293.

Nagata, T., 1944. Variation in earth-current in the vicinity of the Sikano fault. *Bull. Earthquake Res. Inst., Univ. Tokyo*, 22: 72—82 (in Japanese).

Nagata, T., 1969. Tectonomagnetism. *Int. Assoc. Geomagn. Aeron. Bull.* 27: 12-43.

Nagata, T., 1970. Effects of a uniaxial compression on remanent magnetizations of igneous rocks. *Pure Appl. Geophys.*, 78: 100—109.

Nagata, T. and Kinoshita, H., 1965. Studies on piezo-magnetization, 1. Magnetization of titaniferous magnetite under uniaxial compression. *J. Geomagn. Geoelectr.*, 17: 121—135.

Nagumo, S., 1973. The role of submarine seismometry in earthquake prediction research. *Proc. Symp. Earthquake Prediction*, December 12, 1972. Seismological Society of Japan, Tokyo, pp. 61—65 (in Japanese).

Nason, R.D., 1973. Fault creep and earthquakes on the San Andreas fault. In: R.L. Kovach and A. Nur (Editors), *Proceedings of the Conference on Tectonic Problems on the San Andreas Fault System*. Stanford Univ. Publ., Geol. Sci., 13: 275—285.

Nasu, N., 1950. Crustal deformation. In: H. Tsuya (Editor), *The Fukui Earthquake of June 28, 1948*. Committee for the Study of Fukui Earthquake, Science Council Japan, Tokyo, pp. 93—130.

National Oceanic and Atmospheric Administration (NOAA), 1973. *Earthquake History of the United States*. Washington, D.C., 208 pp.

National Research Center for Disaster Prevention, 1969. *Quaternary Tectonic Map of Japan*. Tokyo, 6 sheets.

National Research Center for Disaster Prevention, 1973. *Explanatory Text of the Quaternary Tectonic Map of Japan*. Tokyo, 167 pp.

National Research Center for Disaster Prevention, 1974. Earthquakes occurring in the Tokyo area, observed at the Iwatsuki Observatory. *Rep. Coord. Comm. Earthquake Prediction*, 12: 20—22 (in Japanese).

Nersesov, I.L., 1970. Earthquake prognostication in the Soviet Union. *Bull. New Zealand Soc. Earthquake Eng.*, 3: 108—119.

Nersesov, I.L., Semenov, A.N. and Simbireva, I.G., 1973. Space—time distribution of shear and longitudinal wave travel time ratios in the Garm area. In: M.A. Sadovsky (Editor), *Experimental Seismology*. Science Press, Moscow, 1971, 423 pp. Translated in English from Russian by D.B. Vitaliano, U.S. Geological Survey.

Nersesov, I.L., Latynina, L.A. and Karmaleyeva, R.M., 1974a. On the relationship of crustal strain to earthquake on the basis of data of the Talgar station. In: M.A. Sadovsky, I.L. Nersesov and L.A. Latynina (Editors), *Earthquake Precursors*. Acad.

Sci. U.S.S.R., Moscow, 1973, 216 pp. Translated in English from Russian by D.B. Vitaliano, U.S. Geological Survey.

Nersesov, I.L., Lukk, A.A., Ponomarev, V.S., Rautian, T.G., Rulev, B.G., Semenov, A.N. and Simbireva, I.G., 1974b. Possibilities of earthquake prediction, exemplified by the Garm area of the Tadzhik S.S.R. In: M.A. Sadovsky, I.L. Nersesov and L.A. Latynina (Editors), *Earthquake Precursors.* Acad. Sci. U.S.S.R., Moscow, 1973, 216 pp. Translated in English from Russian by D.B. Vitaliano, U.S. Geological Survey.

Nishimura, E., 1950. On earth tides. *Trans. Am. Geophys. Union*, 31: 357—376.

Nishimura, E., 1956. On change of state of the materials in the earth's crust with relation to seismic activity. In: *Memorial Issue of the Fifth Anniversary.* Disaster Prevention Research Institute, Kyoto Univ., pp. 8—13.

Nishimura, E., 1961. On the continuous observation of crustal deformation. *Zisin (J. Seismol. Soc. Japan)*, Ser. 2, 14: 260—266 (in Japanese).

Nishimura, E. and Hosoyama, K., 1953. On tilting motion of ground observed before and after the occurrence of an earthquake. *Trans. Am. Geophys. Union*, 34: 597—599.

Nordquist, J.M., 1945. Theory of largest values applied to earthquake magnitudes. *Trans. Am. Geophys. Union*, 26: 29—31.

Nur, A., 1972. Dilatancy, pore fluids, and premonitory variations of t_s/t_p travel times. *Bull. Seismol. Soc. Am.*, 62: 1217—1222.

Nur, A., 1974a. The Matsushiro earthquake swarm: a confirmation of the dilatancy—fluid flow model. *Geology*, 2: 217—221.

Nur, A., 1974b. Tectonophysics: the study of relations between deformation and forces in the earth. *Proc. 3rd Congr. Int. Soc. Rock Mech.*, National Academy of Sciences, U.S.A., Vol. 1, Part A, pp. 243—317.

Nur, A. and Simmons, G., 1969. The effect of saturation on velocity in low porosity rocks. *Earth Planet. Sci. Lett.*, 7: 183—193.

Nur, A., Bell, M.L. and Talwani, P., 1973. Fluid flow and faulting, 1. A detailed study of the dilatancy mechanism and premonitory velocity changes. In: R.L. Kovach and A. Nur (Editors), *Proceedings of the Conference on Tectonic Prolems on the San Andreas Fault System.* Stanford Univ. Publ., Geol. Sci., 13: 391—404.

O'Connel, R.J. and Budiansky, B., 1974. Seismic velocities in dry and saturated cracked solids. *J. Geophys. Res.*, 79: 5412—5426.

Ohnaka, Y. and Kinoshita, H., 1968. Effects of uniaxial compression on remanent magnetization. *J. Geomagn. Geoelectr.*, 20: 93—99.

Ohtake, M., 1973. Changes in the V_p/V_s ratio related with the occurrence of some shallow earthquakes in Japan. *J. Phys. Earth*, 21: 173—184.

Ohtake, M., 1974. Seismic activity induced by water injection at Matsushiro, Japan. *J. Phys. Earth*, 22: 163—176.

Oike, K., 1973. Results of microearthquake observation. *Proc. Symp. Earthquake Prediction*, December 12, 1972. Seismol. Society of Japan, Tokyo, pp. 76—80 (in Japanese).

Okada, A. and Tsubokawa, I., 1969. Vertical displacements accompanied by the swarm earthquakes in Matsushiro area. *Rep. Coord. Comm. Earthquake Prediction*, 2: 34—40 (in Japanese).

Okano, K. and Hirano, I., 1970. Recent microseismicity in the Kyoto—Osaka—Kobe region. *Rep. Coord. Comm. Earthquake Prediction*, 4: 52—54 (in Japanese).

Oliver, J., 1964. Earthquake prediction. *Science*, 144: 1364—1365.

Oliver, J., 1970. Recent earthquake prediction research in the U.S.A. *Tectonophysics*, 9: 283—290.

Ostrovskiy, A.E., 1972. On changes in tilts of the earth's surface before strong near earthquakes. In: M.A. Sadovsky (Editor), *Physical Bases of Seeking Methods of Predicting Earthquakes.* Acad. Sci. U.S.S.R., Moscow, 1970, 152 pp. Translated in English from Russian by D.B. Vitaliano, U.S. Geological Survey.

Ostrovskiy, A.E., 1974. Tilts and earthquakes. In: M.A. Sadovsky, I.L. Nersesov and L.A. Latynina (Editors), *Earthquake Precursors.* Acad. Sci. U.S.S.R., Moscow, 1973, 216 pp. Translated in English from Russian by D.B. Vitaliano, U.S. Geological Survey.

Ozawa, I., 1971. Observations of the secular and annual changes of the crustal strains at Osakayama. *Spec. Contrib. Geophys. Inst., Kyoto Univ.*, 11: 205–212.

Packard, M. and Varian, R., 1954. Free nuclear induction in the earth's magnetic field. *Phys. Rev.*, 93: 941.

Page, R. (Editor), 1966. *Proceedings of the Second United States–Japan Conference on Research Related to Earthquake Prediction Problems.* Lamont Geological Observatory, Columbia Univ., New York, N.Y., 106 pp.

Pakiser, L.C. and Healy, J.H., 1971. Prédiction et contrôle des tremblements de terre. *La Recherche*, 2: 717–725.

Pakiser, L.C., Eaton, J.P., Healy, J.H. and Raleigh, C.B., 1969. Earthquake prediction and control. *Science*, 166: 1467–1473.

Pan, C., 1973. Analysis of tidal strains from crustal Colorado strainmeter network. Preprint (personal communication by J.C. Harrison).

Papazachos, B.C., 1973. The time distribution of the reservoir-associated foreshocks and its importance to the prediction of the principal shock. *Bull. Seismol. Soc. Am.*, 63: 1973–1978.

Parkin, E.J., 1948. Vertical movement in the Los Angeles region, 1906–1946. *Trans. Am. Geophys. Union*, 29: 17–26.

Parkin, E.J., 1969. Horizontal crustal movements determined from surveys after the Alaskan earthquake of 1964. In: *The Prince William Sound, Alaska, Earthquake of 1964 and Aftershocks*, Vol. 3. Environmental Science Services Administration, U.S. Government Printing Office, Washington, D.C., pp. 35–98.

Plafker, G., 1965. Tectonic deformation associated with the 1964 Alaska earthquake. *Science*, 148: 1675–1687.

Plafker, G., 1972. Alaskan earthquake of 1964 and Chilean earthquake of 1960: implications for arc tectonics. *J. Geophys. Res.*, 77: 901–925.

Press, F., 1965a. Displacements, strains, and tilts at teleseismic distances. *J. Geophys. Res.*, 70: 2395–2412.

Press, F., 1965b. Earthquake prediction: a challenge to geophysicists. *Geophysics*, 30: 1242.

Press, F., 1968. A strategy for an earthquake prediction research program. *Tectonophysics*, 6: 11–15.

Press, F., 1975. Earthquake prediction. *Sci. Am.*, 232 (5): 14–23.

Press, F. and Brace, W.F., 1966. Earthquake prediction. *Science*, 152: 1575–1584.

Press, F., Benioff, H., Frosch, R.A., Griggs, D.T., Handin, J., Hanson, R.E., Hess, H.H., Housner, G.W., Munk, W.H., Orowan, E., Pakiser Jr., L.C., Sutton, G. and Tocher, D., 1965. *Earthquake Prediction: a Proposal for a Ten Year Program of Research.* Office Sci. Technol., Washington, D.C., 134 pp.

Raleigh, C.B. and Paterson, M.S., 1965. Experimental deformation of serpentine and its tectonic implications. *J. Geophys. Res.*, 70: 3965–3985.

Reid, H.F., 1910. *The California Earthquake of April 18, 1906, 2. The Mechanics of the Earthquake.* Carnegie Institution of Washington, Washington, D.C., 192 pp.

Research Group for Microearthquakes, Tohoku University, 1971. An earthquake that occurred in Southeast Akita Prefecture. *Rep. Coord. Comm. Earthquake Prediction*, 5: 14–21 (in Japanese).

Research Group for Microearthquakes, Tohoku University, 1974. Variations in the travel time of compressional wave before the southeastern Akita earthquake of 1970 and the

Niigata earthquake of 1964. *Rep. Coord. Comm. Earthquake Prediction*, 11: 56—59 (in Japanese).

Reyes, A., Brune, J., Canales, L., Madrid, J., Rebollar, J. and Munguia, L., 1975. A microearthquake survey of the San Miguel fault zone, Baja California, Mexico. *Geophys. Res. Lett.*, 2: 56—59.

Reynolds, O., 1886. Dilatancy. An abstract of a lecture delivered to the Royal Institute of Great Britain. *Nature*, 33: 429—430.

Richter, C.F., 1958. *Elementary Seismology*. W.H. Freeman and Co., San Francisco, Calif., 768 pp.

Rikitake, T., 1947. Changes in the Dogo hot spring associated with the Nankai earthquake. Spec. *Bull. Earthquake Res. Inst., Univ. Tokyo*, 5: 189—194 (in Japanese).

Rikitake, T., 1958. Oscillations of a system of disk dynamos. *Proc. Cambridge Philos. Soc.*, 54: 89—105.

Rikitake, T., 1966a. A five-year plan for earthquake prediction research in Japan. *Tectonophysics*, 3: 1—15.

Rikitake, T., 1966b. Elimination of non-local changes from total intensity values of the geomagnetic field. *Bull. Earthquake Res. Inst., Univ. Tokyo*, 44: 1041—1070.

Rikitake, T., 1966c. *Electromagnetism and the Earth's Interior*. Elsevier, Amsterdam, 308 pp.

Rikitake, T., 1968a. Earthquake prediction. *Earth-Sci. Rev.*, 4: 245—282.

Rikitake, T. (Editor), 1968b. *Earthquake Prediction — Tectonophysics*, 6: 1—92.

Rikitake, T., 1968c. Geomagnetism and earthquake prediction. *Tectonophysics*, 6: 59—68.

Rikitake, T., 1969a. Prediction of magnitude and occurrence time of earthquakes. *Bull. Earthquake Res. Inst., Univ. Tokyo*, 47: 107—128 (in Japanese).

Rikitake, T., 1969b. An approach to prediction of magnitude and occurrence time of earthquakes. *Tectonophysics*, 8: 81—95.

Rikitake, T., 1969c. The undulation of an electrically conductive layer beneath the islands of Japan. *Tectonophysics*, 7: 257—264.

Rikitake, T., 1970a. Prévision des tremblements de terre. *Sciences*, 65: 4—9.

Rikitake, T. (Editor), 1970b. *Earthquake Mechanics — Tectonophysics*, 9: 95—300.

Rikitake, T., 1972a. Earthquake prediction studies in Japan. *Geophys. Surv.*, 1: 4—26.

Rikitake, T., 1972b. Problems of predicting earthquakes. *Nature*, 240: 202—204.

Rikitake, T., 1972c. An earthquake prediction operation in an area south of Tokyo. *Proc. Symp. Results of Upper Mantle Investigations with Emphasis on Latin America*. Comite Argentino del Manto Superior, Buenos Aires, 2: 95—106.

Rikitake, T., 1974a. Japanese national program on earthquake prediction. *Tectonophysics*, 23: 225—236.

Rikitake, T., 1974b. Probability of earthquake occurrence as estimated from crustal strain. *Tectonophysics*, 23: 299—312.

Rikitake, T. (Editor), 1974c. *Focal Processes and Prediction of Earthquakes — Tectonophysics*, 23: 217—318.

Rikitake, T., 1975a. Statistics of ultimate strain of the earth's crust and probability of earthquake occurrence. *Tectonophysics*, 26: 1—21.

Rikitake, T., 1975b. Dilatancy model and empirical formulas for an earthquake area. *Pure Appl. Geophys.*, in press.

Rikitake, T., 1975c. Earthquake precursors. *Bull. Seismol. Soc. Am.*, in press.

Rikitake, T., 1975d. Crustal dilatancy and geomagnetic variations of short period. *J. Geomagn. Geoelectr.*, in press.

Rikitake, T. and Yamazaki, Y., 1967. Small earth strains as detected by electric resistivity measurements. *Proc. Japan Acad.*, 43: 477—482.

Rikitake, T. and Yamazaki, Y., 1969. Electrical conductivity of strained rocks (5th paper). Residual strains associated with large earthquakes as observed by a resistivity variometer. *Bull. Earthquake Res. Inst., Univ. Tokyo*, 47: 99—105.

Rikitake, T. and Yamazaki, Y., 1970. Strain steps as observed by a resistivity variometer. *Tectonophysics*, 9: 197—203.

Rikitake, T., Yamazaki, Y., Hagiwara, Y., Kawada, K., Sawada, M., Sasai, Y., Watanabe, T., Momose, K., Yoshino, T., Otani, K., Ozawa, K. and Sanzai, Y., 1966a. Geomagnetic and geoelectric studies of the Matsushiro earthquake swarm, 1. *Bull. Earthquake Res. Inst., Univ. Tokyo*, 44: 363—408.

Rikitake, T., Yamazaki, Y., Hagiwara, Y., Kawada, K., Sawada, M., Sasai, Y. and Yoshino, T., 1966b. Geomagnetic and geoelectric studies of the Matsushiro earthquake swarm, 2. *Bull. Earthquake Res. Inst., Univ. Tokyo*, 44: 409—418.

Rikitake, T., Yukutake, T., Yamazaki, Y., Sawada, M., Sasai, Y., Hagiwara, Y., Kawada, K., Yoshino, T. and Shimomura, T., 1966c. Geomagnetic and geoelectric studies of the Matsushiro earthquake swarm, 3. *Bull. Earthquake Res. Inst., Univ. Tokyo*, 44: 1335—1370.

Rikitake, T., Yamazaki, Y., Sawada, M., Sasai, Y., Yoshino, T., Uzawa, S. and Shimomura, T., 1966d. Geomagnetic and geoelectric studies of the Matsushiro earthquake swarm, 4. *Bull. Earthquake Res. Inst., Univ. Tokyo*, 44: 1735—1758.

Rikitake, T., Yamazaki, Y., Sawada, M., Sasai, Y., Yoshino, T., Uzawa, S. and Shimomura, T., 1967a. Geomagnetic and geoelectric studies of the Matsushiro earthquake swarm, 5. *Bull. Earthquake Res. Inst., Univ. Tokyo*, 45: 395—416.

Rikitake, T., Yukutake, T., Sawada, M., Sasai, Y., Watanabe, T. and Tachinaka, H., 1967b. Geomagnetic and geoelectric studies of the Matsushiro earthquake swarm, 6. *Bull. Earthquake Res. Inst., Univ. Tokyo*, 45: 919—944.

Rikitake, T., Yoshino, T. and Sasai, Y., 1968. Geomagnetic noises and detectability of seismo-magnetic effect, 1. *Bull. Earthquake Res. Inst., Univ. Tokyo*, 46: 137—154.

Robinson, R., Wesson, R.L. and Ellsworth, W.L., 1974. Variation of P-wave velocity before the Bear Valley, California, earthquake of 24 February 1972. *Science*, 184: 1281—1283.

Rothé, J.P., 1968. Earthquakes and dams. *New Scientist*, 39: 75—78.

Rothé, J.P., 1970. Seismes artificiels. *Tectonophysics*, 9: 215—238.

Rothé, J.P., 1973. Summary: geophysics report. In: W.C. Ackermann, G.F. White and E.B. Worthington (Editors), *Man-Made Lakes: Their Problems and Environmental Effects*. Am. Geophys. Union, Geophys. Monogr., 17: 441—454.

Sacks, I.S., Suyehiro, S., Evertson, D.W. and Yamagishi, Y., 1971. Sacks-Evertson strainmeter, its installation in Japan and some preliminary results concerning strain steps. *Papers Meteorol. Geophys.*, 22: 195—208.

Sadeh, D.S. and Meidav, M., 1973. Search for siderial periodicity in earthquake occurrences. *J. Geophys. Res.*, 78: 7709—7716.

Sadovsky, M.A. and Nersesov, I.L., 1974. Forecasts of earthquakes on the basis of complex geophysical features. *Tectonophysics*, 23: 247—255.

Savosky, M.A., Nersesov, I.L., Nigmatullaev, S.K., Latynina, L.A., Lukk, A.A., Semenov, A.N., Simbireva, I.G. and Ulomov, V.I., 1972. The processes preceding strong earthquakes in some regions of Middle Asia. *Tectonophysics*, 14: 295—307.

Sassa, K., 1948. *Earthquakes and Disasters*. Kobunsha, Kyoto, 204 pp. (in Japanese).

Sassa, K. and Nishimura, E., 1951. On phenomena forerunning earthquakes. *Trans Am. Geophys. Union*, 32: 1—6.

Sassa, K. and Nishimura, E., 1955. On phenomena forerunning earthquakes. *Publ. Bur. Central Séismol. Int.*, Ser. A, 19: 277—285.

Sassa, K., Ozawa, I. and Yoshikawa, S., 1952. Observation of the tidal strain of the earth. *Bull. Disas. Prev. Res. Inst., Kyoto Univ.*, 3: 1—3.

Sato, H., 1973. A study of horizontal movement of the earth crust associated with destructive earthquakes in Japan. *Bull. Geogr. Surv. Inst.*, 19: 89—130.

Sato, H. and Ichihara, M., 1971. On the revision of triangulation after the great Kanto earthquake. *J. Geod. Soc. Japan*, 17: 178—186 (in Japanese).

Savage, J.C. and Burford, R.O., 1970. Accumulation of tectonic strain in California. *Bull. Seismol. Soc. Am.*, 60: 1887—1896.

Savage, J.C. and Burford, R.O., 1971. Discussion of paper by C.H. Scholz and T.J. Fitch "Strain accumulation along the San Andreas fault". *J. Geophys. Res.*, 76: 6469—6479.

Savage, J.C. and Burford, R.O., 1973. Geodetic determination of plate motion in central California. *J. Geophys. Res.*, 78: 832—845.

Savage, J.C., Prescott, W.H. and Kinoshita, W.T., 1973. Geodimeter measurements along the San Andreas fault. In: R.L. Kovach and A. Nur (Editors), *Proceedings of the Conference on Tectonic Problems on the San Andreas Fault System*. Stanford. Univ. Publ., Geol. Sci., 13: 44—53.

Savarensky, E.F., 1968. On the prediction of earthquakes. *Tectonophysics*, 6: 17—27.

Savarensky, E.F., 1974. Introductory remarks and Soviet national program on earthquake prediction. *Tectonophysics*, 23: 221—224.

Savarensky, E.F. and Rikitake, T. (Editors), 1972. *Forerunners of Strong Earthquakes —Tectonophysics*, 14: 177—348.

Savarensky, E.F., Hagiwara, T. and Rikitake, T., 1972. Geophysical principles for studying forerunners of earthquakes. *Tectonophysics*, 14: 179—181.

Schmidt, P., 1971. Zu Fragen der Erdbebenprognose, 1. *Acta Geodaet., Geophys. et Montanist. Acad. Sci. Hung.*, 6: 449—457.

Schmidt, P., 1973. Zu Fragen der Erdbebenprognose, 2. *Acta Geodaet., Geophys. et Montanist. Acad. Sci. Hung.*, 8: 451—460.

Scholz, C.H., 1967. *Microfracturing of Rock in Compression*. Thesis, Massachusetts Institute of Technology, Cambridge, Mass., 160 pp.

Scholz, C.H., 1968a. Experimental study of the fracturing process in brittle rock. *J. Geophys. Res.*, 73: 1447—1454.

Scholz, C.H., 1968b. The frequency—magnitude relation of microfracturing in rock and its relation to earthquakes. *Bull. Seismol. Soc. Am.*, 58: 399—415.

Scholz, C.H. and Fitch, T.J., 1969. Strain accumulation along the San Andreas fault. *J. Geophys. Res.*, 74: 6649—6665.

Scholz, C.H. and Fitch, T.J., 1970. Strain and creep in central California. *J. Geophys. Res.*, 75: 4447—4453.

Scholz, C.H., Sykes, L.R. and Aggarwal, Y.P., 1973. Earthquake prediction: a physical basis. *Science*, 181: 803—809.

Schuster, A., 1897. On lunar and solar periodicities of earthquakes. *Proc. R. Soc. Lond.*, Ser. A, 61: 455—465.

Sekiya, H., 1971. On the seismic activity in the southern part of Kanto. *Q. J. Seismol., Japan Meteorol. Agency*, 36: 13—27 (in Japanese).

Sekiya, H. and Tokunaga, K., 1974. On the seismicity near the sea of Enshu. *Rep. Coord. Comm. Earthquake Prediction*, 11: 96—101 (in Japanese).

Semyenov, A.N., 1969. Variations in the travel time of traverse and longitudinal waves before violent earthquakes. *Izv. Acad. Sci. U.S.S.R.* (*Phys. Solid Earth*), 4: 245—248 (English edition).

Shakal, A.F. and Willis, D.E., 1972. Estimated earthquake probabilities in the North Circum-Pacific area. *Bull. Seismol. Soc. Am.*, 62: 1397—1410.

Shamsi, S. and Stacey, F.D., 1969. Dislocation models and seismomagnetic calculations for California 1906 and Alaska 1964 earthquakes. *Bull. Seismol. Soc. Am.*, 59: 1435—1448.

Sheng, C.K., Chang, C.H., Chen, H.C., Li, T.C., Huang, L.S., Wan, T.C., Yan, C.J. and Lo, H.H., 1973. Earthquakes induced by reservoir impounding and their effect on the Hsinfengkiang dam. Paper presented at the 11th Congress on Large Dams, Madrid, 44 pp.

Shichi, R., 1973. Continuous observation of crustal movement: development of research and its possible improvement. *Proc. Symp. on Earthquake Prediction*, December 12, 1972. Seismol. Society of Japan, Tokyo, pp. 26—34 (in Japanese).

Shimazaki, K., 1971a. Periodicity of earthquake occurrence. *Kagaku*, 41: 688—689 (in Japanese).

Shimazaki, K., 1971b. Unusually low seismic activity in the focal region of the great Kanto earthquake of 1923. *Tectonophysics*, 11: 305—312.

Shimazaki, K., 1972a. Where should we set up a new crustal-deformation observatory in Japan? *Tectonophysics*, 15: 255—261.

Shimazaki, K., 1972b. Focal mechanism of a shock at the northwestern boundary of the Pacific Plate: extensional feature of the oceanic lithosphere and compressional feature of the continental lithosphere. *Phys. Earth Planet. Inter.*, 6: 397—404.

Shimazaki, K., 1972c. Hidden periodicities of destructive earthquakes at Tokyo. *Zisin (J. Seismol. Soc. Japan)*, Ser. 2, 25: 24—32 (in Japanese).

Shimazaki, K., 1974a. Preseismic crustal deformation caused by an underthrusting oceanic plate, in eastern Hokkaido, Japan. *Phys. Earth Planet. Inter.*, 8: 148—157.

Shimazaki, K., 1974b. Nemuro-oki earthquake of June 17, 1973: a lithospheric rebound at the upper half of the interface. *Phys. Earth Planet. Inter.*, 9: 314—327.

Simbireva, I.G., 1973. Focal mechanism of weak earthquakes in the Naryn River Basin. In: M.A. Sadovsky (Editor), *Experimental Seismology*. Science Press, Moscow, 1971, 423 pp. Translated in English from Russian by D.B. Vitaliano, U.S. Geological Survey.

Skovorodkin, Y.P., Bezuglaya, L.S. and Vadkovskiy, V.N., 1973. Magnetic investigations in an epicentral zone. In: M.A. Sadovsky (Editor), *Experimental Seismology*. Science Press, Moscow, 1971, 423 pp. Translated in English from Russian by D.B. Vitaliano, U.S. Geological Survey.

Small, J.B., 1969. Veritcal displacements determined by surveys after the Alaskan earthquake of March 1964. In: *The Prince William Sound, Alaska, Earthquake of 1964 and Aftershocks*, Vol. 3. Environmental Science Services Adminsitration, U.S. Government Printing Office, Washington, D.C., pp. 21—33.

Smith, B.E., Johnston, M.J.S. and Myren, G.D., 1974. Results from a differential magnetometer array along the San Andreas fault in Central California. *EOS (Trans. Am. Geophys. Union)*, 56: 1113.

Smith, P.J., 1974. Earthquakes predicted. *Nature*, 252: 9—11.

Sobolev, G.A., 1974. Prospects for routine prediction of earthquakes on the basis of electrotelluric observations. In: M.A. Sadovsky, I.L. Nersesov and L.A. Latynina (Editors), *Earthquake Precursors*. Acad. Sci. U.S.S.R., Moscow, 1973, 216 pp. Translated in English from Russian by D.B. Vitaliano, U.S. Geological Survey.

Sobolev, G.A. and Morozov, V.N., 1972. Local disturbances of the electrical field on Kamchatka and their relation to earthquakes. In: M.A. Sadovsky (Editor), *Physical Bases of Seeking Methods of Predicting Earthquakes*. Acad. Sci. U.S.S.R., 1970, 152 pp. Translated in English from Russian by D.B. Vitaliano, U.S. Geological Survey.

Stacey, F.D., 1963. Seismo-magnetic effect and the possibility of forecasting earthquakes. *Nature*, 200: 1083—1085.

Stacey, F.D., 1964. The seismo-magnetic effect. *Pure Appl. Geophys.*, 58: 5—22.

Stacey, F.D. and Westcott, P., 1965. Seismomagnetic effect — limit of observability imposed by local variations in geomagnetic disturbances. *Nature*, 206: 1209—1211.

Steinbrugge, K.V. and Zacher, E.G., 1960. Creep on the San Andreas fault — fault creep and property damage. *Bull. Seismol. Soc. Am.*, 50: 389—396.

Stewart, G.S., 1973. Prediction of the Pt. Mugu earthquake by two methods. In: R.L. Kovach and A. Nur (Editors), *Proceedings of the Conference on Tectonic Problems on the San Andreas Fault System*. Stanford Univ. Publ., Geol. Sci., 13: 473—478.

Stuart, W.D., 1974. Diffusionless dilatancy model for earthquake precursors. *Geophys. Res. Lett.*, 1: 261—264.

Sugimura, A. and Matsuda, T., 1965. Atera fault and its displacement vectors. *Geol. Soc. Am. Bull.*, 76: 509—522.

Sugimura, A. and Naruse, Y., 1954. Changes in sea level, seismic upheavals, and coastal terraces in the southern Kanto region, Japan, 1. *Japan. J. Geol. Geogr.*, 24: 101—113.

Sugimura, A. and Naruse, Y., 1955. Changes in sea level, seismic upheavals, and coastal terraces in the southern Kanto region, Japan, 2. *Japan. J. Geol. Geogr.*, 25: 165—176.

Suh, J.H., 1973. *The Influence of Site Characteristics on the Measurement of Tidal Strain.* Thesis, Colorado School of Mines, Golden, Colo. (personal communication by J.C. Harrison).

Sutton, D.J., 1974. A fall in P-wave velocity before the Gisborne, New Zealand, earthquake of 1966. *Bull. Seismol. Soc. Am.*, 64: 1501—1508.

Suyehiro, S., 1966. Difference between aftershocks and foreshocks in the relationship of magnitude to frequency of occurrence for the great Chilean earthquake of 1960. *Bull. Seismol. Soc. Am.*, 56: 185—200.

Suyehiro, S., 1969. Difference in the relationship of magnitude to frequency of occurrence between aftershocks and foreshocks of an earthquake of magnitude 5.1 in central Japan. *Papers Meteorol. Geophys.*, 20: 175—187.

Suyehiro, S. and Sekiya, H., 1972. Foreshocks and earthquake prediction. *Tectonophysics*, 14: 219—225.

Suyehiro, S., Asada, T. and Ohtake, M., 1964. Foreshocks and aftershocks accompanying a perceptible earthquake in Central Japan. *Papers Meteorol. Geophys.*, 15: 71—88.

Suyehiro, Y., 1934. Some observations on the unusual behaviour of fishes prior to an earthquake. *Bull. Earthquake Res. Inst., Univ. Tokyo, Suppl.*, 1: 228—231.

Sykes, L.R., 1967. Mechanism of earthquakes and nature of faulting on the mid-ocean ridges. *J. Geophys. Res.*, 72: 2131—2153.

Sykes, L.R., 1971. Aftershock zones of great earthquakes, seismicity gaps, and earthquake prediction for Alaska and the Aleutians. *J. Geophys. Res.*, 76: 8021—8041.

Sylvester, A.G. and Pollard, D.D., 1972. Observation of crustal tilt preceding an aftershock at San Fernando, California. *Bull. Seismol. Soc. Am.*, 62: 927—932.

Takada, M., 1959. On the crustal strain accompanied by a great earthquake. *Bull. Disas. Prev. Res. Inst., Kyoto Univ.*, 27: 29—46.

Takahashi, H., 1970. Water injection experiments — deep drilling at Matsushiro (3rd report). *Rep. Coord. Comm. Earthquake Prediction*, 3: 43—45 (in Japanese).

Takahashi, H. and Hamada, K., 1975. Deep bore-hole observation of the earth's crust activities around Tokyo — introduction of the Iwatsuki Observatory. *Pure Appl. Geophys.*, in press.

Takemoto, S., 1970. Strain steps and the dislocation fault model. *Bull. Disas. Prev. Res. Inst., Kyoto Univ.*, 20: 1—15.

Tanaka, T. and Kato, M., 1974. On the change of crustal elasticity and earth tides. *J. Geod. Soc. Japan*, 20: 125—132.

Tanaka, Y., 1965. On the stages of anomalous crustal movements accompanied with earthquake. *Annual Rep. Disas. Prev. Res. Inst., Kyoto Univ.*, 8: 91—108 (in Japanese).

Tanakadate, A. and Nagaoka, H., 1893. The disturbance of isomagnetics attending the Mino—Owari earthquake of 1891. *J. College Sci., Imperial Univ., Japan*, 5: 149—192.

Tazima, M., 1968. Accuracy of recent magnetic survey and a locally anomalous behavior of the geomagnetic secular variation in Japan. *Bull. Geogr. Surv. Inst.*, 13: 1—78.

Terada, T., 1931. On luminous phenomena accompanying earthquakes. *Bull. Earthquake Res. Inst., Univ. Tokyo*, 9: 225—255.

Terada, T., 1932. On some probable influence of earthquakes upon fisheries. *Bull. Earthquake Res. Inst., Univ. Tokyo*, 10: 393—401.

Terada, T. and Miyabe, N., 1929. Deformation of the earth crust in Kwansai districts and its relation to the orographic feature. *Bull. Earthquake Res. Inst., Univ. Tokyo*, 7: 223—239.

Tocher, D., 1960. Creep on the San Andreas fault — creep rate and related measurements at Vineyard, California. *Bull. Seismol. Soc. Am.*, 50: 396—404.

Tsuboi, C., 1932. Investigation on the deformation of the earth's crust in the Tango district connected with the Tango earthquake of 1927, 4. *Bull. Earthquake Res. Inst., Univ. Tokyo*, 10: 411—434.

Tsuboi, C., 1933. Investigation on the deformation of the earth's crust found by precise geodetic means. *Jap. J. Astron. Geophys.*, 10: 93—248.

Tsuboi, C., 1958. On seismic activities in and near Japan. In: H. Benioff, M. Ewing, B.F. Howell and F. Press (Editors), *Contributions in Geophysics, in Honor of Beno Gutenberg*. Pergamon Press, London, pp. 87—112.

Tsuboi, C., 1964. Time rate of energy release by earthquakes in and near Japan — Its general uniformity and variability. *J. Phys. Earth*, 12: 25—36.

Tsuboi, C., Wadati, K. and Hagiwara, T., 1962. *Prediction of Earthquakes — Progress to Date and Plans for further Development. Rep. Earthquake Prediction Res. Group Japan*. Earthquake Research Institute, Univ. of Tokyo, Tokyo, 21 pp.

Tsubokawa, I., 1969. On relation between duration of crustal movement and magnitude of earthquake expected. *J. Geod. Soc. Japan*, 15: 75—88 (in Japanese).

Tsubokawa, I., 1973. On relation between duration of precursory geophysical phenomena and duration of crustal movement before earthquake. *J. Geod. Soc. Japan*, 19: 116—119 (in Japanese).

Tsubokawa, I., Ogawa, Y. and Hayashi, T., 1964. Crustal movements before and after the Niigata earthquake. *J. Geod. Soc. Japan*, 10: 165– 171.

Tsumura, K., 1963. Investigation of mean sea level and its variation along the coast of Japan, 1. Regional distribution of sea level variation. *J. Geod. Soc. Japan*, 9: 40—90 (in Japanese).

Tsumura, K., 1970. Investigation of mean sea level and its variation along the coast of Japan, 2. Changes in ground level at various places in Japan as deduced from tidal data and earthquake prediction. *J. Geod. Soc. Japan*, 16: 239—275.

Tsumura, K., 1973. Microearthquake observation and earthquake prediction. *Proc. Symp. Earthquake Prediction*, December 12, 1972. Seismol. Society of Japan, Tokyo, pp. 81—89 (in Japanese).

Ulomov, V.I., 1968. On the way to prognosis of earthquakes. *Zemlya i Vselennaya, Acad. Sci. U.S.S.R.*, 3: 23—30 (in Russian).

Undzendov, B.A. and Shapiro, V.A., 1967. Seismomagnetic effect in a magnetite deposit. *Izv. Acad. Sci. U.S.S.R. (Phys. Solid Earth)*, 1: 69—72 (English edition).

Usami, T. (Editor), 1975. *Rikanenpyo* (Science Calendar, Tokyo Astronomical Observatory), Maruzen, Tokyo, 225 pp. (in Japanese).

Usami, T. and Hisamoto, S., 1970. Future probability of a coming earthquake with intensity V or more in the Tokyo area. *Bull. Earthquake Res. Inst., Univ. Tokyo*, 48: 331—340 (in Japanese).

Usami, T. and Hisamoto, S., 1971. Future probability of a coming earthquake with intensity V or more in the Kyoto area. *Bull. Earthquake Res. Inst., Univ. Tokyo*, 49: 115—125 (in Japanese).

Utsu, T., 1969. Aftershocks and earthquake statistics, I. *J. Fac. Sci., Hokkaido Univ.*, Ser. 7, 3: 129—195.

Utsu, T., 1971. Aftershocks and earthquake statistics, III. *J. Fac. Sci., Hokkaido Univ.*, Ser. 7, 3: 380– 441.

Utsu, T., 1972a. Large earthquakes near Hokkaido and the expectancy of the occurrence of a large earthquake off Nemuro. *Rep. Coord. Comm. Earthquake Prediction*, 7: 7—13 (in Japanese).

Utsu, T., 1972b. Aftershocks and earthquake statistics, IV. *J. Fac. Sci., Hokkaido Univ.*, Ser. 7, 4: 1—42.

Utsu, T., 1973. Temporal variations in travel time residuals of P waves from Nevada sources. *J. Phys. Earth*, 21: 475—480.

Utsu, T., 1974. Space—time pattern of large earthquakes occurring off the Pacific coast of the Japanese Islands. *J. Phys. Earth*, 22: 325—342.

Utsu, T. and Hirota, T., 1968. A note on the statistical nature of energy and strain release in earthquake sequences. *J. Fac. Sci., Hokkaido Univ.*, Ser. 7, 3: 49—64.

Utsu, T. and Seki, A., 1955. Relation between the area of aftershock region and the energy of the main shock. *Zisin* (*J. Seismol. Soc. Japan*), Ser. 2, 7: 233—240 (in Japanese).

Uyeda, S., 1971. *A New Picture of the Earth*. Iwanami Shoten, Tokyo, 197 pp. (in Japanese).

Vacquier, V., 1972. *Geomagnetism in Marine Geology*. Elsevier, Amsterdam, 185 pp.

Vine, F.J. and Matthews, D.H., 1963. Magnetic anomalies over oceanic ridges. *Nature*, 199: 947—949.

Wakita, H., 1975. Water well as a possible indicator of tectonic strain. *Science*, in press.

Wallace, R.E., 1974. Goals, strategy and task of the earthquake hazard reduction program. *U.S. Geol. Surv. Circ.* No. 701, 26 pp.

Wang, C.Y., 1974. Earthquake prediction and oriented microcracks in rocks. *Nature*, 251: 405—406.

Watanabe, H., 1974. Variation of seismic velocities before the earthquake of the central part of Kyoto Prefecture, Aug. 18, 1968, as derived from the data of the routine observations of microearthquakes. *Rep. Coord. Comm. Earthquake Prediction*, 11: 112—116 (in Japanese).

Weibull, W., 1951. A statistical distribution function of wide application. *J. Appl. Mech.*, 18: 293—297.

Whitcomb, J.H., Garmany, J.D. and Anderson, D.L., 1973. Earthquake prediction: variation of seismic velocities before the San Fernando Earthquake. *Science*, 180: 632—635.

Whitcomb, J.H., Kanamori, H. and Hadley, D., 1974. Earthquake prediction: variation of seismic velocities in Southern California. *EOS* (*Trans. Am. Geophys. Union*), 55: 355.

Whitten, C.A., 1955. Measurements of earth movements in California. *Calif. Dept. Natural Resources, Div. of Mines. Bull.*, 171: 75—80.

Whitten, C.A., 1956. Crustal movement in California and Nevada. *Trans. Am. Geophys. Union*, 37: 393—398.

Whitten, C.A., 1957. Geodetic measurements in the Dixie Valley area. *Bull. Seismol. Soc. Am.*, 47: 321—325.

Wideman, C.J. and Major, M.W., 1967. Strain steps associated with earthquakes. *Bull. Seismol. Soc. Am.*, 57: 1429—1444.

Wilson, J.T., 1965. A new class of faults and their bearing on continental drift. *Nature*, 207: 343—347.

Wilson, J.T., 1972. Mao's almanac: 3,000 years of killer earthquakes. *Saturday Rev. Sci.*, February 19: 60—64.

Wood, M.D., 1973. Time dependent tilt response to ocean loading for sites across the San Andreas fault. In: R.L. Kovach and A. Nur (Editors), *Proceedings of the Conference on Tectonic Problems on the San Andreas Fault System*. Stanford Univ. Publ., Geol. Sci., 13: 124.

Wood, M.D. and Allen, R.V., 1971. Anomalous microtilt preceding a local earthquake. *Bull. Seismol. Soc. Am.*, 61: 1801—1809.

Wyss, M., 1974. Will there be a large earthquake in Central California during the next two decades? *Nature*, 251: 126—128.

Wyss, M., 1975a. Sea level, magnetic field and P-residuals before the Sitka earthquake 1972. *Pure Appl. Geophys.*, in press.

Wyss, M., 1975b. Precursors to the Garm earthquake of March 1969. *J. Geophys. Res.*, in press.

Wyss, M. and Holcomb, D.J., 1973. Earthquake prediction based on station residuals. *Nature*, 245: 139—140.

Wyss, M. and Johnston, A.C., 1974. A search for teleseismic P residual changes before large earthquakes in New Zealand. *J. Geophys. Res.*, 79: 3283—3290.

Wyss, M. and Lee, W.H.K., 1973. Time variations of the average earthquake magnitude in Central California. In: R.L. Kovach and A. Nur (Editors), *Proceedings of the Conference on Tectonic Problems on the San Andreas Fault System.* Stanford Univ. Publ., Geol. Sci., 13: 24—42.

Yamada, J., 1973. A water-tube tiltmeter and its applications to crustal movement studies. *Spec. Bull. Earthquake Res. Inst., Univ. Tokyo*, 10: 1—147 (in Japanese).

Yamaguti, S., 1937. Deformation of the earth's crust in Idu Peninsula in connection with the destructive Idu earthquake of Nov. 26, 1930. *Bull. Earthquake Res. Inst., Univ. Tokyo*, 15: 899—934.

Yamazaki, Y., 1965. Electrical conductivity of strained rocks (1st paper), Laboratory experiments on sedimentary rocks. *Bull. Earthquake Res. Inst., Univ. Tokyo*, 44: 783—802.

Yamazaki, Y., 1966. Electrical conductivity of strained rocks (2nd paper), Further experiments on sedimentary rocks. *Bull. Earthquake Res. Inst., Univ. Tokyo*, 44: 1553—1570.

Yamazaki, Y., 1967. Electrical conductivity of strained rocks (3rd paper), A resistivity variometer. *Bull. Earthquake Res. Inst., Univ. Tokyo*, 45: 849—860.

Yamazaki, Y., 1968. Electrical conductivity of strained rocks (4th paper), Improvement of the resistivity variometer. *Bull. Earthquake Res. Inst., Univ. Tokyo*, 46: 957—964.

Yamazaki, Y., 1974. Coseismic resistivity steps. *Tectonophysics*, 22: 159—171.

Yamazaki, Y., 1975. Precursory and coseismic resistivity changes. *Pure Appl. Geophys.*, in press.

Yamazaki, Y. and Rikitake, T., 1970. Local anomalous changes in the geomagnetic field at Matsushiro. *Bull. Earthquake Res. Inst., Univ. Tokyo*, 48: 637—643.

Yanagihara, K., 1966. Geomagnetic changes associated with the Matsushiro earthquakes. In: T. Nagata (Editor), *Proc. Symp. Geomagnetic Changes Associated with Earthquakes and Volcanic Activities.* Geophys. Institute, Univ. of Tokyo, Tokyo. pp. 22—24 (in Japanese).

Yanagihara, K., 1972a. Secular variation of the electrical conductivity anomaly in the Kanto district. *Rep. Coord. Comm. Earthquake Prediction*, 8: 37—41 (in Japanese).

Yanagihara, K., 1972b. Secular variation of the electrical conductivity anomaly in the central part of Japan. *Mem. Kakioka Magn. Obs.*, 15: 1—11.

Yoshikawa, T., Kaizuka, S. and Ota, Y., 1964. Crustal movement in the late Quaternary revealed with coastal terraces on the southeast coast of Shikoku, southwestern Japan. *J. Geod. Soc. Japan*, 10: 116—122.

Yoshimatsu, T., 1957. Universal earth-currents and their local characteristics. *Mem. Kakioka Magn. Obs., Suppl.*, 1: 1—76.

Yukutake, T. and Tachinaka, H., 1967. Geomagnetic variation associated with stress change within a semi-infinite elastic earth caused by a cylindrical force source. *Bull. Earthquake Res. Inst., Univ. Tokyo*, 45: 785—798.

AUTHOR INDEX

Abdullabekov, K.N., 198, 206, 207, 315
Abe, N., 10, 321
Aggarwal, Y.P., 192, 193, 241, 315, 332
Aki, K., 184, 189, 245, 250, 254, 307, 315, 318
Alba, J., 318
Alewine, III, R.W., 146, 315
Alldredge, L.R., 200, 315
Allen, C.R., 165, 195, 221, 315, 317
Allen, J.H., 206, 321
Allen, R.V., 146, 276, 337
Alsop, L.E., 48, 315
Alt, J.N., 317
Al'tgauzen, N.M., 213, 315
Amand, P.S., 315
Ambraseys, N.N., 222, 223, 315
Anderson, D.L., 136, 157, 239, 243, 244, 315, 323, 336
Anderson, J.M., 146
Ando, M., 65, 70, 99, 103, 183, 315
Antsyferov, M.S., 177, 315
Arieh, E., 232, 287, 316
Armbruster, J., 315
Asada, T., 334

Bakun, W.H., 192, 316, 317, 323
Balazs, E.I., 317
Baldwin, A.L., 75, 76, 77, 321
Barsukov, O.M., 213, 286, 315, 316
Bartels, J., 200, 317
Båth, M., 1, 316
Beaumont, C., 149, 219, 316
Bell, M.L., 328
Bendefy, L., 117, 316
Benioff, H., 127, 316, 329
Bennet, J.H., 94, 320
Berger, J., 128, 136, 149, 219, 316
Bezuglaya, L.S., 315, 333
Bilham, R.G., 136, 324
Boldyrev, S.A., 319
Bolt, B.A., 2, 3, 56, 165, 317
Bonchkovskiy, V.F., 143
Bouricius, G.M.B., 84, 317
Boyes, W.S., 110, 317
Brabb, E.E., 325
Brace, W.F., 1, 213, 236, 238, 239, 317, 329
Brady, B.T., 243, 244, 317

Breiner, S., 198, 205, 206, 317
Bronson, W., 25, 76, 317
Brown, R., 192, 317
Brune, J.N., 165, 317, 330
Budd, J., 25
Budiansky, B., 241, 328
Bufe, C.G., 172, 214, 282, 317
Burford, R.O., 94, 269, 332
Butler, D., 149
Byerlee, J.D., 236, 317

Caloi, P., 147, 317
Canales, L., 330
Carder, D.S., 305, 317
Castle, R.O., 117, 118, 273
Chang, C.H., 332
Chapman, S., 200, 317
Chen, H.C., 332
Chen, P.S., 253, 254, 317
Chin, P.Y., 325
Chinnery, M.A., 65, 68, 76, 77, 135, 318
Chou, E.L., 56
Chung, W.Y., 195, 323
Coe, R.S., 1, 3, 56, 165, 209, 212, 230, 232, 318
Cole, D., 316
Cook, K.L., 126, 127, 146, 318
Cox, A., 154, 318

Dalrymple, G.B., 318
Dambara, T., 88, 115, 118, 119, 243, 257, 272, 318
Davis, P.M., 206, 318
Defazio, T., 189, 315, 318
Derr, J.S., 21, 318
Dickson, G.O., 322
Doell, R.R., 318
Dolbilkina, N.A., 319, 327
Dutta, T.K., 305, 318

Earnshaw, K.B., 84, 317
Eaton, J.P., 48, 165, 329
Eaton, M.S., 325
Eisler, J.D., 189, 318
Ellsworth, W.L., 331
Engdahl, E.R., 192, 284, 324
Epstein, B., 253, 318
Evans, D.M., 237, 303, 318

Evertson, D.W., 331
Evison, F.F., 237, 318
Ewing, J., 27

Fedotov, S.A., 55, 177, 183, 212, 286,
     319
Feng, H.T., 325
Feng, T.Y., 194, 195, 215, 231, 258, 288,
     319
Fiedler, B.G., 172, 282, 319
Fisher, R.A., 247, 319
Fitch, T.J., 72, 94, 269, 319, 332
Forsch, R.A., 329
Freiberger, W.F., 256, 319
Fujii, Y., 229, 319
Fujita, N., 124, 198, 208, 229, 285, 319

Garland, G.D., 151, 319
Garmany, J.D., 336
Gedney, L., 172, 174
Golovkov, V.P., 315
Gordon, F.R., 111, 112, 230, 320
Gough, D.I., 305, 320
Gough, W.I., 305, 320
Gouin, P., 198, 206, 320
Greensfelder, R.W., 94, 320
Griggs, D.T., 243, 320, 321, 329
Gumbel, E.J., 253, 320
Gupta, H.K., 305, 320
Gupta, I.N., 176, 196, 239, 285, 320
Gusev, A.A., 319
Gutenberg, B., 158, 248, 320

Haas, J.E., 311, 312
Hagiwara, T., 1, 2, 36, 47, 57, 105, 126,
     127, 133, 134, 136, 233, 276, 280,
     287, 305, 320, 321, 335
Hagiwara, Y., 62, 106, 107, 227, 228,
     265, 299, 300, 321, 331
Hamada, K., 185, 334
Hamilton, R.M., 307, 309, 321, 322
Handin, J., 329
Hanson, R.E., 329
Harada, T., 180, 321
Harada, Y., 83, 321, 327
Harrison, J.C., 137, 321
Hasbrouck, W.P., 206, 321
Hasegawa, A., 196
Hatai, S., 10, 11, 212, 321
Hayakawa, M., 189, 193, 321
Hayashi, T., 335
Hayford, J.F., 75, 76, 77, 321
Healy, J.H., 2, 145, 164, 165, 303, 306,

307, 321, 322, 329
Heaton, T.H., 146, 315
Heirtzler, J.R., 154, 322
Helmberger, D.V., 195, 315
Herron, E.M., 322
Hess, H.H., 152, 322, 329
Hirano, I., 280, 328
Hirota, T., 248, 336
Hisamoto, S., 247, 335
Hofmann, R.B., 93, 94, 221, 272, 305,
     322
Holcomb, D.J., 195, 285, 337
Holmes, A., 152, 332
Hosoyama, K., 139, 274, 322, 328
Housner, G.W., 329
Huang, L.S., 332
Hubbert, M.K., 237, 322
Hughes, W.J., 219, 322
Huzita, K., 158, 225, 322

Ichihara, M., 65, 332
Ichikawa, M., 162, 293, 322
Iida, K., 141, 158, 281, 322, 323
Iijima, H., 107, 322
Iizuka, S., 189, 322
Imamura, A., 27, 121, 137, 138, 192,
     273, 322
Isacks, B., 155, 323
Ishibashi, K., 178, 323
Ishido, T., 326
Ishimoto, M., 29, 125, 158, 323
Ispir, Y., 198, 206, 323
Iwata, T., 323
Izutuya, S., 326

Jackson, D.D., 320
Johnson, A.G., 230, 323
Johnson, L.R., 192, 195, 325
Johnston, A.C., 195, 285, 337
Johnston, J.R., 323
Johnston, M.J.S., 2, 147, 197, 205, 206,
     208, 243, 277, 288, 323
Jungels, P., 136, 323

Kaizuka, S., 337
Kaminuma, K., 68, 73, 97, 102, 103, 104,
     105, 113, 272, 278, 279, 280, 323
Kanamori, H., 1, 36, 65, 66, 68, 72, 168,
     169, 195, 279, 280, 323
Kaneko, S., 225, 227, 324, 326
Karmaleyeva, R.M., 127, 144, 277, 278,
     325, 327
Kasahara, J., 281, 324

Kasahara, K., 65, 68, 127, 132, 133, 181, 276, 321
Kassai, A., 180, 321
Kato, M., 50, 149, 334
Kato, Y., 197, 198, 324
Kawada, K., 218, 324, 331
Kawasumi, H., 84, 246, 324
Kayano, I., 323
Kelleher, J., 171, 180, 183, 324
King, G.C.P., 136, 324
Kinoshita, H., 210, 327
Kinoshita, W.T., 332
Kisimoto, Y., 280, 322, 324
Kisslinger, C., 2, 48, 56, 126, 146, 148, 165, 172, 174, 176, 185, 191, 192, 228, 229, 283, 324
Knopoff, L., 320
Kokubo, S., 321
Kondratenko, A.M., 190, 324
Koresawa, S., 324
Kovach, R.L., 230, 323, 325
Krasniuk, P.D., 316
Ku, K.S., 56
Kuno, H., 223, 324
Kuo, T.K., 231, 258, 325

Latham, G., 282, 325
Latynina, L.A., 127, 144, 277, 278, 325, 327
Lee, W.H.K., 28, 56, 172, 243, 281, 282, 322, 325, 337
Lensen, G.J., 58, 110, 116, 117, 325
Le Pichon, X., 322
Li, T.C., 332
Lin, P.H., 253, 254, 317
Listov, N.A., 316
Lo, H.H., 332
Lomnitz, C., 1, 245, 250, 253, 318, 325
Lukk, A.A., 328

Madden, T.R., 317
Madrid, J., 330
Major, M.W., 127, 133, 134, 148, 217, 218, 336
Malvasia, Count, 24
Matsuda, T., 69, 94, 224, 225, 325, 334
Matsui, T., 326
Matsumura, K., 158, 159, 160, 161, 325
Matsushima, S., 238, 325
Matthews, D.H., 154, 336
Matumoto, T., 282, 325
Mazzella, A., 214, 286, 325
McEvilly, T.V., 192, 195, 325

McGarr, A., 195, 325
Meade, B.K., 77, 78, 83, 92, 93, 326
Meidav, M., 24, 331
Merzer, A.M., 232, 287, 316
Mescherikov, J.A., 109, 110, 116, 120, 273, 326
Mickery, W.V., 305, 326
Milne, J., 16, 18, 19, 24, 26, 27, 197, 211, 326
Minster, B., 326
Miyabe, N., 62, 98, 326, 335
Miyakoshi, J., 219, 326
Miyamura, S., 65, 226, 323, 326
Mizutani, H., 193, 288, 326
Mogi, K., 46, 166, 167, 171, 172, 184, 192, 235, 237, 243, 244, 279, 281, 326
Mohan, I., 320
Momose, K., 331
Moore, G.W., 198, 206, 326
Mori, T., 202, 203, 326
Morozov, V.N., 212, 286, 319, 327, 333
Morrison, H.F., 214, 286, 325
Mortensen, C.E., 147, 243, 277, 323
Mukuhira, H., 21
Munguia, L., 330
Munk, W.H., 329
Murai, I., 226, 327
Musha, K., 9, 10, 11, 12, 14, 15, 20, 22, 23, 24, 166, 278, 327
Muto, K., 64, 72, 327
Myachkin, V.I., 195, 271, 285, 319, 327

Nagaoka, H., 197, 334
Nagata, T., 210, 212, 327
Nagumo, S., 187, 324, 327
Nakamura, I., 324
Narain, H., 320
Naruse, Y., 226, 334
Nason, R.D., 221, 283, 327
Nasu, N., 72, 327
Nersesov, I.L., 1, 2, 55, 155, 165, 173, 174, 177, 190, 191, 273, 283, 288, 324, 327, 328, 331
Nishida, R., 280, 324
Nishimura, E., 138, 139, 140, 141, 147, 148, 273, 274, 277, 331
Nordquist, J.M., 253, 315, 328
Nur, A., 192, 228, 235, 241, 325, 323, 325, 328

O'Connell, R.J., 241, 328
Ogawa, Y., 335
Ohnaka, Y., 210, 328

Ohtake, M., 193, 284, 304, 305, 320, 323, 328, 334
Oida, T., 322
Oike, K., 158, 159, 160, 161, 325, 328
Okada, A., 107, 326, 328
Okano, K., 280, 328
Okuda, T., 327
Oliver, J.E., 1, 47, 48, 325, 323, 324, 328
Omori, F., 27
Orange, A.S., 213, 239, 317
Orowan, E., 329
Ostrovskiy, A.E., 143, 144, 147, 275, 329
Ota, Y., 337
Otani, K., 331
Otway, P.M., 110, 325
Ozawa, I., 127, 329, 331
Ozawa, K., 331

Packard, M., 200, 329
Page, B., 47, 329
Pakiser, L.C., 1, 2, 237, 303, 322, 323, 329
Pan, C., 148, 329
Papazachos, B.C., 167, 305, 329
Parkin, E.J., 81, 107, 329
Paterson, M.S., 237, 329
Paulding, Jr., B.W., 317
Perrey, A., 24
Pitman, III, W.C., 322
Plafker, G., 81, 107, 108, 329
Pollard, D.D., 146, 276, 334
Ponomarev, V.S., 328
Preobrazensky, V.B., 319
Prescott, W.H., 332
Press, F., 1, 49, 50, 51, 52, 53, 133, 134, 135, 329

Raleigh, C.B., 237, 321, 322, 329
Rastogi, B.K., 320
Rautian, T.G., 328
Reasenberg, P., 315
Rebollar, J., 330
Reid, H.F., 88, 329
Reyes, A., 165, 330
Reynolds, O., 238, 330
Richards, P.G., 315
Richter, C.F., 28, 74, 76, 77, 78, 79, 109, 111, 158, 166, 222, 248, 281, 315, 320, 330
Rikitake, T., 1, 2, 3, 31, 35, 36, 48, 57, 58, 69, 73, 79, 82, 88, 105, 119, 126, 147, 148, 154, 156, 172, 174, 183, 185, 197, 198, 201, 202, 204, 205,

212, 215, 217, 219, 229, 243, 249, 251, 252, 255, 257, 258, 259, 260, 261, 262, 263, 264, 265, 267, 269, 269, 271, 272, 289, 291, 292, 293, 294, 295, 296, 321, 324, 330, 331, 337
Robinson, R., 192, 288, 325, 331
Roming, P.R., 149
Rothé, J.P., 167, 282, 305, 331
Rubey, W.W., 237, 321, 322
Rulev, B.G., 328

Sacks, I.S., 128, 331
Sadeh, D.S., 24, 331
Sadovsky, M.A., 2, 144, 165, 173, 174, 175, 176, 177, 191, 230, 232, 258, 273, 283, 287, 331
Sanzai, Y., 331
Sasai, Y., 331
Sassa, K., 127, 138, 139, 140, 189, 193, 273, 274, 277, 331
Sato, H., 62, 65, 67, 71, 331, 332
Savage, J.C., 94, 269, 317, 331, 332
Savarensky, E.F., 1, 2, 3, 5, 54, 55, 57, 190, 332
Savino, J., 171, 324
Sawada, M., 331
Sbar, M.L., 315
Schmidt, P., 2, 332
Scholz, C.H., 72, 172, 174, 215, 219, 233, 236, 238, 241, 2242, 243, 244, 269, 270, 282, 283, 284, 287, 295, 298, 317, 319, 332
Schuster, A., 245, 332
Seki, A., 243, 336
Sekiya, H., 170, 182, 332
Sekiya, K., 27
Semyenov, A.N., 191, 243, 284, 327, 328, 332
Sezawa, K., 29
Shakal, A.F., 253, 332
Shamsi, S., 211, 332
Shapiro, V.A., 207, 335
Sheng, C.K., 305, 332
Shibukawa, S., 25
Shichi, R., 141, 142, 276, 277, 322, 333
Shimazaki, K., 84, 177, 178, 179, 180, 181, 247, 265, 301, 333
Shimomura, T., 331
Shiono, K., 322
Shreve, R.L., 320
Simbreva, I.G., 176, 283, 327, 328, 332
Simmons, G., 328

Simpson, D.W., 315
Skovorodkin, Y.P., 209, 288, 315, 332
Small, J.B., 107, 333
Spadea, M.C., 147, 317
Stacey, F.D., 201, 206, 211, 318, 332, 333
Steinbrugge, K.V., 221, 333
Stewart, G.S., 194, 284, 285, 333
Stewart, R.M., 316
Stuart, W.D., 243, 333
Sugimura, A., 224, 226, 326, 334
Suh, J.H., 148, 334
Sutton, D.J., 195, 288, 344
Sutton, L.C., 329
Suyehiro, S., 170, 280, 282, 331, 334
Suyehiro, Y., 13, 14, 334
Sykes, L.R., 157, 183, 315, 323, 324,
    332, 334
Sylvester, A.G., 146, 276, 334

Tachinaka, H., 211, 331, 337
Tago, K., 14
Tajima, H., 227, 300, 321
Takada, M., 140, 277, 334
Takahashi, H., 185, 304, 334
Takahashi, T., 324
Takemoto, S., 133, 135, 334
Talwani, P., 328
Tan, A.N., 319
Tanaka, T., 148, 149, 334
Tanaka, Y., 140, 141, 274, 275, 334
Tanakadate, A., 197, 334
Tarr, A.C., 323
Tazima, M., 198, 207, 208, 285, 334, 335
Terada, T., 14, 16, 17, 21, 22, 23, 25, 62,
    254, 334
Tocher, D., 221, 316, 317, 329, 335
Tokunaga, K., 182, 332
Tsuboi, C., 1, 3, 33, 47, 63, 64, 65, 66,
    67, 68, 82, 96, 97, 98, 99, 100, 101,
    113, 162, 163, 249, 263, 272, 335
Tsubokawa, I., 107, 118, 123, 227, 228,
    243, 258, 270, 272, 273, 293, 328
Tsumura, K., 123, 162, 178, 280, 323,
    324, 335

Ulomov, V.I., 232, 335
Unzendov, B.A., 207, 335
Usami, T., 7, 247, 335
Utsu, T., 179, 196, 243, 248, 278, 281,
    335, 336
Uyar, O., 198, 206, 323

Uyeda, S., 155, 336
Uzawa, S., 331

Vacquier, V., 153, 336
Vadkovskiy, V.N., 333
Van Wormer, J., 172, 174
Varian, R., 200, 329
Vine, F.J., 154, 336
Von Humboldt, A., 197

Wadati, K., 335
Wakita, H., 230, 336
Wallace, R.E., 52, 306, 307, 336
Wan, T.C., 332
Wang, K.F., 319
Wang, C.Y., 239, 336
Watanabe, H., 336
Watanabe, T., 331
Weibull, W., 265, 336
Wesson, R.L., 325, 331
Westcott, P., 201, 333
Whitcomb, J.H., 147, 192, 194, 195, 243,
    244, 270, 284, 295, 315, 336
Whitten, C.A., 78, 80, 81, 107, 336
Wideman, C.J., 127, 133, 134, 217, 218,
    336
Williams, F.J., 323
Willis, D.E., 253, 332
Wilson, J.T., 56, 76, 157, 336
Wood, M.D., 146, 148, 276, 322, 336, 337
Wyss, M., 172, 176, 195, 208, 243, 281,
    282, 285, 288, 337

Yamada, J., 126, 131, 132, 135, 136, 276,
    321, 337
Yamada, K., 322
Yamaguti, S., 67, 102, 337
Yamazaki, Y., 204, 205, 215, 217, 218,
    286, 330, 331, 337
Yan, C.J., 332
Yanagihara, K., 198, 219, 337
Yokoyama, I., 215
Yoshikawa, S., 331
Yoshikawa, T., 226, 337
Yoshimatsu, T., 211, 337
Yoshino, T., 202, 203, 326, 331
Yukutake, T., 211, 331, 337

Zacher, E.G., 221, 333
Zubkov, S.I., 271, 327

SUBJECT INDEX

Aburatsubo, 124, 131, 133, 215, 286
Aburatsubo tide-gauge station, 124
Activity, aftershock, 170, 179
—, Matsushiro, 228
—, seismic, 151, 186, 303, 304
—, swarm, 264
Adirondack Mountains, 192
AE (acoustic emission), 235
AEC (Atomic Energy Commission), 8, 54
Aftershock, 172
AGU (American Geophysical Union), 8
Alaska, 172, 174, 183
Alma-Ata, 55
Alps, Japan, 98
Amagi, Mt., 22
Analysis, Weibull distribution, 265
Anisotropy, V_s, 196, 285
Anatolia (Asia Minor), 222
Ankara, 222
Anomaly, focal mechanism, 258
—, fault creep, 283, 289, 290
—, geomagnetic variation, 218, 219
—, magnetic, 153
—, underground water, 258
—, V_p/V_s, 258
Aqueduct, 92
Arc, Aleutian, 109, 155
—, Aleutian—Alaska, 253
—, island, 156, 157
—, Japan, 155, 156, 162
—, Kamchatka, 155
—, Kamchatka—Kurile—Japan, 171
—, Kurile, 155
—, Kurile—Hokkaido, 179
—, Kurile—Kamchatka—Aleutian—Alaska, 183
—, Peru—Chile, 109
Area, Bakersfield—Arvin, 107
—, Dixie Valley, 79
—, Eastern Hokkaido, 179
—, Fort Ross, 75
—, Fort Tejon, 177, 221, 269
—, Garm, 209, 214
—, Hokkaido, 163
—, Hokkaido—Tohoku, 162
—, Hollister, 165, 230
—, Izu, 254
—, Izu—Kanto, 189

—, Kakegawa—Pt. Omaezaki, 114
—, Kanto, 162, 169, 230, 249, 250, 251, 252, 257, 260, 262, 265
—, Kii, 225
—, Matsushiro, 128, 167, 195, 204, 212, 228
—, Mina, 307
—, North Izu, 87, 269
—, Pt. Arena, 75
—, San Andreas fault, 269
—, San Fernando, 312
—, San Francisco, 177, 221, 269
—, San Francisco—Colma, 75
—, Seward—Anchorage, 107
—, Shikoku, 225
—, Shikoku—Kyushu, 164
—, South Kanto, 37, 84, 85, 86, 87, 95, 177, 178, 183, 227, 267, 268
—, Tashkent, 116, 209
—, Tokai, 37, 95, 163, 181, 182, 187, 230
—, Tokyo, 185, 186, 217, 246
—, Tokyo Metropolitan, 246
—, Tokyo—Yokohama, 246
—, Tomales, 75
—, Wakayama, 168, 169
Area of concentrated observation, 37, 262
Area of intensified observation, 37, 260
Area of special observation, 36, 37
Arvin, 78
Asamushi Biological Station, 11
Ashkhabad, 55, 109, 110

Baja California, 165
Bakersfield, 78
Bandojima, 134
Base line, rhombus, 82, 272
Basin, Tashkent, 232
Bay, Mikawa, 69
—, Russian, 286
—, Sagami, 12, 16, 29, 44, 64, 86, 98, 178, 186, 189, 264
—, San Francisco, 145, 165
—, Suruga, 16
—, Tokyo, 14, 15, 186
Belt, Alpide-Asiatic, 151
—, Circum-Pacific, 151
Bench mark, 94, 96, 106, 124, 132, 141, 226

Bench mark, base, 95, 124
— —, tidal, 108
BENHAM, 307
Berkeley, 146
Blue Mountain Lake, 192, 193, 284
Blueprint, 3, 33, 125, 186
Bonito, 14, 15
Buildup, stress, 173
b-value, 4, 171, 172, 238, 242, 243, 282, 289

California Department of Water Resources, 92
California Division of Mines and Geology, 92
California Institute of Technology, 136, 165
CANNIKIN, 206, 207
Caracas, 18
Carp, 14
—, crucian, 14, 15
Cat, 18
Catfish, 9, 10, 11, 14
CCEP (Coordinating Committee for Earthquake Prediction), 8, 36, 37, 38, 260
Centipede, 18, 19
Central Meteorological Observatory, 29, 31
CERECIS (Centro Regional de Sismologia), 8
Change, geomagnetic, 290
Chardchow, 109, 110
Chengtu, 254
Chevron Oil Company, 306
Chiki, 19, 20
Cholame, 92, 93
CIRES (Cooperative Institute for Research in Environmental Sciences), 8
City, Fukui, 72
—, Fukuoka, 14
—, Hamada, 121, 122
—, Hamamatsu, 181
—, Iwatsuki, 185
—, Kakegawa, 113
—, Koshoku, 280
—, Kyoto, 29
—, Matsumoto, 98
—, Matsuyama, 229
—, Nagano, 106
—, Nagaoka, 112
—, Nagoya, 17, 28
—, Niigata, 35
—, Salt Lake, 48, 126, 146

—, Sendai, 29, 104
Cluster, 51
—, super-, 51
Cock, 19
Cod, 12, 16
College, 208
Committee for Earthquake Prediction, 35
Compression, 156, 157
Compression axis, reorientation of, 175, 196, 244
— —, rotation of, 174
Conference, U.S.—Japan, 3, 49, 148
Convection, mantle, 152
Cooperation, U.S.—Japan, 46
Corralitos, 93
Correction, free-air, 227
Council, Geodetic, 34, 38
County, Hanfung, 231
—, Los Angeles, 117
—, Martin, 76
—, Tsinchiang, 231
Crab, 13
Crack, 241
Creation of sea bottom, 153
Creep movement, 221
Creepmeter, 221
Criterion, Schuster's, 247
Crustal Activity Monitoring Center, 36
Crustal deformation, non-seismic, 119
Crustal movement, continuous observation of, 125
Cumana, 197
Cuttlefish, 12, 15

Dace, 16
Dai Nihon Jishin Shiryo, 20, 22, 25
Dam, Hoover, 305
—, Hsinfengkiang, 305
—, Kariba, 305
—, Koyna, 305
—, Kremasta, 304, 305
—, Kurobe, 305
—, Monteynard, 305
—, Talbingo, 206
Danville, 145, 146, 276
Data processing, 46
Delay, P-, 195, 208, 288
—, P-wave, 194
Denver, 148, 237, 303
Department of Geodesy and Geophysics, 128
Diffusion, 243
Dilatancy, 137, 196, 213, 219, 233, 238,

241, 244
—, local, 211
Dilatation, 62, 82, 83
Disaster Prevention Research Institute, 138
Distribution, Gaussian, 256, 257, 259, 265
—, Poisson, 250
—, Weibull, 265, 267, 296
District, Chugoku, 167
—, Chugoku—Kinki, 192
—, Kinki, 135
—, Kinki—Chubu, 223
—, Kinki—Chugoku, 158
—, Mino-Owari, 27
—, North Izu, 87, 88
—, South Kanto, 37, 44
—, Tokai, 37, 92
Djirgital, 190
Djungarskoie Ala-Tau, 144
Dog, 18
Dogo, 229
Donan, 231
Donkey, 18
Dowerin, 111
Dragonfly, red, 19
Dushambe, 55, 143, 144, 145

Ear shell, 12, 121
Earth current, 11, 211, 285, 289, 290
Earthquake, Afghanistan, 144, 275
—, Ajikazawa, 121, 122, 273
—, Alaska, 47, 49, 81, 82, 107, 108, 109, 144, 198, 211, 264
—, Alma Ata, 275
—, Amami-oshima, 280
—, Ashkhabad, 109, 275
—, Atsumi Peninsula, 141, 142, 276, 281
—, Bear Valley, 288
—, Bear Valley North, 282
—, Bear Valley South, 281, 282
—, Belen, 281
—, Borrego Mountain, 195
—, Boso-oki, 169, 171, 280
—, Calabrian, 16, 19
—, Caracas, 172
—, Central Gifu, 276, 277, 286
—, Central Gifu Prefecture, 141, 142, 288
—, 1929 Central Kumamoto, 279
—, 1937 Central Kumamoto, 279
—, Central Kyoto, 279
—, Central Saitama, 286
—, Central Yamanashi, 279

—, Chilean, 7, 109, 172, 282
—, Chizu, 280
—, Choshi-oki, 286
—, conspicuous, 162, 163
—, Corralitos, 272
—, Daishoji-oki, 139, 274
—, deep-focus, 171
—, Djungarskoie Ala-Tau, 278
—, Dunaharaszti, 116, 117, 272
—, Dushambe, 278
—, East Hokkaido-oki, 171
—, East Kumamoto, 279
—, East Yamanashi, 279
—, Echigo, 20
—, Echizenmisaki-oki, 141, 275
—, Edo, 9, 14, 17, 18, 19, 22, 23, 25, 166, 186, 197, 278
—, Ellensburg, 281
—, Erimozaki-oki, 286
—, Erzincan, 222
—, Ethiopia, 198
—, Elsimore, 281
—, Fairbanks, 282, 283
—, Fairview Peak, 79, 80, 107, 198, 264
—, Fort Tejon, 165, 177
—, Fukui, 15, 72, 73, 104, 134, 264, 276
—, 1966 Garm, 283
—, 1969 Garm, 273, 283, 285
—, Genroku, 22, 25
—, Gifu, 135
—, Gisborne, 195, 285, 288
—, Hachijojima Island, 286
—, Hachijojima Island-oki, 281
—, Hachinohe-oki, 278
—, 1763 Hachinohe-oki, 278
—, Hamada, 121, 166, 273, 278
—, Hamamli, 222
—, Hawthorne, 281
—, Hayward Fault, 77
—, Hidaka, Hokkaido, 196
—, Hindu Kushu, 278
—, Hiroshima, 198
—, 1960 Hollister, 94, 272
—, 1961 Hollister, 283
—, 1971 Hollister, 282
—, Hollister area, 277, 286
—, Hsintai, 18, 56, 231
—, Hyuganada, 141, 275
—, 1931 Hyuganada, 279
—, Iga, 166, 278
—, Imaichi, 198, 279
—, Imperial Valley, 77, 264
—, Inangahua, 110

Earthquake, induced, 305
—, Izu Peninsula, 226, 286
—, Kamikochi, 280
—, Kamitakai, 278
—, Kanto, 4, 10, 11, 12, 14, 15, 16, 17,
    22, 28, 44, 64, 65, 74, 83, 84, 85, 92,
    98, 137, 138, 169, 170, 178, 179, 184,
    186, 219, 226, 246, 247, 264, 272,
    273, 279
—, Kariba Lake, 167
—, Kern County, 78, 79, 107, 264, 281
—, Koyna Reservoir, 167
—, Kremasta, 282
—, Kremasta Lake, 167
—, Kyoto, 20, 22
—, laboratory, 6, 235
—, Long Beach, 107
—, man-made, 47, 48
—, Managua, 18, 186, 282
—, Meckering, 111, 112, 230, 287
—, Mikawa, 69, 70, 103, 279
—, Mina, 285
—, moderately conspicuous, 162, 163
—, Montana, 281
—, Nagano, 102, 264, 279
—, Nagaoka, 112, 113, 272
—, Nankai (Nankaido), 15, 71, 72, 74,
    103, 104, 169, 182, 198, 226, 229
—, Nanki, 139, 274
—, Naryn, 283
—, 1894 Nemuro-oki, 278
—, Nobi, 12, 17, 18, 19, 22, 27, 62, 96,
    197, 198, 224, 264
—, Niigata, 35, 47, 114, 115, 123, 132,
    193, 198, 208, 233, 272, 273, 276,
    284, 285
—, Niijima Island, 280
—, North Gifu, 279
—, 1927 North Hiroshima, 279
—, 1930 North Hiroshima, 279
—, North Izu, 21, 22, 29, 67, 87, 100,
    101, 166, 198, 223, 263, 264, 279
—, North Kumamoto, 279
—, North Mino, 118, 141, 272, 275
—, North Miyagi, 104, 105, 193, 198, 264,
    284
—, North Nagano, 193, 284
—, Northeast Arizona, 281
—, Northwest Turkey, 198
—, Noto, 264, 267
—, occurrence time of, 250
—, Odaigahara, 140, 274
—, off East Hokkaido, 286

—, 1958 off Itrup, 281
—, 1963 off Itrup, 281
—, off Kii Peninsula, 280
—, off Shikotan, 281
—, 1972 off Sitka, 208
—, off South California, 281
—, Omachi, 97, 264, 278
—, Omi, 118, 272
—, Osaka, 198
—, Oshima Peninsula, 280
—, Pamirs, 278
—, Parkfield, 48, 221, 281, 283
—, Pleasant Valley, 281
—, Pt. Mugu, 194, 284, 285
—, Przhevalsk, 287
—, Rat Islands, 281
—, reservoir-associated, 305
—, Rikuu, 17, 19, 166, 198, 278
—, Riverside, 284
—, Sado, 121, 122, 273
—, Sakata, 198
—, San Fernando, 117, 118, 146, 186,
    192, 194, 273, 284, 311
—, San Francisco, 25, 49, 75, 76, 165,
    177, 198, 211, 264, 266, 269
—, 1896 Sanriku, 16
—, 1933 Sanriku, 12, 13, 14, 15, 16, 18,
    171, 198, 279
—, Seddon, 195, 285
—, Sekihara, 112, 272, 279
—, Shensi, 56
—, Shimabara, 279
—, Shinshu, 20, 22
—, Shirahama-oki, 141, 275
—, 1935 Shizuoka, 198
—, 1965 Shizuoka, 198
—, Sichi, 193, 194, 195, 214, 288
—, Slate Mt., 285
—, Soccoro, 281
—, South Bulgaria, 264, 266
—, South Nagasaki, 279
—, South Tien Shan, 277
—, Susaka, 198
—, Southeast Akita, 193, 198, 205, 280,
    284
—, statistical prediction of, 245
—, Takata, 23
—, Tanabe, 198, 285
—, Tango, 12, 14, 29, 65, 66, 99, 158,
    264, 273
—, Tashkent, 116, 232, 273
—, Thanksgiving Day, 208
—, Tokachi-oki, 36

—, 1843 Tokachi-oki, 278
—, 1952 Tokachi-oki, 171, 198, 279
—, 1968 Tokachi-oki, 171, 183, 187, 217, 280, 286
—, Tokyo Bay, 286
—, Tonankai, 15, 71, 113, 114, 138, 169, 182, 183, 226, 272, 273
—, Tottori, 68, 69, 102, 139, 162, 212, 264, 273
—, Ugosen, 97, 264, 279
—, Wachi, 280
—, West Oita, 279
—, Whittier, 166, 281
—, Windy Islands, 284
—, 1880 Yokohama, 27
—, Yoshino, 274, 277
—, Yunan, 23
Earthquake magnitude, 11, 218, 231, 248
Earthquake Mechanism Laboratory, 145
Earthquake modification and control, program on, 307
Earthquake precursor, 270
Earthquake prediction, response to, 311
— —, short-range, 218
— —, theory of, 245
Earthquake Prediction Observation Center, 36, 46
Earthquake risk, 246
— —, rating of, 260
Earthquake swarm, Danville, 172
— —, Ito, 100
— —, Matsushiro, 5, 47, 174, 218, 227, 255
— —, Wakayama, 169
— —, Western Hyogo, 141
Earthquakes, BML, 284
—, Chugoku-Kinki, 284
—, Danville, 276, 281, 282
—, Denver, 48, 303
—, Garm, 283, 284, 286
—, Gulf of Suez, 287
—, Kamchatka, 285, 286
—, Matsushiro, 21, 35, 119, 133, 198, 204, 264, 276, 280, 285, 287
Earthworm, 19
Edo, 22, 166
Eel, 12
Effect, cavity, 137
—, geoelectric, 197
—, geomagnetic, 197
—, precursory, 165, 176
—, premonitory, 239, 253, 255
—, pressure, 210
—, site, 136

—, seismomagnetic, 5, 197, 199, 200, 201, 203, 204, 205, 206, 211
EHRP (Earthquake Hazards Reduction Program), 8, 52, 54, 307
El Centro, 77
Elastic wave velocity, change in, 238
Electric currents, stray, 203, 212
Electric resistivity, change in, 239
— —, decrease in, 241
Electronics, quantum, 200
Element, prediction, 256, 258
Emission, radon, 242, 290
Energy, strain, 157, 249
EOS (Transaction of the American Geophysical Union), 309
Epoch reduction, 208
ERI (Earthquake Research Institute), 8, 29, 35, 46, 100, 107, 126, 185, 198, 205, 215, 227, 228, 229, 309
ESC (European Seismological Commission), 8
ESSA (Environmental Science Services Administration), 8, 51, 81
Experience at Matsushiro, 309
Experiment, Denver, 305
—, laboratory, 235, 241
—, Matsushiro, 184, 305
—, rock-breaking, 235
—, water injection, 304
Experiments at Rangely Oil Field, 306
Explosion, nuclear, 307
Extensometer, 127
Extreme values, theory of, 253
Extrusion, 152
Exudation, water, 204

Failure rate, cumulative, 265
Failure time, 265
Fairbanks, 172, 174
Fairview Peak, 79, 196
Fallon, 79
Fault, active, 44, 221
—, Aizu basin, 225
—, Alpine, 157
—, Anatolian, 6, 222, 223
—, Atera, 224, 225
—, Atotsugawa, 224, 225
—, Calaveras, 165, 221, 222
—, Fukozu, 225
—, Fukushima basin, 225
—, Garlock, 206
—, Gomura, 65, 99, 224, 264
—, Hanaore, 224

Fault, Hayward, 165, 221, 222
—, Imperial, 77
—, Morioka, 225
—, Nagaoka plain, 225
—, Neodani (Neo Valley), 27, 62, 96, 224, 225
—, North Izu, 225
—, Rikuu, 225
—, Rokko, 225
—, San Andreas, 5, 6, 76, 77, 78, 79, 92, 94, 157, 164, 165, 177, 189, 192, 193, 205, 208, 214, 221, 222, 223, 230, 264, 269, 307
—, Shikano, 68, 69
—, Sierra, 205
—, strike-slip, 157, 162, 211
—, submarine, 264
—, subsurface, 264
—, Sylmar, 146
—, Tango, 225
—, Tanna, 67, 87, 88, 101, 223, 264
—, Tottori, 225
—, transform, 76, 157
—, White Wolf, 78
—, Yamada, 65, 99
—, Yamazaki, 224, 225
—, Yanagase, 224
—, Yoshioka, 68, 69
—, Zenkoji basin, 225
Fault system, San Andreas, 93
— —, Wasatch, 48
Fault zone, San Andreas, 48, 51, 53
Faulting, aseismic, 181
Ferganda, 233
Folding, active, 44, 221
Foreshock, 165, 166, 167, 171, 172, 238, 278, 279, 280, 281, 282, 289
Foretelling earthquakes, 9
Formula, Dambara, 119
—, Dambara-Utsu, 243
—, Gutenberg-Richter, 158, 172, 248
Fort Tejon, 74
Fracture, brittle, 236, 237
Fremantle, 111
Frog, 18
Frunze, 55
Function, failure density, 265
Fuji, Mt., 15

Gabilan Range, 189
Gap, seismicity, 5, 177, 180, 181, 183, 184, 258
Garm, 5, 54, 165, 173, 175, 177, 190,

191, 192, 196, 289
Generation, dilatancy, 6, 7, 230, 270
Geodimeter, 83, 92, 133, 272
—, Type 8, 40
Geoelectric Division, Lanchou Seismology Brigade, 214
Geological Survey of Japan, 189, 223
Geomagnetic change, precursory, 207
Geomagnetism, 285, 289
Geophysical Institute, Kyoto University, 138
Ginza, 18
Golden Gate, 76
Goose, 19
Granite, Westerly, 236, 242
Gravity, 227
Gravity station, first-order, 106, 228
Gravimeter, 227
Grenoble, 58
Group, Kyoto, 138
—, Kyoto University, 141
GSI (Geographical Survey Institute), 8, 36, 40, 41, 45, 62, 69, 71, 82, 83, 85, 86, 88, 89, 90, 91, 92, 104, 107, 113, 114, 124, 180, 200, 207, 227, 228, 229, 272
Gulf, Kamchatka, 183
—, Kronotskiy, 286
Gulf of California, 151
Gulf of Suez, 232

Hachinohe, 13
Haiyuen, 231
Halfbeak, 15
Hamamatsu, 114
Hangting, 231
Hantan, 231
Hardening, dilatancy, 174, 242
Hawks Crag, 110
Helium, 53
Hen, 19
Hokkaido, 90, 162, 179, 180, 181, 217, 265, 300
Hollister, 92, 93, 136, 147, 192, 214, 221, 309
Hongshan, 209, 231
Honshu, 71, 86, 91, 104, 121, 162, 167, 192, 205, 226
Horse, 18
House of Peers, 189
Hsian, 56
Hsingtai, 209, 212, 231
HUD (Housing and Urban Development), 8, 54

IAG (International Association of Geodesy), 8, 57
IAGA (International Association of Geomagnetism and Aeronomy), 8, 57
IASPEI (International Association of Seismology and Physics of the Earth's Interior), 8, 57
IAVCEI (International Association of Volcanology and Chemistry of the Earth's Interior), 8
ICEP (International Commission on Earthquake Prediction), 8, 57, 58
ICG (Inter-Union Commission on Geodynamics), 8, 58, 89
ICSU (International Council of Scientific Unions), 8, 89
Iduna, Mt., 22
Imperial Earthquake Investigation Committee, 20, 22, 23, 27, 28, 29, 30
Imperial Fisheries Institute, 17
Imperial Valley, 77
Inangahua, 110
Induction, magnetic, 209
Institute of Engineering Mechanics, Academia Sinica, 56
Institute of Geology, Academia Sinica, 56
Institute of Geophysics, Academia Sinica, 56, 57
Institute of Physics of the Earth, Academy of Sciences of the U.S.S.R., 55
Invar-wire, 59
Ionosphere, 201
Isabella, 136
Island, Amchitka, 206
—, Itrup, 177
—, Kodiak, 108
—, Montague, 108, 109
—, Oshima, 29, 44, 64, 85, 87, 169, 189, 202
—, Sado, 19, 121
—, South, 110
—, Windy, 192
Islands, Aleutian, 53, 192, 195, 206
—, Andreanof, 183
—, Commander, 183
—, Japan, 89, 95, 186, 300
—, Japanese, 180
—, Kurile, 177, 179, 180, 183
—, North Kurile, 183
—, Rat, 183
Ito, 100
IUGG (International Union of Geodesy and Geophysics), 8, 55, 57, 58, 89

IUGS (International Union of Geological Sciences), 8, 89
Iwamuro, 132

JMA (Japan Meteorological Agency), 8, 21, 29, 36, 43, 106, 162, 178, 181, 309
JSPS (Japan Society for Promotion of Science), 8, 47

K, energy class, 174
K, index, 173
Kakegawa, 114
Kakioka, 227
Kamakura, 246
Kamchatka, 171, 183, 195, 212
Kanozan, 201, 204
Kashiwazaki, 123
Kazakh, 55
Kazakhstan, 206
Khait (near Garm), 177, 288
Kirghiz, 55
Krasnovodosk, 109, 110
Kuji, 15
Kyoto, 68, 135, 158, 192, 247
Kyushu, 14, 92, 141, 147, 148, 167, 300
—, North, 59

Lake, Hamanako, 181
—, man-made, 167, 206, 304, 305
—, Yamanakako, 15
Lanchou, 214, 215, 254
Land deformation, 59, 96, 121, 271, 272, 289
— —, area of, 118
— —, precursory, 256, 257
Land uplift forerunning an earthquake, 112
Lapilli tuff, 216
Laser, He-Cd, 84
—, He-Ne, 83, 84
—, iodine absorption-cell, 128
Layer, basaltic, 152
—, granitic, 152
Level, bubble, 276, 289
—, precise, 95
—, underground water, 230
Levelling, 124, 272
Levelling route, first-order, 95
Life, mean, 265
Lineation, magnetic, 153
Loach, 12
Lobster, 12
Los Angeles, 74, 165, 166

Luenyuen, 231
Luho, 215

M_2, 148, 149
Macaw, 19
Mackerel, 13, 14
—, horse, 17, 254
Mackerel pike, 11
Magnet, 23
Magnetism, piezo-remanent, 209
Magnetization, remanent, 210
Magnetometer, GSI-type, 207
—, optical-pumping rubidium, 205
—, proton precession, 44, 153, 199, 200,
    201, 202, 204, 206, 207, 208
Magnetosphere, 201
Magnitude, prediction of, 255
Makimine, 148
Map, microseismicity, 159, 160, 161
Marianas, 195
Maruoka, 134
Matsushiro, 105, 106, 136, 201, 204, 304
Mechanism, focal, 64, 174
—, source, 283, 289
Meckering, 111, 112
Medeo, 206
Menlo Park, 165, 306
Merredin, 111
Metamorphism, 162
Method, electro-optical, 59, 128
—, P-residual, 194, 195
—, V_p anomaly, 194
Microcrack, 238
Microearthquake, 158, 162, 164, 165,
    184, 303, 304, 305
—, deep-well observation of, 185
—, ultra-, 158, 168
Microfracture, 235, 237, 238
Microseismicity, 162, 165, 168, 173, 184,
    225, 283
Microshock, 235, 304
Mikura, 114
Millipede, 19
Mina, 196
Minakami, Mt., 21, 106, 228, 304
Mini-scenario, 312
Misaki, 13
Mitaka, 82
Model, dilatancy, 5, 44, 119, 172, 241,
    243, 270
—, dry, 243, 244
—, Rikitake, 219
—, wet, 241

Modification and control, earthquake, 303
Monkey, 18
Moon phase, 24
Mountain range, North Anatolian, 222

Naples, 16
Naryn, 144
National Academy of Sciences, 54
National Committee for Geodesy and
    Geophysics, 35
National Diet, 181
National Research Center for Disaster
    Prevention, 44, 185, 186, 223, 304
NCER (National Center for Earthquake
    Research), 8, 48, 145, 165, 208, 306
Nemichthys avocetta, 13
Neotectonics, 225
Network, first-order triangulation, 39
Network of Crustal Movement Observa-
    tories, 135
Nevada Test Site, 136
Newton, 110
Nezugaseki, 123
Nihon Jishin Shiryo, 9, 12, 20
Niigata, 208
Nishiki-e, 9
NOAA (National Oceanic and Atmo-
    spheric Administration), 8, 52, 54, 74,
    151, 281
Noise elimination, 200, 201, 203, 208
Nokogiriyama, 133
Northam, 111
NRM (Natural remanent magnetization),
    209
Nuclear explosion, underground, 206
NSF (National Science Foundation), 3, 8,
    47, 51, 52, 54

O_1, 148
Observation, tide-gauge, 41, 122, 124, 271
Observation of crustal movement, contin-
    uous, 42
Observatory, Aburatsubo Crustal Move-
    ment, 131, 132, 136, 215
—, Akibasan, 274
—, Alma Ata, 275
—, Ashkhabad, 275
—, Bandojima, 276
—, Berkeley, 276
—, Cecil H. Green Geophysical, 134
—, crustal deformation, 42, 301
—, crustal movement, 129, 130, 132
—, Garm, 278

—, Granite Mountain, 126, 146
—, Ide, Kyoto University, 140, 277
—, Ikuno, 273, 275
—, Inuyama Crustal Movement, 141, 142, 276, 277
—, Kakioka Magnetic, 218
—, Kamigamo Geophysical, Kyoto University, 139, 273, 274, 275
—, Kamikineusu Microearthquake, 196
—, Kamioka, 275
—, Kamitakara Crustal Movement, 142, 276
—, Kanozan Geodetic, 60, 205
—, Kishu, 274, 275
—, Kochi, 139, 274
—, Kondara, 143, 144, 145, 275, 278
—, Kronoki, 286
—, Lamont-Doherty Geological, 47
—, Libby, 277
—, magnetic, 200
—, Makimine Crustal Movement, 147, 275
—, Matsushiro Seismological, 104, 106, 128, 133, 135, 136, 171, 195, 196, 228, 229, 276
—, Maze Crustal Movement, 132, 141, 276
—, microearthquake, 43, 185
—, Mizusawa Geodetic, 205
—, Nokogiriyama Crustal Movement, 129, 130
—, Nutting, 277
—, Ogoya, 274, 275
—, Osakayama, Kyoto University, 140, 277
—, Oura, 275
—, Peking, 57
—, Sage, 277
—, Shionomisaki, 274
—, Talger, 277, 278
—, Tamamizu, 139, 274
—, Tokyo Astronomical, 7, 82
—, Tokyo University, 273
—, Yahiko Crustal Movement, 132
—, Yura, 274, 275
Occurrence time, prediction of, 258
Octopus, 14
Odawara, 13
Ogdenburg, 189
Ogi, 121
Ogoya, 139
Oil flow, 232, 287, 289, 290
Omachi, 97
Operations research, 299, 301
Organism, intertidal sessile marine, 108

Osaka, 158

Palaeomagnetism, 154
Paleozoic, 148
Palmadale, 118
Pamirs, 55
Parkfield, 48, 221
Pattern recognition, 53
Peking, 18, 56, 165, 209
Peninsula, Alaska, 183
—, Boso, 15, 29, 44, 64, 85, 87, 98, 178, 183, 185, 226, 227
—, Izu, 12, 16, 17, 29, 44, 85, 87, 100, . 101, 225, 230
—, Kii, 15, 138, 139, 140, 162, 168, 182, 207, 226, 269
—, Miura, 29, 44, 85, 87, 98, 124, 178, 226, 227
—, Oga, 14
—, San Francisco, 165
Peridotite, 152
Perth, 111
Pheasant, 19
Pigeon, 19
Plain, Kanto, 185
Plate, Asian, 156
—, Pacific, 89, 90, 156, 162, 171
—, Philippine Sea, 86, 89, 169, 182
Plate tectonics, 4, 76, 90, 151, 154, 155, 156, 169
PPBS (Planning-Programming-Budgeting-System), 8, 299
Precursor, 241
—, A-type, 295, 296
—, A_1-type, 296, 298, 299
—, A_2-type, 296, 297, 298
—, B-type, 294
—, earthquake, 7
—, geomagnetic, 208, 209
—, resistivity, 218
Precursor time, 166, 168, 176, 218, 231, 242, 244, 258, 270, 271, 289, 293, 294, 295
— —, histogram of, 297
Prediction, medium- and short-term, 297
—, statistical, 297
Prediction of extremely short range, 298
Prefecture, Aichi, 12, 27, 69, 181, 225
—, Akita, 14, 17, 97, 205, 225
—, Aomori, 11, 14
—, Chiba, 169
—, Ehime, 104
—, Fukushima, 225

Prefecture, Gifu, 225
—, Hiroshima, 167
—, Hyogo, 225
—, Ibaragi, 170
—, Ishikawa, 139
—, Iwate, 13, 15, 25, 225
—, Kagawa, 104
—, Kanagawa, 13, 15, 16
—, Kochji, 104
—, Kyoto, 12, 21, 59, 225, 280
—, Mie, 104
—, Miyagi, 13
—, Nagano, 20, 35, 97, 225
—, Niigata, 19, 20, 23, 119, 121, 132, 225
—, Shimane, 167
—, Shizuoka, 16, 113, 181, 182, 225
—, Tokushima, 104
—, Tokyo, 16
—, Tottori, 68, 225, 280
—, Toyama, 225
—, Wakayama, 104, 279, 280
—, Yamanashi, 16
Presidio of San Francisco, 145, 146
Pressure, confining, 213, 236
—, pore, 237, 241, 304
Prince William Sound, 81, 108
PRM (Piezo-remanent magnetization), 210
Probability, a posteriori, 256
—, a priori, 256
—, preliminary, 255, 259
—, synthesized, 256
Program, earthquake prediction, 33, 171
—, — —, American, 49
—, — —, Japanese, 34
—, — —, U.S.—Japan Scientific Coopera-
    tion, 46, 48
Project, Geodynamics, 89
Province, Hopei, 18, 56, 231
—, Kansu, 56, 215
—, Ningsia, 193, 194, 215, 231, 288
—, Szechwan, 215
—, Taiwan, 231
—, Tsinghai, 231
—, Yunan, 231
Promontory, Kii, 104
—, Muroto, 104, 226
Przhevalsk, 230
Pt. Arena, 76
Pt. Mugu, 146
Pt. Omaezaki, 114, 226

Quadrilateral, 83, 146
Quartz, fused, 125

Radon, 53, 55, 287, 289
Radon content, 232, 233
Radon emission, increase in, 241
Range, Zaliyskiy, 144
Rangely, 306
Rangely Oil Field, 48, 306, 307
Rainbow Mountain, 79
Rat, 17, 18
Rat House, 17
Rate, free-air, 228
Rebound, 156, 157, 169, 226
Reefton, 110
Region, Boso Peninsula, 187
—, Garm, 198, 213
—, Hokkaido, 187
—, Kanto-Tokai, 181
—, Naryn, 177
—, northeastern Honshu, 187
—, Shikoku, 187
—, South Kanto, 178, 179
—, Tashkent, 198
—, Tohoku, 162
—, Tokai, 181, 182, 187
Republic, Uzbek, 116
Research Group for Microearthquakes,
    Tohoku University, 193, 196, 280,
    284, 285
Residual, P, 194, 195, 196
Residual time, 194
Resistivity, 286, 289, 290
—, earth, 212, 213, 214, 215, 219
Return period, 246, 247, 253
— —, mean, 254
Reversal of the geomagnetic field, 153,
    154
Rhombus, 83
Ridge, Mid-Atlantic, 152, 153
Rift, East African, 151
Rikanenpyo (Science Calender, Tokyo
    Astronomical Observatory), 7
Rise, East Pacific, 152, 155
River, Kuzuryu, 15
Riverside, 194, 195
Rockville, 51
Rocky Mountains, 48
Rocky Mountain Arsenal, 303
Rotation, 62
Rotokohu, 110
Routes, first-order levelling, 41
Rumbling, 166
Rupture, creep-like, 218
—, main, 172, 218
—, mean time to, 265

S_2, 148
Sakai, 168
Sakhalin, 171
Salinas, 189
Samurai, 20, 23
San Fernando, 118, 136
San Francisco, 74, 76, 77, 92, 93, 145, 165, 221
San Gabriel mountain range, 117
Sardina melanosticta, 12, 13
Sardine, 12
Scale, JMA, 246
—, modified Mercalli, 232, 246
—, Richter, 12
Scandinavia, 119
Schmidt Institute of Earth Physics, 54
Science Council of Japan, 35
Sea, Caspian, 110
—, Kashimanada, 170
—, Okhotsk, 180
—, Red, 151
—, Setonaikai, 162
Sea retreat, 121, 122, 273
— —, anomalous, 271
Sea-floor spreading, 89
Secular variation, geomagnetic, 202
Seward, 108
Seismic activity, Matsushiro, 24, 136
Seismic wave velocity, 44
— — —, change in, 189, 194, 196, 238
Seismicity, 4, 43, 151, 172, 174
—, regional, 158
Seismicity Monitoring Center, 36
Seismograph, borehole, 186
—, deep-well, 186
—, Omori-type horizontal pendulum, 137, 138
—, sea-bottom, 187
—, submarine, 186
Seismological Society of Japan, 27
Seismological station, Gifu, 193
Seismology, explosion, 189
—, submarine, 186
Seismomagnetic effect, interpretation of, 210
Sekihara, 112, 113
Shark, 16
Shear, 62
—, maximum, 62
Shichinohe, 14
Shihchiachung, 231
Shikoku, 72, 74, 104, 162, 226, 229
Shogun, 25

Sichi, 193, 231
Sicily, 16
Sierra Nevada, 79
Sikhote-Alin, 171
Sinchu, 231
Sitka, 209
Slate Mountain, 196
Sliding, frictional, 236, 237
Snake, 18
—, blue-green, 18
—, grass, 18
Snowy Mountains, 206
Solar wind, 201
South Kanto, 124
Spanish stallion, 18
Spreading, ocean-floor, 154, 156
S.S.R., Turkmenian, 109, 110
Stage, dilatancy generation, 297
—, immediately prior to main rupture, 298
—, preliminary, 297
—, strain accumulation, 297
Station, Alma-Ata, 143
—, Ashkhabad, 143
—, deep-well, 186
—, Garm, 145
—, gravity, 228
—, Hongshan, 57
—, Imperial Fisheries Experimental, 14
—, magnetic, 200, 207
—, reference, 203
—, Talgar, 144
—, tide-gauge, 122
—, triangulation, 60
Stanford Research Institute, 311
Step, resistivity, 217, 218
—, strain, 133, 134, 136, 214, 218
—, tilt, 133, 134, 135, 208
Stick-slip, 237
Strain, 271, 273, 274, 275, 276, 278, 289
—, maximum shearing, 66, 68, 82, 83, 87
—, ultimate, 4, 7, 64, 263, 267, 297
Strainmeter, 127, 136, 277, 289, 291, 292
—, laser-beam, 128
—, quartz, 136
—, quartz-tube, 127, 128, 129, 130
—, Sacks-Evertson, 128
—, super-invar-wire, 127
Strike-slip, 192, 193
Subduction, 155
Subsidence, land, 181
Survey, geodetic, 297
—, geodimeter, 221, 271
—, levelling, 180, 264, 271, 299

Survey, magnetic, 200, 207
—, microearthquake, 165
—, Military Land, 62, 100
—, traverse, 89, 180
—, triangulation, 59, 180, 264
Susceptibility, magnetic, 209
Swallow, 19
Swarm activity, Matsushiro, 193
Sweetfish, 15

Tajik, 55
Tadjik S.S.R., 165
Tadjikistan, 190
Taichung, 231
Talcahuano, 18
Talgar, 145
Tanabe, 207, 208
Tashkent, 55, 58, 116, 207, 219, 232, 233
Technique, Delphi, 311
—, finite-element, 137
—, weighted difference, 201
Tectonic line, Itoigawa—Shizuoka, 224, 225
— —, Median, 162, 224, 225
Tectonomagnetism, 107
Telluric currents, 211
Terrace, coastal, 226
Test, rock breaking, 46
Theorem, Bayes', 256
Theory, dilatancy, 55, 148, 229
—, dislocation, 65, 135, 218
Tidal load, oceanic, 215
Tidal loading, 216
Tide, earth, 189
Tide-gauge, 108, 122, 273
Tien Shan, 55, 144
Tien-shen, 254
T'ienshui, 214, 215
Tilt, 271, 273, 274, 275, 276, 278, 289
Tiltmeter, borehole, 126, 127, 143, 147, 277, 289, 291, 292
—, buoy, 127
—, horizontal pendulum, 125, 129, 273, 289, 291, 292
—, water tube, 126, 129, 130, 133, 134, 136, 276, 289, 291, 292
Tokyo, 9, 11, 27, 28, 82, 84, 90, 124, 129, 162, 166, 169, 170, 186, 189, 197, 201, 202, 219, 223, 227, 246, 247, 249, 267, 271, 286, 301
Town, Kamiyamada, 280
—, Matsushiro, 35
—, Sanada, 280

—, Togura, 280
Transcursion, 157
Transducer, capacitance, 127
—, inductance, 127
Traverse Range, 182
Tremor, mining, 195
Trench, Japan, 92, 162, 169
—, Japan—Kurile, 90
Trepang, 16
TRM (Thermo-remanent magnetization), 209, 210
Trough, Nankai, 72, 183
—, Sagami, 29, 64, 86, 169, 171, 186
Tsinghai, 254
Tsunami, 121, 122, 181
—, 1896 Sanriku, 25
—, 1933 Sanriku, 18
Tsunghai, 231
Tuna, 14
Turkmen, 55
Type, A, 294
—, A_1, 294, 295, 298
—, A_2, 294, 295
—, anchored buoy, 187
—, self-falling and self-rising, 187

UMC (Upper Mantle Committee), 8, 57
UMP (Upper Mantle Project), 8
Units, SI, 197
University, Colombia, 47
—, Kyoto, 127, 135, 142, 147
—, Nagoya, 141
—, Tokyo Imperial, 29, 137, 138
—, Peking, 56
University of California, Berkeley, 145
University of Colorado, 48, 311
University of Tokyo, 29, 36, 47
University of Utah, 126
Uplift, coseismic, 226
—, land, 123, 181, 204, 233, 241, 244
—, post-glacier, 119
U.S. Coast and Geodetic Survey, 107, 108, 151
USGS (United States Geological Survey), 3, 8, 52, 54, 92, 145, 309
Uzbek, 55

Variometer, resistivity, 216
Victoria, 208
Village, Azuma, 280
—, Sakai, 280
V_p and V_s, 284, 289, 290
V_p anomaly, 284

V_p decrease, 288
V_p residual, 285
V_p/V_s, 283, 284, 289
V_p/V_s change, 243
V_p/V_s ratio, 190, 191, 192, 193, 194, 195, 241, 244, 290, 297

Warning, earthquake, 309, 310
Water, impounding of, 206
—, underground, 23, 227, 229, 287, 289, 290
Weasel, 17
Westport, 110
Work, geodetic, 39
—, geoelectric, 44
—, geomagnetic, 44
—, laboratory, 46

—, levelling, 95
Working Group on Earthquake Prediction, 57

Yokohama, 11, 27, 28, 124, 131, 132
York, 111

Zone, aftershock, 183
—, Hyuganada, 167
—, Izu—Nagano, 167
—, Kurile—Kamchatka—Aleutian—Alaska, 183
—, Miyoshi—Hamada, 167
—, Oita—Kumamoto—Nagasaki, 167
—, Taiyuan—Hsian, 56
Zotei Dai Nihon Jishin Shiryo, 20